Campaigns on the North-West

Frontier

H. L. Nevill

Alpha Editions

This edition published in 2019

ISBN : 9789353299866

Design and Setting By
Alpha Editions
email - alphaedis@gmail.com

CAMPAIGNS ON THE NORTH-WEST FRONTIER

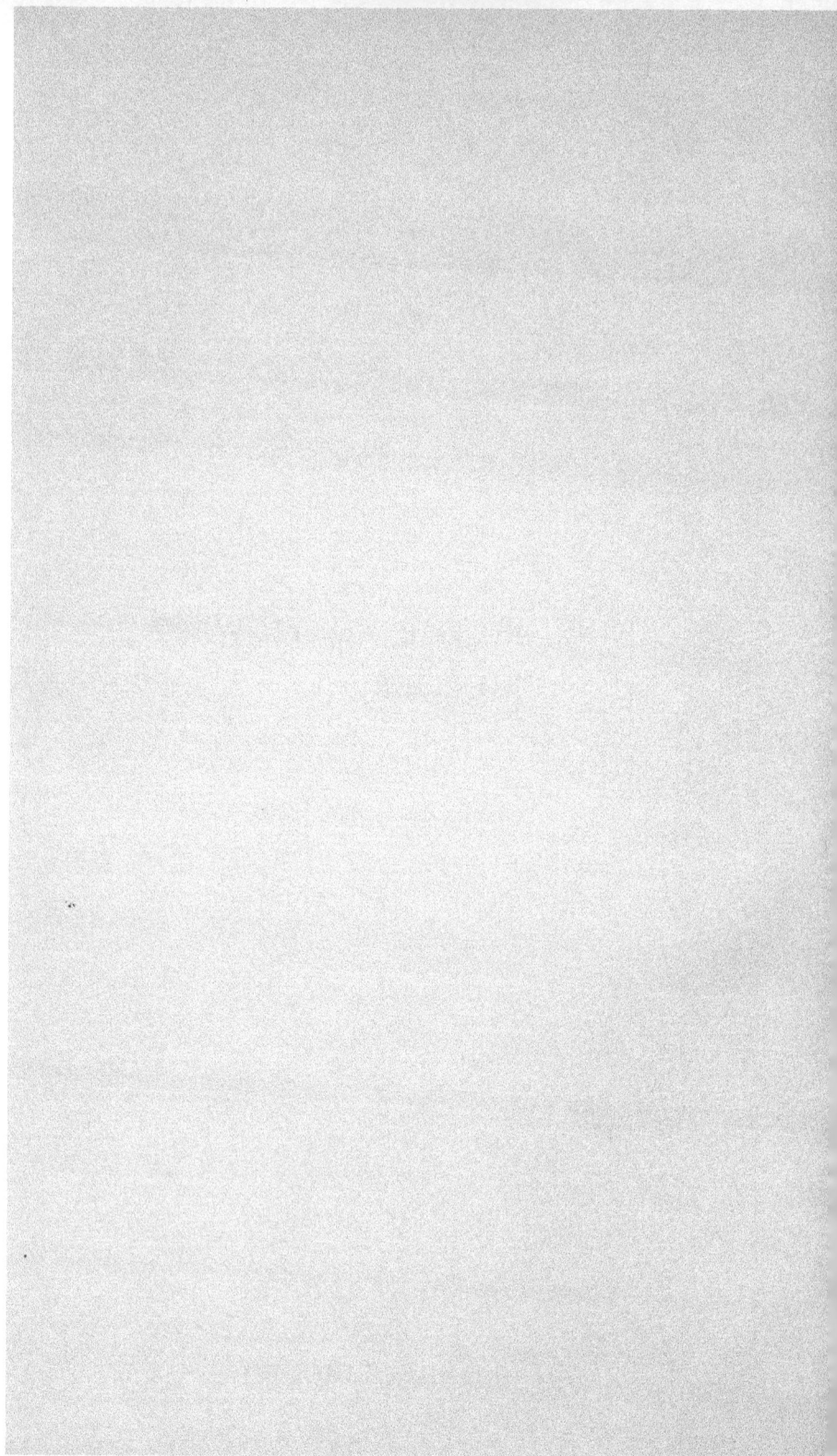

CAMPAIGNS ON THE
NORTH-WEST FRONTIER

BY CAPTAIN H. L. NEVILL, D.S.O.

ROYAL FIELD ARTILLERY

WITH MAPS

LONDON
JOHN MURRAY, ALBEMARLE STREET, W.
1912

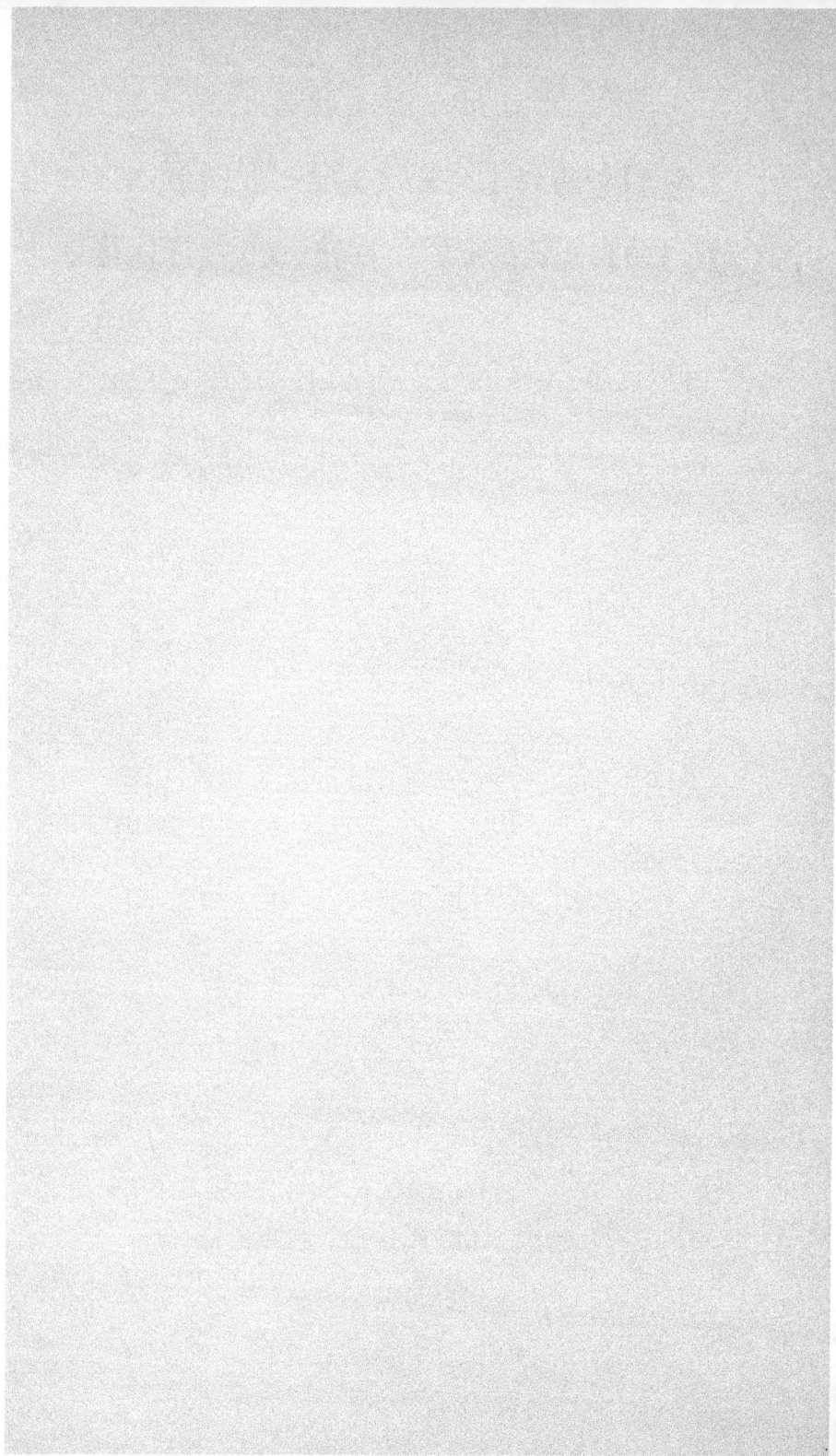

CONTENTS

CONTENTS

APPENDICES

LIST OF ILLUSTRATIONS

MAPS

(IN THE TEXT)

MAPS

(IN POCKET AT END)

TABLES OF TROOPS ENGAGED

LIST OF WORKS CONSULTED

CALLWELL, COLONEL C. E.: Small Wars: their Principles and Practice.
HOLDICH, COLONEL SIR T. H.: The Indian Borderland.
HUTCHINSON, COLONEL H.: The Campaign in Tirah, 1897-98.
JAMES, LIONEL: The Indian Frontier War, 1897.
KNIGHT, E. F.: Where Three Empires Meet.
OFFICIAL: Chitral Expedition, The.
       ,,   Correspondence relating to the Despatch of Expeditions against the Samil Clans of the Orakzai Tribe on the Miranzai Border of the Kohat District.
       ,,   Expedition against the Black Mountain Tribes, 1888.
       ,,   Expedition against the Hassanzai and Akazai Tribes of the Black Mountain.
       ,,   Field Service Regulations (Part I.: Operations), 1909.
       ,,   Mahsud Waziri Operations.
       ,,   Operations of the Buner Field Force, 1898.
       ,,   Operations of the Malakand Field Force, 1897.
       ,,   Operations of the Mohmand Field Force, 1897.
       ,,   Operations of the Tochi Field Force, 1897-98.
       ,,   Operations of the Zhob Field Force, 1890.
       ,,   Papers regarding the Zakha Khel Afridis (Operations).
       ,,   Papers regarding the Mohmands (Operations).
PAGET, LIEUTENANT-COLONEL W. H., and MASON, LIEUTENANT A. H.: A Record of the Expeditions against the North-West Frontier Tribes.
PIONEER, THE: Risings on the North-West Frontier, 1897-98.
ROBERTSON, SIR G. S.: Chitral: the Story of a Minor Siege.
YOUNGHUSBAND, CAPTAINS G. J. and F. E.: The Relief of Chitral.

And others acknowledged in the text.

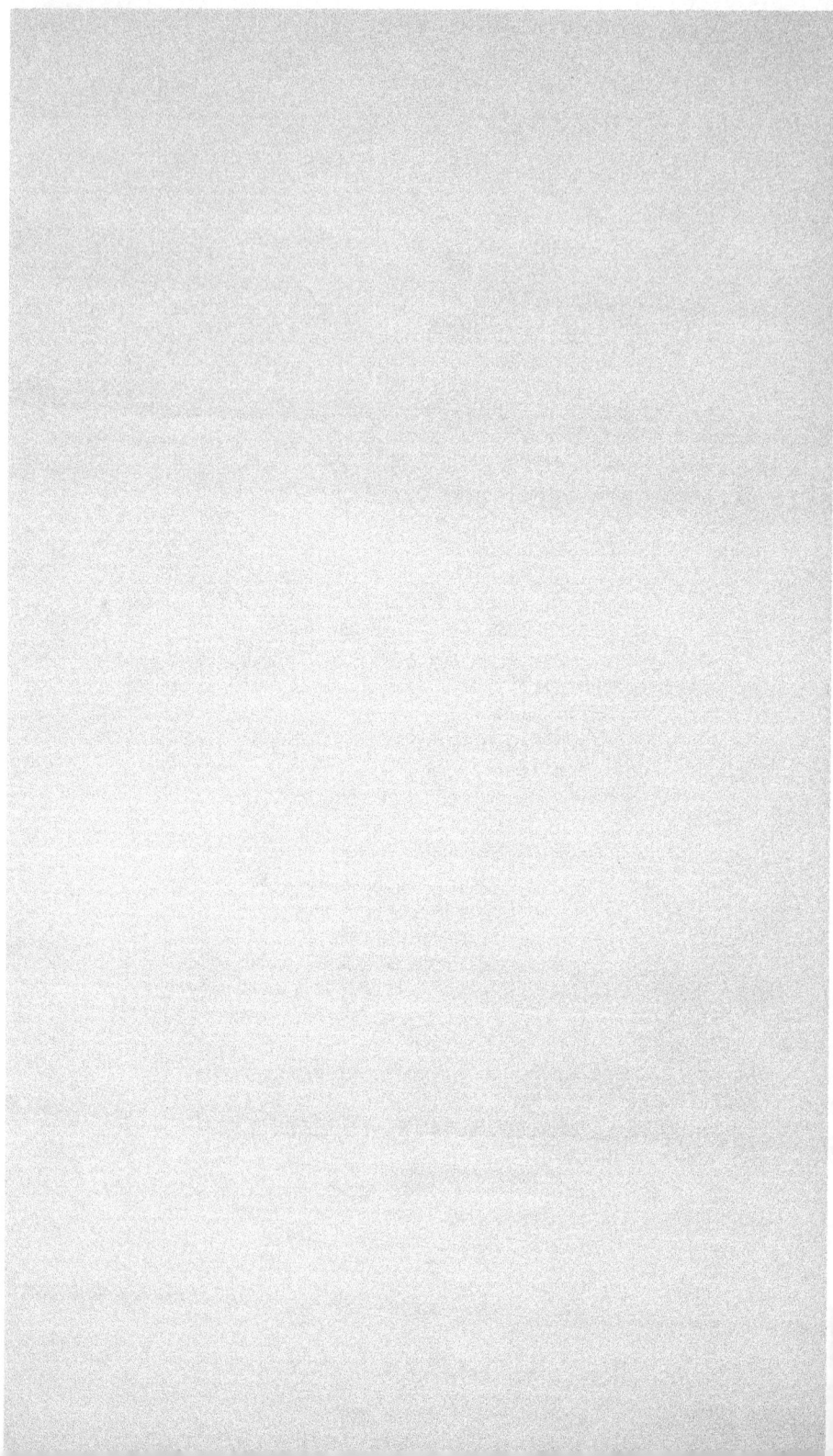

GLOSSARY OF HINDUSTANI WORDS AND MILITARY TERMS

Abatis—an obstacle made of trees or branches of trees. This is the spelling adopted in the official textbook on military engineering.

Akhund—a teacher.

Amir—a ruler.

Badmash—a bad character.

Badmashi—villainy.

Bania—a grain-dealer.

Bazar—a trading quarter.

Bhisti—a water-carrier.

Bhoosa. See *Bhusa.*

Bhusa—chopped straw.

Cantonment—the quarter occupied by the garrison of Indian towns.

Chaprasi—a messenger.

Contain—to keep in check.

Coolie—a labourer. The Hindustani word is *kuli.*

Dafadar—a rank in the Indian cavalry corresponding to sergeant.

Dandi—a sort of sedan chair carried on the shoulders of men.

Doolie. See *Duli.*

Duli—a palanquin swung on a long bamboo pole.

Enfilade—to attack in flank with fire from guns or rifles.

Ghazi—a religious maniac.

Godown—a storeroom.

Havildar—a rank in the Indian infantry corresponding to sergeant.

Jagir—a freehold.

Jehad—a holy war by Muhammadans against "infidels."

Jemadar—the lowest commissioned rank in the Indian Army.

Jirga—a deputation.

Jungle—a forest or wood, but is also a term applied to any uninhabited part.

Kahar—a Hindu caste furnishing *duli*-bearers.

Kajawah—a pannier.

Kot—a hamlet.

Kotal—the summit of a pass.

Lakh—100,000.

Lashkar—an armed force.

Maidan—a plain.

Malik—a headman, an owner.

Maulvi—a teacher.

Maund—80 pounds.

Mehtar—ruler.

Moral—a French word signifying mental faculties or spirit. *Morale* is another French word meaning morals, and in some phrases a rebuke.

Mullah—a Muhammadan religious authority.

Naik—a rank in the Indian Army corresponding to corporal. A Lance-Naik is a man on probation for the rank of Naik.

Nala—a watercourse with or without water.

Nullah. See *Nala*.

Pakhal—a leather water-bag.

Palki—a palanquin.

Purdah—a curtain.

Pushtin—a short coat lined with sheep-skin.

Ressaldar—the second commissioned rank in the Indian cavalry.

Sangar—a breastwork made of stones.

Sarkar—the Government.

Second line transport—baggage and stores not required on the field of battle.

Sepoy—a term derived from the Hindustani word *sipahi*, meaning a soldier.

Serai—a resting-place for travellers.

Shikari—a hunter.

Sowar—a mounted man.   Indian cavalry soldiers are called *sowars*.

Subadar—the second commissioned rank in the Indian infantry.

Tahsildar—a native official in charge of a district.

Tangi—a defile.

Terrain—ground in a general sense.

Thana—a police post.

Tomtom—a native drum.

Tonga—a two-wheeled conveyance common in India.

Tulwar—a curved sword.

Ziarat—a shrine.

FOREWORD

THE history of the North-West Frontier of India is one long record of strife with the wild and war-like tribes that inhabit the difficult mountainous region which is the Borderland between British India and Afghanistan. From pre-Mutiny days down to the present time the trouble has been there, though there have been intervals of rest more or less frequent; and all the factors which contribute to a fiery and fanatical outbreak are still present, and may at any moment compel a fresh expedition to punish an outrage, to enforce restitution, and to restore order.

This being so, it is very desirable that all officers whose duty takes them to India should be acquainted with the military history of the North-West Frontier; and should endeavour by study to familiarize themselves with the conditions under which they will very probably some day have to fight, and lead their men. Many excellent accounts have been written in the past about particular expeditions, but this is the first time that what may be called a student's history of *all* the campaigns of this Frontier has been compiled within the limits of a single volume, and presented in such a way as to exhibit the gradual progress and development in arms and tactics on either side, and to enable comparison to be profitably made. Captain Nevill's history is, therefore, particularly valuable to soldiers ; and I can cordially recommend it, not only to those who may have to participate in future fighting on the Frontier, but also to those who may be concerned in the administration of our policy on that wild border ; and also to all who desire to take an intelligent interest in one of the most difficult and delicate problems which concern the welfare of our great Indian Empire. A discussion of the policy which regulates our dealings with the tribes on the North-West Frontier is outside the scope of this book, but it may be remarked that our relations with these restless and war-like people constitute a very real and ever-present difficulty, which will increase, and not diminish, in gravity as time goes by ; and no study of the question can be complete without a judicial survey of its military aspects, such as can be gained by an attentive perusal of Captain Nevill's work.

ROBERTS, F.M.

October 29, 1910.

PREFACE

IT is feared that the action of an obscure junior officer
in embarking upon so large a subject as the history of
the North-West Frontier Wars of the Indian Empire
will seem not a little presumptuous, especially when it
is found that an attempt has been made to dogmatize
in addition to the presentation of bare narrative. The
interesting nature of the subject, and the difficulty of
acquiring information about the military history of the
Indian border in a short course of study, must be the
principal excuses. There are many works, official and
otherwise, which deal with Indian frontier wars either
wholly or in part, but the writer knows of no single
work which presents to the reader a brief survey of the
whole. It is in the hope of supplying this want that
the following pages have been written. No attempt has
been made to go into minute detail, but rather to offer
a description of the operations in question, which will
satisfy all ordinary requirements and prepare the way
for a more detailed study of the literature of any special
campaign. Whenever a detailed account of some minor
operation is given, it will be found that it owes its inclusion to the fact that the incident in question serves to
point some military moral, to which it is desired to call
attention in the review of the campaign, or group of
campaigns, following the narrative. Furthermore, minute

military or personal detail has been avoided, in the hope of arousing the interest of the non-military reader as well as his countryman in the Imperial Army. Ignorance of India and its affairs has been a standing disgrace in the past to the bulk of the British nation. Improved communication between India and the Mother Country has done much to remove the reproach, but it is to be feared that there are still numerous individuals who would betray the same ignorance as one of Thackeray's minor characters in their allusions to "that odious India."

The historical facts admit of practically no question ; but, whatever may be said of the value of any deductions or opinions drawn from them by a writer of modest experience, the junior officer, writing for junior officers, has one sure line of defence—a Torres Vedras, behind which he can retreat when hard pressed—and that is, that he is more in touch with the needs, the doubts, the difficulties, and the aspirations of his contemporaries than those who are much their seniors can be. Moreover, young officers are brought up to accept the words of teachers of acknowledged standing and capacity without question, whereas they will pause for reflection, and inwardly criticize the remarks of one of their own number, and this is just what is wanted. They will see for themselves if the principle enunciated is borne out by history, or is in accordance with the letter and spirit of the official textbooks of the day.

Throughout the following pages endeavour has been made to illustrate by historical instances the lessons set forth in standard works, such as "Field Service Regulations (Operations)" in particular, rather than to attempt to enlarge upon the instructions already clearly expressed therein. It only remains, then, to acknowledge with the deepest gratitude the kindness of those officers who have been good enough to help with criticism and advice, and to submit the pages that follow to the judgment of those for whom chiefly they have been compiled.

H. L. NEVILL, Captain.

September 20, 1911.

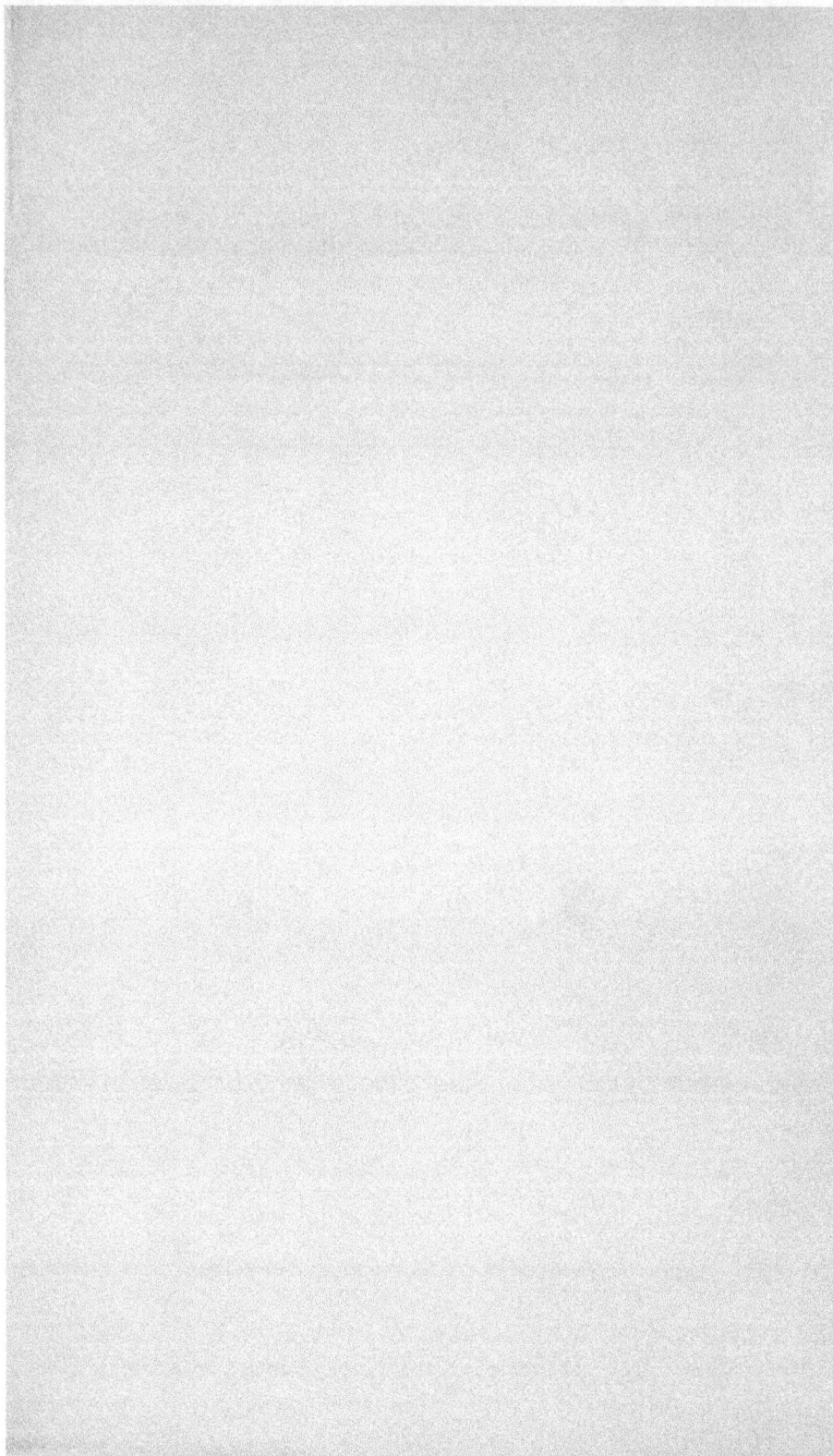

CAMPAIGNS ON THE NORTH-WEST FRONTIER

INTRODUCTION

THE North-West Frontier of India is marked throughout its length by a well-defined natural wall, running north and south, which varies in height from 20,000 feet in the north to 5,000 feet in the south. Though there are points where this wall can be scaled by an active climber who knows his ground, the really practicable breaches are but few in number, and even these are susceptible of easy defence against direct attack. To the west of the wall lie the dominions of His Majesty, the Amir of Afghanistan, but in the extreme north a narrow strip of Afghanistan, 200 miles in length, projects towards the east, constituting a finger * stretched out by request from the hand which keeps the two great European Powers in Asia apart. On the British side there lies another well-defined line of defence — another of the three chief natural obstacles of which military science takes count.† Parallel to the mountain - wall, forming the recognized frontier, and at an average distance of 100 miles from it, runs the historic bed of the mighty Indus. It is a saying in Southern Afghanistan that all roads lead to Quetta ; it might be said in Northern India, with even less hyperbole, that all streams flow to the Indus. Practically the whole of the Punjab, the whole of Kashmir, the whole of the North-West Frontier Province and adjacent tribal territory, and Afghanistan east of Kabul, are drained by tributaries of the Indus, the size of whose basin is two and a half times that of

* Wakhan.
† The third is, of course, deserts. The Bikanir Desert constitutes a third obstacle to an invader seeking to reach the heart of India from the direction of Quetta.

I

Great Britain and Ireland. Between the Indus and the frontier lies the country of which this volume treats; the Black Mountain District is alone to the east of the former boundary.

The general character of the country is a tangled mass of mountains and valleys, like an exaggerated Switzerland. Among the former are included peaks which tower to a height of over 26,000 feet, and the valleys are often mere gorges where man is obliged to struggle with raging mountain-torrents for a right of way. The general level of the country decreases from north to south, but Nature is little more tractable on that account. The well-watered valleys and pine-clad slopes of the north give place in the south to arid, waterless tracts, where the very rocks seem to be built on a different system, and radiate a heat infernal during the summer months. In the Zhob District the strata of the rocks seem to run vertically rather than horizontally, and even the Takht-i-Suliman itself gives the impression that it is unable to account for its presence amid its comparatively humble surroundings. Where water is obtainable the soil is fertile, cereals being extensively grown; pasturage is generally scanty and of a poor description. From north to south the people are Muhammadans of uncertain origin, but the strictness of their views varies a good deal, particularly in the Gilgit District and in Hunza, where they may be characterized as distinctly broad.

The rivers of the North-West Frontier are all, from the Indus downwards, very variable in volume. In the winter months the smaller of them are either dry altogether or dwindle to mere streams, but when the summer sun thaws the snowy mantle of the hills, and in rainy weather, the mountain watercourses, fed by hundreds of small tributary streams, become raging torrents, which rush headlong down their rock-strewn paths to help in swelling the River Indus to a mighty flood.

In a country consisting either of valleys or precipitous hillside the courses of the roads and streams are either literally identical or closely adjacent to one another. Except along a very few short stretches close to British territory wheeled traffic is impracticable, and in some parts even mules have to be discarded in favour of the sturdy but evasive coolies obtainable in such localities.

The climate of the Indian borderland in winter varies in severity according to the altitude, but is bracing throughout, while in summer the heat in the valleys is oppressive, and in the case of the Swat Valley is distinctly unhealthy. The best proof, however, of the climate of a particular district is afforded by the people who inhabit it, and on the whole the Pathans are decidedly a good advertisement for their country.

Enough has been said now of a general character to introduce a stranger-reader to the region to which his attention is about to be invited, but some further details must be given regarding the breaches which have been mentioned as existing in the mountain-wall defining the frontier, the approaches to them, and the strength and characteristics of the various tribes living in the neighbourhood.

Attention has already been drawn to the fact that the Indus receives tributaries from Afghan territory east of Kabul. Where these break through the mountains, passages are formed which afford facilities for a highway. At other points, although no stream actually breaks through, there are depressions in the mountain-chain which may be approached by means of water-courses, thus forming a convenient place of passage. The most important of these breaches or passes will now be dealt with briefly in order from north to south.

1. KILIK PASS (15,600 feet).—Due north of Hunza; approached from Gilgit by way of the Hunza Valley; leads across extreme east of Afghan territory (Wakhan) into Russian Turkestan through Kanjuti territory.

Kanjutis.—These include the inhabitants of Hunza and Nagar. Formerly they were notorious marauders, but have now settled down to peaceful cultivation of the soil, which is of considerable fertility. Their fighting strength is about 5,000.

2. BAROGHIL PASS (12,400 feet).—Due north of Yasin; approached from south by way of the Yasin Valley through Punial and Yasin; leads into the centre of projecting finger of Afghan territory; is an easier pass than the others north of Chitral.

Gilgitis.—These are not a people of martial instincts, but might be able to put 3,000 men into the field.

Punialis.—Punial is situated in the Gilgit Valley above Gilgit. The inhabitants are of a much more warlike nature than the Gilgitis, and did good service in 1895; but their fighting strength is only about 400.

Yasinis.—These are an agricultural race of hardy physique; they can muster about 1,200 men for military service.

3. DORAH PASS (14,800 feet).—North-west of Chitral; leads into the Badakshan District of Afghanistan.

4. SHAWAL PASS (14,100 feet).—South-west of Chitral; leads into Kafiristan.

5. KUNER RIVER.—Breaks through the frontier mountain-chain fifty miles below Chitral.

Chitralis.—The Chitralis possess several martial qualities, have pleasing manners, and are fond of music and dancing, but they are treacherous, cruel, avaricious, and revengeful. The cultivation of the soil is somewhat neglected, and supplies are scarce. Their fighting strength is about 7,000.

Between the above and India lie—

6. BURZIL PASS (13,800 feet). — On the direct road between Srinagar and Gilgit, about twenty miles on the Srinagar side of the halfway point. The Rivers Astor and Indus are bridged on this route.

7. SHANDUR PASS (12,250 feet). — On the road from Gilgit to Chitral.

8. LOWARAI PASS (10,250 feet).—On the road from Nowshera to Chitral, Chitral lying to the north, Dir to the south.

All the passes mentioned above are snow-bound in winter, and are impracticable for wheeled traffic.

9. BINSHI PASS (8,020 feet).—On the road between Dir and the Afghan garrison town of Asmar.

Dir can be reached from India by two routes after crossing the Malakand and Katgola Passes:

(i.) By the Panjkora Valley.
(ii.) By the Jandol Valley, and Janbatai Pass.

Both roads pass through country inhabited by a branch of the Yusafzai tribe.

Yusafzais. — It will be necessary to deal with this important tribe in some detail. Its branches cover a large area, stretching from the Black Mountain in the east to the Afghan frontier in the west, and will be mentioned again and again throughout the following pages. The number of sections and subsections, with their various names, is very large, and not a little bewildering; but for the purpose of this work a glance at the table appended will make the situation sufficiently plain. The figures in brackets give the approximate fighting strength of the tribe whose name they follow.

It will be seen from the table that of the two sons of

MANDAI.

USZAR.

YUSAF.

MANDAN.   RAZAR.

Usmanzais.   Utmanzais.

URIA.   MALIZAIS.   MUSA.   ISAZAIS.

Akozais (Swatis).

Baizais.   Ranizais.   Iliaszais.

Bunerwals (8,000), and to the north-east of them Chagarzais (5,000).

Abazais.   Khadakzais.   Khwazazais.

Black Mountain Tribes:
Hassunzais (2,200).
Akazais (1,500).
Mada Khel (1,600).

Left bank of Swat River.

Right bank of Swat River.

Malizais (36,000).
Dir and Panjkora Valley.

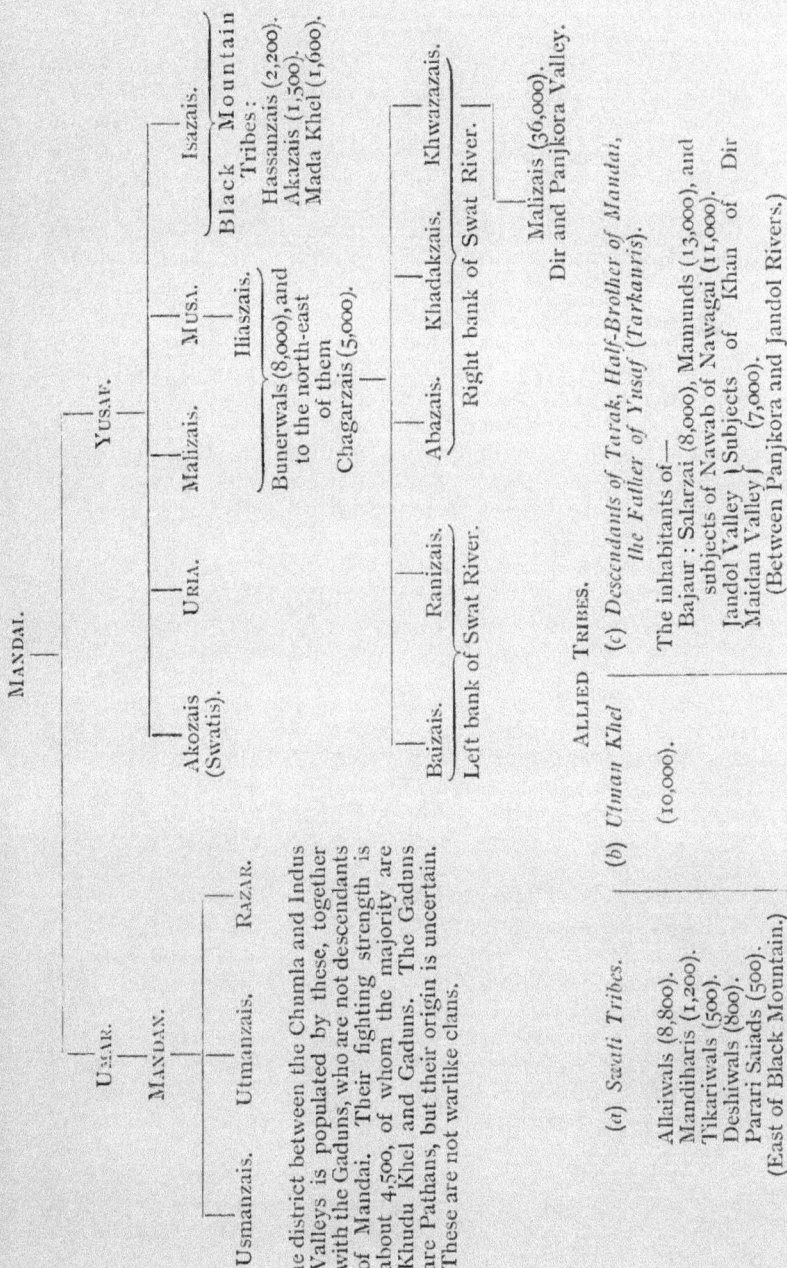

The district between the Chumla and Indus Valleys is populated by these, together with the Gaduns, who are not descendants of Mandai. Their fighting strength is about 4,500, of whom the majority are Khudu Khel and Gaduns. The Gaduns are Pathans, but their origin is uncertain. These are not warlike clans.

ALLIED TRIBES.

(*a*) *Swati Tribes.*

Allaiwals (8,800).
Mandiharis (1,200).
Tikariwals (500).
Deshiwals (800).
Parari Saiads (500).
(East of Black Mountain.)

(*b*) *Utman Khel*
(10,000).

(*c*) *Descendants of Turak, Half-Brother of Mandai, the Father of Yusaf (Tarkanris).*

The inhabitants of—

Bajaur: Salarzai (8,000), Mamunds (13,000), and subjects of Nawab of Nawagai (11,000).
Jandol Valley } Subjects of Khan of Dir
Maidan Valley } (7,000).
(Between Panjkora and Jandol Rivers.)

Mandai the descendants of Yusaf, or the Yusafzais, are by far the more important.

Swatis.—These inhabit an unhealthy district, and in consequence their physique is not so good as that of other frontier tribes. They are, nevertheless, industrious cultivators of the soil, but are treacherous and vindictive by nature. They were formerly not rated highly as fighting men, but events in 1895 and 1897 proved that this estimate was wide of the mark. The Swati tribes of the Black Mountain District inhabit a broken, wooded country. They are quarrelsome and avaricious, but are wanting in soldierly qualities.

Tarkanris.—Now in a fairly settled condition, especially as the distance from the Afghan frontier increases, but liable to excitement by religious zealots. They have proved themselves good fighters in the past. The Nawab of Nawagai has considerable influence in Bajaur. The Khan of Dir has entered into an agreement to keep open the road to Chitral. His annual subsidy was fixed in 1895 at Rs. 10,000.

Utman Khel.—A clan living on both banks of the Swat River at the lower part of its course. Agriculture is the chief occupation of the people, who have always succeeded in preserving their independence of their neighbours.

Bunerwals.—These are probably the best representatives of the Pathan race. They do not possess the bloodthirsty marauding instincts of the majority of their ilk, but are a simple and comparatively trustworthy people. They have little intercourse with British India. Stock raising and agriculture are their occupations.

Chagarzais.—Their territory lies on both banks of the Indus at the northern end of the Black Mountain. They do not possess the same virtues as their neighbours the Bunerwals, but display more of the military spirit than the Isazais.

Isazais.—In these are included the Hassanzais, Akazais, and Mada Khel, of whom the two first will receive frequent mention in the accounts of the various Black Mountain expeditions. Their military reputation does not stand high.

10. KABUL RIVER.—The valley of the Kabul River is the route for the projected railway from Peshawar into Afghan territory. The Mohmands are owners of the neighbouring country.

Mohmands.—This is an important Pathan tribe living partly in Afghanistan, partly in independent territory, and partly in the Peshawar District. They are divided into nine clans, and with the Safis to the north and the Shilmanis to the south, both of whom are claimed as vassals, their full fighting strength is about 25,000 men.

Mohmand territory is rocky and arid in character. Water is scarce, many of the villages being dependent on rain water collected in tanks. No very decisive engagement has ever been fought by British troops against the Mohmands, but occasional encounters, such as their attacks on the Swat Valley posts in 1908, show that they are not wanting in bravery. The Baizais, who live on both sides of the Afghan border, constitute their most martial clan. Where water is obtainable the soil is cultivated with success.

Mullagoris.—A small clan of obscure origin living on the British border south of the Kabul River. They are not well armed, but are courageous, and have succeeded in preserving their independence of the Mohmands and Afridis. Their fighting strength is only about 600, and they have caused little trouble since they came in contact with the British Government.

11. KHAIBAR PASS.—This is by far the most important channel of communication between India and Kabul. It is traversed by a good road suitable for wheeled traffic as far as Kabul. The pass is dominated by the Afridis, who have agreed to keep it open for trade in return for a yearly subsidy of just under £6,000. In addition, a force of 1,700 men, recruited from the neighbouring tribes and commanded by British officers (called the Khaibar Rifles), is employed in guarding the forts and smaller posts from Landi Kotal at the western end to Jamrud. The British Government have also the right to construct a railway as well as a road through the Khaibar Pass.

Afridis.—This is the most powerful of the frontier tribes. The members of it are endowed with many martial qualities, but are rapacious, untrustworthy, and lawless by nature. They are constantly at feud with one another, but are always ready to unite in defence of their independence. Their territory is bounded on the north by the Khaibar Pass, on the east by the Peshawar District, on the south by the Mastura Valley, and on the west by the Safed Koh Mountains and Afghanistan. They are divided into eight clans, whose fighting strength and territories are as under:

Zakha Khel (Maidan, Bara, and Bazar Valleys)	...	5,000
Kuki Khel (Rajgal Valley) ...	...	5,000
Malikdin Khel (Maidan and Bara Valley)	...	4,500
Kambar Khel (Maidan and Bara Valley)	...	5,000
Kamrai Khel (Maidan and Bara Valley, and the means of communication between them)	...	700
Sipah (Bara Valley)	...	1,400
Aka Khel (Waran and Bara Valleys)	...	2,000
Adam Khel, including the Jowakis (between Peshawar and Kohat)	...	6,500
		30,100

The Afridis are a people of nomadic instincts, for in winter months they leave their upland homes, and take up quarters in caves in the Khaibar district and Kajurai. The only trade they carry on is in fuel, grass, and salt.

The Zakha Khel are the most important of the Afridi clans, chiefly by reason of their geographical position, which enables them to control the direct route from the lowlands bordering the Peshawar District to the summer homes of the tribe in Tirah. They have always been far less tractable than the other clans, and have never shown the same readiness to accept service in the Indian Army.

There are three main valleys running parallel to one another through Afridi territory from west to east, which vary in height from about 5,000 feet above sea-level at the upper or western end, to 2,000 feet at the eastern, where they all join the basin of the Kabul River. From north to south these are the Bazar, Bara, and Waran Valleys, and they vary in width from about six miles to mere mountain gorges, but all afford means of access to Tirah.

12. KURRAM RIVER.—This was the line of advance into Afghanistan of the forces under Major-General (Lord) Roberts in 1878-79. At Thal, some eighty miles down the valley from the frontier, the roads from Kohat and Bannu meet. In addition to the road, Kohat is in railway communication with Thal by way of the Miranzai Valley, which is separated from Orakzai territory to the north by the Samana Ridge. Ascending the valley from Thal Zaimukht territory lies to the right or north, Waziri to the south, and the upper portion of the valleys belongs to the Turis. The Miranzai Valley is inhabited by the Bangash, a branch of the Pathan race.

Orakzais.—These are less warlike than their kinsmen, the Afridis. They are divided into seven clans, of whom the Massuzai, living at the head of the Khanki Valley on the border of Tirah Maidan, will receive mention in the account of the Tirah Campaign. Among the subdivisions of these seven clans are the Chamkannis, living at the extreme western end of Orakzai territory; the Bizotis, living north of the Ublan Pass, near Kohat; and the Rubia Khel, who live on the Samana Ridge. The fighting strength of the tribe is about 30,000.

Zaimukhts. — This tribe inhabits a broken country between that of the Orakzais and the Kurram and Miranzai Valleys. They are a fine race, and have given little trouble to the British Government. They can muster about 4,000 men.

Turis.—The Turis originally gained their present possessions by conquest. They were formerly Afghan vassals, but threw off their allegiance at the outbreak of the Afghan War in 1878, and since then have rendered valuable service to the British arms on several occasions. They are quarrelsome among themselves, but are vigorous and brave; their fighting strength is about 7,000, of whom some are mounted.

13. KAITU RIVER. — Rises in the rugged district of Khost, a favourite refuge of the lawless characters of this part of the frontier. Passes through territory of the Darwesh Khel Waziris.*

14. TOCHI RIVER. — Affords a direct route to Ghazni from Bannu. Passes through territory of the Darwesh Khel Waziris.

15. GOMAL RIVER AND PASS.—A route largely used by camel caravans between Ghazni and Dera Ismail Khan. The Gomal Valley is very barren, and villages are few. The Waziris live to the north, and Zhob Valley tribes to the south.

Waziris.—This important tribe inhabits the tract of country between the Kurram and Gomal Rivers. The district is rugged and mountainous throughout, especially in the part inhabited by the Mahsuds. The valleys run roughly from west to east, as in Afridi territory, falling towards the Indus, their watercourses being unimportant features in dry weather, but capable of rapidly becoming formidable obstacles at other times. Roads worthy of the name are practically non-existent, except along the Tochi and Gomal Valleys, the rocky beds of watercourses being usually the sole channels of communication. These watercourses vary in width from about three-quarters of

* Also known, and perhaps more correctly, as Wazirs.

a mile to mere defiles, called "tangis," which form the usual places of resistance to an invader.

Agriculture is carried on where possible, but, speaking generally, the pasturage, which suffices to maintain large flocks and herds, alone redeems the barren and inhospitable nature of the country. The effect of the inability of the soil to support the inhabitants is that they have to find other means of supplying themselves with the necessaries and all the luxuries of life, and plunder and robbery under arms are the result.

There are four Waziri clans, particulars of which are tabulated below.

	Fighting Strength.	Where Located.
1. Darwesh Khel ...,	29,000	Between Kurram and Tochi Rivers, Wana District, and Gomal Valley.
2. Mahsuds ...	14,000	Between the Shaktu and Shahur Valleys.
3. Dawaris ...	6,500	Tochi Valley.
4. Bhittanis ...	6,500	Hill country near Bannu and Tank.

Darwesh Khel.—This is the principal Waziri clan. Its members are of migratory instincts, and their habitations are of a distinctly temporary nature; they are a hardy, warlike race, and more united among themselves than their neighbours to the north, but hostile to the Mahsuds. The Madda Khel and Kabul Khel are branches of this clan.

Mahsuds.—This clan occupies the centre and most mountainous part of Waziristan. Their inaccessibility has always been their safeguard, and is responsible for the independence which has long been their boast. They are the most daring and accomplished freebooters on the whole North-West Frontier; their hands may, indeed, be said to be against all men, and the hands of all men against them. They are united in themselves, but are ignorant and unscrupulous at the same time.

Dawaris.—Agriculture is their chief occupation; they are not a warlike clan.

Bhittanis.—The main characteristics of the Bhittanis resemble those of the rest of the Waziri tribe, but they are more civilized than the Mahsuds, and more warlike than the Dawaris.

16. KHOJAK PASS.—Close to the Afghan frontier on the road between Quetta and Kandahar. It is now threaded by a road and railway, the latter of which terminates at Chaman. Between Quetta and India lie the Harnai and Bolan Passes.

17. HARNAI PASS.—A defile through which the Harnai branch of the Sibi-Quetta railway runs.

18. BOLAN PASS.—This was once a formidable obstacle, but is now traversed by both a railway and a first-class road.

Baluchis.—The three last-named passes are situated in territory inhabited by the Baluchi tribes, of whom the inhabitants of the Zhob Valley are a branch. They are a virile race, and have been friendly to the British Government for a considerable time. Their country is rocky, arid, and in the summer months intensely hot. There are several places at which the frontier may be crossed between Chaman and the Gomal River, but the scarcity of water and bad roads are great obstacles to the movements of large bodies of men.

There are several British posts in the Zhob Valley and to the south of it, of which the two most important are Fort Sandeman and Loralai, so that clans like the Marris and the Shiranis, who have given trouble in the past, are, strategically speaking, surrounded.

Before closing this topographical and ethnological description of the country, of which the following pages treat, it will be well to draw attention to the strategical positions of Gilgit, Chitral, Peshawar, Kohat, Bannu, Dera Ismail Khan, and Quetta, with reference to the avenues of approach just enumerated and the tribes whose territory they traverse.

The history of our wars against the tribes of the North-West Frontier may be divided into two main sections covering unequal periods of time :

(1) Prior to 1890 ;
(2) 1890 and after.

It is suggested that the date selected marks the time when the armament of the tribesmen all along the frontier began to improve, necessitating some changes in the minor tactics of both sides. Before 1890 the Pathan tribes were very indifferently armed ; they therefore depended for success on the *arme blanche* rather than on firearms ; but as their weapons improved, and they realized the value of a long-range rifle for firing into a camp, throwing a convoy into confusion, or harassing a retirement, so they showed less inclination to commit themselves to a hand-to-hand struggle in broad daylight without preparing the way by fire first.

The Hunza-Nagar Expedition took place in 1890, and it will be seen in the account of the campaign, not only how important captures of arms of European manufacture were made, but also how the tribesmen were able to use their weapons with effect, and to keep the British force at bay for nearly three weeks. Each campaign subsequent to 1890 marked an improvement in the armament of our enemies. In the Chitral Campaign Colonel Kelly at any rate found the force opposed to him almost as well armed as himself; in 1897 there was further improvement, which aided materially the guerilla tactics of the Afridis. At the present time the improvement is still going on, and has become a very serious question; but as an attempt will be made to deal with the subject in a later chapter, the matter will not be discussed here.

The year 1890 marks another change in the history of the North-West Frontier of India, and that is in the published records of the expeditions which took place. In 1890 a fortunate chance enabled Mr. E. F. Knight to accompany the Hunza-Nagar Expedition as a volunteer, and compile the interesting account of the operations which is to be found in his book, " Where Three Empires Meet." The literature of the Chitral Campaign is most complete; in fact the incidents of this instructive campaign are better and more fully described than those of any other frontier war. Then, again, the events of 1897 are dealt with fully or in part in several volumes; but before 1890 it is very difficult to gain access to any accounts other than official records. This difficulty is for the general reader an insuperable barrier to a knowledge of the process by which British influence was built up among the frontier tribes of North-West India, and at the best a somewhat laborious task for the military student. Colonel Paget's book—" Record of Expeditions against the North-West Frontier Tribes of India"—as revised by Lieutenant Mason, is really the only one in which the history of a considerable number of years is included between the covers of a single volume, and is the standard work on the frontier wars down to 1883. Though many of the incidents described are of deep interest, still the mass of minute detail of little military importance swells the size of the book to such an extent

as undoubtedly to frighten all but the most determined.*

The record of the North-West Frontier campaigns
before 1890 embraces a number of small expeditions, the
leading points of which, with the exception of the Ambela
Campaign of 1863, can be dealt with in a few words; if
greater detail is desired, it will be found supplied in
Colonel Paget's book. It has been thought best to deal
with these expeditions in chronological sequence rather
than in any order suggested by the geographical situation
of the theatre of war. It is to be feared that this arrangement will have the drawback of shifting the reader's attention from one part of the frontier to another with, perhaps,
bewildering rapidity; but, on the other hand, the advantage will be gained of seeing clearly how one expedition
followed, or was led up to by, another. The earlier frontier
campaigns are not so prolific of military lessons as those
of a later date, so no attempt will be made to extract the
moral from events described until the narrative of the
first section is complete. A short review will then be
made of the whole period.

* This work has been embodied recently in a new official publication,
entitled " Frontier and Overseas Expeditions from India "; but the latter is
for official use only, and is also written in great detail.

CHAPTER 1

BEFORE THE MUTINY

THE BAIZAIS, 1849. (*Map I.*)

THE annexation of the Punjab in 1849 was followed by a series of encounters with almost every tribe along the whole of the North-West Frontier. Difficulties at once arose over the payment of dues with the Baizais, a Swat clan living between British territory and the Swat River. Other means having failed, two expeditions were despatched under Lieutenant-Colonel J. Bradshaw, C.B., into the country of the recalcitrant tribe during December, 1849, in which the troops named below took part, and the principal villages were destroyed. No serious fighting took place before the tribesmen were reduced to submission, and, although further troubles arose at intervals during the course of the next few years, no military expedition was necessary, the fine demanded for any act of misconduct that occurred being invariably paid without prevarication.

> 2nd Troop 2nd Brigade Horse Artillery (52nd Battery Royal Field Artillery).
> 13th Irregular Cavalry (mutinied at Benares, 1857).
> 1st Company Bombay Sappers and Miners (3rd Sappers and Miners).
> 3rd Bombay Native Infantry (103rd Mahratta Light Infantry) ; and
> Detachments from—
> > 60th Rifles (King's Royal Rifle Corps), 200.
> > 61st Foot (2nd Battalion Gloucestershire Regiment), 300.

THE KOHAT PASS AFRIDIS, 1850. (*Map II.*)

The next quarter in which trouble arose was in the neighbourhood of Kohat. When the annexation of the Punjab brought the frontier of British India up to the north-western hills the Indian Government decided to continue the payments to the Kohat Pass Afridis which had been customary in the past in return for the protection of the road through the Pass. On February 2, 1850, however, a serious attack was made on a party working on the road near Kohat within British territory. An expedition, as shown below, was then organized, under the command of Brigadier-General Sir Colin Campbell, K.C.B., for the purpose of reinforcing the garrison of Kohat and exacting punishment from the authors of the raid.

> 2nd Troop 2nd Brigade Horse Artillery (52nd Battery Royal Field Artillery), elephant transport.
> Two 5½-inch mortars.
> Two Companies 60th Rifles (King's Royal Rifle Corps), 61st and 98th Foot (2nd Battalions Gloucestershire and North Staffordshire Regiments).
> 1st Punjab Cavalry (21st Cavalry).
> 15th Irregular Cavalry (disbanded in 1861).
> 1st Punjab Infantry (55th Coke's Rifles).
> 23rd Native Infantry (mutinied at Mhow, 1857).
> 31st Native Infantry (2nd Queen's Own Rajput Light Infantry).
> 1,600 tribal levies.

The force left Peshawar on February 9, 1850, accompanied by the Commander-in-Chief, General Sir Charles Napier, G.C.B., who happened to be in Peshawar at the time. Akhor was reached and destroyed on the 10th, after a short fight for the possession of the heights overlooking the place. This village marked the northern end of the Kohat Pass, so a force consisting of the 15th Irregular Cavalry and tribal levies was left to hold it, while the remainder continued the advance on Kohat. Other villages along the line of advance, or adjacent to it, were destroyed, the enemy harassing the flanks and rear of the column as it wound its way through the pass. Camp was formed at the foot of the Kohat Kotal early in the afternoon of February 11, and on the same day the 1st Punjab Cavalry pushed on into Kohat ; the piquets on the surrounding hills were at times briskly engaged with the enemy, and several casualties occurred. A village about four miles to the north-west was destroyed on the 12th, and the next day the return to Peshawar began, the 1st Punjab Infantry moving on into Kohat. Some sharp fighting occurred at the Peshawar end of the pass, but the enemy were driven off without real difficulty.

The tribal levies, with the exception of one detachment,

proved most unsatisfactory during these operations; both during the attack on Akhor on the 10th, and during the withdrawal from the pass, they failed to carry out the duties assigned to them. The single exception was a small band of Khaibaris of the Malikdin clan, under one Fateh Khan, who had already distinguished himself in the British service. In recognition of the gallant conduct of Fateh Khan and his standard-bearer, the Commander-in-Chief directed that they should be mounted on an elephant and precede the column into Peshawar.

A fortnight after the conclusion of Sir Colin Campbell's expedition the tribesmen made an attack on the British police post stationed in a tower on the Kohat Kotal. The garrison were hard pressed for some time, but help arrived from Kohat in time to save the situation, and a company of the 1st Punjab Infantry was left to reinforce the police. Two days later another attack was made on the same post; the enemy were beaten off, but took up a position surrounding the garrison, until forced to withdraw on the arrival of troops from Kohat. After this second attack it was decided to occupy the Kotal no longer, so the garrison returned to Kohat; the tower was then destroyed by the enemy. In November, 1850, a settlement was made with the Afridi clans of the neighbourhood after much haggling, based on a readjustment of the annual subsidies paid by Government for the maintenance of order along the Kohat road, and the construction of a fort at the Peshawar end of the pass, called Fort Mackeson, was begun.

MOHMANDS, 1851-52. (*Map I.*)

Four months after the conclusion of peace with the Kohat Pass Afridis trouble broke out with the Mohmands. The Indian Government first came into contact with this tribe during the first Afghan War of 1838-1842, but the latter came into little prominence on one side or the other. When, however, the Indian frontier reached the foot of the hills after the second Sikh War, only a few months elapsed before the Mohmands began to make attacks on Shabkadr, Matta, and other posts within British territory. In March, 1851, several small brushes occurred between the tribesmen and the frontier garrisons, and some of the neighbouring Mohmand villages were destroyed by way of reprisal. During the next six months the raids on British villages grew so frequent

and assumed so serious a character that a force was sent
out from Peshawar under Sir Colin Campbell in October
to exact punishment. No fighting occurred, and the troops
had to be content with merely destroying the villages
whence the attacks were believed to have emanated.
Even after this punishment the raids did not cease;
Peshawar itself was not immune, and several small
cavalry skirmishes occurred, in one of which a good
opportunity was lost through the misconduct of the
troops engaged. The following is an account of this
incident:

"On the 30th March (1852) news was received at Fort
Shabkadr that the Mohmands had collected in the hills
in front, and detachments were held ready to turn out at
a moment's warning. About 3.30 a.m. on the 31st, a shot
being fired at the village of Shabkadr, Captain J. L.
Walker, of the 71st Native Infantry commanding the
outpost, immediately moved out with sixty bayonets, but
the enemy were in retreat before he could come up with
them. Lieutenant F. R. Tottenham, commanding a troop
of the 7th Bengal Light Cavalry, had at once detached a
division (forty sabres) of the troop to cut off the retreat of
the enemy whilst he followed with the remainder. The
position taken up by this division was most favourable
for the purpose, and, as 250 of the enemy were advancing
on it with a brisk matchlock fire, Lieutenant Tottenham,
who had joined it with eight or nine men after posting
the second division to cut off the enemy's retreat in
another direction, advanced to charge; but with the
exception of the subadar* and a havildar and a trumpeter
not a man followed him. Riding back, he entreated his
men to follow him as the enemy passed their flank,
but in vain; and although Lieutenant Tottenham subsequently induced this detachment to follow the enemy to
the foot of the hills, no order, no entreaty, no example
could get them to charge. Both the subadar and the
trumpeter had their horses wounded. The second
division appear to have behaved well, killing one man,
and having themselves several horses wounded."†

On April 15, 1852, Sir Colin Campbell, who had taken
over command of the force assembled at Shabkadr,
observed a threatening movement on the part of the

---

* In the old Bengal Light Cavalry Regiments the native officers and non-
commissioned officers held the same ranks as in the infantry.

† "Record of Expeditions against the North-West Frontier Tribes," p. 238
(Paget and Mason).

enemy between Shabkadr and Matta. He immediately moved his troops out to try and cut the tribesmen off from the hills; but the latter perceived the manœuvre in time to make good their escape and even harass the retirement. Though no serious engagement took place, the moral effect of the presence of Sir Colin Campbell with a strong force was sufficient to secure the dispersal of the hostile gatherings. In order to strengthen the frontier defences still further, a fort was constructed about this time at Michni, on the left bank of the Kabul River close to where it issues from the border hills.

The troops who took part in the operations under Sir Colin Campbell in 1851-52 were:

> Detachment 3rd Company 1st Battalion Artillery, with
>   No. 17 Light Field Battery (No 1 Mountain
>   Battery Royal Garrison Artillery) attached.
> 2nd Troop 1st Brigade Horse Artillery (56th Battery
>   Royal Field Artillery), 2 guns.
> 2nd Irregular Cavalry (2nd Lancers).
> 15th Irregular Cavalry (disbanded in 1861).
> 7th Bengal Light Cavalry (5th Light Cavalry).
> 53rd Foot (1st Battalion Shropshire Light Infantry).
> Guides.
> 66th Gurkha Regiment (1st Battalion 1st Gurkhas).
> Detachments of 61st and 98th Foot (*vide ante*) and
>   71st Native Infantry (mutinied at Lucknow, 1857).
> 2nd Company Sappers and Miners.

RANIZAIS AND UTMAN KHEL, 1852. (*Map I.*)

In addition to the Mohmands military operations became necessary in March, 1852, against the Ranizais, a Swat clan living between British territory and the Swat River, in consequence of various raids which were made across the border and the asylum afforded to outlaws. The expedition, which was under the command of Brigadier-General Sir Colin Campbell, K.C.B., secured the promise of payment of a fine without fighting; but as the fine remained unpaid two months later, Sir Colin Campbell again invaded Ranizai territory, and after a sharp fight captured and destroyed the village of Shakot. At the close of the engagement the Guides Cavalry had an opportunity of closing with the fugitive tribesmen and inflicting considerable loss. Other Ranizai villages were destroyed, and the clan submitted to the British terms.

The troops employed under Sir Colin Campbell were :

1st Troop 1st Brigade Horse Artillery (Field Battery Royal Horse Artillery).
Detachment 3rd Company 4th Battalion Royal Artillery, and No. 19 Light Field Battery (6th Mountain Battery Royal Garrison Artillery) attached, 2 guns.
H.M.'s 32nd Regiment (1st Battalion Duke of Cornwall's Light Infantry).
2nd Irregular Cavalry (2nd Lancers).
Guides Cavalry.
1st Punjab Cavalry (21st Cavalry).
15th Irregular Cavalry (disbanded in 1861).
2nd Company Sappers and Miners.
28th Native Infantry (mutinied at Shahjahanpur, 1857).
66th Gurkha Regiment (1st Battalion 1st Gurkhas).
Guides Infantry.
1st Punjab Infantry (55th Coke's Rifles).
29th Native Infantry (mutinied at Moradabad, 1857).

In addition to his operations against the Mohmands, Sir Colin Campbell was employed, during the interval between his two expeditions against the Ranizais, in command of detachments of the same troops against the Utman Khel, a clan living along the banks of the Swat River between the Ranizais and Mohmands. This clan had also been making raids into British territory. A successful cavalry skirmish took place on May 2, and ten days later Sir Colin Campbell turned his attention to the hostile villages, which were destroyed with little difficulty, together with the crops surrounding them.

The concentration of the force for operations against the Utman Khel was remarkable for a very fine feat of marching on the part of the 1st Punjab Cavalry and 1st Punjab Infantry.

" The letter from the Commissioner sent by express to Captain Coke at Kohat, calling for his services, had miscarried, and that officer only got his orders in a second letter sent by post. The 1st Punjab Infantry and the two squadrons of the 1st Punjab Cavalry marched from Kohat at 2 a.m. on May 8, 1852, and reached Peshawar, forty miles, the same day. On arriving at the bridge of boats over the Kabul River, Captain Coke found it had been swept away, and the boats carried down-stream. On the evening of the 10th the troops had got across, and on that night marched for Abazai, halting for two hours under the Shabkadr Fort; and when, on reaching Abazai at daybreak, it was found that the force under Sir Colin Campbell had gone out to attack Nawadan,

Captain Coke pushed on, joining the force as the attack was commencing, having marched more than forty miles when Abazai was reached after the operations."*

Waziris, 1852. (*Map II.*)

The Waziris, who inhabit a tract of country stretching for 140 miles along the North-West Frontier of India, between the Miranzai Valley and the Gomal Pass, were next to come into prominence. Their two chief clans are the Darwesh Khel, or Waziris proper, and the Mahsuds, the former inhabiting the northern portion of Waziri territory, the latter the southern. They are a Pathan tribe of nomadic instincts, but differ in some essential respects from the Afridis, Mohmands, and others of their ilk. Like other Pathans, the Waziris are thieves of an extremely daring and bloodthirsty character, but, unlike their neighbours, especially to the north, they are united in themselves. The little family feuds, so common among the Afridis, are practically unknown, so that it is easy for the tribesmen to unite for the disputes which continually occur with their neighbours on every side. The Darwesh Khel (who call themselves Waziris) and Mahsuds, however, do not combine with one another; each section is left to fight its own battles by itself. The Waziris are a great stock-raising tribe, for which purpose parts of their country are very favourable, and the small but hardy breed of pony which is reared among these border hills provides the fighting forces of the tribe with mounts for a certain proportion of their men.

Trouble arose with the Waziris directly after the annexation of the Punjab, and has continued at intervals ever since. The first expedition against them took place in 1852, when a force was assembled secretly at Bannu and Latammar under Major John Nicholson, the Deputy-Commissioner, for the chastisement of the most troublesome clan. The troops that took part in these operations were organized in three columns, as shown below :

    1st Column :
        2nd Punjab Infantry (56th Punjabi Rifles).

---

* " Record of Expeditions against the North-West Frontier Tribes," p. 216 (Paget and Mason).

2nd Column :
    Two Companies 1st Punjab Infantry (55th Coke's
        Rifles), 140.
    4th Punjab Infantry (57th Wilde's Rifles), 350.

3rd Column :
    2nd Punjab Cavalry (22nd Cavalry), 40.
    Mounted Police, 50.
    6th Punjab Police Battalion, 400.

The objectives were the villages of Sapari and Garang. Starting on the night of December 20/21, 1852, the first column marched direct on Garang through the Gumatti Pass; the second, or Latammar column, on Sapari through the Barganatta Pass; and the third took a circular right-handed course from Bannu up the Kurram Valley for about twelve miles and back, with the remainder of the force through the Gumatti Pass. The surprise of the enemy was so complete that very little resistance was offered; the villages were destroyed, a large quantity of cattle and sheep carried off, and Major Nicholson returned to Bannu on December 22, having bivouacked the previous night at Gumatti.

During these successful operations the following mishap occurred to the 4th Punjab Infantry :

"On reaching their bivouac, twenty-three men of the regiment were reported missing. It was ascertained afterwards that these men had either fallen out, overcome by sleep and fatigue, or, straggling behind, had missed the road, when they were killed by the Waziris in detail after the corps had descended from the heights."[*]

Shortly afterwards peace was concluded for a time on the Waziri border.

THE BLACK MOUNTAIN EXPEDITION, 1852. (*Map IV.*)

While the Waziris were being reduced to submission British troops became engaged also at the northern end of the Punjab frontier. If a line fifty miles long be drawn slightly to the west of north from Rawal Pindi, or one twenty miles in length north-west from Abbottabad, both will strike the Indus near Amb, a place nearly due west of Srinagar. At Amb the Indus flows due south, and if its course be followed up-stream for fifty miles, a point will be reached where the river bed makes a rectangular bend about seven miles long to the east before

[*] "Record of Expeditions against the North-West Frontier Tribes," p. 469 (Paget and Mason).

it runs again in a northerly direction. If a rectangle be drawn, taking as the sides the fifty-mile stretch of the Indus above Amb, and the seven-mile arm of the right angle to the east, the area so enclosed will cover practically the whole of the Black Mountain District. The Black Mountain consists of a main ridge running north and south at an average height of 8,000 feet above sea-level, access to the summit being gained by several tracks running up spurs, which branch off roughly at right angles from the main watershed. Many of these tracks are steep and stony, and most of them pass through thickly wooded country. The Indus, which is the western boundary of the rectangle, is from 70 to 150 yards broad, and flows over a rocky bed in a deep and rapid stream.

The expedition, which took place in 1852, was directed against the Hassanzais, one of the clans inhabiting the western slopes of the mountain. The Hassanzais are described as members of the Yusafzai tribe; like the rest of their ilk, they were at this period constantly at feud with neighbouring clans, but all private quarrels were held in abeyance when it became necessary to face a common danger. The *casus belli* in 1852 was the unprovoked murder by the Hassanzais of two British officers of the Customs Department, employed in connection with the prevention of the importation of trans-Indus salt into the Punjab. The two Englishmen entered Hassanzai territory in spite of the warnings of the Deputy-Commissioner, and paid the penalty with their lives. The tribesmen refused to surrender the murderers, and seized the two forts of Chamberi and Shanglai, which belonged to a friendly Khan, who tried to bring about a peaceful compliance with the British demands.

No alternative remained, therefore, but to send a punitive expedition into Hassanzai territory, in spite of the season of the year. Accordingly, in December, 1852, a force assembled at Shergarh, under the command of Lieutenant-Colonel F. Mackeson, C.B., the Commissioner of Peshawar. The force was divided into three columns and a reserve, as shown in Table I., and on December 20, after a reconnaissance of Shanglai the previous day, the fort at that place was occupied by Major Abbott, the Deputy-Commissioner, and the three columns prepared to enter the Black Mountain territory by three parallel routes from Chutta, Shanglai, and Sasni ; the reserve remained at Shergarh.

Before resuming his advance Colonel Mackeson re-

TABLE I

THE BLACK MOUNTAIN EXPEDITION, 1852

LIEUTENANT-COLONEL F. MACKESON, C.B.

RIGHT COLUMN.	CENTRE COLUMN.	LEFT COLUMN.	RESERVE.
*Lieutenant-Colonel R. Napier, R.E.**	*Major J. Abbott.*	*Captain W. W. Davidson, 16th Irregulars.*	5th Troop 1st Brigade Horse Artillery ("T" Battery Royal Horse Artillery).
Mountain Train Battery, 2 guns.	Two Companies Police.	Mountain Train Battery, 4 guns.	7th Company Sappers and Miners.
Corps of Guides, 350.	Two Companies Kashmir Dogras.	16th Irregular Cavalry (disbanded in 1882).	3rd Native Infantry (disbanded in 1861).
1st Sikh Infantry (51st Sikhs), 300.	1,400 levies.	Two Regiments Kashmir Dogras less 2 Companies.	Kelat-i-Ghilzai Regiment (12th Pioneers).
Rawal Pindi Police, 176.	11 light native guns.		

* Afterwards Lord Napier of Magdala.

paired the fort at Shanglai, to act as a *point d'appui*, and made one more attempt to induce the Hassanzais to comply with the demands already communicated to them. The tribesmen, however, maintained a defiant attitude, and were found to be so strongly posted in the hills that Colonel Mackeson determined to transfer his reserve to the Indus Valley, and so take the enemy in rear before committing his other three columns to the frontal attack of the formidable position before him. In pursuance of this plan Lieutenant-Colonel Butler marched from Shergarh on December 24, but the troops were so delayed by the enormous quantity of baggage that accompanied them that it took this column three days to reach Darband, only seventeen miles distant. "The orders of* the Board of Administration were that these troops (the regular troops) were not to be employed on the mountain-top at that late season, and at Shergarh they were in a confined, narrow valley, encumbered with impedimenta, double-poled tents, doolies, palkies, and hundreds of camels—in short the column was equipped as if for an ordinary march, and not for mountain warfare, and yet it had passed through mountain defiles to its present position, and must pass through such defiles whatever direction it took. It was fortunate that the points occupied by the irregular portion of the force at Chutta, Shanglai, and Sasni, formed, with the assistance of intermediate posts, a complete screen, behind which the encumbered regular column laboriously, but securely, threaded its way through the mountain defile."

On reaching Darband Colonel Butler was ordered to send four companies to Chamberi to demonstrate on the heights to the south of the enemy's position facing Shanglai, and to march the remainder to Bruddur. It was thought that the difficulties of the ground were too great to render advisable any further advance of the regular troops up the Valley of the Indus. In his instructions to the three attacking columns, Colonel Mackeson named Panji Gali, the pass over the Black Mountain ridge due west of Shanglai, as the point of concentration, and warned his subordinate commanders that they could expect no reinforcements, and that in the event of a reverse they were to take ground to the south towards the reserve column at Bruddur and Chamberi.

Colonel Butler's dispositions were completed on

* "Record of Expeditions against the North-West Frontier Tribes," p. 36 (Paget and Mason).

Plate 1

FRONTIER SCENERY, NO. 1

To face p. 24

December 28, and on the next day the advance into
Hassanzai territory was begun. The columns started
before dawn, and by evening had united successfully on
the main ridge and occupied Panji Gali. Colonel Napier,
commanding the right column, encountered the most
opposition; but his infantry, covered by the fire of the
guns, carried everything before them, and in spite of the
abatis constructed by the tribesmen in front of their
position, a heavy matchlock fire, and a series of desperate
charges by the enemy, turned the hostile left flank and
insured the success of the whole attack.

The centre column under Major Abbott found the
enemy in strong force about halfway up the hill, but
by means of a turning movement succeeded in gaining
the summit and effecting a junction with the left column
about 2 p.m. The Hassanzais then took up another
strong position, but, finding their retreat threatened by
Colonel Napier, soon evacuated it, and took to flight.

The left column met with practically no resistance,
and, uniting as we have seen early in the day with Major
Abbott, merely remained in observation of the enemy till
the appearance of Colonel Napier's column caused the
tribesmen to abandon finally their position.

The three following days were devoted to the destruction of the Hassanzai villages as far as the left bank of
the Indus, and on January 2, 1853, the whole force concentrated at Bruddur, at which point operations came to
an end except for the small affair at Kotla against the
Hindustani fanatics, which will now be described.

Hindustani Fanatics, Kotla, 1853. (*Map IV.*)

The individuals known as the Hindustani fanatics were
the followers of a mullah named Ahmad Shah, a native of
Bareilly. This man had been to Mecca and returned to
India with all the prestige conferred by his pilgrimage
by way of Kandahar and Kabul. Establishing himself
in 1823 on the Peshawar border in what was then the
Sikh kingdom, Ahmad Shah proceeded to attract to his
side a large following of co-religionists from among the
Pathan tribes of the frontier hills. He "gave out that
he was a man of peculiar sanctity and divinely commissioned to wage a war of extermination with the aid of all
true believers against the infidel."[*]

---

[*] " Record of Expeditions against the North-West Frontier Tribes," p. 81
(Paget and Mason).

It was not long before Ahmad Shah and the non-Moslem Sikhs came to blows, till finally, in 1829, in a series of encounters in the main favourable to the forces of Ranjit Singh, the saintly mullah himself was slain, together with the greater part of his followers. The remnant of the Hindustani fanatics, some 300 in number, escaped to the hills on the right bank of the Indus, and took refuge with one Syad Akbar Shah, a man of considerable influence in the neighbourhood, who had been a follower of Ahmad Shah, and was known to be an enemy of the Sikhs. Akbar Shah's stronghold was at Sittana, a village about a mile from the right bank of the Indus, and near here (two miles to the north) the fugitives from the Sikhs constructed a fort which they called Mandi.

During the disturbances of 1852 the Hindustani fanatics sided with the Hassanzais, and even seized a small fort at Kotla belonging to the Khan of Amb, who was friendly to the British Government. Accordingly, after the conclusion of the operations against the Hassanzais, Lieutenant-Colonel Mackeson moved down the left bank of the Indus to Kirpilian on the opposite side of the river to Kotla. On January 6, 1853, two mountain guns, two regiments of Sikh infantry, and two regiments of Kashmir Dogras with twelve native guns were sent across the river under cover of the Horse Artillery guns, two of which were held in readiness to be sent across to ascend the mountain on elephants, or to be dragged* up on sledges formed of hollow trees; at the same time a demonstration was made opposite Sittana. The day before the Khan of Amb's men had ascended the hills to the west of Kotla and established themselves in a position from which the interior of the fort could be commanded.

The place was soon in the hands of the attacking troops, for as soon as the Sikhs and mountain guns began to climb the hill, the defenders, numbering between 200 and 300, took to flight, pursued by the Khan of Amb's contingent, who accounted for over thirty of the enemy.

The British casualties during the expedition of 1852 amounted only to fifteen; the Hassanzais were taught a severe lesson, the effect of which lasted till the disturbances of 1863, which led to the Ambela Campaign, and some useful experience of mountain warfare was gained by the army in India of the time.

* " Record of Expeditions against the North-West Frontier Tribes," p. 83 (Paget and Mason).

SHIRANIS, 1853. *(Map III.)*

It is now necessary to turn for a moment to the southern half of the North-West Frontier of India.

The Shiranis are a Pathan tribe inhabiting the district surrounding the peak known as Takht-i-Suliman due west of Dera Ismail Khan and south of the Gomal Pass. So numerous and so wholesale were their depredations in the early years of their connection with the Indian Government that Major John Nicholson, then Deputy-Commissioner of Dera Ismail Khan, reported in 1853 that "the Shiranis have regularly plundered and taken blackmail from this border since it came into our possession."

Some small engagements took place near Draband in 1853, and in April the same year the force named below devastated the Shirani country under the command of Brigadier-General J. S. Hodgson, commanding the Punjab Irregular Force.

> No. 2 Punjab Light Field Battery (21st Kohat Mountain
>   Battery).
> Detachment Garrison Artillery.
> 5th Punjab Cavalry (25th Cavalry).
> Sind Camel Corps.
> Wing 1st Punjab Infantry (55th Coke's Rifles).
> Wing 3rd Punjab Infantry.
> 2nd Police Battalion.
> 6th Police Battalion.
> Total, 2,795.

After demonstrations to the south, General Hodgson entered Shirani territory by the most northern route, through the Shekh Haidar Pass. The task of protecting the troops from surprise was well carried out, and no fighting took place.

KOHAT PASS AFRIDIS, 1853.

Turning north once more, the doings of the Kohat Pass Afridis again claim attention. The peace concluded by Sir Colin Campbell in 1850 was of short duration, for the Jowakis, who inhabit the country east of the Kohat Pass, began to make raids in 1851, which increased in daring and frequency till, after exclusion from Peshawar and Kohat had proved futile, an expedition had to be organized against them in November, 1853.

Peshawar Mountain Train Battery (23rd Peshawar
   Mountain Battery).
Two 9-pounder guns, elephant transport.
22nd Foot (Cheshire Regiment).
7th Irregular Cavalry (5th Cavalry), 1 squadron.
Corps of Guides.
Sappers and Miners.
20th Native Infantry (mutinied at Meerut, 1857).
66th Gurkhas (1st Battalion 1st Gurkhas).

The force named above assembled near Fort Mackeson under the command of Colonel S. B. Boileau for
operations in the Bori Valley, which was the origin of
the recent raids. The Bori Valley is about twelve miles
long, running roughly east and west, and is closed at
each end by a somewhat formidable defile. Two points
were discovered, however, in the northern watershed
where troops could cross—one near a village called
Kandao, and the other about a mile farther to the east
at the Sarghasha Pass. The latter was the easier route
of the two, so it was arranged that the main body should
cross there while a detachment ascended by the Kandao
route to turn the flank of any opposition that might be
offered at the Sarghasha Pass. The Sarghasha Pass
was found to be "steep, winding, and long, and, though
quite practicable for horses and any beasts of burden, it
only admitted of troops ascending in single file."[*]

Colonel Boileau had intended that the 9-pounder guns
should be left under escort at the foot of the pass on
account of the difficulties of the road and the possibility
of the absence of any occasion for their employment;
but owing to some mistake the guns, transported by
their elephants, had already started before orders to
remain at the bottom of the hill reached the officer in
command. As the guns had moved off in front of the
sappers and miners, who were equipped with mule
transport, the latter were so delayed in getting past
when the order for the guns to return was received that
they were unable to come up in time to demolish the
Bori towers, and the infantry had to be content with
setting fire to the houses in the villages on the south
side of the pass. There was some sharp fighting during
the process of crossing the heights, and reinforcements
had to be sent more than once to one point in particular.

When the work of destruction had been carried out, it
was decided to withdraw from the valley by the eastern

---

[*] "Record of Expeditions against the North-West Frontier Tribes,"
p. 333 (Paget and Mason).

defile instead of taking the road over the Sarghasha Pass again. The enemy harassed the retirement, but the protection of the rear and flanks was efficiently carried out by a happy combination of all three arms, and no difficulty was experienced at the defile, although a large number of Afridis were in the vicinity; these preserved a strictly neutral attitude, and even warned the Bori Jowakis not to proceed beyond the limits of their own territory. The troops returned to camp, after a long and arduous day, between 8 and 11 p.m., the latter hour being the time at which the last detachments got in.

Disheartened for the time being by the destruction of the Bori villages, the Jowakis, after prolonged haggling, made an unconditional surrender on February 24, 1854. Twelve years later fresh difficulties arose, and an expedition was on the point of starting to restore order when the submission of the Jowakis was received; so the necessity for military operations passed away.

MOHMANDS, 1854. (*Map I.*)

After the events of 1852 the Mohmands remained quiet for a short time, but then fell into arrears with the tribute due from them, and one of their chiefs—Rahim Dad by name—who had been summoned to Peshawar in connection with the matter fled before a settlement had been reached. An expedition, as shown below, then left Michni on August 31, 1854, under Colonel S. J. Cotton, and captured Rahim Dad's cattle in payment of the sum due. Some frontier villages were destroyed, but very little fighting took place.

> Mountain Train Battery (manned by 62nd Company
>   Royal Garrison Artillery).
> 1st Sikh Infantry (51st Sikhs).
> 9th Native Infantry (21st Punjabis).
> Detachments :
>   22nd Foot (Cheshire Regiment), 2 companies.
>   10th Light Cavalry, 1 troop.
>   2nd Company Sappers and Miners.

After the expedition of 1854 fresh Mohmand outrages occurred, but owing to the political situation of the time the Government of India were unwilling to undertake any military operations which could be deferred to a more convenient season. The Mohmands gave no special trouble during the Mutiny, and after the crisis was over an arrangement was made between them and the British authorities which had the effect of securing peace for a time. The chief bone of contention was the possession of certain lands within British territory which had been confiscated from the Mohmands; these the latter were very anxious to regain, and the British political authorities equally reluctant to relinquish. The situation is well summed up in a letter to one of the Mohmand chiefs written by Colonel H. B. Edwardes, C.B., the Commissioner, in which he says: "From all you write I believe you sincerely desire to put an end to the disturbances on the Mohmand frontier and to come to friendly terms. I have this day addressed my own Government in your favour and asked that your past offences may be forgiven and bygones be bygones; and, as your son undertakes to be responsible for the rest of the Mohmand maliks, I have recommended that the pardon be extended to all other Mohmands (except such individuals as may be known to have committed murder or other serious crimes of which justice must take notice) and that the blockade be taken off, and the Mohmands be admitted to come and go and trade in the Peshawar Valley. For I conceive it is beyond my discretion to forgive and condone an old-standing enmity like this, though I have every hope that Government will listen to my representations.

"As to any jagirs that have been confiscated, I do not think it at all advisable that they should be released, for they will only be a future bone of contention. Whoever sits on a barren hillside and enjoys a fine estate in the plain below for doing nothing must necessarily get wind in his head. He thinks he owes it to his own strength and the fears, not the generosity, of Government. So after a year or two he gets full and proud and rebels, and then the whole fight comes over again, and the tribe is plunged into war to please him, and many lives are lost. In short, jagirs in the plain are not good for the men on the hills, and they will never be given with my consent. Don't think I say this for the sake of the money. To a great Government the sum is of no consequence, but it is bad for the administration. If there be any Mohmand mortgages in the hands of our subjects, the Mohmands will be free to sue in our courts, where every justice will be done them. And as to the prisoners in our gaols, to please you I will release every Mohmand who has been seized merely because he was a Mohmand, on condition that he pay whatever reward was given for his own seizure. But no highwayman, or murderer, or other criminal will be released; justice must take its course with such offenders.

"My friend, I have spoken my mind out, for it is best to be plain. For the rest, I desire the honour and welfare and strength of you and your family, and I conceive that they will be better served by the friendship than by the enmity of the British Government."[*]

AFRIDIS, 1854. (*Map II.*)

At the end of 1854 the Afridis claimed the attention of the frontier garrisons for the first time. It is true that some dealings with this important tribe had already taken place during the first Afghan War fifteen years before; but the year 1854 marked the first military conflicts since the British and Afridi borders became contiguous. The Aka Khel were the clan concerned. This section thought themselves aggrieved by non-participation in the grants made by the Indian Government in connection with the Kurram Pass. They commenced therefore a series of depredations on the Peshawar border, which resulted in a blockade of their country and several retaliatory raids, by which large numbers of their cattle were carried off, and it became very unsafe for them to send their animals to graze anywhere within reach of the British posts. These raids and counter raids went on till the end of 1855, when the circumstances of the Aka Khel became so reduced through loss of their cattle and exclusion from trade with India that, despairing of assistance from the other sections of the tribe, they tendered an unwilling submission to the British Commissioner. The Aka Khel adopted every device to escape the payment in full of the fine demanded, and to obtain access to the Peshawar market before they had satisfied all claims against them; but the blockade was rigorously enforced until a complete settlement had been made.

During the Indian Mutiny the Afridis, like their kinsmen to the north, caused no embarrassment to the Government; small differences occurred, but none of a serious or insuperable nature.

---

[*] "Record of Expeditions against the North-West Frontier Tribes," p. 247 (Paget and Mason).

ORAKZAIS, 1855. *(Map II.)*

The Orakzais, a Pathan tribe inhabiting the mountains to the north-west of Kohat, were the next to come into prominence. Up to the year 1855 they had caused no serious trouble to the British authorities, but during the operations of the Miranzai Field Force in the same year they committed several acts of hostility, which continued after the troops had been withdrawn, and necessitated the reinforcement of the frontier posts.

In August, 1855, the attitude of the Orakzais became so menacing that the force shown below assembled at Hangu on the 25th, under the command of Brigadier-General N. B. Chamberlain, for the destruction of the villages of Nasin, Sangar, and Katsah belonging to the most disaffected of the Orakzai clans.

> Peshawar Mountain Train Battery (23rd Peshawar Mountain Battery), 4 guns.
> No. 3 Punjab Field Battery (22nd Derajat Mountain Battery), 5 guns.
> 4th Punjab Cavalry.
> 1st Punjab Infantry (55th Coke's Rifles).
> 2nd Punjab Infantry (56th Punjabi Rifles).
> 3rd Punjab Infantry.
> A number of tribal levies.

Nasin and Sangar were both situated high up among the hills bordering the Miranzai Valley on the north side, and their facilities for defence were so great that the only chance of decisive success lay in simultaneous surprise. Two detachments of the regular troops were detailed for the attack on Nasin and Sangar, while the levies were deputed to destroy Katsah; the main body followed the column directed on Nasin, to act as a reserve to the whole force. The troops left Hangu between 9 and 11 p.m. on September 1, 1855, and had about fourteen miles to traverse before their objectives were reached. The assaults were delivered at dawn; the enemy were completely surprised, but the fighting men contrived to make good their escape, leaving large quantities of cattle in the hands of the assailants. The villages and crops were destroyed, and the retirement began about 10 a.m. The enemy then followed up with some determination, and succeeded in overpowering a small party of the 2nd Punjab Infantry before they were driven back by a counter-attack of the same regiment. The clans whose territory had just been invaded came to terms soon afterwards, and General Chamberlain returned to Kohat on October 7.

THE MIRANZAI AND KURRAM VALLEYS, 1855-56.
(*Map II.*)

An entirely new district now renders its contribution to the history of the time.

The Miranzai Valley, which runs due west from Kohat as far as the Kurram River, is divided into two nearly equal portions by a watershed running north and south slightly nearer to the Kurram River than Kohat. The eastern portion is bounded on the north by the territory of the Orakzais, that on the west by the territory of the Zaimukhts, the Kohat District lying to the south of both sections.

From Thal, the point where the Miranzai and Kurram Valleys meet, the latter runs upwards in a north-westerly direction to Kurram Fort and the Peiwar Kotal through country inhabited by a tribe of obscure origin, called the Turis. Soon after the annexation of the Punjab the Afghans set up a claim to the Kurram and Miranzai Valleys, and even sent troops to occupy places therein. The inhabitants at once protested to the Indian Government, and offered to pay an annual tribute in return for inclusion of their country in British territory. The offer was accepted, and the Afghans were forced to withdraw.

Shortly afterwards the presence was reported in the neighbourhood of the Miranzai Valley of bands of Waziri raiders, so the force named below moved out from Kohat on October 14, 1851, under the command of Captain J. Coke, to cause the dispersion of these bands, and clear the road for a visit by the Deputy-Commissioner of the district. Captain Coke reached Thal without any fighting, but while camped at that place his piquets were frequently attacked at night, until the inhabitants were informed that they would be held responsible for such disturbances under penalty of the destruction of their villages ; the attacks then ceased, and Captain Coke returned to Kohat on November 12.

> No. 1 Punjab Light Field Battery, 3 guns.
> 1st Punjab Cavalry (21st Cavalry).
> Half Company Sappers and Miners.
> 1st Punjab Infantry (55th Coke's Rifles).

During the next three years, however, things grew from bad to worse in the Miranzai Valley; the Turis fell into arrears with their tribute, and, as the Deputy-Commissioner said, the valley became the asylum of all the robbers and murderers of the neighbouring districts. Early in 1855, therefore, the force shown below was organized at Kohat under the command of Brigadier-General N. B. Chamberlain, and advanced up the Miranzai Valley on April 4. General Chamberlain reached Darsamand on April 28, receiving the unwilling submission of the various villages passed *en route*. At Darsamand a spirited little affair took place, in which the cavalry and infantry acted in admirable combination, and inflicted so severe a defeat on the enemy that no further resistance of any kind was offered, and after Thal had been visited the force returned to Kohat on May 21.

> No. 1 Punjab Light Field Battery, 3 guns.
> No. 3 Punjab Light Field Battery (22nd Derajat Mountain Battery), 6 guns.
> 4th Punjab Cavalry.
> Detachment Sappers and Miners.
> Four Companies 66th Gurkhas (1st Battalion 1st Gurkhas).
> 1st Punjab Infantry (55th Coke's Rifles).
> 3rd Punjab Infantry.
> Scinde Rifle Corps, afterwards 6th Punjab Infantry (59th Scinde Rifles).

In his report on this expedition Major Edwardes, the Commissioner, drew attention to the difficult position of many of the rank and file of the 1st and 3rd Punjab Infantry, whose homes were among the very tribes against whom the operations of the force had been directed. At the same time he testified to the unswerving loyalty of both regiments in spite of the efforts of tribal emissaries, whom it was impossible to exclude altogether from the camps, to induce the men to join in a religious war against the infidel. Colonel Paget* says also that " Major Edwardes alluded in terms (which the events of 1857 made truly prophetic) to the danger of not having mixed races in the native army." It is to be hoped that in view of the large number of men now recruited for the Indian Army in the Punjab the allusion will not become prophetic again.

---

* " Record of Expeditions against the North-West Frontier Tribes," p. 441 (Paget and Mason).

Miranzai Valley, 1856. (*Map II.*)

Raids in the Miranzai Valley soon recommenced, so the troops which had taken part in the expedition of 1855 again moved out from Kohat on October 21, 1856, under the command of Brigadier-General N. B. Chamberlain, together with the reinforcements named below. The total strength of the force was 4,876 of all ranks, with fourteen guns. The inhabitants received the troops in a friendly spirit, which was very different from their attitude in 1855, and no hostility was met till General Chamberlain approached Torawari, a Zaimukht stronghold a little to the north of the usual route through the valley. Colonel Paget's account of the surprise and capture of Torawari is most graphically put, and, though not of any great military importance, is quoted here as an interesting episode in the history of Indian Frontier campaigns.

> Detachment Peshawar Mountain Train Battery (23rd Peshawar Mountain Battery).
> Detachment 1st Punjab Cavalry (21st Cavalry).
> Four Companies 66th Gurkha Regiment (1st Battalion 1st Gurkhas).
> 2nd Punjab Infantry (56th Punjabi Rifles).
> 5th Punjab Infantry (58th Vaughan's Rifles).
> Khotah levies.

"It was therefore decided to surprise the village. Orders were issued for the usual march to Nariab on the following morning. The Nariab road was reconnoitred by the engineer officers, and improved by the sappers, and the ground at Nariab was selected for the camp. The criminals from this place no doubt congratulated themselves that they were snug in Torawari. An hour before the appointed time the morning bugle sounded. From Kai to Torawari is about nine miles, and for half the distance the road is the same as that to Nariab. Up to this point the whole force proceeded leisurely, and none but commanding officers knew what was going to happen. At length, however, the troops broke into two columns, one keeping the road to Nariab, and the other striking off to Torawari. The friends of the Zaimukhts then became uneasy, but no man was allowed to go ahead. When within four miles of the place, and as day was fast breaking, the cavalry pushed on in two bodies, one led by Captain Henderson, the Deputy-Commissioner, the other under the Brigadier himself, accompanied by Lieutenant-Colonel H. B. Edwardes, the Commissioner. The broken nature of the ground prevented any rapid movements, but, by keeping a tolerably wide circle, the cavalry succeeded in surrounding the place before the inhabitants had any warning, and the Zaimukhts and their guests awoke to find themselves caught in a net.

"So entirely helpless were these boasters now that not a sign of resistance was made. The head-men were summoned from the village to hear the terms dictated to them, but after two hours' negotiation nothing could be settled, and they were sent back with the intimation that they must either surrender the criminals known to be harboured by them, pay a fine for previous misconduct, and give security for future good behaviour, or stand the consequences.

"In the meanwhile the Peshawar Mountain Train Battery and the 6th Punjab Infantry came up, shortly followed by the mountain guns of No. 1 Punjab Light Field Battery and the 1st and 2nd Punjab Infantry; these were all placed in position ready to act if required. Half an hour had been allowed to the maliks for the surrender of the criminals, and this time expired without any sign of compliance on their part being shown. A further quarter of an hour was granted to enable them to send out their women and children, and during this period every endeavour was made to induce them to place their families in security, but with no effect; and the time having expired, the guns were opened with blank cartridge in the hope of intimidating the inhabitants, but without success. At length shells were thrown into the village, and after about thirty rounds the women were seen rushing out of the village and running towards our position, waving clothes and holding up the Koran. The fire of the guns was instantly stopped, and the women were sent back to tell the men that they must now come out and lay down their arms or the batteries would re-open. Slowly and angrily they came out and threw their swords, daggers, pistols and muskets down upon the plain, but only by twos and threes; and still there was no sign of giving up the criminals. The 1st and 2nd Punjab Infantry were therefore ordered into the village to search for arms and refugees. One sepoy was wounded in a house, and the Zaimukht assailant was killed on the spot. Still the criminals were concealed. At length the stacks of winter fodder for the cattle were fired, and the wind carried the flames from house to house, setting off loaded muskets that had been hidden in the straw. Then, one by one, the criminals were brought out, each with protestations that he was the last. But Captain Henderson had the list of them in his hand, and patiently demanded the remainder. The troops were then recalled from the village and the inhabitants allowed to extinguish the flames which had destroyed about one-third of their houses.

" The arms* that had been surrendered and the thirteen criminals who had been captured were all sent off to our camp at Nariab ; and 100 hostages with 200 or 300 head of cattle were also carried away as security, till a fine of Rs. 2,000 should be paid for the long-standing scores of Torawari."†

On November 6 and 7 an entrenched camp was formed at Thal on the left bank of the Kurram River, which was garrisoned by 600 men, while the remainder of the force continued the advance up the Kurram Valley. After an arduous march along a very bad track, partly along the bed of the nullah, Kurram Fort was reached on the 11th by way of the Darwaza Pass. No fighting took place, but the opportunity was seized to survey the surrounding country and reconnoitre the Peiwar Pass.

General Chamberlain's threat to destroy the neighbouring villages if the tribesmen fired into his camp proved sufficient to secure immunity from annoyance of this kind. The return march to Thal was made by way of the Kurram Valley to the east of the route taken during the advance. The road lay along the bed of the nullah, but proved to be easier than was anticipated.

From Thal an expedition was made against a band of Waziris about seven miles down the Kurram Valley, who had murdered five grass-cutters near the British camp. After a night march a column moving down the left bank of the river succeeded in surprising the enemy and cutting off their retreat, while another column on the right bank closed in on the Waziri encampment. The Waziris soon realized the futility of resistance, gave up the men demanded, and agreed to the terms imposed as compensation for the outrage. Satisfactory terms were concluded soon afterwards with all the neighbouring clans, and General Chamberlain returned to Kohat at the end of December.

The results of the Miranzai Expeditions of 1855 and

---

* Matchlocks, 90 ; swords, 176 ; pistols, 11 ; knives, 8 ; shields, 29.
† " Record of Expeditions against the North - West Frontier Tribes," pp. 445, 446 (Paget and Mason).

1856 were most satisfactory; the old attitude of sullen hostility gave way to contented acquiescence in British rule, and even to a cordiality which secured the assistance of the Turis in subsequent operations in or near their valley. The Turis were given their independence on October 7, 1880, before the evacuation of the Kurram Valley at the conclusion of the second Afghan War; but as internal dissensions began immediately, it is questionable whether they would not have been better off if they had continued to be British subjects.

TRIBES NEAR DERA GHAZI KHAN, 1853-1857. (*Map III.*)

Events near the southern end of the frontier line now claim a brief description.

Expeditions against the predatory tribes inhabiting the district lying to the north-west of Dera Ghazi Khan were undertaken in 1853 by Brigadier-General J. S. Hodgson with a portion of the force employed against the Shiranis, and in 1857 by Brigadier-General N. B. Chamberlain with the troops named below. The force assembled at Taunsa, a place about fifty miles north of Dera Ghazi Khan, and had one sharply contested engagement on March 7 with the enemy at a point called Khan Bund, in a pass giving access to the territory of the Bozdars. The enemy were found barring the way in a strong position, but a combined flank and frontal attack, well supported by artillery fire, had the effect of causing its speedy evacuation. After considerable loss of property had been inflicted on the tribesmen, satisfactory terms were arranged without further fighting.

No. 1 Punjab Light Field Battery, 4 field guns.
No. 2 Punjab Light Field Battery, 4 mountain guns.
No. 3 Punjab Light Field Battery, 4 mountain guns.
2nd and 3rd Punjab Cavalry (22nd and 23rd Cavalry),
    113.
Sappers and Miners, 58.
1st Sikh Infantry, 443.
3rd Sikh Infantry, 445.
1st Punjab Infantry, 471.
2nd Punjab Infantry, 476.
4th Punjab Infantry, 484.

CHAPTER II

THE MUTINY PERIOD

THE HINDUSTANI FANATICS, 1857-58. (*Map I.*)

DURING the Indian Mutiny the only quarter in which trouble arose with any of the border tribes was to the north-west of Rawal Pindi beyond the Indus. The Hindustani fanatics, sustained by assistance in men and money from India, were at the bottom of the outbreak. They and the neighbouring clans were held in check by the Fort of Mardan, which was, as now, usually garrisoned by the Corps of Guides. At the beginning of the Mutiny this corps left to form part of the Punjab Movable Column, and its place was taken by the 55th Native Infantry. The latter regiment mutinied in the middle of May, but was attacked and defeated with heavy loss by Colonel John Nicholson, and the remnant scattered in disorganized bodies over the country. Mardan was then garrisoned by the 5th Punjab Infantry and two guns of the Peshawar Mountain Battery, under the command of Major J. L. Vaughan. This officer was soon called upon to utilize his men, assisted by a detachment of the 2nd Punjab Cavalry, to restore order in the hilly country west of the Indus. Marching rapidly from Mardan, he attacked the village of Shekh Jana, which was the centre of the disturbance, early on July 2, drove the enemy in disorder to the hills, and burnt the village.

A fortnight later another outbreak instigated by the Hindustani fanatics occurred at Narinji. As this place was difficult of access, it was desired to take the enemy by surprise, so supplies were collected at Salim Khan, as if the country to the east of Narinji was destined to be the objective. After a night march Narinji was reached at dawn on July 21, 1857; the enemy were taken completely by surprise, and the troops carried the lower part of the village without waiting to crown the heights and

39

draw a cordon around the place. The men had executed a long march at a trying time of year, so it was not considered advisable to expose them to the risk of becoming exhausted by arduous hill-climbing and to the danger of small detachments being attacked in overwhelming numbers by the large hostile force in the neighbourhood. The enemy made several unavailing counter-attacks, but the work of destroying the lower part of the village was soon carried out, and Major Vaughan withdrew his men without opposition. The enemy suffered severely, fifty, mostly Hindustanis, being killed in the lower village alone; the British loss was five killed and twenty-one wounded.

It was not long before another expedition to Narinji had to be undertaken. At 1 a.m. on August 3 Major Vaughan moved out from his camp at Shewa with a composite force* made up of detachments from various regiments which had joined him during the past month, and arrived at Narinji before sunrise. While the guns opened fire on the village from a nala skirting its north side, a detachment of 300 men was sent to work round by the British right to the reverse side of the village. In spite of determined opposition this detachment carried out its orders without a check, and occupied the upper portion of the village. In the meantime another force was detached to the left of the British main attack to intercept the enemy's retreat, while the lower half of the village was occupied by Major Vaughan's infantry. As soon as the destruction of the village was complete the force was withdrawn without molestation. "Not a house was spared; even the walls of many were destroyed by elephants. . . . Three prisoners were taken—one was a Bareilly maulvi, the second a Chamla standard-bearer, and the third a vagrant of Charonda; they were all subsequently executed."†

---

* 24-pounder howitzers, 2 guns.
Peshawar Mountain Battery, 4 guns.
27th Regiment (1st Battalion Royal Inniskilling Fusiliers), 50 bayonets.
70th Regiment (2nd Battalion East Surrey Regiment), 50 bayonets.
87th Regiment (1st Battalion Royal Irish Fusiliers), 50 bayonets.
21st Native Infantry (1st Brahmans), 50 bayonets.
5th Punjab Infantry (58th Vaughan's Rifles), 400 bayonets.
6th Punjab Infantry (59th Scinde Rifles), 200 bayonets.
16th Punjab Infantry (24th Punjabis), 150 bayonets.
Police and levies, 325.
2nd Punjab Cavalry (22nd Cavalry), 150 sabres.

† "Record of Expeditions against the North-West Frontier Tribes," p. 89 (Paget and Mason).

Three months had not elapsed after the destruction of Narinji when an attack on the British Assistant Commissioner of the district encamped at Shekh Jana rendered another punitive expedition necessary. The force shown in Table II. assembled in the following spring near Nowshera on the left bank of the Kabul River, under the command of Major-General Sir Sydney Cotton, K.C.B., and occupied Salim Khan on April 25.

At 1 a.m. on the morning of April 26 Sir Sydney Cotton started with the first column, *viâ* the Daran Pass, for Chinglai, which was occupied and destroyed almost without opposition. The first column returned to Salim Khan the next day by way of Panjtar, finding the two routes to Chinglai almost equal in length, but the Daran Pass road much the easier for troops. While Sir Sydney Cotton was carrying out the destruction of Chinglai, the second column visited Panjtar, and, having carried out the same work there, returned to Salim Khan; the third column remained in charge of the camp at Salim Khan.

Another hostile stronghold at Mangal Thana was destroyed, without fighting, on April 29, and on May 3 Sir Sydney Cotton's force reached Khabal with a view to proceeding against the last remaining Hindustani stronghold at Sittana, in co-operation with Major Becher's column from the left bank of the Indus. An enveloping attack was made on the morning of the 4th by a portion of Sir Sydney Cotton's force and Major Becher's men; the enemy were caught by a cross-fire, and, after a short hand-to-hand struggle, "every Hindustani in the position was either killed or taken prisoner."*

Of this decisive engagement it is stated that "the fighting of the Hindustanis was strongly marked with fanaticism; they came boldly and doggedly on, going through all the preliminary attitudes of the Indian prizering, but in perfect silence, without a shout or a word of any kind. All were dressed in their best for the occasion, mostly in white, but some of the leaders wore velvet cloaks."†

As the troops withdrew some attempt was made to harass the retreat by parties of tribesmen, who had been observed assembling in the hills, but no difficulty was experienced in beating them off. During the operations under Sir Sydney Cotton just described the Enfield rifle

---

* "Record of Expeditions against the North-West Frontier Tribes," p. 95 (Paget and Mason).
† *Ibid.*

TABLE II

EXPEDITION AGAINST THE HINDUSTANI FANATICS, 1858

MAJOR-GENERAL SIR SYDNEY COTTON, K.C.B.

FIRST COLUMN.	SECOND COLUMN.	THIRD COLUMN.	MAJOR J. R. BECHER'S COLUMN.
	Lieutenant-Colonel H. Renny, 81st Foot.	*Major A. T. Allen, 81st Foot.*	
Peshawar Light Field Battery (manned by 35th Battery Royal Field Artillery), 4 guns. Peshawar Mountain Train Battery (23rd Peshawar Mountain Battery), 2 guns. 98th Foot (2nd Battalion North Staffordshire Regiment), 260. 7th Irregular Cavalry (5th Cavalry), 100. Guides Cavalry, 200. Peshawar Light Horse,* 30. Sappers and Miners, 100. 9th Punjab Infantry (21st Punjabis), 400. 18th Punjab Infantry (26th Punjabis), 400. 21st Native Infantry (1st Brahmans), 300. Guides Infantry, 300.	81st Foot (2nd Battalion Loyal North Lancashire Regiment), 200. 18th Irregular Cavalry,* 100. Sappers and Miners, 47. Kelat-i-Ghilzai Regiment (12th Pioneers), 200. 8th Punjab Infantry (20th Punjabis), 450.	81st Foot, 105. 98th Foot, 100. 7th Irregular Cavalry, 25. 18th Irregular Cavalry, 25. Guides Cavalry, 60. 8th Punjab Infantry, 54. 9th Punjab Infantry, 137. 18th Punjab Infantry, 185. 21st Native Infantry, 155. Kelat-i-Ghilzai Regiment, 254. Guides Infantry, 76.	Peshawar Mountain Train Battery (23rd Peshawar Mountain Battery), 2 guns. Hazara Mountain Train Battery (24th Hazara Mountain Battery), 3 guns. 2nd Sikh Infantry (52nd Sikhs), 300. 6th Punjab Infantry (50th Scinde Rifles), 450. 12th Punjab Infantry,* 300.

* No modern representative.

was used for the first time in hill warfare ; it "was found most effective and evidently made a great impression, both on the minds of the enemy as well as on those of the native chiefs who accompanied the force."*

Before the troops left the neighbourhood an ultimatum was sent to the clans inhabiting the hilly country west of Sittana, requiring them to enter into an agreement not to assist the Hindustani fanatics in any way. The demand was supported by a mixed force of cavalry and infantry, which occupied Maini so as to be ready for action in case of refusal. The British terms were complied with, however, and Sir Sydney Cotton marched back to Nowshera.

WAZIRIS, 1859-60. (*Map II.*)

Seven years elapsed after the conclusion of Major John Nicholson's expedition against the Waziris before another became necessary against the same tribe. On this occasion the theatre of operations lay in the north-west of that of 1852, against a clan called the Kabul Khel, who had been implicated in the murder of a British officer on the road between Bannu and Kohat in November, 1859.

Brigadier-General N. B. Chamberlain was appointed to the command of the troops named below, and marched out from Kohat on December 15, 1859, arriving at Thal four days later. The force crossed to the right bank of the Kurram River on December 20, and camped for the night in the territory of the Amir of Kabul, whose good offices had already been secured. Here it was ascertained that the Waziris had taken up a position at Maidani, a place eight miles west of Biland Khel, where General Chamberlain was encamped. The approaches to the place lay through two narrow gorges, one giving access from the east, named Gandiob, the other from the south, called Zaka. The gorges were reconnoitred on December 21, and it was decided to use the one by Gandiob. The advance on Maidani was made the next day ; the infantry and mountain guns made a simultaneous attack on the ridges flanking the gorge, and, after two hours' rough climbing, the heights above the Waziri encampments were won.

* " Record of Expeditions against the North-West Frontier Tribes," p. 95 (Paget and Mason).

Detachment No. 1 Punjab Light Field Battery, 2 guns.
Detachment No. 2 Punjab Light Field Battery
(21st Kohat Mountain Battery), 4 guns.
Detachment Peshawar Mountain Train Battery, 4 guns.
Detachment Hazara Mountain Train Battery, 3 guns.
Detachment Guides Cavalry.
Detachment Sappers and Miners.
Detachment Guides Infantry.
4th Sikh Infantry (54th Sikhs).
1st Punjab Infantry.
3rd Punjab Infantry.
4th Punjab Infantry.
6th Punjab Infantry.
24th Punjab Infantry Pioneers (32nd Sikh Pioneers).
1,456 levies.

Total, 5,372.

The column on the right of the gorge, from the point of view of the attackers, met with practically no resistance, but that on the left came in for some sharp fighting. The Waziris had been deceived as to the probable line of advance by the more careful examination made of the Zaka route, and by the presence there of Pioneer working parties, who were engaged in improving the road. Little attempt had been made therefore to prepare the hills on the right or north of the Gandiob defile, but breast-works had been thrown up on the opposite side, which were held with resolution for some time. These breast-works, however, could be enfiladed by the mountain guns on the other side of the gorge, so soon became untenable. The following tribute is paid to the gallantry of the Waziri defenders on this occasion :

" The charge by a small body of Waziri footmen, with some ten or twelve horsemen, upon the skirmishers of the Guides Infantry, whilst ascending to the attack of the first breastwork, was most gallant, and elicited the admiration of our officers and men. It was wonderful how the horsemen, mounted on small but wiry mares, managed to charge down over the rocks and declivities. . . . Another party of a dozen footmen, behind a low breast-work on the summit of a hill, endeavoured to keep their ground against a company of rifles. Having exhausted their ammunition, they took to stones, which, in Waziri hands, are formidable missiles, and, coming out in front, kept up an incessant discharge, wounding several sepoys. At last, finding that their foes were closing in upon them, several came down, sword in hand, to die." *

* " Record of Expeditions against the North-West Frontier Tribes," p. 477 (Paget and Mason).

All Waziri property in Maidani was either carried off or destroyed, and General Chamberlain returned to camp at dusk without molestation. Maidani was visited again the next day, and, by means of a combined advance from the Gandiob and Zaka defiles, a large number of sheep, cattle, and camels fell into the hands of the force. During the night a clan, which had professed neutrality, and therefore had been left unharmed, was called upon to piquet the heights, with the result that no disturbance took place.

General Chamberlain's force concentrated on December 24 at Shiwa, a place in the Kurram Valley ten miles below Biland Khel. Here representatives of various clans came in to make terms, and advantage was taken of the four days' halt which ensued to survey the surrounding country.

No further fighting took place, but the country was scoured for some twelve miles west, south-west, and east of Shiwa ; several Waziri encampments were destroyed, and further captures of stock made. Some valuable survey work was accomplished, and, satisfactory terms having been arranged with the tribesmen, General Chamberlain returned by the way he had come to Kohat on January 14, 1860.

Other troubles arose with the Waziris between 1860 and 1883, but the threat of renewed military operations or a counter-raid by a small detachment was sufficient to restore order and reduce the tribesmen to submission. During the Afghan War of 1878-1880 the Waziris, as distinct from the Mahsuds, gave little trouble, though urged thereto by the Afghan authorities ; their opportunities were certainly favourable, but besides the traditional absence of cordiality between the two parties, the presence of a considerable British force in the Kurram Valley may have been sufficient to deter the tribesmen from hostile enterprises. The only expedition of any size was one commanded by Brigadier-General J. J. H. Gordon, C.B., in October, 1880, which, after a rapid march from Thal, succeeded in surprising and capturing 200 prisoners and 2,000 head of cattle. The force was back at Thal in twenty-four hours. The troops engaged were :

> 1—8th Royal Artillery, 2 guns.
> 85th King's Own Light Infantry (2nd Battalion Shrop-
>   shire Light Infantry), 250.
> 18th Bengal Cavalry (18th Lancers), 250.
> 20th Punjab Native Infantry (20th Punjabis), 250.

Mahsuds, 1860. (*Map III.*)

Three months later General Chamberlain again took the field against the second of the two chief Waziri clans. From the first the Mahsud Waziris were a thorn in the side of the British authorities in this part of the north-west frontier line on account of their repeated forays and the difficulty of effecting the capture of any of the raiders. For various reasons no military expedition was undertaken against them until 1860 ; but the first conflict, though only the affair of a small body of cavalry, was cleverly planned and most efficiently carried out by the native officer in command. Colonel Paget's account of this brilliant little affair is as follows : " Emboldened by years of immunity, and believing that they could success-fully oppose any attempt to penetrate their mountains, the Waziris had on March 13, 1860, without provocation or pretext of any kind, come out into the plains to the number of some 3,000, headed by their principal men, with the intention of sacking the town of Tank, which stands on the plains some five miles from the foot of the hills. The Nawab's agent, having obtained previous notice of their gathering, on the 12th informed Saadat Khan, the native officer in command of the troop of the 5th Punjab Cavalry then holding Tank. This officer at once summoned the sowars in the neighbouring regular outposts, besides collecting twenty of the Nawab's horse-men, and some other irregular horse ; so that the force at his disposal was 158 sabres 5th Punjab Cavalry, and 37 mounted levies. On the morning of the 13th the whole party moved out towards the mouth of the Tank Zam, on arriving near the entrance of which they found the Waziris drawn up about half a mile on the plain side of the pass. The Waziris immediately opened fire upon the cavalry, on which Ressaldar Saadat Khan ordered his detachment to retire with the intention of drawing the enemy farther into the plains. The stratagem was successful, and the enemy followed with shouts of deri-sion ; but when they had come nearly a mile, the cavalry turned, and, having first cut off their retreat to the hills, charged in the most dashing manner. The Waziris, per-sonally brave, and invariably of vigorous, muscular frames, wanted the power of combination to resist effectually the charge of our cavalry. Cut down and ridden over, they fled in confusion, the men in front forcing back the men behind till all became a helpless rabble, struggling, striving, straining to regain the safety of the mountain-pass. The result was that about 300 Mahsuds were killed, including six leading maliks, and many more wounded. Our loss was one jemadar of levies killed, two non-commissioned officers, and eleven sowars of the 5th Punjab Cavalry, and three of the levies wounded."* The principal chief of the whole Mahsud tribe was killed in this encounter.

After the affair just narrated it was decided to despatch an expedition against the clans mainly responsible for the border outrages. In April, 1860, the force named below assembled at Tank, under the command of Brigadier-General N. B. Chamberlain. On April 17, 1860, General Chamberlain crossed the border by the Tank Zam, and, after destroying the Mahsud villages at hand, camped at Palosin two days later.

> No. 2 Punjab Light Field Battery, 3 guns.
> No. 3 Punjab Light Field Battery, 3 guns.
> Peshawar Mountain Train Battery, 4 guns.
> Hazara Mountain Train Battery, 3 guns.
> Guides Cavalry, 108.
> 3rd Punjab Cavalry, 131.
> Multani Cavalry (15th Lancers), 100.
> 1st Company Sappers and Miners, 60.
> Guides Infantry, 407.
> 4th Sikh Infantry, 427.
> 1st Punjab Infantry, 397.
> 2nd Punjab Infantry, 684.
> 3rd Punjab Infantry, 373.
> 4th Punjab Infantry, 387.
> 6th Punjab Infantry, 400.
> 14th Punjab Infantry (disbanded), 207.
> 24th Punjab Infantry (Pioneers), 418.
> Hazara Gurkha Battalion (1st Battalion 5th Gurkhas), 464.
> 6th Police Battalion, 394.
> 1,600 levies.

On the 20th General Chamberlain started up the Shahur Zam, taking with him part of his force, while the remainder remained to guard the camp at Palosin. The road which lay along the bed of the nala was so narrow and difficult that progress was slow. Very few of the enemy were seen, and, after the villages and crops found *en route* had been destroyed and about twenty-three miles of the valley reconnoitred, General Chamberlain returned to Palosin by the same road on April 26.

* "Record of Expeditions against the North - West Frontier Tribes," pp. 507, 508 (Paget and Mason).

In the meantime a determined attack was made on the British camp at Palosin, and for some time the situation was extremely critical. The camp was pitched on the left bank of the Tank Zam, while the ground commanding it to the south-east was held by piquets. Great difficulty had been experienced in getting information of the enemy's movements ; but all appeared tranquil until daybreak on April 23, when firing broke out in the piquet-line to the south-east. In a few minutes the Waziris, having over-powered the piquets, were in the portion of the camp occupied by the levies and supplies, cutting down all they met. The confusion at first was considerable ; but the tribesmen were eventually driven out at the point of the bayonet, while the 4th Sikhs, Gurkhas, and Guides fell upon the enemy's left on the high ground, driving them back into the hills to the east in confusion. The losses on both sides were considerable ; the British casualties were 37 killed and 132 wounded, including camp fol-lowers,* while 132 dead bodies of the enemy were found round the camp.

After a halt of four days to give time for the sick and wounded to be sent back to Tank, and for the ambulance litters to return, General Chamberlain resumed his ad-vance north on May 2. No opposition was encountered till two days later, when the enemy were found occupying a strong position across the Barari Pass. The mouth of the gorge had been blocked by a well-constructed abatis, and both flanks rested on steep hills strengthened with sangars. The troops were organized for the assault into two wings for the attack of the flanks of the position, a support in the gorge, and a general reserve. The attack was begun by the right wing, and, after a stiff climb, the foremost men got to within a short distance from the enemy's sangars. Here, however, the ground became so steep and the showers of stones hurled by the enemy as well as their fire became so thick, that the assaulting infantry had to take cover behind the rocks, and could only direct a desultory fire on the hostile sangars. The Mahsuds were not slow to profit by the check thus caused, and the dispersion of the troops into small parties by the difficulties of the ascent, for, leaping their breastworks, they charged down on the assailants, and threw them back in confusion down the hill. For a short time the situation was critical, but was retrieved by the steady fire of the Hazara Mountain Battery, and

* Sixteen killed, twenty-three wounded.

a resolute counter-attack by a portion of the local reserves on the British right. The Mahsuds now fled back up the hill, hotly pursued ; the main breastwork was carried, and in a short time the left of the enemy's position was won. The success of the right wing insured that of the left, who met with only a feeble resistance ; the abatis was cleared away, and camp pitched three miles beyond the northern end of the pass. The British loss was 30 killed and 86 wounded.

Continuing his advance the next day, General Chamberlain visited the important tribal centre of Kaniguram, and then, marching due north as far as the limit of Mahsud territory, turned east, and reached Bannu without serious fighting on May 20. No settlement could be made with the tribesmen, so the villages and crops passed *en route* were destroyed, and the tribe put under blockade till June, 1862, when the loss caused to their trade compelled them to submit. Raids and outrages of all kinds were committed at frequent intervals after the return of General Chamberlain's expedition, but no further military operations on anything like a large scale were undertaken till 1881.

CHAPTER III

THE AMBELA CAMPAIGN, 1863

(Map I.)

THE story of the most important of the early frontier campaigns must now be told. After the destruction of Sittana by Sir Sydney Cotton in 1858, the Hindustani fanatics settled at Malka, but after three years of tranquillity again began to disturb the peace of the surrounding district, aided and abetted by the clans bordering on British territory. Matters soon came to such a pass as to render military operations necessary once more, and it was determined that an effort should be made to extirpate for good and all the troublesome gang which was so fruitful a source of bloodshed and rapine on both banks of the River Indus.

Counting on the neutrality of the Bunerwals, who were known to have little in common with the Hindustani fanatics, though next-door neighbours on the north, it was decided to attack the enemy from that direction so as to drive them out of the sanctuary afforded by the hills in a south-easterly direction towards the Indus Valley, which was to be held by another force. Brigadier-General Sir Neville B. Chamberlain was appointed to the command of the expedition, consisting of the troops enumerated in Table III., who were drawn from the garrisons of the Punjab.

The foremost troops assembled at Nawakila, but to facilitate supply the bulk of the force remained farther to the south, till all preparations for the advance were complete. In order to deceive the enemy as to the real line of advance a demonstration was made on October 18, 1863, in the direction of the Daran Pass, the road taken by Sir Sydney Cotton in 1858, and at 9 p.m. on the 19th a strong detachment was pushed forward towards the Surkhawai or Ambela Pass, under Lieutenant-Colonel

TABLE III

THE AMBELA CAMPAIGN, 1863

Brigadier-General Sir Neville B. Chamberlain, K.C.B.

succeeded by

Major-General J. Garvock

First Brigade.	Second Brigade.	Divisional Troops.
Colonel W. W. Turner, C.B., 97th Foot.	*Lieutenant-Colonel A. T. Wilde, C.B., Corps of Guides.*	11th Bengal Cavalry (11th Lancers), 100. Guides Cavalry, 100. Sappers and Miners.
C—19th Royal Artillery (35th Battery Royal Field Artillery), 3 guns. Peshawar Mountain Train Battery (23rd Peshawar Mountain Battery). 71st Foot (1st Battalion Highland Light Infantry). 1st Punjab Infantry (55th Coke's Rifles). 3rd Punjab Infantry.* 5th Punjab Infantry (58th Vaughan's Rifles). 20th Punjab Native Infantry (20th Punjabis). 32nd Punjab Native Infantry Pioneers (32nd Sikh Pioneers). 5th Gurkha Regiment.	No. 3 Punjab Light Field Battery (22nd Derajat Mountain Battery), 3 guns. Hazara Mountain Train Battery (24th Hazara Mountain Battery). 101st Royal Bengal Fusiliers (1st Battalion Royal Munster Fusiliers). 6th Punjab Infantry (59th Scinde Rifles). 14th Native Infantry (14th Sikhs). Guides Infantry. 4th Gurkha Regiment.	REINFORCEMENTS WHICH ARRIVED IN DECEMBER.
		7th Foot (Royal Fusiliers). 93rd Foot (2nd Battalion Argyll and Sutherland Highlanders). 3rd Sikhs (53rd Sikhs). 23rd Punjab Native Infantry Pioneers (23rd Sikh Pioneers).

* No modern representative.

A. T. Wilde, C.B., followed four hours later by the main body. Little opposition was encountered in forcing the Ambela Pass, which was accomplished without loss by 2 p.m. on the 20th, but the progress of the main body was extremely slow. Sir Neville Chamberlain, describing the Ambela Pass, said :

"As a road for troops it certainly presents great difficulties. The track lies up the bed of a stream encumbered with boulders and large masses of rock, and is overgrown with low trees and jungle. The hills on either side rise to some height, but for the most part with a gradual slope, so that infantry can ascend them without difficulty, except for the obstacle presented by thick, thorny jungle."

Of this march through the Ambela Pass it is recorded that "the guns were drawn by horses as far as possible and then transferred to elephants; . . . in most parts it was only practicable to march in single file. The British troops were much fatigued, but the plentiful stream of water which flowed through the pass prevented their suffering from thirst, and late in the afternoon the rear of Lieutenant-Colonel Wilde's column was reached. Lieutenant-Colonel Wilde's force had not been strong enough to post flanking parties at more than a few of the most important points in the pass. Detachments were therefore posted from the main column wherever it seemed necessary, and the entire 5th Gurkha Regiment, which had advanced with the main body, was left about three-quarters of a mile from the crest of the pass in a commanding situation, where it served as a support to the small flanking parties, and also protected the baggage. The 32nd Punjab Native Infantry formed the rear-guard, but did not get beyond Surkhawai on the night of the 20th. It was 10 p.m. before the guns reached camp. The whole of the cavalry had been sent with the advanced column, under the idea that the pass was much easier and shorter than it proved to be, with a view to pushing them forward, supported by some infantry and mountain guns, to reconnoitre the road down the pass and the head of the Chamla Valley. But when it was found what difficulties the pass presented even to the march of the troops, and how long it would necessarily be before the whole of the baggage could come up, it was thought prudent to make no further movement in advance. The ammunition mules of the infantry had with difficulty been able to keep up in the rear of their respective regiments, but with this exception not a single

SIR NEVILLE CHAMBERLAIN'S POSITION
ON THE AMBELA PASS

OCTOBER 20 — DECEMBER 16, 1863

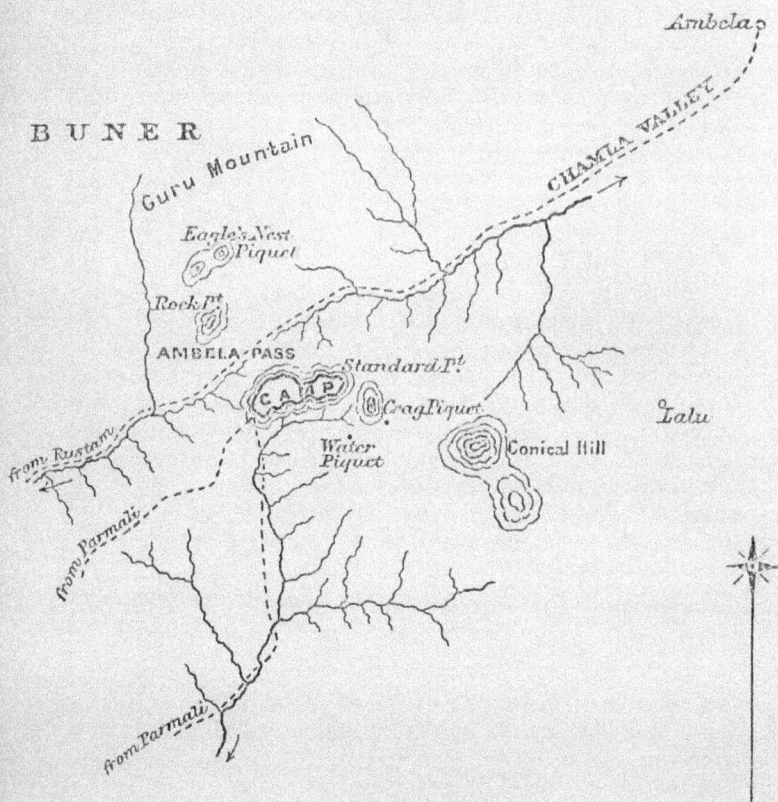

BUNER

Ambela

CHAMLA VALLEY

Guru Mountain

Eagle's Nest Piquet

Rock Pt

AMBELA-PASS

Standard Pt

CAMP

Crag Piquet

Water Piquet

Conical Hill

Lalu

from Rustam

from Parmali

from Parmali

Scale 1 in. = 1 mile.
Miles

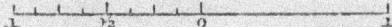

from 'Record of Expeditions against the N.W. Frontier tribes.'

baggage animal reached the camp during the night of the 20th."*

The road through the Ambela Pass to the Chamla Valley runs roughly from west to east, and is crossed at right angles by the watershed which marks the top of the pass. Sir Neville Chamberlain's camp was formed just below the watershed on the western side, with his piquets posted on commanding points on the summit.

On the north side of the pass rose a succession of steep ridges parallel to the road on which small plateaux and knolls were found affording good positions for piquets. These ridges culminated in what was known as the Guru Mountain, which marked the boundary of Buner on the south. The southern side of the pass was guarded by a lower range of hills, on which also piquets were posted. The sides of the hills were wooded, but unobstructed with brushwood.

On October 19 a proclamation had been sent to the Bunerwals disclaiming any hostility towards them, and a reply was received to the effect that the people of Buner would preserve a strict neutrality as long as their country was not threatened. The effect of this proclamation was, however, considerably discounted by a somewhat remarkable letter sent to the same clan by one Syad Amran, who imputed the most sinister meaning to the presence of the British force. As this letter is typical of such documents a translation of it is appended here.

Translation of a Persian letter from Syad Amran and Ubaidula (commonly known as Maulvi Abdulla) to the address of Ahmad Khan of Bugra.

AFTER COMPLIMENTS : A large force of the infidels has arrived at Salim Khan, Yar Husain, and Shekh Jana with the object of plundering this country. It is therefore incumbent on you, immediately on receipt of this letter, to gird your waist and proceed to Chamla, and, after issuing notices to the other allies, prepare and bring them up with yourself. We are posted in strength on the crest of the pass, and you ought to occupy Sarpatti and Landai—that is, the Chinglai village—and maintain a firm hold of your position. You should not allow a moment's delay in carrying out the above instructions. Should, however, any delay occur, the evil-doing infidels

* "Record of Expeditions against the North-West Frontier Tribes," p. 109 (Paget and Mason).

will plunder and devastate the whole of the hilly tract, especially the provinces of Chamla, Buner, Swat, etc., and annex these countries to their dominions, and then our religion and worldly possessions would be entirely subverted. Consequently, keeping in consideration a regard for Islam, the dictates of faith and worldly affairs, you ought by no means to neglect the opportunity. The infidels are extremely deceitful and treacherous, and will, by whatever means they can, come into these hills and declare to the people of the country that they have no concerns with them; that their quarrel is with the Hindustanis; that they will not molest the people, even as much as touch a hair of their heads, but will return after having extirpated the Hindustanis; and that they will not interfere with their country. They will also tempt the people with wealth. It is therefore proper for you not to give in to their deceit, or else, when they should get an opportunity, they will entirely ruin, torment, and put you to many indignities, appropriate to themselves your entire wealth and possessions, and injure your faith. You will then obtain nothing but regret. We impress this matter on your attention.

Sealed by Syad Amra.
Sealed by Ubaidulla.

The first move forward took place on October 22, when a reconnaissance was made of the Chamla Valley for eleven miles to Kuria. A considerable number of Bunerwals were seen among the hills on the left, or north, of the road, but pains were taken to avoid anything which might bring on a conflict. When, however, the withdrawal began, the Bunerwals descended from the hills with the object of cutting off the reconnoitring party; and to keep this movement in check, the cavalry, under Lieutenant-Colonel D. M. Probyn, V.C., C.B., delivered a successful charge which relieved the pressure for the time. But, emboldened by the continued retirement of the troops, the enemy soon plucked up courage again, and a rear-guard action ensued, which ended in a series of general attacks on the piquets.

On October 22 the last of Sir Neville Chamberlain's baggage arrived in camp, and two days later the sick and all superfluous baggage and transport were sent to the rear. The delay in the arrival of the baggage was due to the inferior nature of the transport and incompetence of the drivers as much as to the difficulties of

the road, and it is stated that "time had not sufficed
after the assembly of the troops for the arrangement of
all details, such as the careful distribution of loads according to the strength and efficiency of the cattle. The large
amount of mule and pony carriage necessary had naturally
resulted in the presence of a good many animals very
little fitted for their work. Loads were knocked off or
thrown by cattle unfit to take them up again, and this, of
course, choked the line."[*]

The declared hostility of the Bunerwals was a most
serious matter, owing to their geographical position with
reference to the line of communication. Reinforcements
had to be called up for the protection of the long stretch
of road which connected Sir Neville Chamberlain's force
with the base, and it was considered advisable to open
up a new line farther to the east, which would not be so
exposed to attack as that skirting the southern slopes of
Guru Mountain. Moreover, the project of advancing
against the Hindustani fanatics from the north had to be
abandoned as long as the rear of the force was exposed
to the attack of enemies from Buner.

The unexpected complications caused by the hostile
attitude of the Buner tribesmen thus necessitated a complete change in the plan of operations, and a long halt
ensued at the head of the Ambela Pass while fresh dispositions were made to cope with the altered political
situation. As usual in this class of warfare, the effect of
a prolonged pause in the progress of operations was
most unfortunate ; enemies multiplied on all sides, and
a series of determined attacks was made on the British
piquets, which, though ultimately unsuccessful in every
case, entailed some severe fighting and one or two
initial reverses.

The line of piquets surrounding the camp and marking
the line of resistance was divided into three sections.
The front or eastern piquets overlooking the Chamla
Valley were under the command of Colonel W. Hope,
71st Highland Light Infantry ; while the northern and
southern sections protecting the camp and road down
the pass were entrusted respectively to Lieutenant-
Colonel J. L. Vaughan, 5th Punjab Infantry, and
Lieutenant-Colonel A. T. Wilde, Corps of Guides.
Loop-holed stone walls and abatis were freely used to
strengthen the posts, but the broken and wooded nature

---

[*] " Record of Expeditions against the North-West Frontier Tribes," p. 110
(Paget and Mason).

of the ground often enabled the enemy to get to close quarters unobserved.

The first engagement on the defensive perimeter took place on October 25, when an attack was made on the enemy, who had taken up a position on Conical Hill. The troops concerned were able to advance within 600 yards before they were obliged to show themselves. The mountain guns then opened fire at 600 yards, while two battalions moved forward to the assault, covered also by rifle fire from the same position as that occupied by the guns. The enemy suffered severely from the accurate covering fire, and declined to await the assault.

The Bunerwals were the aggressors the next day. At noon they were seen moving down the slopes of the Guru Mountain, in force amounting to about 2,000, towards the Eagle's Nest piquet. Their swordsmen advanced to the attack in a most determined manner covered by the fire of matchlock men in rear, and, aided by the ground, they succeeded in getting right up to the breastwork surrounding the post before they were finally driven off. During the assault on the Eagle's Nest an attack was made on another piquet posted on the slopes of Guru Mountain, but was repelled by the fire of the Hazara Mountain Battery. As the tribesmen fell back, a counter-attack was delivered by the 6th Punjab Native Infantry, but, being carried a little too far, the regiment lost somewhat heavily in its retirement.

The first temporary success gained by the enemy occurred on the night October 29/30, when the Crag Piquet, held by twelve men, was carried. The piquet, however, retreating without loss of *moral*, took up a position a little lower down the hill, where it was joined at dawn by a party of twenty men under Major Keyes. Recognizing the importance of the post, commanding as it did several of the lower piquets, Major Keyes suggested to Major Brownlow, the senior officer present in the neighbourhood, that the latter should threaten the enemy in rear, while he (Major Keyes) attacked in front. This was agreed to, and Major Keyes divided his small force up into three parties, who proceeded to climb the hill by three different paths. A hand-to-hand fight ensued on the summit, but eventually the enemy were driven out at the point of the bayonet, and the post was re-occupied.

While these events were taking place on the right or south, an unsuccessful attack was made on the centre of the defensive perimeter by a contingent which had lately arrived from Swat. Some of the enemy succeeded in getting up to the 9-pounder battery in the gorge, but were immediately slain; and as the remainder of the assailants fell back they were pursued by the 5th Gurkhas and driven down the hill in confusion.

Nothing of importance occurred between October 31 and November 5, but the defences of all the piquets were strengthened considerably; work was begun on the new line of communication, and efforts were made to open political negotiations with the Bunerwals.

On November 6 the enemy gained a distinct success to set against their repulse a week before. Working parties had been sent out to improve the road towards Ambela, covered by detachments from various regiments; but the retirement was begun too late. A detachment was isolated, and seventy-eight casualties occurred before camp was reached, the officer commanding the covering troops being himself killed.

After the temporary loss of the Crag Piquet post on the night of October 29/30 the position had been considerably enlarged and strengthened; the garrison, now consisting of 160 men and 2 guns of the Peshawar Mountain Battery, were posted below to sweep the approaches as far as possible with shrapnel. The southern and western slopes of the crag were precipitous, but the left or northern face was in a military sense distinctly weak, owing to the cover afforded by rocks and trees to within a few yards of the top. During the daytime, on November 11, the enemy were seen moving south from Ambela in considerable force as if for an attack on the southern piquets. Accordingly the defences of the Crag Piquet, commanded by Major Brownlow, were improved as much as possible, and all preparations made for a night attack. The graphic account given by Colonel Paget of the fight which ensued is now transcribed:

"About 10 p.m. the enemy's watch-fire showed that they were in movement and descending in great numbers to the hollow in front of the piquet, which in half an hour was full of them. Their suppressed voices soon broke into yells of defiance, and they advanced in masses to the attack, their numbers being, as far as could be judged, at least 2,000. They were allowed to approach within 100 yards of the piquet, when a rapid and well-sustained fire was opened upon them from the front face, which Major Brownlow believed did great execution, and soon silenced their shouts, and drove them under cover, some to the broken and wooded ground on the left, and the remainder into the ravine below. In half an hour they rallied, and, assembling in increased numbers, rushed to the attack, this time assaulting both the front and left of the piquet. They were received with the greatest steadiness, and again recoiled before our fire. These attacks continued until 4 a.m., each becoming weaker than the last, many of them being mere feints to enable them to carry off their dead and wounded.

"The post was at one time in great danger of being forced at its left front angle, which from its position was badly protected by our fire. The enemy clambered up, and, assailing its occupants with stones from the breast-work, stunned and drove them back. At this critical moment the gallantry of the men of the 20th Punjab Native Infantry, whose names are noted below, saved the post.

"Answering Major Brownlow's call when others wavered, they followed him into the corner, and, hurling stones on the enemy who were close under the wall and sheltered from musketry, they drove them back and rebuilt the parapet, holding that point for the rest of the night. The Peshawar Mountain Train Battery rendered Major Brownlow very valuable assistance during the night. From its position, about 250 yards below, and in the right rear of the crag, it made most successful practice, being guided as to direction and range by voice from the parapet. Two shells were pitched by it into the watch-fire of the enemy before the attack commenced, and must have done considerable damage."*

> Havildar Alam Khan.
> Naick Chatar Singh.
> Sepoy Gulbadin.
> Sepoy Muhammad Khan.
> Sepoy Ala Mir.

The work of the Peshawar Mountain Battery is an interesting example of the employment of guns at night.

Two days after the unsuccessful night attack on the Crag Piquet the enemy again succeeded in capturing the post. Heavy firing had been heard for some time from the direction of this piquet, and a request for reinforcements was received from the officer in command on the summit. Shortly after this the men of the Crag Piquet

---

* " Record of Expeditions against the North - West Frontier Tribes," pp. 127, 128 (Paget and Mason).

were seen rushing down the hill in confusion. Major
Keyes, who was commanding the piquet on Standard
Hill, promptly collected all the men he could, and, taking
up a position at a breastwork across the road leading to
the Crag Piquet, opened a heavy fire on the pursuing
enemy, which had the effect of checking their advance.
The garrison of the crag, however, could not be rallied
at the breastwork, but, rushing on towards camp in a
complete state of demoralization, produced a most unfortunate moral effect. A successful counter-attack was
absolutely necessary to restore the situation; this was
immediately carried out under a covering fire from the
breastwork by the troops at Major Keyes's disposal, and,
though the force was not strong enough to retake the
crag, the enemy's progress was effectually stopped.
The 101st Foot (Royal Bengal Fusiliers) were then
ordered out from camp to recapture the position; this
they soon did, assisted by detachments from various
native regiments who joined in on the way, and drove
the enemy over the hills in the direction of Ambela, with
the total loss of 230 killed and wounded. The British
loss on this day was 158.

During the next four days no serious fighting took
place, and, in addition to further improvements to the
defences, preparations were made for concentrating the
force on the south side; but the communications to the
rear were at this time very unsafe, and the construction
of the new road was much delayed by the scarcity and
inferior quality of the tools available. From considerations of supply every animal not urgently needed at the
front was sent back to Parmalai. The new camp was
occupied early on the morning of November 18, and,
thanks to the careful precautions taken, the move came
as a surprise to the enemy, who offered no interference
till too late. When the tribesmen became aware of the
change of position, they at once concluded it was a movement in retreat, and, swarming down into the gorge,
made repeated attacks on the breastworks guarding the
north face of the new camp. The British loss was severe,
amounting to 118 killed and wounded, but the enemy
were known to have lost nearly twice as many.

On November 20 the crag was again captured by the
enemy, but retaken the same afternoon by the 71st Highland Light Infantry, supported by the 5th Gurkhas, and
detachments of the 5th and 6th Punjab Infantry. In this
affair Sir Neville Chamberlain, who accompanied the

71st, was severely wounded, and forced to relinquish the command of the expedition in favour of Major-General J. Garvock. The total casualties sustained in the third recapture of the crag were 137, the enemy's loss being estimated at about a hundred more.

During the next ten days signs were not wanting that the enemy were wearying of the struggle. Although fresh reinforcements kept pouring in from Bajaur and other parts, numerous desertions took place, and the Buner and Chamla tribes began to enter into negotiations, the result of which was that the Bunerwals agreed— (1) To co-operate in the destruction of Malka ; (2) to expel the Hindustani fanatics from their country.

This compact, however, was not ratified without yet another fight. The British force had now been reinforced by two European and two Indian battalions, which had arrived from India. On December 15 the troops having been formed into two columns and a camp guard, the former moved out in an easterly direction against a large hostile gathering at Lalu. The first objective was the enemy posted on Conical Hill, a position which was carried by a combined assault of the two columns, and the pursuit vigorously pressed as far as Lalu. The enemy then made a determined counter-attack on the British left from Ambela, but were driven back with considerable loss. The fight was over about 2 p.m., and the troops bivouacked on the ground they had won. Ambela was occupied the next day, and the enemy again suffered so severely that the Bajauris and many other hostile contingents took to flight in the direction of their homes, leaving the Bunerwals no alternative but to carry out the engagements already mentioned. It was then arranged that the men of Buner should be called upon to destroy Malka themselves, without assistance from the British troops, but in the presence of a party of officers, accompanied by a suitable escort, to see that the work of destruction was properly carried out. This the Bunerwals agreed to do, and also undertook to dismiss the armed men stationed on the Buner Pass, and to give their chief men as hostages for the fulfilment of their engagements.

Malka was reached without *contretemps* on December 21, the place was completely destroyed the next day, and on the 23rd the party was back again in camp in the Ambela Pass. The mission was a delicate one, and not unattended with risk; but the Bunerwals carried out their promise faithfully, and, although the demeanour of some of the tribesmen met was far from friendly, no rupture of any kind occurred.

The active work of the Ambela Campaign was now at an end ; the toll taken of officers and men had been heavy. No less than 238 officers and men had been killed, and 670 wounded, but the enemy * had suffered much more severely, and the power of the Hindustani fanatics was gone for ever. Their one remaining stronghold at Mandi was also destroyed by representatives of the Gaduns and Utmanzais after a little demur, in obedience to the British demand, backed by a brigade, that they should do this in proof of the sincerity of their friendly protestations.

* Their loss was estimated at 3,000 killed and wounded.

CHAPTER IV

1863—1878

MOHMANDS—1863-64. (*Map I.*)

DURING the Ambela Campaign trouble again rose with the Mohmands, owing to the intrigues of the Akhund of Swat. Some skirmishes occurred near Shabkadr in December, 1863, and, as the attitude of the tribesmen grew more menacing, the garrison of that post was increased to the force shown below, which was under the command of Colonel A. Macdonell, C.B., of the Rifle Brigade. On January 2, 1864, the enemy advanced towards Shabkadr in force, amounting to about 5,600, and took up a position on the plateau to the north - west of the fort. Colonel Macdonell tried to tempt the tribesmen to come farther away from the hills by concealing his strength, in which object he was partly successful, for the sight of the enemy's line pressing on presented a favourable opportunity to the cavalry, which the 7th Hussars promptly seized. The enemy's right was thrown back on the centre, was enfiladed by the fire of the guns; three times the Hussars rode through the hostile ranks, which were assailed at the same time in front by the Rifle Brigade. In a very short time the Mohmands were in full flight to the hills, having received a most salutary lesson. This is the only occasion on which British cavalry have had an opportunity of distinguishing themselves as a body in Indian border warfare, but the one and only charge to their credit in this class of campaign ranks high among the achievements of the mounted arm. The enemy's loss in killed and wounded was about eighty.

D Battery 5th Brigade Royal Horse Artillery (S Battery
    Royal Horse Artillery).
7th Hussars, 140.
3rd Battalion Rifle Brigade.

Detachments of—
    2nd Bengal Cavalry (2nd Lancers).
    6th Bengal Cavalry (6th Cavalry).
    2nd Gurkha Regiment (1st Battalion 2nd Gurkhas).
    4th Sikh Infantry.
           Total, 1,800.

BLACK MOUNTAIN EXPEDITION, 1868. (*Map IV.*)

In 1868 fresh troubles arose with the Black Mountain tribes, due to the ambition and lawless conduct of the Khan of Agror, a chief who owed his position to the Sikhs, but had been allowed by the British Government to remain in possession of his lands after the annexation of the Punjab. As a check to the evil practices prevalent in Agror a police post of twenty-two men was established at Aghi at the end of 1867. The Khan resented this step from the first, and lost no time in trying to induce the clans on the western side of the Black Mountain to join him in procuring the removal of the obnoxious post.

Early on the morning of July 30, 1868, a body of about 500 tribesmen attacked the police, but were driven off successfully after a sharp fight. Reinforcements were sent up immediately from Abbottabad, consisting of the Peshawar Mountain Battery and 350 men of the 5th Gurkhas under Lieutenant-Colonel O. E. Rothney. These troops started at four hours' notice, and covered the forty-two miles to Aghi in twenty-five hours. As the enemy increased in number and further fighting occurred, additional reinforcements were sent to Colonel Rothney, who was able then to take the offensive and drive the hostile tribesmen out of the Agror Valley. In these operations a contingent furnished by the Khan of Amb, and led by that chief in person, rendered loyal and valuable service. As, however, the force at Colonel Rothney's disposal was insufficient to exact punishment for the attack on the police post, it was decided to despatch an expedition into the Black Mountain District which would be strong enough to overcome any opposition likely to be encountered.

Owing to disquieting news as to the state of affairs on the Peshawar border, it was resolved not to draw the necessary troops from the frontier garrisons, but to call on stations down-country to supply the men required. In spite of the unfavourable season some very fine feats of marching were accomplished by several of the regiments detailed. It is recorded that "the 20th Punjab

Native Infantry marched a distance of 232 miles, from Lahore to Abbottabad, in ten days in the month of August, the 31st Punjab Native Infantry marched a distance of 422 miles, and the two companies of Sappers and Miners actually covered nearly 600 miles by forced marches in twenty-nine days."[*] The concentration was complete on September 24, the troops being organized and distributed as shown in Table IV.

The moral effect of the assembly of the British force was soon apparent, for the Hassanzais, warned by their experiences in 1852, and influenced by the friendly offices of the Khan of Amb, at once dissociated themselves from their neighbours, and other clans followed their example. The theatre of operations of 1868, therefore, lay to the north of that of 1852.

The advance north from Aghi was begun at daybreak on October 3, and good progress was made, the 1st Brigade reaching Mana-ka-Dana, with the 2nd Brigade posted about three miles to the east, in case of hostility from that direction, and the reserve at Kangali, on the Aghi road. The 1st Brigade came in for some fighting, and a battalion of Gurkhas was sent up as a reinforcement from the reserve, but the shooting both of guns and rifles was good, and the opposition of the enemy was easily overcome.

At dawn, on October 4, the 2nd Brigade moved up to Mana-ka-Dana, and the advance of the 1st Brigade (General Bright) was resumed in a westerly direction up the spur leading to Chittabut, the levies moving up the parallel spur to the south through Barchar. General Bright began his advance, covered by the fire of D Battery, F Brigade, Royal Horse Artillery, whose guns had been brought up on elephants, and were directed against a position which the enemy had occupied on a grassy knoll, and strengthened with sangars and abatis. The mountain guns also came into action, but before the Gurkhas, who were detailed for the assault, could reach the position the enemy had taken flight into the hills. After an arduous climb up a precipitous path, General Bright reached Chittabut early in the afternoon, and immediately fortified his position. In the meantime the levies working up the Barchar spur overcame the slight resistance offered, and joined General Bright at Chittabut. The 2nd Brigade remained at Mana ka-Dana, occupying the position from which the enemy

[*] " Record of Expeditions against the North-West Frontier Tribes," p. 45 Paget and Mason).

TABLE IV

BLACK MOUNTAIN EXPEDITION, 1868

Brigadier-General A. T. Wilde, C.B., C.S.I.

First Brigade.	Second Brigade.	Divisional Troops and Reserve.	
Brigadier-General R. O. Bright.	*Brigadier-General J. L. Vaughan, C.B.*	D — F Royal Horse Artillery (S Battery Royal Horse Artillery).	16th Bengal Cavalry, 188.* Guides Cavalry, 131. 2nd and 7th Companies Sappers and Miners.
1st Battalion 19th Foot (1st Battalion York-shire Regiment). 20th Punjab Native In-fantry (20th Punjabis). 1st Gurkha Regiment.	1st Battalion 6th Foot (1st Battalion Royal Warwickshire Regi-ment). 3rd Sikh Infantry (53rd Sikhs). 2nd Gurkha Regiment.	E — 19th Royal Artillery (59th Battery Royal Field Artillery). 2 — 24th Royal Artillery (4th Mountain Battery Royal Garrison Artillery). Peshawar Mountain Battery (23rd Peshawar Mountain Battery). Hazara Mountain Battery (24th Hazara Mountain Battery).	Detachment Telegraph Sappers. 2nd Punjab Infantry (56th Pun-jabi Rifles). 24th Punjab Native Infantry (24th Punjabis). 4th Gurkha Regiment. 5th Gurkha Regiment. Levies and police, 518.
		At Darband.	
		38th Foot (1st Battalion South Staffordshire Regiment). 9th Bengal Cavalry (9th Hodson's Horse). 31st Punjab Native Infantry (31st Punjabis).	

* No modern representative. The present 16th Cavalry was raised as the 16th Regiment of Bengal Cavalry in 1885.

had been driven in the morning, with two battalions, in order to maintain communication with General Bright.

On October 5 Muchai was occupied by the 1st Brigade, reinforced by the 2nd Gurkhas and both mountain batteries. A little skirmishing took place, but the accurate covering fire of the guns, and the steady advance of the infantry shook the nerve of the tribesmen so much that they abandoned a very strong position practically without a struggle. An abundant supply of water was soon found near the various bivouacs of the whole force, and Muchai was prepared for defence to act as a pivot for further expeditions into hostile territory. It is interesting to note that at Muchai the officer commanding the Royal Artillery "succeeded in bringing two elephants up to the top of the peak, establishing the fact that, if required, the field-guns could have been brought up there also."*

Some villages near Mana-ka-Dana were destroyed on the 7th, but by the 10th all the clans between the Black Mountain and the Indus had tendered their submission. The terms imposed were not exacting, as the tribesmen in these parts were poor, and any attempt to force compliance by military operations in the broken mountain country would have been fraught with considerable difficulty. It was considered enough to have "lifted the purdah," and let those concealed behind behold the power of the British arms. No fighting took place near Muchai, the only disturbance being caused by intermittent sniping at the sentries and piquets by night. Muchai was evacuated on October 12, and, except for an attack on the rear-guard near Mana-ka-Dana, the latter place was reached without any molestation by the enemy.

Instead of returning to Aghi by the direct route, Major-General Wilde marched the troops back by a circular movement to the north and east, which had the effect of spreading British prestige still further among the neighbouring tribes, and Aghi was reached on October 22. The total British casualties during the operations were five killed and twenty-nine wounded.

Eighty miles of hill country were covered by the force in this march; roads were practically non-existent, and had to be made, but Major-General Wilde spoke in high terms of the mobility and endurance displayed by the men, both European and Indian. It was hoped at first to reach the Indus to the north, but when the difficult nature

* " Record of Expeditions against the North-West Frontier Tribes," p. 54 (Paget and Mason)

of the ground was seen it was thought that the results to be achieved did not justify the risk and hardships involved.

After the conclusion of the expedition of 1868, the usual raids common on the Indian frontier continued for some years, but punishment was inflicted without difficulty, and no further important operations took place in the Black Mountain District till 1888. The Agror Valley was occupied by a small permanent force, which proved sufficient for all purposes.

ORAKZAIS, 1868. (*Map II.*)

After General Chamberlain's expedition in 1855 the Orakzais remained peaceful for thirteen years, when the Bizotis, a small clan living close to Kohat on the northwest, became so troublesome that their presence could no longer be ignored. On March 10, 1868, the Bizotis made a demonstration against the police posts stationed at the foot of the Ublan Pass, six miles out of Kohat. At the foot of the pass on the British side, and a little to the east of the road leading up to the Kotal, was a small hill, an under-feature of the main ridge. The police guarding the pass were told to remain strictly on the defensive, and it was hoped that, if the hills on the west of the road were occupied, the tribesmen would be induced to descend from the high hills flanking the Kotal, and seize the small hill on the east of the road. A force could then be sent to cut off the enemy's retreat, while the remainder attacked the position in front.

On the morning of March 11 the plan was put into execution by the force shown below under Major L. B. Jones, 3rd Punjab Cavalry, with the result that the small hill was occupied precisely as had been anticipated. A detachment was sent to close the road over the Kotal, a troop of cavalry watched the British right, and the 3rd and 6th Punjab Infantry advanced to the attack of the enemy's position, supported by the cavalry and guns at the foot of the pass. The hill was carried without loss, but the tribesmen made good their escape to a commanding peak in the main ridge, where they had constructed a sangar. An unfortunate misunderstanding of orders then occurred through which the 3rd Punjab Infantry followed up the retreating enemy, and tried unsuccessfully to capture the sangar. The orders given to the assaulting infantry were "to advance to the summit, take the position, and halt until further orders." This was intended to mean that the infantry were to halt on the summit of the small hill, but apparently the officer in command of the 3rd Punjab Infantry took it to mean the main hill beyond. The assault was gallantly made, but was repulsed at the foot of the sangar, and the officer commanding killed. The 3rd Punjab Infantry then fell back down the hill, and the 6th Punjab Infantry came up to their assistance, supported by the guns, but again the attack was unsuccessful. Encouraged by their success, the enemy now began to move forward down the hill, whereupon a third attack was made, which also failed. As darkness was then approaching, no further attempt was made to take the position, and the troops returned to Kohat; the retirement was not harassed, owing possibly to losses already sustained by the enemy. In this unsuccessful affair the British casualties amounted to eleven killed and forty-four wounded.

> No. 2 Punjab Light Field Battery, 2 guns.
> 3rd Punjab Cavalry, 80.
> 3rd Punjab Infantry, 280.
> 6th Punjab Infantry, 200.

It is not surprising to find that after their success the tribesmen showed no inclination to desist from their depredations and bow to the inevitable. A blockade of their country proved totally ineffective, and on February 13, 1869, an attack was made on the police post at the foot of the Kohat Kotal, whereby one man was killed and three others were carried off. If there had been any question about it before, no alternative now remained but to despatch a force into Orakzai territory to punish the marauding clans. It was decided to seize the Ublan Pass by a *coup de main*, and then to try to capture the villages of Gara and Dana Khula, which were Bizoti strongholds, before arrangements could be made for their defence. Secrecy was essential, but two native officers and two other prominent native gentlemen were taken into the confidence of the British authorities in order to obtain local information. The order for the troops to be got in readiness having been deferred as late as possible, the force shown below moved out from Kohat on February 25, 1869, under Lieutenant-Colonel C. P. Keyes, C.B., followed by a small reserve. Careful preparations had been made for rushing any piquet found on the pass, in order to prevent the alarm being given, but not a sign of the enemy was seen. Four Bizoti head-

men who professed themselves to be friendly were then
sent on to Gara ahead of the troops to warn the inhabitants that if no resistance was offered the troops would
pass on to Dana Khula, but that if the inhabitants were
hostile their village would be destroyed. The headmen,
however, so far from allaying the fears of the villagers,
merely gave warning that the troops were coming, and
immediately began removing their property and driving
away their cattle, an example which was followed at once
by the rest of the inhabitants. The result was that when
Colonel Keyes arrived, scarcely a quarter of an hour later,
the village was practically deserted. The place was then
rushed and destroyed, but as the alarm had now been
effectually given the idea of passing on to Dana Khula
was abandoned. During the retirement the enemy pressed
forward with great determination, and the British force
sustained a loss of three killed and thirty-three wounded
before Kohat was reached.

> No. 1 Punjab Light Field Battery, 2 mountain guns.
> 1st Punjab Infantry.
> 4th Punjab Infantry.

While Colonel Keyes was carrying out the operations
just described, a force from Peshawar demonstrated on
the north side of the Kohat Pass; it had no fighting, but
its presence undoubtedly had a mystifying and restrain-
ing effect on the neighbouring clans which contributed
to the success of the expedition under Colonel Keyes.
The Bizotis tendered their submission on April 4, 1869,
since when no further military operations have been
undertaken against them in particular. Various raids
were committed from time to time, but punishment,
usually in the shape of a fine, was always exacted without difficulty.

DAWAR, 1872. (*Map II.*)

After the conclusion of the operations against the
Orakzais, in 1869, peace reigned on the North-West
Frontier for three years, when the Tochi Valley became
the scene of the next conflict. The Tochi Valley, which
lies due west of Bannu, is inhabited by a tribe called the
Dawaris. The territory belonging to this tribe lies
between the Darwesh Khel Waziris to the north and
the Mahsuds to the south; it "is entered by three passes
from British territory—the Tochi Pass the best known,

Plate II

A FRONTIER NALA

To face p. 70

the Baran Pass, and the Khaisora Pass."* The inhabitants are chiefly cultivators, who wander little beyond the limits of their own country, and show few of the warlike qualities which characterize their Waziri neighbours to the north and south.

The first occasion on which the Indian Government came in contact with the Dawaris was in 1851, when the latter took part in an attack on one of the border posts, but were driven off with heavy loss. After this little trouble arose until 1871, when the Dawaris lent their assistance to the Waziris in acts of hostility towards the Indian Government. As a punishment for their complicity in these outrages the Dawaris were ordered to pay a fine, but half of the tribe not only refused to comply with this demand, but sent an insulting letter to the British authorities, in addition to treating the envoys despatched to them with great indignity. Brigadier-General C. P. Keyes, commanding the Punjab Frontier Force, was therefore ordered to proceed with the troops named below, and chastise the refractory section of the Dawari tribe.

On the night March 5/6, 1872, the levies were sent forward up the Tochi Valley to seize the Shinki Kotal, which lay on the road from Bannu to the hostile villages. The remainder of the force, marching out from Bannu on the morning of the 6th, camped at the eastern end of the Tochi Pass, while the Brigadier-General and Staff rode forward to reconnoitre. When the party reached the Kotal, where the levies were stationed, some firing was going on, and it was evident that the levies could not be relied on to hold their ground if attacked in strength. It was then about 4 p.m., and therefore too late to send forward reinforcements from camp before darkness set in, so General Keyes ordered the headmen of the levies to hold his position till morning, and started to return to camp. The General's party, however, had not gone far, when the Waziris abandoned the position and took to flight. Nevertheless, as time was an important consideration, it was decided to adhere to the original line of advance, in spite of the possibility of some severe fighting, rather than make a *détour* by a more circuitous route. Leaving a detachment to guard the camp, General Keyes started at 4 a.m. on March 7 for the Shinki Kotal, which was occupied five hours later without opposition.

* "Record of Expeditions against the North-West Frontier Tribes," p. 564 (Paget and Mason).

It appeared that the Dawaris had thought from the fact
that the levies had not been reinforced the day before,
that no advance would be made the following morning,
so they had returned to their homes. A halt was made
on the Kotal, while the road was made practicable for
guns ; the force then pushed on and carried out the
brilliant and decisive little series of operations which
are now described in Colonel Paget's own words :

> No. 3 Punjab Light Field Battery, 2 howitzers.
> 1st Punjab Cavalry, 149.
> 2nd Punjab Cavalry, 206.
> 1st Sikh Infantry, 534.
> 4th Sikh Infantry, 424.
> 1st Punjab Infantry, 448.
> Waziri levies, 400.

" The howitzers and ammunition wagons, having been
got over the Kotal about noon, the Brigadier-General,
accompanied by the Commissioner, pushed on with the
cavalry, and, after an hour's ride over the rocky bed of
the river, ascending a slight rise, found themselves on
the edge of a broad plateau, with the three refractory
villages of Haidar Khel, Hassu Khel, and Aipi, in their
front. Here they were met by two Hassu Khel maliks,
who expressed willingness on the part of the people of
Dawar to agree to any terms which might be imposed.
They were then informed by the Commissioner that the
fines originally proposed would be levied, with an
additional Rs. 1,000 from Hassu Khel, and Rs. 500 from
Haidar Khel, as a mark of our further displeasure at
their conduct. Blood money at the usual rate would be
demanded for the Bannuchi found dead in their pass that
day, and two towers in each of the villages would be
burnt for the previous day's misconduct of the Hassu
Khel malik, as well as for the recusancy of the leading
men of lower Dawar, which had necessitated the march
of a British force into the valley.

The maliks acquiesced in these demands, but they
begged for time. However, the afternoon was advancing,
and if the force was to return to camp that night no time
was to be lost. A quarter of an hour's delay was, therefore, granted to the villagers, in which to collect the fine
money, the cavalry remaining halted on the plain. A
large body of the enemy was, however, seen assembling
in front of the village of Haidar Khel, defiantly waving
their tulwars, and apparently inciting to an attack. On
the arrival of the infantry and guns the assurances of

obedience and submission were repeated, and the force
advanced on the village of Haidar Khel, partly with the
purpose of receiving the fine imposed, and partly to
carry out the terms on which their submission was
accepted—viz., the burning of the village towers. In
strange contrast with the submissive tone of the emissaries was the attitude of the great mass of the enemy,
who, far from dispersing, still maintained their position
in front of the village. The authorities were, however,
so confident of the honesty of the Dawaris, that the
force, covered by the skirmishers of the 1st Sikh Infantry,
advanced to within matchlock range of the enemy without
firing a shot. When the skirmishers had arrived within
200 yards of the Dawaris a shot was fired, apparently as
a signal, which was followed by a volley from the rest of
the enemy, who at once took shelter behind the walls
and in the ditches. The guns were promptly brought
into action on the village, while the 1st Sikh Infantry
made a spirited advance on the enemy. A wing of the
4th Sikh Infantry (the other wing having been left to
hold the Shinki Kotal) was at the same time sent round
to the left flank of the village, and the cavalry to its right
and rear, to cut off any attempt to escape. The 1st Sikh
Infantry stormed the closed gates of the village, and
effected an entry, driving the inhabitants to the north
corner, where for some time they made a stand behind
some high-walled houses. The 1st and 4th Sikh Infantry,
having obtained entire possession of the left portion of
the village, set it on fire. The 1st Punjab Infantry was
then brought up and sent to the right flank of the village,
to aid the cavalry in cutting off the retreat of the villagers.
The fire, and the determined bearing of the two Sikh
regiments, was soon too much for the defenders of the
village, and, abandoning their position, they fled towards
the plain, only to find themselves surrounded by the
cavalry on the left, the dark coats of the Punjab Infantry
in their front, the guns on their right, and behind them
the deadly Enfields of the two Sikh regiments. The
cavalry was speedily down upon them, and sabred ten of
their number, when the rest, seeing that all was lost,
made a rush for the guns and headquarters, and, throwing
down their arms as they ran, surrendered as prisoners."*

Aipi was surrounded in a similar manner, and the
inhabitants of Hassu Khel sent in an unconditional sur-

* " Record of Expeditions against the North-West Frontier Tribes,"
pp. 569, 570 (Paget and Mason).

render, whereupon the troops returned to camp unmolested, having been under arms for eighteen hours.

Jowakis, 1877-78. (*Map II.*)

After the admission of the Jowakis to a share of the
Kohat Pass allowances in 1853, this section of the Afridi
tribe gave no trouble till 1877, when, being affected by
the general unrest prevalent among the neighbouring
clans, or to show their resentment at a proposal to dis-
continue their allowances in consequence of the meagre
services rendered in return, the Jowakis committed a
series of raids on the main road connecting Kohat with
India. In August, 1877, therefore, an expedition organized
and composed as in Table V. was ordered to penetrate
the Jowaki hills from the south-west, and carry out
punitive measures against the refractory clan.   The
command of the expedition was given to Brigadier-
General C. P. Keyes, C.B., commanding the Punjab
Frontier Force, but owing to a sudden illness that
officer was unable to assume the direction of operations,
and the command devolved on Colonel D. Mocatta,
commanding the 3rd Sikh Infantry.

The force under Colonel Mocatta invaded the enemy's
territory on August 30, 1877, by three routes — the
western column through the Tortang Defile under
Colonel Mocatta himself, a column from the south
through the Gandiali Pass, and a third from the east,
from a starting-place on the River Indus.   Each column
directed its march towards Turkai, by which plan it was
hoped to enclose the enemy between the converging
forces and inflict a severe defeat.   In spite of efforts to
keep secret the British plan of attack, however, the
Jowakis managed to get timely warning, so the expedition failed to achieve any decisive result.   The three
columns met in the Turkai Valley, traversed it from end
to end, and withdrew to British territory by the Kuka-
chana Pass all in the same day; the only fighting that
took place occurred during the withdrawal from the
Turkai Valley.

As was only natural, no lasting result followed from
these indecisive operations. The raids were resumed at
once with increased daring, and in November, 1877,
preparations were made on a larger scale for an effective
invasion of Jowaki territory. One of these raids, however, deserves special mention before proceeding to a

TABLE V

JOWAKI EXPEDITION, 1877

COLONEL D. MOCATTA, 3RD SIKH INFANTRY

WESTERN COLUMN.	SOUTHERN COLUMN.	EASTERN COLUMN.
No. 1 Mountain Battery Royal Artillery (1st Mountain Battery Royal Garrison Artillery).	2nd Punjab Cavalry, 104.	Guides Infantry, 201.
2nd Punjab Cavalry (22nd Cavalry), 45.	1st Sikh Infantry, 220.	
1st Sikh Infantry (51st Sikhs), 103.	6th Punjab Infantry (59th Scinde Rifles), 297.	
3rd Sikh Infantry (53rd Sikhs), 278.		
4th Sikh Infantry (54th Sikhs), 245.		

description of the subsequent military operations, because
it contains a warning of the result of the neglect of
ordinary precautions in an unsettled country. On the
night of October 25, 1877, an attack was made on a party
of infantry who, "in gross disregard of all rules for
insuring the safety of troops on the march, and in the
neighbourhood of an enemy's country, had encamped on
the edge of a ravine immediately on the Afridi border.
Fourteen of their number were killed and wounded, and
eight rifles were carried off."*

Two main columns were organized at Peshawar and
Kohat to enter the enemy's country simultaneously from
north and south. Details concerning these two columns
will be found in Table VI.; that from Kohat was entrusted to Brigadier-General C. P. Keyes, the one from
Peshawar to Brigadier-General C. C. G. Ross. Both
Generals subdivided their forces into two or three smaller
columns, which operated on separate enterprises as circumstances required. The account of the operations given
in " Record of Expeditions against the North-West
Frontier Tribes " is somewhat difficult to follow, owing
to the number of small detachments into which the
troops were divided; but as there was very little fighting
from beginning to end, and there is not much to be learnt
from a study of the operations, the history of the campaign may be summed up in a few words. If details are
desired, they will be found in plenty in the standard work
just mentioned, which contains a careful record of all the
early wars on the North-West Frontier of India.

The work of both columns was greatly delayed throughout by rain, bad roads, and lack of topographical information. General Keyes began his advance on November 9,
1877, by the Tortang and Gandiali Defiles, and effected
a junction at Paiah with a small column under Colonel
Gardiner. For the rest of the month important military
movements were rendered practically impossible by continuous heavy rain, but reconnaissances and surveys
were actively carried on of what was then a *terra in-
cognita*. At the beginning of December General Keyes
tried to initiate a combined movement by the two main
columns on Jamu, which was one of the principal Jowaki
strongholds, but General Ross had been so delayed by the
state of the country during the heavy rains that he was
only able to occupy the ridge dominating the Bori Valley

---

* " Record of Expeditions against the North-West Frontier Tribes," p. 348
(Paget and Mason).

TABLE VI
JOWAKI EXPEDITION, 1871-78

KOHAT COLUMN.	PESHAWAR COLUMN.	
BRIGADIER-GENERAL C. P. KEYES, C.B.	BRIGADIER-GENERAL C. C. G. ROSS, C.B.	
	FIRST BRIGADE.	SECOND BRIGADE.
	Colonel J. Doran, C.B.	*Colonel H. J. Buchanan.*
No. 1 Mountain Battery Royal Artillery (No. 1 Mountain Battery Royal Garrison Artillery). No. 4 Hazara Mountain Battery (24th Hazara Mountain Battery). 2nd Punjab Cavalry (22nd Cavalry), 50. Corps of Guides, 380. 1st Sikh Infantry (51st Sikhs), 225. 3rd Sikh Infantry (53rd Sikhs), 225. 4th Punjab Infantry (57th Wilde's Rifles), 350. 6th Punjab Infantry (59th Scinde Rifles), 300.	I—C Royal Horse Artillery,* 3 guns. 51st Foot (1st Battalion King's Own Yorkshire Light Infantry). Two companies Sappers and Miners. 22nd Punjab Native Infantry (22nd Punjabis). 27th Punjab Native Infantry (27th Punjabis).	I—C Royal Horse Artillery,* 3 guns. 13—9th Royal Artillery (53rd Company Royal Garrison Artillery). 9th Foot (Norfolk Regiment). 4th Battalion Rifle Brigade. 14th Native Infantry (14th Sikhs). 20th Punjab Native Infantry (20th Punjabis).
JOINED AT PAIAH.		
Colonel P. F. Gardiner, 5th Gurkhas.		
No. 2 Mountain Battery Royal Artillery (2nd Mountain Battery Royal Garrison Artillery), 2 guns. 5th Punjab Infantry (58th Vaughan's Rifles), 250. 5th Gurkha Regiment, 280.		

* No modern representative.

on December 4; General Keyes, therefore, was obliged to
effect the capture of Jamu single-handed. This was done
without difficulty by the combined attack of three detachments, and a fresh tract of country was subjected to
survey. From Jamu also the important village of Ghariba
was captured and destroyed after a combined movement,
which was both well planned and resolutely carried out.

In the meantime General Ross assembled his force at
Fort Mackeson, but the completion of his arrangements
was greatly delayed by rain, as has been mentioned
already, and also by the destruction by flood of the bridge
of boats at Attock, which caused a serious block on the
line of communication with Rawal Pindi. The line of
advance selected was that adopted by Colonel Boileau in
1853—namely, by Kandao and the Sarghasha Pass—and
on December 4 both passes were carried after a somewhat feeble resistance. The main camp was formed at
the top of the ridge overlooking the Bori Valley, from
which point parties were sent out during the next four
days to destroy the villages and towers below ; the opposition encountered was again extremely slight.

On December 8 rain fell so continuously and the
weather was so cold that tents were sent up from Fort
Mackeson and the main body of the force was withdrawn
from the ridge to the foot of the pass on the north side,
while six companies and two guns were left to hold the
crest. During the next fortnight much was done to
improve the roads, and reconnaissances were made of
the approaches to the Pastaoni Valley to the south,
which were found to be so bad that General Ross took
his force no farther than the Sarghasha Pass. A simultaneous advance was then made towards the Pastaoni
Valley by Generals Keyes and Ross ; neither met with
serious resistance, and the two columns met at Pastaoni
on December 31. Some reconnaissances were carried
out, and the two columns withdrew south and north
respectively the next day. Further operations, however, were undertaken during January, 1878, in the heart
of the Jowaki country, during which General Ross, at
the request of General Keyes, abandoned his line of
communication over the Sarghasha Pass, and both
columns were based on Kohat. There was a little fighting, but only affairs of piquets and small detachments,
one of which, however, deserves mention, as it points a
lesson. On one of these occasions Captain A. G. Hammond, finding his men annoyed by the fire of a small

party of the enemy, " conceived the idea, after examin-
ing the ground, that it was possible to get above them
without his movements being seen or suspected. Taking
with him only four of his men, he succeeded in ascending
the hill and getting above the enemy, and, with his own
hand, shot three of them and captured their arms, the
others flying before his party. This gallant exploit was
a useful service to the regiment (Guides) and saved the
men from further annoyance." *

On January 22 the withdrawal of the troops from
Jowaki territory began ; the whole force marched into
Kohat, whence the column under General Ross withdrew to Peshawar. Soon afterwards the Jowakis came
to terms with the Indian Government after the usual
prevarications, and since then no military expedition
against them has taken place. During the operations
just concluded the neighbouring clans remained as bodies
strictly neutral. The Jowakis tried, however, to induce
not only their neighbours, but even the Akhund of Swat
and the Amir to espouse their cause, but in no case were
their efforts rewarded with success.

UTMAN KHEL, 1878. *(Map I.)*

The conduct of the Utman Khel was entirely satisfactory between 1852 and 1876, but on December 9 in the
latter year a dastardly attack was made on the camp of a
number of unarmed coolies employed in the construction
of the Swat Canal near Abazai. The tents were surrounded during the night, and, at a given signal, the
ropes were cut, and several of the unfortunate men
killed or wounded as they struggled beneath the canvas.
The camp was then plundered. Although the necessity
for it was clear, no punitive expedition could be undertaken immediately owing to the impending outbreak of the
Afghan War with Sher Ali, the Amir, but on February 14,
1878, a force consisting of 280 men of the Guides left
Mardan under Captain Wigram Battye to exact punishment for the outrage and pecuniary compensation for the
relatives of the murdered coolies.

Mian Khan, the organizer of the raid, was located at
Sapri, a hill village about five miles north-west of Abazai,
and careful precautions were taken to avoid giving him
the alarm. Captain Battye left Mardan at 7 p.m., and,

* " Record of Expeditions against the North-West Frontier Tribes," p. 365
(Paget and Mason).

avoiding all villages *en route*, reached Sapri at 4 a.m. the following morning, having left his horses near Abazai, and covered the last few miles on foot. The village was rushed at dawn, and it was a complete surprise. Mian Khan was killed, and, retiring with the utmost deliberation, Captain Battye reached Abazai at 11 a.m., having traversed about forty-five miles in twenty-eight hours. Certain fines and scales of compensation were imposed on the Utman Khel, which were all paid within a month, except the shares allotted to a few villages; these, however, submitted also on the reappearance of the Guides on March 20.

In addition to coercing the Utman Khel, the Guides had another little brush with the Ranizais, who had been quiet since 1852, but had lately been committing raids and harbouring outlaws. The village of Shakot was surrounded at dawn on March 14, 1878, and the unconditional surrender of the tribesmen was received at once.

CHAPTER V

SIDE ISSUES OF THE SECOND AFGHAN WAR

Zakha Khel, 1878-79. (*Map II.*)

During the British advance into Afghanistan in 1878 through the Khaibar Pass the Zakha Khel caused great annoyance by their harassing tactics. Accordingly, operations against them were undertaken on December 19, 1878, by two columns from Dakka and Jamrud, under the direction of Lieutenant-General F. F. Maude, V.C., C.B., commanding the 2nd Division. Brigadier-General J. A. Tytler commanded the Dakka Column, and marched into the Bazar Valley by way of Chenar and the Sisobi Pass, the route taken by General Maude being through Chora and Walai. The only fighting that took place occurred during the withdrawal of the columns, but the operation in question was skilfully conducted, and the total casualties of the whole force only amounted to ten killed and wounded. All the villages were found deserted, but large quantities of supplies were discovered which were destroyed after the requirements of the troops had been satisfied. The villages and towers were razed to the ground, and the two columns returned to their respective stations after an absence of only three days, General Tytler taking the Tabai Pass route on his return journey, and covering twenty-two miles of bad hill-road on the last day in the presence of the enemy.

It was not long, however, before another expedition against the Zakha Khel became necessary in consequence of continued acts of hostility in the Khaibar Pass. Five columns were organized under the direction of Lieutenant-General F. F. Maude, and converged on the Bazar Valley from Jamrud, Ali Masjid, Landi Kotal, Dakka, and Basawal, in January, 1879. Many towers and villages were destroyed, but no enemy were seen except at considerable distances. A reconnaissance of the Bokar Pass leading

TABLE VII

ZAKHA KHEL EXPEDITION, 1878

LIEUTENANT-GENERAL F. F. MAUDE, V.C., C.B.

DAKKA COLUMN.	JAMRUD COLUMN.
Brigadier-General J. A. Tytler, V.C., C.B.	*Lieutenant-General F. F. Maude, V.C., C.B.*
11—9th Royal Artillery (65th Company Royal Garrison Artillery), 2 guns.	D—A Royal Horse Artillery (O Battery Royal Horse Artillery), 3 guns.
Detachments from—	1st Battalion 5th Fusiliers (1st Battalion Northumberland Fusiliers), 300.
1st Battalion 17th Foot (1st Battalion Leicestershire Regiment).	51st Foot (1st Battalion King's Own Yorkshire Light Infantry), 200.
8th Company Bengal Sappers and Miners (8th Company 1st Sappers and Miners).	11th Bengal Lancers (11th Lancers), 1 troop.
27th Punjab Native Infantry (27th Punjabis).	13th Bengal Lancers (13th Lancers), 1 troop.
45th Sikhs.	Mhairwara Battalion (44th Merwara Infantry), 400.
Total, 718.	2nd Gurkha Regiment, 500.

TABLE VIII

ZAKHA KHEL EXPEDITION, 1879

LIEUTENANT-GENERAL F. F. MAUDE, V.C., C.B.

JAMRUD COLUMN.	BASAWAL COLUMN.	ALI MASJID COLUMN.	LANDI KOTAL COLUMN.
Lieutenant-General F. F. Maude, V.C., C.B. D—A Royal Horse Artillery (O Battery Royal Horse Artillery), 2 guns on elephants. 11—9th Royal Artillery (65th Company Royal Garrison Artillery), 2 guns. Detachments from— 1st Battalion 5th Fusiliers (1st Battalion Northumberland Fusiliers). 1st Battalion 25th Foot (1st Battalion King's Own Scottish Borderers). 13th Bengal Cavalry (13th Lancers). Madras Sappers and Miners. 24th Punjab Native Infantry (24th Punjabis). Total, 1,185. Route taken: Jamrud — Chura — China — Jamrud.	*Brigadier-General J. A. Tytler, V.C., C.B.* 11—9th Royal Artillery, 2 guns. Detachments from— 1st Battalion 17th Foot (1st Battalion Leicestershire Regiment). 4th Battalion Rifle Brigade. Guides Cavalry. Bengal Sappers and Miners. 4th Gurkha Regiment. Total, 847. Route taken: Basawal — Chenar — Sisobi Pass — China — Sisobi Pass — Dakka.	*Brigadier-General F. E. Appleyard, C.B.* 11—9th Royal Artillery, 2 guns. Detachments from— 51st Foot (1st Battalion King's Own Yorkshire Light Infantry). Madras Sappers and Miners. Mhairwara Battalion (44th Merwara Infantry). 2nd Gurkha Regiment. Total, 876. Route taken: Ali Masjid — Karamna — Barar Kas — China — Ali Masjid.	6th Native Infantry (6th Jat Light Infantry). 311. Joined Brigadier-General Appleyard at Karna. DAKKA COLUMN. Detachments from— 1st Battalion 17th Foot. 27th Punjab Native Infantry (27th Punjabis). 45th Sikhs. Total, 413. Joined Brigadier-General Tytler at Chenar.

to the Bara Valley showed that the Afridis of all clans were gathering there to dispute any further advance. Under these circumstances General Maude did not think it advisable to bring on a campaign against the entire Afridi tribe without definite instructions from the Government of India.   While, however, the troops remained halted awaiting orders, satisfactory terms were arranged with the Zakha Khel; but though sanction was given for a further advance if General Maude thought such a course desirable, that officer considered that the situation warranted the withdrawal of the troops, particularly as the return of General Tytler's column had been urgently desired.   The troops taking part in the two expeditions under General Maude are shown in Tables VII. and VIII.; these had evacuated the Bazar Valley by February 4, 1879.

Further annoyance was caused by the Zakha Khel during 1879-80, but, in February, 1881, an agreement was made with the Khaibar tribes by which the independence of the Afridis was recognized under British suzerainty, and the tribesmen undertook to keep the Khaibar Pass open, and to abstain from outrages in British territory in return for an annual subsidy of Rs. 85,860.

MOHMANDS, 1878. (*Map II.*)

In 1879 there was trouble with the Mohmands in addition to the Zakha Khel.   When the Afghan War broke out in 1878, the Mohmands sent a contingent to join the Amir's troops at Ali Masjid, but proved themselves worthless as allies, for they fled without firing a shot, and tendered their submission to Lieutenant-General Sir S. J. Browne shortly afterwards at Dakka. Small expeditions were despatched from time to time from the frontier posts, near the Afghan border, in consequence of raids committed, but order was restored without difficulty, and no fighting with the Mohmands took place for some time.

On February 28, 1879, an attack was made on a British surveyor, near Michni, for which a fine of Rs. 2,000 was imposed.   Two months later information was received at Dakka, which was held by a British garrison, to the effect that a large force of Mohmands was in the neighbourhood.   Accordingly a reconnaissance was made the next day to Kam Dakka, a small village on the south or right bank of the Kabul River, seven miles east of Dakka. The inhabitants seemed friendly, and asked for the protection of the party; but no enemy were seen, and the reconnoitring column returned to Dakka. On being informed of the situation, Lieutenant - General F. F. Maude, V.C., C.B., commanding the 2nd Division Peshawar Valley Field Force at Landi Kotal, ordered a reconnaissance to be made from that place through the Shilman Valley towards Kam Dakka, and at the request of the political officer two companies of the Mhairwara Battalion were sent from Dakka to Kam Dakka for the protection of the villagers.

The two companies of the Mhairwara Battalion left Dakka under Captain O'Moore Creagh* at 5 p.m. on April 21, 1879, but owing to the difficulties of the road did not reach the village till 11.15 p.m. On arriving there the British force was received in a very unfriendly manner by the inhabitants, who expressed themselves as not desirous of protection, and so compromising themselves with the rest of the tribe. They said the troops would be attacked, but added that they would remain neutral, and not allow the tribesmen to enter the village.

At 4 a.m. on April 22 Captain Creagh made dispositions to protect the village, and an hour later the enemy appeared in sight on the opposite bank of the Kabul River, and soon afterwards opened fire. News of the impending attack had already been sent to Dakka, but it was nearly twelve hours before assistance arrived. In consequence of the hostile demeanour of the villagers the troops were withdrawn from the village to a position between the Kam Dakka Road and the river. At about 8 a.m. a party of thirty-six men arrived with ammunition from Dakka, from whom Captain Creagh learned that he could not expect reinforcements that day. Accordingly he constructed a stone breastwork near the river, and the troops had no sooner been brought inside as well as a supply of water, than the position was surrounded on all sides. The fighting was desperate; counter-attacks with the bayonet were made several times, but at about 3 p.m., just as ammunition was beginning to run short and the situation to look most critical, the advanced troops of the relief column appeared. The Mohmands were charged by a troop of the 10th Bengal Lancers, supported by the Kam Dakka detachment, and driven across the river. The retirement to Dakka was begun without delay, and successfully carried out, in spite of difficulties caused by the

* Now General Sir O'Moore Creagh, V.C., G.C.B.

badness of the road, the delay occasioned by transport animals and wounded, the attacks of the enemy, and the failing light. The rear-guard reached Dakka at 8.30 p.m.

On April 23 a strong column of all arms marched from Dakka to Kam Dakka, but found the enemy already moving off. While at Kam Dakka it was joined by the reconnoitring column sent out from Landi Kotal on the 21st, but, no more of the enemy being seen, the two columns returned to their starting-points.

In December, 1879, and January, 1880, the Mohmands again became aggressive, and a body of some 5,400 men took up a position about two miles from Dakka, in the hills between the fort and Kam Dakka. A combined movement against them was then arranged: a column from Dakka was to attack the enemy in front, while another column moved against their rear from Landi Kotal, the effect of which, it was hoped, would be to drive the tribesmen back on the unfordable Kabul River. The advance was begun on January 15, the Landi Kotal Column starting six hours in advance of the one from Dakka. The troops engaged are shown in Table IX.

The enemy were found in occupation of a strong position, but were easily dislodged by the infantry, supported by the artillery of the Dakka Column under Colonel Boisragon. In spite of Colonel Boisragon's very deliberate advance, however, the combined action failed, owing to the delay caused to the Landi Kotal Column by the difficulties of the road. This force did not reach Kam Dakka till 6.30 p.m., and then without its baggage, which only arrived on the morning of January 18 with great difficulty, and with assistance both from Landi Kotal and Kam Dakka. Two villages were destroyed on the left bank of the Kabul River on the 16th without opposition, and two days later the troops returned to their respective stations. The Mohmands suffered so severely in the action of January 15 that the gathering was completely dispersed, and a long period of peace followed before they took up arms again against the British Government.

ZAIMUKHTS, 1878-79. (*Map II.*)

Another side-show to the main spectacle being enacted in Afghanistan has now to be described. The Zaimukhts inhabit a triangular district bordering on the

TABLE IX

EXPEDITION TO KAM DAKKA, 1880

DAKKA COLUMN.	LANDI KOTAL COLUMN.
Colonel T. W. R. Boisragon, 30th Punjab Native Infantry.	*Brigadier-General J. Doran, C.B.*
I—C Royal Horse Artillery,* 4 guns.	11—9th Royal Artillery (65th Company Royal Garrison Artillery), 2 guns.
6th Dragoon Guards, 94.	1st Battalion 5th Fusiliers (1st Battalion Northumberland Fusiliers), 200.
1st Battalion 25th Foot (1st Battalion King's Own Scottish Borderers), 110.	1st Battalion 25th Foot, 200.
17th Bengal Cavalry (17th Cavalry), 50.	17th Bengal Cavalry, 20.
8th Native Infantry (8th Rajputs), 100.	C Company Madras Sappers and Miners (C Company 2nd Sappers and Miners).
30th Punjab Native Infantry (30th Punjabis), 300.	1st Madras Native Infantry (61st Pioneers), 300.
	4th Madras Native Infantry (64th Pioneers), 200.
	31st Punjab Native Infantry (31st Punjabis), 300.

* No modern representative.

Kurram Valley to the south and Orakzai territory to the north. No trouble arose with them until the Afghan War of 1878, when they proceeded to harass the line of communication of the British force operating in Afghanistan. Transport difficulties prevented at first the despatch of an expedition against the Zaimukhts, but early in December, 1879, the force shown below concentrated at Balish Khel under Brigadier-General J. A. Tytler, V.C., C.B., and, moving in a south-easterly direction, invaded the hostile territory on the 8th, after some preparatory reconnaissances of the route had been made.

> 1—8th Royal Artillery (92nd Company Royal Garrison
>   Artillery), 4 guns.
> No. 1 Kohat Mountain Battery, 2 guns.
> 2nd Battalion 8th Regiment (Liverpool Regiment), 41.
> 85th Regiment (2nd Battalion Shropshire Light
>   Infantry), 733.
> 1st Bengal Cavalry (1st Lancers), 57.
> 13th Bengal Lancers (13th Lancers), 155.
> 18th Bengal Cavalry (18th Lancers), 55.
> 8th Company Sappers and Miners, 57.
> 13th Native Infantry (13th Rajputs), 323.
> 4th Punjab Infantry, 557.
> 20th Punjab Infantry, 399.
> 29th Punjab Infantry, 568.

Having destroyed the villages on the way, General Tytler reached Chinarak on the 12th, where a detachment was left, while the main body continued its advance the next day on Zawo, the chief Zaimukht stronghold. A narrow ravine seven miles long leads from Chinarak to Zawo, flanked on either side by a difficult path across the hills. It was decided that the main body should advance by the ravine, with a flanking force on the right, or eastern, route. Owing to the difficulties of the road the progress of the main body was very slow, and General Tytler halted for the night at Bagh. The force on the right of the main line of advance, under Colonel J. J. H. Gordon, met with some resistance from the enemy, who were found occupying a strong position along a ridge due east of Bagh, running at right angles to the direction of march. The attempt by four companies of the 85th Regiment to carry the position by a frontal attack having failed, two companies of the 29th Punjab Native Infantry, supported by two mountain guns, were directed to make a turning movement to the left and attack the enemy's right. At the same time the 85th Regiment renewed their attack from two different directions, and after a

short hand-to-hand struggle Colonel Gordon was in possession of the whole ridge, where he remained for the
night.

The advance was resumed early the next morning, and
the pass leading to Zawo gained after a short fight.
Colonel Gordon, as on the day before, guarded the right
of the main column, and was able to drive off some
hostile reinforcements that were seen moving on Zawo
from the east, besides clearing the ground to his front,
and destroying a group of villages in rear. As soon as
the heights around Zawo had been crowned, a detachment
was sent down from the pass to destroy the place, while
the main body waited on the kotal. The withdrawal
was not molested, and General Tytler returned to
Chinarak on December 15. The British casualties during
these operations only amounted to four officers and men,
but the enemy were believed to have suffered severely ;
the vaunted purdah of their seemingly inaccessible
stronghold had been rudely lifted, and they tendered
their submission six days after the destruction of Zawo.
General Tytler then marched his column back to the
Kurram Valley in a southerly direction to Thal, destroying
some refractory villages on the way. Thal was reached
on December 23, and there the force was broken up. No
further expedition has been undertaken against the
Zaimukht tribe.

MARRIS, 1880. (*Map V.*)

At the close of the second Afghan War an expedition
was organized from troops guarding the line of communication through the Harnai Pass for the punishment
of the Marris, a Baluchi tribe living south-west of Dera
Ghazi Khan, for various raids committed during the
progress of the war. It was not the first time that
British arms had penetrated the district, for during the
first Afghan War the successful defence of Kahan, and
the disasters and privations entailed by efforts for its
relief, form a memorable chapter in the military history
of the period. These operations, however, form incidents
in the record of the Afghan wars rather than Indian
North-West Frontier campaigns, so are for this reason
beyond the scope of this work.

Although the tribesmen of the extreme south of the
North-West Frontier of India were as notorious for their
raiding propensities as their neighbours to the north, no

regular military expedition was undertaken against them until 1880, when Brigadier-General C. M. MacGregòr assembled the troops mentioned below at Mandai, and marched north from there on October 17, 1880. The plan was to skirt the northern boundary of Marri territory, so as to cut them off from the assistance of the tribes to the north, and then, turning south, to advance upon their chief stronghold at Kahan. This was successfully carried out without opposition from the enemy, but in face of great difficulties presented by the nature of the road. Kahan was reached on November 6, but the Marris had already tendered their submission, so General Mac-Gregor marched in an easterly direction over better ground into British territory.

> 11—9th Royal Artillery (65th Company Royal Garrison Artillery).
> 2nd Battalion 60th Rifles.
> 3rd Punjab Cavalry.
> 2nd Sikh Infantry.
> 3rd Sikh Infantry.
> 4th Gurkha Regiment.
> 5th Gurkha Regiment.

MAHSUDS, 1881. (*Map III.*)

In addition to the expedition against the Marris, sanction was accorded, after the conclusion of the Afghan War, for a combined expedition against the Mahsuds, under Brigadier-Generals T. G. Kennedy and J. J. H. Gordon, starting from Tank and Bannu respectively. The object of the expedition was to exact punishment for a long list of outrages committed before and during the second Afghan War. The composition of the columns is shown in Table X.

General Kennedy left Tank on April 18, 1881, and reached Jandola without incident four days later. The advance was continued up the difficult Shahur Gorge on April 24, and thence into the Khaisora Valley. Very few of the enemy were seen, property of all kinds was devastated, and the submission of some of the neighbouring clans received. On May 4 a small engagement occurred at Shah Alam, where the enemy had taken up a strong position on some wooded hills. Three battalions were detailed for the attack, supported by the guns and another battalion in the centre; but, just as the assaulting infantry had got into position, the tribesmen charged down on the left battalion, who, however, stood firm,

TABLE X

MAHSUD EXPEDITION, 1881

BANNU COLUMN.	TANK COLUMN.
Brigadier-General J. J. H. Gordon, C.B.	*Brigadier-General T. G. Kennedy, C.B.*
No. 1 Battery 8th Brigade Royal Artillery (92nd Company Royal Garrison Artillery).	No. 2 (Derajat) Mountain Battery† (22nd Derajat Mountain Battery), 3 guns.
No. 1 (Kohat) Mountain Battery* (21st Kohat Mountain Battery), 2 guns.	No. 3 (Peshawar) Mountain Battery (23rd Peshawar Mountain Battery).
4th Battalion Rifle Brigade, 480.	No. 4 (Hazara) Mountain Battery† (24th Hazara Mountain Battery), 3 guns.
18th Bengal Cavalry (18th Lancers), 326.	1st Punjab Cavalry (21st Cavalry), 100.
No 6. Company Sappers and Miners (6th Company 1st Sappers and Miners), 124.	4th Punjab Cavalry,†‡ 190.
5th Punjab Infantry (58th Vaughan's Rifles), 596.	8th Company Sappers and Miners† (8th Company 1st Sappers and Miners), 70.
14th Native Infantry (14th Sikhs), 503.	1st Sikh Infantry (51st Sikhs), 465.
20th Punjab Native Infantry (20th Punjabis), 641.	4th Sikh Infantry (54th Sikhs), 466.
21st Punjab Native Infantry (21st Punjabis), 610.	1st Punjab Infantry (55th Coke's Rifles), 423.
30th Punjab Native Infantry (30th Punjabis), 426.	2nd Punjab Infantry (56th Punjabi Rifles), 460.
	3rd Punjab Infantry,‡ 461.
	4th Punjab Infantry (57th Wilde's Rifles), 464.
	6th Punjab Infantry (59th Scinde Rifles), 475.
	32nd Punjab Native Infantry Pioneers† (32nd Sikh Pioneers), 378.

* Transferred to Tank Column at Raznak.   † Transferred to Bannu Column at Makin.   ‡ No modern representative.

and following close on the enemy's heels when the latter fell back, rapidly gained possession of the position. General Kennedy arrived at Kaniguram, the important Mahsud centre visited by General Chamberlain in 1860, on May 5; thence communication was opened with General Gordon, and after a day's halt, during which some valuable survey work was accomplished, General Kennedy resumed his march north to Makin.

General Gordon left Bannu on April 16, and, marching west up the Khaisora Valley without opposition, reached Raznak on May 9. It was arranged then that General Gordon should return to Bannu by the unexplored Shaktu Valley, the next valley to the south of that by which the Bannu column had advanced, while General Kennedy marched back to Tank by way of the Barari Pass, which was the route taken by General Chamberlain in his advance on Kaniguram in 1860. Neither column was molested during the withdrawal, the tribesmen were submissive, and Tank was reached on May 18, Bannu four days later. Much valuable survey work was accomplished during these operations, the purdah had been effectually lifted and the tribesmen overawed, but the absence of any decisive military success somewhat discounted the value of these results. The Mahsuds failed to comply fully with the British terms, so it was necessary to continue the blockade, which lasted till September 7, 1881, when, despairing of outside assistance, the Mahsuds finally complied with the last demand.

CHAPTER VI

1882—1889

EXPEDITION TO THE TAKHT-I-SULIMAN, 1883. (*Map III.*)

AFTER General Hodgson's expedition in 1853 the conduct of the Shiranis improved, so that it was not found necessary to send troops into their country again till 1883, when the survey of the Takht-i-Suliman Mountain was undertaken. The legend of the Takht-i-Suliman* is that Solomon carried off a bride from India, and as he was returning with her over the mountains on a throne supported in the air by genii, he called on the genii to set his throne down on the summit of the peak, to allow his Princess to take one last farewell of the plains of India.

The escort to the survey party, under Major T. H. Holdich, R.E., consisted of the troops named below, under the command of Brigadier-General T. G. Kennedy, C.B.

No. 4 Hazara Mountain Battery.
1st Punjab Cavalry, 42.
1st Sikh Infantry, 500.
4th Punjab Infantry, 500.
5th Punjab Infantry, 496.

After pledges for the good behaviour of the Shiranis had been secured, the party left Dera Ismail Khan on November 15, 1883, and marching by way of Draband, entered Shirani territory through the Shekh Haidar Pass. Considerable delay was caused at a narrow defile by a large fallen rock, and even when a way had been cleared for mules it was so narrow that most of the camels had to be unloaded and loaded on opposite sides of the rock. It is stated that " the difficulty here experienced was due chiefly to the large space (nearly 8 feet) required by the camels loaded with uncompressed bhoosa. For a

* " Throne of Solomon."

hill expedition, where narrow defiles have to be passed, compressed bhoosa only should be carried."*

Pazai, whence the ascent of the Takht-i-Suliman was to be made, was reached on November 25. Here it was discovered that the enemy were holding a kotal, barring the way up the peak, but a combined turning and frontal attack on the 26th had the effect of clearing the way for the accomplishment of the object of the expedition. Survey operations were carried out on November 27 to 30, and the expedition returned on December 8 to Dera Ismail Khan by the way it had come. This, as well as other survey operations, is described in Sir. T. H. Holdich's book, "The Indian Borderland."

BLACK MOUNTAIN EXPEDITION, 1888. (*Map IV.*)

IN 1888 the Black Mountain again became the scene of military operations. For some years the country in these parts had been in a very unsettled state; a considerable sum was owing from the tribesmen for various offences, without much prospect of early payment, and numerous raids had been made across the British border, particularly in the Agror Valley. To assist the inhabitants of friendly villages in repelling these incursions, arms and ammunition were distributed by Government, and a military post was maintained at Aghi, the chief place in the district. On September 12, 1884, a successful skirmish took place between a detachment of 150 Sikhs and Gurkhas, assisted by twenty-five police, under Lieutenant A. A. Barrett,† 5th Gurkhas, and the tribesmen, in which the latter received a decided check; but the raids continued at varying intervals, until matters were brought to a head in 1888 by the murder of two British officers. This incident is described as follows in the official account of the work of the expedition which ensued:

"On June 18 a serious affair occurred on the Agror frontier, which resulted in the death of two British officers and four men of the 5th Gurkhas. Early on the morning of June 18, Major Battye, 5th Gurkhas, with sixty men of his regiment and nineteen police, and, accompanied by Captain Urmston, 6th Punjab Infantry, left Aghi Fort and ascended the Barchar spur, to make

---

* "Record of Expeditions against the North-West Frontier Tribes," p. 591 (Paget and Mason).
† Now Major-General Sir A. A. Barrett, K.C.B.

himself acquainted with the features of the surrounding country, the water-supply, etc. Shortly before reaching the crest, and while still within British territory, the party was fired on by some Gujar graziers, who were tenants of the Akazais. The fire was not returned, and Major Battye pushed on towards Chittabut, keeping within our own territory; but finding the enemy were becoming more numerous and their fire heavier, he decided to retreat, and accordingly the retirement of the party was ordered, covered by a small rear-guard. A havildar in the rear-guard having been wounded, the two British officers went back to his assistance with a stretcher, and while they were putting the wounded man into it the enemy charged, and in the hand-to-hand fight which ensued Major Battye and Captain Urmston were killed. The main body in the meanwhile, unaware of what had occurred, continued their retirement down the mountain-side. Subadar Kishenbir, who had been with the officers, though himself wounded, succeeded in escaping, and, rejoining the main body at the village of Atir, led them back and recovered the bodies of the officers. Four of the Gurkhas were left dead on the field and six rifles were lost. Of the enemy six were killed."*

This incident, as such incidents usually are, was the signal for the general gathering of the tribesmen and increased audacity, so that no alternative remained to the Government of India but to sanction the despatch of a punitive expedition against the offending clans. On September 7, 1888, orders were issued for the mobilization of the force shown in Table XI., under the command of Major-General J. W. McQueen, C.B., A.D.C., in which, it will be noticed, contingents of Kashmir troops and Khaibar Rifles were included. Proclamations were sent to the Hassanzais, Akazais, Parari Saiads, and Tikariwals, setting forth the terms on which their submission would be received if they wished to save their territory from invasion, and at the same time assurances of the friendly attitude of the Indian Government were given to other neighbouring clans not involved in the recent disturbances. October 2, 1888, was fixed as the limit of the time which could be allowed for reflection.

The 1st, 2nd, and 3rd Columns, into which the expeditionary force was divided, concentrated at Aghi, while

* "Expedition against the Black Mountain Tribes, 1888," p. 11 (Captain A. H. Mason, R.E.).

TABLE XI

BLACK MOUNTAIN EXPEDITION, 1888

ORIGINAL DISTRIBUTION

MAJOR-GENERAL J. W. McQUEEN, C.B., A.D.C.

FIRST BRIGADE. Brigadier-General G. N. Channer, V.C.		SECOND BRIGADE. Brigadier-General W. Galbraith.		RESERVE COLUMN.
Colonel J. M. Sym, 1st Battalion 5th Gurkhas.	Colonel R. H. O'G. Haly, 1st Battalion Suffolk Regiment.	Lieutenant-Colonel M. S. J. Sunderland, 2nd Battalion Royal Sussex Regiment.	Colonel A. C. W. Crookshank, C.B., 34th Pioneers.‡	2nd Battalion Seaforth Highlanders. 15th Bengal Cavalry (15th Lancers). 2nd Sikhs (52nd Sikhs). Kashmir Contingent, 1,392.
No. 4 Hazara Mountain Battery* (24th Hazara Mountain Battery), 4 guns. 1st Battalion Northumberland Fusiliers. 3rd Sikhs (53rd Sikhs). 1st Battalion 5th Gurkhas. Half No. 3 Company Sappers and Miners. Two Gatlings.	3—1st South Irish Division Royal Artillery† (6th Mountain Battery Royal Garrison Artillery), 2 guns. 1st Battalion Suffolk Regiment. 34th Pioneers (34th Sikh Pioneers), 4 Companies. 40th Bengal Infantry (40th Pathans). 45th Sikhs.	3—1st South Irish Division Royal Artillery,† 2 guns. No. 2 Derajat Mountain Battery* (22nd Derajat Mountain Battery), 2 guns. 2nd Battalion Royal Sussex Regiment. 14th Sikhs. 24th Punjab Infantry (24th Punjabis). Half No. 3 Company Sappers and Miners. Khaibar Rifles, 296.	2—1st Scottish Division Royal Artillery (1st Mountain Battery Royal Garrison Artillery). 2nd Battalion Royal Irish Regiment. 4th Punjab Infantry (57th Wilde's Rifles). 29th Punjab Infantry (29th Punjabis). 34th Pioneers, 4 Companies. Two Gatlings.	

* 7-pounder rifled muzzle-loader.   † 2·5-inch rifled muzzle-loader.

‡ Succeeded by Colonel Beddy, 29th Punjab Infantry, and then by Colonel Pratt, 2nd Sikhs.

the 4th assembled at Darband. This, it will be remembered, was a repetition of the strategy of the 1852 campaign, under Colonel Mackeson, whereby the crest of the Black Mountain was approached in front by a number of columns advancing up parallel spurs, while the rear of the hostile position was threatened from the beginning by the detachment at Darband. The task of improving the roads up the spurs was begun without delay, and on October 2, as nothing had been heard from the four offending clans, and working and reconnoitring parties had been fired on, orders were issued for the advance to be begun on October 4, the delay of twenty-four hours being necessary to complete the equipment of some corps.

On October 4 the 1st, 2nd, and 3rd Columns reached Mana-ka-Dana, Barchar, and Sambalbat, respectively, practically without opposition, though the camp of the 1st Column was fired into, and part of it attacked during the night. The lack of resistance to the frontal advance was probably due to the fact that the tribesmen had gathered near Towara to oppose the 4th Column, which threatened to make the position along the crest of the Black Mountain untenable : Towara was, in fact, the decisive point. While General McQueen's main body was toiling up the arduous slopes of the Black Mountain on the eastern side, a sharp engagement was fought on the western between Towara and Kotkai. The enemy were found in position about 800 yards north-east of Towara, between the hills and the river on the far bank of a nala, with their flanks resting on the river to their right, and on sangars constructed on the slopes of the hills to their left ; sharpshooters and some useless guns were also posted on the right bank of the Indus. While the 4th Punjab Infantry and 34th Pioneers cleared the right and left flank, respectively, of the British advance, the guns opened fire on the enemy's main position, and the Royal Irish deployed a little in advance of the artillery. This was the situation at 1.30, when "the enemy's position having been well searched by artillery and machine-gun fire, and the flanking parties being abreast of the line, the Royal Irish advanced without firing a shot, and, as steadily as if on parade, charged the enemy, Lieutenant W. Gloster particularly distinguishing himself by rushing to the front and capturing a standard. At this moment a body of fanatical swordsmen, who had been concealed in a masked nala, running

7

diagonally towards our left front, made a desperate
attempt to break our line. All were at once shot down
by the Royal Irish and the Gatlings except thirteen, who
were followed and accounted for by two companies of
the 29th Punjab Infantry and 34th Pioneers in the jungle
near the river. Eighty-eight dead were subsequently
counted at this spot, among whom forty-eight were
identified as Hindustanis."*

As the tribesmen fell back the 4th Column followed,
and Kotkai and the sangars on both banks of the river
were shelled, the enemy making little reply, and speedily
taking to flight towards Kunhar. Kotkai was occupied
at 4.30 p.m., but, owing to the difficulties of the road for
supply purposes, the greater part of the force returned
to Towara.

On October 5 the three columns ascending the
eastern side reached the crest of the Black Mountain
after a stiff climb, but with very little fighting, and on
the next day the 2nd Column moved south along the
crest for a distance of a little over a mile, to the place
where the 3rd Column had bivouacked the previous
evening, the 3rd Column moving about one and a half
miles farther west to a place called Kaima. The 1st
Column remained at Chittabut, the point reached on
October 5, but, owing to the scarcity of water and difficulty
of supply, the baggage-mules were sent back to Dilbori.

The country round Kaima proved to be much more
difficult than had been anticipated from the map available ;
in fact the road was so bad, and water so scarce, that the
3rd Column was obliged to return to the crest of the
main ridge on October 7, being harassed by the enemy
as it withdrew. The following fortnight was spent by
all three columns on the crest of the Black Mountain in
carrying out reconnaissances, improving the communications, and destroying hostile villages. The tribesmen
kept at a respectful distance throughout, but during the
night October 8/9 an attack was made on one of the
piquets of the 1st Column, which resulted in the death
of a native officer, and the wounding of two men. In
consequence of this incident, orders were issued that
" all fires and lights in bivouac should be extinguished at
sunset, and that trees should be fired at a distance of
from 50 to 100 yards in front of the bivouac, so as to
prevent the unseen approach of the enemy."†

* " Expedition against the Black Mountain Tribes, 1888," p. 15.
† d., p. 21.

On October 12 General Channer made his way down the western slopes of the mountain, with an escort of 300 men, and communicated with the 4th Column at Kunhar, returning to his brigade three days later. On the 13th and 16th, respectively, the Akazais and Hassanzais began to show signs of submission, but a jirgah considered sufficiently representative of the former clan was not received till the 19th, when an armistice for seven days was granted to them to comply with the British demands. As their villages became at the mercy of the 4th Column, all hostilities on the part of the Hassanzais ceased automatically; their fine was paid on October 30, four days after the Akazais had made their settlement.

While the columns on the crest of the Black Mountain were carrying out the foregoing operations, the 4th Column was engaged in work of a similar nature. The advance up the Indus Valley was greatly delayed by the badness of the roads, which had to be made passable for transport animals before the troops could make permanent progress—in fact, for the first few days, supplies could only be got through to Kotkai by hand. Some assistance, however, was derived from the river, for forage was brought up by this means in boats supplied by the Khan of Amb, who showed his loyalty to the British cause in a most practical manner throughout the campaign.

During a reconnaissance towards Kunhar on October 5 Colonel Crookshank was mortally wounded, and the command of the 4th Column devolved on Colonel Beddy, 29th Punjab Infantry, till Colonel Pratt arrived with the 2nd Sikhs ten days later. Kunhar was occupied on October 11, and from there signal communication was opened with the main body. General Channer arrived at Kunhar, as already mentioned, on the 12th. On October 13 the settlement of the Hindustani fanatics at Maidan, on the right bank of the river, was destroyed, this being the fifth occasion on which this notorious faction had come into collision with British troops in the past forty years, and been compelled to build their homes elsewhere.* Another expedition was made across

---

* The previous occasions were:

    1853. After Black Mountain Expedition of 1852, under Colonel Mackeson.
    1857. Expedition under Major Vaughan.
    1858. Expedition under Sir Sydney Cotton.
    1863. Ambela Campaign (Sir Neville Chamberlain and General Garvock).

the river three days later, and a considerable quantity of
forage and some grain collected. Continuing the advance
up the valley, the 4th Column occupied Led on October 20; this proved to be the most northerly point reached,
for news was received of the submission of the tribesmen,
and the withdrawal began on the 23rd.

The second phase of the campaign had now been
reached; the Akazais and Hassanzais had been brought
to terms, but the clans living to the north had still to be
dealt with. The Parari Saiads, Tikariwals, and subsequently the Allaiwals, were now made to realize the
fatuity of the idea that a British force could not penetrate
their country, difficult as it was, and exact reparation for
misdeeds. It will be remembered that when General
Wilde's force was operating in these parts in 1868 the
northern slopes of the Black Mountain were left untouched. This had given the inhabitants an exaggerated
idea of the security of their position, which it was now
necessary to correct.

Some reorganization of the force at General McQueen's
disposal took place at this juncture, which will be found
shown in Table XII. On the evening of October 20 the
situation of the various columns was as under:

Force Headquarters   ...⎱
Headquarters 1st Brigade ...⎰ Mana-ka-Dana.
1st Column   ...   .⎠
2nd Column ...   . Chittabut.
3rd Column ...   . Distributed along the crest.
4th Column ...   . Indus Valley (Led to Darband).
5th Column (see Table XII.) Dilbori.

The advance north began on October 21, and was
immediately followed by the submission of the Tikariwals. The next two days were devoted to reconnaissance;
Parari Saiad territory was entered on the 24th, and the
destruction of villages began. Marching on in the
direction of Thakot, the force halted on the 28th, while
a detachment under General Channer went forward to
visit that place. During the advance through Parari
Saiad territory the road was bad throughout, and often
very steep as well—in fact, on October 27 only two and
a half miles were covered, and strong working parties,
assisted by coolies, had to be employed in improving the
track throughout the day. The flying column, as shown
below, marching with only one blanket per man, great-
coats, and one day's rations, reached Thakot without
opposition. The village is described as " an insignificant

TABLE XII

BLACK MOUNTAIN EXPEDITION, 1888

DISTRIBUTION ON OCTOBER 20

COMMANDERS AS SHOWN IN TABLE XI

FIRST BRIGADE.		SECOND BRIGADE.		
FIRST COLUMN.	SECOND COLUMN.	THIRD COLUMN.	FOURTH COLUMN.	FIFTH COLUMN.
No. 4 (Hazara) Mountain Battery (34th Hazara Mountain Battery), 4 guns. 1st Battalion Northumberland Fusiliers. 2nd Battalion Seaforth Highlanders, 1 Company. 3rd Sikhs (53rd Sikhs). 34th Pioneers(34th Sikh Pioneers), 4 Companies). 1st Battalion 5th Gurkhas. Half No. 3 Company Sappers and Miners.	No. 2 (Derajat) Mountain Battery (22nd Derajat Mountain Battery), 2 guns. 1st Battalion Suffolk Regiment. 45th Sikhs.	3—1st South Irish Division Royal Artillery (6th Mountain Battery Royal Garrison Artillery), 2 guns. 2nd Battalion Royal Sussex Regiment. 14th Sikhs. 24th Punjab Infantry (24th Punjabis). Half No. 3 Company Sappers and Miners.	2—1st Scottish Division Royal Artillery (1st Mountain Battery Royal Garrison Artillery). 2nd Battalion Royal Irish Regiment. 2nd Battalion Seaforth Highlanders,4 Companies. 2nd Sikhs (52nd Sikhs). 4th Punjab Infantry (57th Wilde's Rifles). 29th Punjab Infantry (29th Punjabis). 34th Pioneers, 4 Companies. Two Gatlings. 15th Bengal Cavalry, 1 Troop at Darband.	*Colonel A. Money, Seaforth Highlanders.* 3—1st South Irish Division Royal Artillery, 4 guns. 2nd Battalion Seaforth Highlanders, 3 Companies. 40th Bengal Infantry (40th Pathans), 4 Companies. Khaibar Rifles. Two Gatlings. RESERVE. 15th Bengal Cavalry (15th Lancers),at Aghi.

place, and from its position (in the bottom of a teacup as
it were) of no importance from a military point of view."*
The troops marched through the village with the pipes
of the Seaforth Highlanders playing, "You're owre lang
in coming, lads," to mark the first visit to the place by a
British force. There was some sniping during the afternoon from a village on the far bank of the river, and from
the high ground to the south, but the guns in the former
case, and the Pioneers and Khaibar Rifles in the latter,
soon caused the annoyance to cease. The villages to
which the snipers were traced were destroyed on October 29, but Thakot was spared, as the inhabitants had
offered no resistance; General Channer then marched
back to join the main body.

> 3—1st South Irish Royal Artillery, 2 guns.
> Seaforth Highlanders, 259 rifles.
> 3rd Sikhs, 250 rifles.
> 34th Pioneers, 269 rifles.
> Khaibar Rifles, 200 rifles.
> Two Gatlings.

The Parari Saiads having received their punishment,
the withdrawal to Maidan began on October 30; and from
there a force, consisting of the 1st and 5th Columns, were
sent into Allai territory to complete the work of the
expedition. Progress was again very slow, owing to the
steep and broken nature of the track leading over the
Ghoraper Pass, which would have been a most formidable obstacle in the hands of a determined enemy. As it
was, the pass was captured without difficulty before
dawn on November 1; the enemy appeared to be present
in some force early in the day, and for some time the
firing was quite brisk, but all opposition soon melted
away before the resolute advance of the Northumberland Fusiliers and Khaibar Rifles, supported by the guns.
The last 500 feet to the summit of the pass was found to
be quite impracticable for mules, and even after the
Pioneers and Sappers and Miners, assisted by coolies,
had been at work on it all the day, the baggage took twelve
hours to make the ascent of the last mile of road on
November 2, and fourteen mules were lost by falling
over the precipice yawning below. The previous night
was "one of great discomfort for the troops, who were,
for the most part, without food or blankets. There was,
moreover, a hard frost during the night, the elevation
being over 9,000 feet. Fortunately, wood was plentiful,

* "Expedition against the Black Mountain Tribes, 1888," p. 30.

the bivouac being in partially cleared forest. The baggage was massed, as far as possible, at the foot of the Chaila crest, with the guns, and the Seaforth Highlanders, with the 3rd Sikhs, held the line of the crest with piquets. Five hundred of the Kashmir troops moved from Batgraon to Mazrai to take the place of the force that had advanced, and to keep open the communications. A letter was received this day from Arsala Khan,* the point of which was contained in the last sentence, 'Kindly wait and stay a little.' His object was evidently to gain time, being aware that, owing to the lateness of the season, operations might at any time be stopped by snow."†

On November 2 a reconnaissance was made in the direction of Pokal, the principal village in Allaiwal territory, and it was decided to send forward a detachment to destroy it the next day. Some opposition was offered to the advance, but Pokal was occupied and entirely destroyed, with the exception of the mosque, by 1 p.m. The enemy suffered considerable loss, for the detachments from the Suffolk and Royal Sussex Regiments, who were all picked marksmen, were able to use their rifles with great effect on the retreating tribesmen. The enemy followed up the retirement with great persistency to within a mile from camp, but the troops fell back in good order, and no mishap occurred—in fact, one company of Northumberland Fusiliers was able to inflict some appreciable loss on the enemy. This company "occupied a knoll, and, waiting for the enemy to collect in groups, soon had an opportunity of pouring in a volley, which effectually drove them back, leaving a good number killed," and the official account goes on to say "our loss during the day had been one man killed and one wounded 5th Gurkhas, and three wounded Khaibar Rifles. Brigadier-General Channer, in his despatch, estimated the enemy's loss at from eighty to a hundred killed, and he considered that the small number of casualties on our side was largely due to the admirable manner in which the troops skirmished during the advance, and performed rear-guard duties during the retirement. The troops all returned to camp before dark, after a heavy day's work. The distance to Pokal was seven miles, and the descent 4,300 feet. The Allai Valley was found to be open and highly cultivated, and dotted with numerous large villages."‡

* Chief of the Allaiwals.
† "Expedition against the Black Mountain Tribes, 1888," p. 37.
‡ *Ibid.*, p. 38.

On November 4 the force which had invaded Allai territory withdrew to Maidan, and by the 13th the whole force under the command of Major-General McQueen was concentrated in the Agror Valley and at Darband. The work of the expedition was now complete, and on November 14 the troops began to disperse to their peace stations.

The results of the campaign just concluded were:

(1) The collection of Rs. 14,000 in fines.
(2) An undertaking from the tribesmen not to—
    (a) molest British subjects on British territory;
    (b) make any claim to territory east of the Black Mountain watershed;
    (c) injure roads constructed.
(3) 177 square miles of unknown country were surveyed.
(4) 222 miles of road suitable for pack transport were constructed.

The British casualty list included twenty-five killed, fifty-four wounded, and seven deaths from disease, total eighty-six; the small number of deaths from disease was attributed to "the men having been specially selected for their physical fitness, the favourable conditions of climate, and the good quality of the rations issued."[*]

The signalling arrangements were particularly successful, and on only two occasions was telegraphic communication with the headquarters of the force interrupted; the General Officer Commanding was in touch with the whole of the force throughout the operations.

The services of the Khaibar Rifles and the troops of His Highness the Maharaja of Kashmir were suitably acknowledged by Major-General McQueen, and of the former in particular the following report was made: "Their rapidity of movement over the hills and familiarity of the tactics pursued by the enemy have proved them to be troops of the very best material for the class of fighting in which we have recently been engaged. Their discipline has been excellent, and no instance of misconduct has been brought to my notice, or that of the Column Commanders under whose immediate orders they have served." Five of the Khaibar Rifles received the Order of Merit for conspicuous gallantry, and the whole contingent were permitted to retain the Snider rifles with which they had been armed throughout the campaign.

[*] " Expedition against the Black Mountain Tribes, 1888," p. 38.

CHAPTER VII

REVIEW OF THE FIRST PERIOD

It is said that tactics alter every ten years. If this be admitted, there must be a reason for the change; occasionally it is an individual who brings it about, but far more frequently it is some important advance in the science which deals with the manufacture of weapons of war. Progress in this respect has been enormous in the last sixty years; consequently it is only natural to expect that the majority of the military lessons which can be drawn from a study of the early Indian frontier wars will be of a general, rather than a particular, interest at the present time. Since 1890 there has undoubtedly been a considerable change in the art of war as practised by the Pathan tribes, which may be traced with certainty to the improvement of their armament. In the preceding pages several instances will be found in which the tribesmen have charged the regular troops sword in hand in broad daylight, but the chapters which follow will reveal a growing disinclination to try the fortune of war by such drastic methods. Instead of the reckless daring characteristic of warriors who depend for success on hand-to-hand encounter, it will be seen that guile and studied prudence have become the chief weapons in the moral armoury of the transfrontier Pathan. Cunning has arisen like a new-born but decadent phœnix from the ashes of the venturesome courage which hurled itself to such purpose against the breastwork of the Crag Piquet. On the other hand it must be remembered that the modern rifle has not only an extensive range, but is also capable of rapid loading. There need now be no material pause between the firing of one round and the next, so the chance of the attacking swordsmen of getting to close quarters is very much less than it was even thirty years ago. Nevertheless, it cannot be denied that the Pathans have taken far greater advantage of the long ranging power of the modern rifle than of its increased rapidity of fire. The necessity for husbanding ammunition may be a predisposing cause, but reluctance to await the assault of regular troops has always been characteristic of wars among the border hills of India, and it is at decisive ranges that the effect of a rapid fire is particularly telling. In short, the long-range rifle has produced the sniper, and relegated the sword to a secondary position.

One of the most notable features of the campaigns just described is the great use made of surprise in the form of a long night march, followed by an attack at dawn. The record of almost every expedition contains an instance, and it says much for the system of intelligence of the Political Officers, and the physical endurance of the men, that operations of this kind should have been so uniformly successful. The use of feints, flank attacks, covering fire, and efforts to draw the enemy into the open, appears again and again. The most decisive action that has been fought by cavalry in an Indian frontier war was the result of the successful employment of the last-mentioned ruse. In the brilliant little engagement near Tank, in 1860, against the Mahsuds, it will be remembered, a native officer of the 5th Punjab Cavalry succeeded in drawing the enemy into the plains by means of a feigned retreat. He then turned, cut off the tribesmen from the hills, and, with about 160 men of his own regiment, and 40 mounted auxiliaries, inflicted a loss of 300 killed. It is not clear how far the figures are trustworthy, but, even if considerably exaggerated, there is ample margin for the most decisive effect.

That there was a certain number of regrettable incidents is only to be expected, but when it is remembered that the foregoing pages cover an interval of over thirty years it will be acknowledged that the number of such mishaps is surprisingly small. As usual, most of them might have been prevented. Many of the outrages, which helped to fill the cup of iniquity of the various tribes against whom the British arms had to be turned, were brought about by the carelessness or neglect of orders of the victims themselves. Again and again it is recorded in Colonel Paget's book how small parties travelling at night, or individuals outside the line of piquets, in both cases contrary to orders, were attacked and paid the penalty for their folly with their lives. Police piquets who lie down to sleep by the roadside in a disturbed country instead of in the defended building provided for them have only themselves to blame if the natural consequences follow, but, unfortunately, the matter does not end there. The elation of the enemy, the loss of prestige in the district by the suzerain power, the necessity for reprisals of some kind, are all consequences which follow in the train of neglect of duty by even an insignificant detachment. The charge of gross disregard of military precautions must be laid at the door of the party of Native Infantry who were cut up on the borders of Jowaki territory in 1877, because they camped for the night near a ravine, which the enemy used as an avenue of approach. The only consolation that it is possible to derive from incidents of this description is that they serve as the best of warnings for the future, if only they can be made widely known.

An example of the necessity for good communications throughout the force is afforded by the mishap to a detachment of the 4th Punjab Infantry, who were isolated, for some reason or other, during the operations against the Waziris in 1852 and annihilated.

In illustration of the principle that a counter-stroke should not be carried too far, the fighting round the Eagle's Nest Piquet, on October 26, 1863, during the Ambela Campaign, may be put forward, for on this occasion the 6th Punjab Infantry, after a successful counter-attack, pursued beyond reach of support, and suffered severely in their retirement.

Misunderstanding of orders, whether from want of clearness or not, is a fruitful source of disaster, and the example of the 3rd Punjab Infantry during the operations against the Orakzais in the Ublan Pass (March, 1868) is a case in point. In this instance it will be remembered that the officer commanding the regiment mistook the hill which was indicated as his objective, and, carrying his pursuit too far, was killed himself, together with several of his men, in an ineffectual attempt to storm a strong position with insufficient force.

The behaviour of the troops throughout the campaigns just described earned the frequent approbation of their commanding officers, in spite of the fact that on some occasions the former were fighting against their own kith and kin; they can therefore, without tarnish to their fame, afford to have two occasions recorded against them on which they failed to reach their own high standard of courage and endurance. One occurred during the attack on the Barari Pass, during General Chamberlain's expedition against the Mahsuds in 1860, when the infantry, assaulting the left of the enemy's position, were driven down the hill in confusion before a charge by the hostile swordsmen. The other occasion was when the Crag Piquet was captured on November 13, 1863, during the Ambela Campaign, and the garrison fell back in such haste as to spread considerable confusion among the troops in rear. These instances, however, are not mentioned here merely as instances of temporary panics, but rather to lead up to the due appreciation of how the crises were met. In each case the tables were successfully turned by a prompt attack on the exultant tribesmen by fresh troops. The situation in both cases was extremely critical, in both cases the remedy applied was the same, and in both cases was immediately effectual; the principle that the best relief from an awkward position is to be found in a resolute counterstroke thus receives the confirmation of history. Fresh troops should, therefore, always be available to carry out, or at least stiffen, such counterstrokes.

One more incident remains to be noticed in which an awkward situation might have been alleviated by more judicious arrangement beforehand. This also occurred during General Chamberlain's expedition against the Mahsuds in 1860. It will be remembered that while General Chamberlain penetrated the Shahur Valley with part of his force, the remainder was left in camp at Palosin, on the left bank of the Tank Zam. This camp was attacked at dawn on April 23, 1860, and the enemy, having rushed the piquets on the east side, poured into the lines occupied by the levies and commissariat, inflicting great loss and causing considerable confusion. The plan of the camp was roughly as shown in the accompanying sketch.

From this it will be seen at once that the least defensible portion of the camp was placed at the end most likely to be attacked, if the camp was attacked at all, instead of being protected by combatant units. The result was considerable loss and confusion before the critical situation could be retrieved.

The Ambela Campaign is quoted in Colonel Callwell's "Small Wars" and elsewhere, as an example of the complications which arise when a hostile people flank an intended line of operations. It will be remembered that, counting at least on the neutrality of the Bunerwals, the British plan was to invade the country inhabited by the

PALOSIN CAMP

APRIL 23, 1860

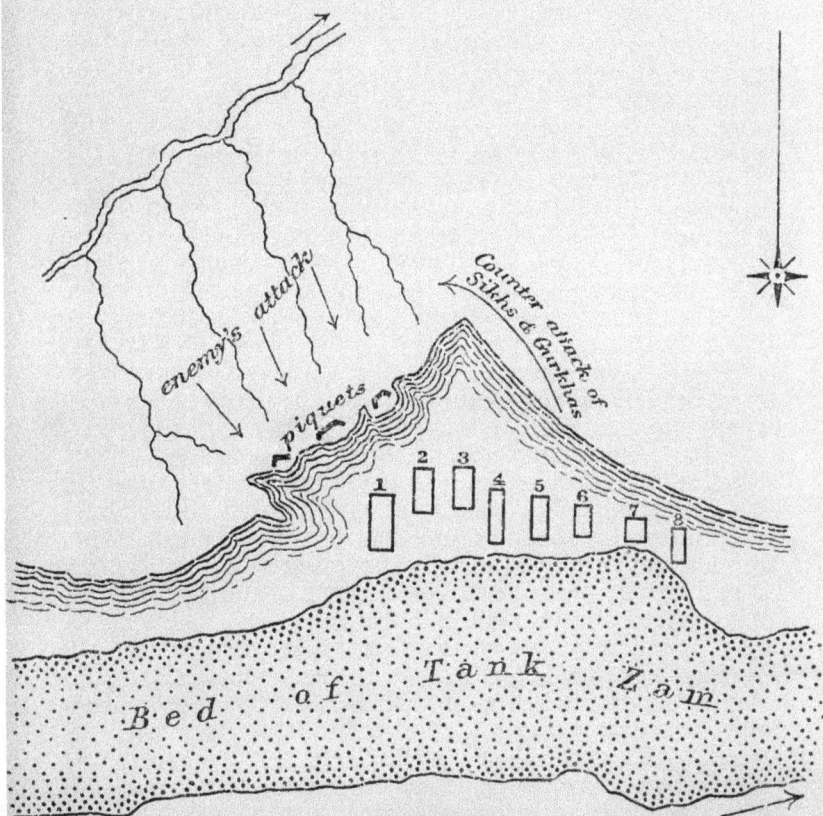

1. *Levies and commissariat*
2. *Guides*
3. *Pioneers*
4. *Artillery*

5. *Gurkhas*
6. *4th Sikhs*
7. *3rd Cavalry*
8. *14th P.N.I.*

Hindustani fanatics from the north, so as to drive them towards the plains of India and away from their mountain fastnesses. When Sir Neville Chamberlain arrived at the summit of the Ambela Pass, however, the Bunerwals adopted so hostile an attitude that it was impossible to carry out the original plan of operations until the left flank and rear of the British column could be secured either by the conciliation of the men of Buner or by additional troops. Accordingly a prolonged halt had to be made at the Ambela Pass to give time for both solutions of the difficulty. In this class of warfare, or in any other for that matter, but especially so in campaigns against irregular forces, a check to the steady progress of operations is greatly to be deprecated. The enemy invariably attribute the pause to weakness, and immediately take courage therefrom. Parties undecided as to which cause, if any, to espouse at once deem it prudent to be on what they think is the winning side. Moreover, when the enemy are relieved from the necessity for confining their attention to parrying the blows of a steady advance, they are free to devote their energies to attacks on the line of communication and other minor enterprises, which may cause great annoyance to the regular troops.

If any permanent result is to be secured by an armed expedition, it must achieve some definite military success; the enemy must be made to recognize their inferiority, the futility of resistance, and the certainty of punishment for outrage of any kind. This well-known fact is well illustrated by the operations against the Bizoti section of the Orakzais in 1868, and by the first expedition in 1877 against the Jowakis. The first example was a distinct British reverse. It will be remembered that the plan of operations was to draw the tribesmen down from the hills bordering the Ublan Pass, and then to attack and cut off their retreat. Up to a certain point the British force was entirely successful, but then came the unfortunate misunderstanding of orders, which has already been mentioned, whereby one of the infantry regiments engaged pushed forward prematurely, and suffered severe loss in attempting to storm a strong position. Further unsuccessful attacks followed, and eventually the force was compelled to withdraw by the approach of darkness. No provision had been made for passing the night in the open, so the enemy had to be left in possession of the field.

The first Jowaki Expedition of 1877 failed, not because

it suffered defeat, but because it was carried out too hurriedly. Moreover, it was hoped to catch the enemy between the fire of three converging columns, but it appears that sufficient precautions were not taken to keep the intended movements secret, so that the tribesmen were able to escape and remove much of their property to a place of safety. Like the attack on the Ublan Pass just mentioned, the operations were confined to one day; a certain amount of property was destroyed, but the Jowakis were not forced to give battle, so that, when the troops withdrew as quickly as they had come, the impression was left that the reason was because they were not strong enough to maintain their position in hostile territory. In both of the cases mentioned further expeditions had to be organized within a year on a larger scale to correct the bad impression left, and reduce the tribesmen to submission.

As is usual in campaigns of this kind, the difficulties to be overcome by the transport were immense. The roads were almost invariably of the worst description, and the transport animals were often inferior; but nevertheless the scale of baggage allowed to officers and men was according to modern ideas extremely liberal. The extract from Colonel Paget's book, quoted in the account of the expedition against the Hassanzais in 1852, presents a striking picture of the laborious progress through mountain defiles of a column encumbered with an excessive quantity of baggage. For the expedition against the Shiranis in 1853 (which lasted four days), one camel was allowed to every two officers.* Now the authorized load for a camel is 5 maunds, or 400 pounds, which gives each officer an allowance of 200 pounds. The quantity allowed by regulations at the present time for a junior officer is 100 pounds, including a tent; but in practice even that amount is seldom permitted. Of course, it was soon found impossible, with a portentous baggage train, to carry on hill warfare against an elusive foe. Sir Neville Chamberlain did much to remedy the evil during the numerous expeditions commanded by him, and many campaigns show a wonderful mobility on the part of the force employed. Fortunately for all concerned, attacks on baggage columns seem to have been the exception during the first period of the history of Indian frontier wars. It has been suggested already

* "Record of Expeditions against the North-West Frontier Tribes," p. 584 (Paget and Mason).

that attacks of this nature, which were so common during the Tirah campaign in particular, are the outcome of a change in Pathan methods of war, due directly to the substitution of the long-range rifle for the sword as the principal weapon of offence.

Lastly, the use of elephants in mountain warfare deserves at least a passing notice. They enabled field-guns to be carried with the troops, but the question of the supply of the 250 to 400 pounds of forage daily that an elephant is supposed to require, according to whether it is dry or green, must have been a veritable thorn in the side of the supply and transport officers of the period. Nevertheless, elephants were employed in hill wars down to a comparatively recent date, for they accompanied the Jamrud Column of the Bazar Valley Expedition under General Maude in 1879, and there seems to be no mention of any complaint against them. On the contrary, the fact that they were used in a hill expedition so late as 1879 indicates that they were considered desirable additions to the force. It is true that their gallantry under fire has been impugned, but they are admirable pack-animals; also, they were often found very useful for demolishing the habitations of refractory tribesmen.

CHAPTER VIII

1890—1891

THE ZHOB VALLEY. (*Map III.*)

THE history of the Zhob Valley, as far as the British Government is concerned, may be dealt with sufficiently for the purposes of this work in a few pages. The district of Zhob constitutes the mountainous portion of Baluchistan, and covers an area of 9,626 square miles, which is approximately the size of the counties of Yorkshire, Lancashire, and Westmorland combined. The Zhob River rises east of the Pishin Valley in the neighbourhood of Quetta, and flows in a north-easterly direction till it joins the Gomal; both then become tributaries of the Indus below Dera Ismail Khan. The basin of the Zhob River forms an immense alluvial plain, studded with numerous villages, and was, according to Huien Tsiang, a celebrated Chinese explorer of the seventh century, the early home of the Afghans.

Attention was first drawn to the Zhob Valley during the Afghan War of 1878-1880, when the inhabitants adopted a hostile attitude, and even went so far as to attack a British column returning to India through the Derajat District. The tribesmen were repulsed with heavy loss, and their leader, who bore the historical name of Shah Jahan, sent envoys to make submission. In 1880, however, a number of outrages were committed, which eventually led to the despatch of the first military expedition under Brigadier-General Sir O. V. Tanner, K.C.B. The operations lasted less than a month, for the arrival of the troops was followed at once by the surprise and capture of Shah Jahan's principal fort, the rout of his supporters, and the flight of that individual himself. A general submission was then made, from which the Indian Government acquired the right to station troops in the Zhob and Bori Valleys.

For the next four years peace was practically undisturbed, but in the meantime the necessity began to be
felt for acquiring trustworthy information regarding the
Gomal route into Afghanistan, and its means of communication with Quetta by way of the Zhob Valley.
Accordingly, in February, 1888, a survey party started
from Dera Ismail Khan with a tribal escort for the
Gomal Pass, but was obliged to return without accom-
plishing its object owing to the hostility of the tribesmen. In December, 1888, however, Sir Robert Sandeman,
the Chief Commissioner of Baluchistan, made a successful expedition down the Zhob Valley to within twenty
miles of the Gomal River, which was followed a year
later by a more extended tour down the same two
valleys. During the negotiations which took place the
tribesmen appeared quite friendly, and one of the results
of this expedition was that the headquarters of the
Political Officer of the Zhob District were established at
Fort Sandeman, close to the village of Apozai, on the
right bank of the Zhob River.

One clan, however, held aloof from the arrangements
made by Sir Robert Sandeman in January, 1890, and
adopted a defiant attitude. This was the Khiddarzai
section of the Shirani tribe, and their territory lay
thirty-five miles north-east of Fort Sandeman in a
straight line. Another centre of unrest lay among the
hills to the west of the British post, where some 250 outlaws and malcontents from all parts were gathered together under the leadership of one Dost Muhammad, the
owner of another historical name. As it was inevitable
that the existence of these two factions would constitute
a serious menace to the peace of the district, the Government of India decided to despatch an expedition against
them under Major-General Sir George White, consisting
of the troops named below, drawn from Quetta, Loralai,
and Hyderabad (Sind).

> Two Squadrons 18th Bengal Lancers.
> No. 7 Mountain Battery Royal Artillery.
> 2nd Battalion King's Own Yorkshire Light Infantry.
> No. 1 Company Bombay Sappers and Miners.
> 29th Bombay Infantry—2nd Baluch Battalion (129th
>   Baluchis).
> 30th Bombay Infantry—3rd Baluch Battalion (130th
>   Baluchis).
> Two Sections British Field Hospital.
> Five Sections Native Field Hospital.

The concentration was ordered to take place at Hindu Bagh, at the upper end of the Zhob Valley, by October 1, 1890, and a letter was sent to the Amir of Afghanistan explaining the objects of the expedition. The original plan was to detach a portion of the force to cut off the retreat into Afghanistan of Dost Muhammad and his followers, while the remainder attacked him in front; but the former part of this project had to be abandoned, owing to the desire of Government to avoid all risk of complications with the Amir. Dost Muhammad having been dealt with, Sir George White was then to turn his attention to the Khiddarzais.

Three columns were formed to march on Thanishpa, Dost Muhammad's stronghold, by different routes, but the place was occupied without a struggle on October 11. The leader of the hostile gang made good his escape into Afghanistan, though hotly pursued by a detachment of the 18th Bengal Lancers. The inhabitants of the surrounding country at once tendered their submission, and Sir George White continued his advance in a north-easterly direction with two lightly equipped columns, moving down two parallel valleys; while the bulk of the cavalry and guns, owing to the difficulties of the road and scarcity of forage, made their way to Fort Sandeman, accompanied by a small force of infantry.

At a point about seven miles south of the Gomal River Sir George White sent the greater part of the troops with him by the direct road to Fort Sandeman, while he himself made a *détour* through Domandi for about eight miles down the Gomal Valley, before following the remainder to Fort Sandeman. During these operations the tribesmen offered no organized opposition whatever; a few shots were fired, but the inhabitants showed a far greater inclination towards peace and a profitable trade in sheep and goats than the rugged vicissitudes of war. On October 29 the force under Sir George White was concentrated at Fort Sandeman, and the first phase of the campaign was over.

To assist in the reduction of the Khiddarzais by containing the rest of the tribe, the force named below was ordered to act against the Shiranis from the east under the immediate command of Colonel A. G. Ross, C.B., 1st Sikh Infantry, but subject to the control of Sir George White. By direction of Sir George White this force occupied Drazand on November 1, after a short skirmish, and threw out a detachment some ten miles to

the south-east to Domandi, which must not be confused
with the place of the same name at the junction of the
Kundar and Gomal Valleys.

> One Troop 1st Punjab Cavalry.
> One Squadron 3rd Punjab Cavalry.
> No. 1 (Kohat) Mountain Battery, 4 guns.
> No. 7 (Bengal) Mountain Battery (27th Mountain
>   Battery), 2 guns.
> Four Companies 1st Sikh Infantry.
> Four Companies 2nd Sikh Infantry.
> Four Companies 2nd Punjab Infantry.
>   Total, 1,651.

For the advance from Fort Sandeman on Namar Kalan,
the stronghold of the Khiddarzais, the British force was
divided into two columns under the command of Sir
George White and Colonel Nicolson, 30th Bombay Infantry, which were to approach the objective by parallel
valleys from the south-west; the considerations which
influenced Sir George White in deciding on his plan of
action being described thus :

" Namar Kalan, the stronghold of the Khiddarzai section, nestles at the foot of, and between three and four
thousand feet below, the Maramazh Heights. These
heights tower almost perpendicularly above Namar
Kalan, and cover it with a back wall most difficult to
scale. From information received, it appeared to Sir
George White that the defiant attitude of the Khiddarzais
was based upon the idea that this higher approach to
their capital was inaccessible to a British force, and that
consequently they could retire unmolested with their
flocks and herds to these heights and adjoining grazing
grounds on the precipitous spurs of the Takht-i-Suliman
before our advance from the easier or eastern line of
approach. The General Officer Commanding determined
therefore to march a small but picked force over the
heights, and to descend upon Namar Kalan, while Colonel
Nicolson was making a practicable road through the
Chuhar Khel Dhana, a very difficult pass from Baluchistan
to the Derajat, which had been closed for some years by
landslips and large boulders blocking the river-bed at its
narrowest parts."*

Sir George White began his advance from Fort Sandeman on October 31, but, as Namar Kalan was approached,
he was compelled by the extreme difficulties of the ground
to form a small lightly equipped column from the troops

* " Operations of the Zhob Field Force, 1890," p. 15.

Plate III

FRONTIER SCENERY, NO. 2

To face p. 116

under his immediate command in order to carry out his intention of approaching the Khiddarzai stronghold over the precipitous hills guarding it. On November 4 the heights overlooking Namar Kalan were gained, and communication established by heliograph with the other portion of the invading force. From this commanding position the headmen of the Khiddarzais, who now hastened to make their submission, were able to realize how completely Sir George White's strategy had cut them off from all hope of assistance from the remainder of the tribe.

On November 6 Sir George White's flying column* reached Namar Kalan, after a stiff climb uphill for about 1,700 feet, and a steep descent of 3,600 feet. In addition to their rifles and forty rounds of ammunition the men carried on their person their bedding, three days' rations, and cooking-pots, and the rear-guard was nearly seventeen hours under arms. The achievement affords a good instance in which men have been called upon to be independent of transport, and points to the necessity for them to be able to do the same again when history repeats itself.

While Sir George White advanced north on Namar Kalan, Colonel Ross moved south towards the same place, and after a short skirmish met and conferred with the General Officer Commanding. Except for some reconnaissances in various directions, during one of which the Takht-i-Suliman† was revisited, the objects of the campaign were now accomplished, and the return of the troops to their stations was begun. Briefly stated, the results of the expedition against the Khiddarzais were twofold—namely, the opening up of the Shirani country, and the establishment of five levy posts within the same area. As regards the operations just concluded as a whole, Sir George White said in his despatch :

"The Zhob Field Force may be said to have been employed for two months. During that time the columns composing it marched in the aggregate 1,800 miles. Of this distance 828 miles were over new routes which had never before been followed by a British force, and to traverse which the troops had often to make their own roads. . . . The results of the operations have been

---

* Consisting of 130 men of the 2nd Battalion King's Own Yorkshire Light Infantry and 170 men of the 29th Bombay Infantry (2nd Baluch Battalion).

† It will be remembered that a survey party visited the Takht-i-Suliman, under suitable escort, in 1883.

rather political than military. All arrangements in the
first phase were made with the studied object of making
friends and not conquering enemies. . . . The operations entailed upon officers and men exertions and
exposure of an exceptional kind. The character of the
country in some instances prevented the use of transport
animals; the men had then to carry bedding, rations, and
cooking-pots for themselves, and to sleep without tents
in a temperature of from 13° to 20° of frost. The
marching was always over rocks and stones, and often in
river-beds, where the water ruined boots and clothing,
entailing heavy expense on the soldiers, both British and
native."

It was, in short, a campaign against Nature rather than
man; but it must not be overlooked that the strategical
combinations were so admirably conceived and carried
out that, when the troops were put in motion, the tribesmen were powerless to offer any opposition worthy of
the name to the unchecked and irresistible advance in
spite of the formidable difficulties of the ground.

The Black Mountain Expedition, 1891. (*Map IV.*)

It will be remembered that, after the Black Mountain
Expedition of 1888, the tribesmen agreed not to molest
troops or officials moving along the crest of the main
ridge which divided British from tribal territory. In
March, 1890, orders were issued for the construction
of several roads leading up to the crest from the Agror
Valley, and in October a force of 1,200 rifles and a mountain battery assembled at Aghi, under Brigadier-General
Sir John McQueen, K.C.B., with orders to assert the
right of the Indian Government to move troops along
the summit of the Black Mountain ridge; but, if the inhabitants were hostile, a collision was to be avoided.
After some delay, due to heavy rain, Sir John McQueen
left Aghi on October 23, and advanced up the Barchar
spur. In spite of their obligations, all reports agreed
that the tribesmen were opposed to the construction of
roads and the visit of troops to their border; moreover,
this impression was confirmed so unmistakably on
October 23 by firing into camp and other acts of hostility,
that Sir John McQueen decided to return to Aghi the
next day, after warning the tribesmen of the possible
consequences of their opposition.

Early in the following year it was decided to send an

TABLE XIII

BLACK MOUNTAIN EXPEDITION, 1891

Major-General W. K. Elles, C.B.

First Brigade.	Second Brigade.	Third Brigade.	Divisional Troops.
Brigadier-General R. F. Williamson.	*Brigadier-General A. G. Hammond, V.C., D.S.O.*	Brigadier-General Sir W.S.A. Lockhart, K.C.B., C.S.I.	11th Bengal Lancers, 1 Squadron. No. 4 Company Bengal Sappers and Miners (4th Company 1st Sappers and Miners).
No. 1 Mountain Battery Royal Artillery* (1st Mountain Battery Royal Garrison Artillery), 3 guns. No. 2 (Derajat) Mountain Battery† (22nd Derajat Mountain Battery), 3 guns. 2nd Battalion Seaforth Highlanders. 4th Sikhs (54th Sikhs). 32nd Bengal Infantry Pioneers (32nd Sikh Pioneers), 4 Companies. 37th Dogras. Guides Infantry.	No. 9 Mountain Battery Royal Artillery* (9th Mountain Battery Royal Garrison Artillery). 1st Battalion Royal Welsh Fusiliers. 11th Bengal Infantry‡ (11th Rajputs). 32nd Bengal Infantry Pioneers, 4 Companies. 2nd Battalion 5th Gurkhas. Khyber Rifles.	No. 1 Mountain Battery Royal Artillery, 3 guns. 11th Bengal Lancers (11th Lancers), 1 Squadron. 1st Battalion King's Royal Rifles. 19th Bengal Infantry (19th Punjabis). 27th Bengal Infantry (27th Punjabis).	At Aghi.
			No. 2 (Derajat) Mountain Battery, 3 guns. 11th Bengal Lancers, 1 Squadron. 28th Bengal Infantry (28th Punjabis).

* 2·5-inch rifled muzzle-loader.   † 7-pounder rifled muzzle-loader.

‡ Replaced at the end of May by the 1st Battalion 1st Gurkhas.

expedition against the Hassanzais and Akazais, under the command of Major-General W. K. Elles, C.B., to enforce recognition of and compliance with the arrangements of 1888. The force was ordered to concentrate at Darband and Aghi, where a detachment was to be left, while the main advance was made up the Indus Valley. The reasons for the selection of this line of operations were—

1. It led straight to the centre of population.

2. The difficult ascent of the Black Mountain on the east was avoided.

3. The ground was more open, and therefore more in favour of regular troops than the broken and wooded slopes of the mountain.

The troops detailed for the expedition were as shown in Table XIII.

Some delay in the concentration was caused by bad weather, but on March 10 everything was in readiness for an advance. The 1st Brigade was ordered to move up the left bank of the Indus on Kanar, while the 2nd Brigade moved along the western slopes of the Black Mountain on Tilli. After these two points had been occupied, General Elles' plan was for "the 1st Brigade to occupy the lower Hassanzai country on both banks, and the Diliarai Peninsula of the Akazai country, and the 2nd Brigade to pass through the middle levels of the mountain by Ril and Kangar, and occupy the Khan Khel country. Thereafter the two brigades to work up and down on the north of the Shal nala, through the Akazai country, till they met."*

While these operations were being conducted in the Indus Valley the Bunerwals were to be contained by a force consisting of 500 men of the Northumberland Fusiliers at Mardan, which was afterwards reinforced by the 9th Bengal Lancers and the 22nd Bengal Infantry.

On March 12 the advance was begun, and the 1st Brigade bivouacked at Towara, the scene of the fight on October 4, 1888. On the next day the advance was continued in face of some slight opposition, the 1st Brigade moving up both banks of the Indus, and Kanar and Tilli were both occupied, but the road constructed three years before had almost entirely disappeared, and had to be remade before further progress was possible. A bridge of boats brought up from Attock was also put in hand at Kotkai. During the next few

* Despatch dated June 22, 1891.

days heavy rain fell, which seriously interfered with the work of improving the communications, but reconnaissances were made of the surrounding country, and a spy was sent to Thakot, who reported a hostile movement down the valley from that direction.

General Elles visited the 2nd Brigade at Tilli on March 15, and, finding the difficulties of supply so great with this column, owing to the nature of the country, decided to modify his plan of operations by leaving detachments at Tilli, Ril, and Makranai, and then bringing the 2nd Brigade down into the Indus Valley to concentrate with the river column at Palosi; there would then be a single chain of supply along the left bank of the river for the whole force. General Williamson was then to operate on the right, and General Hammond on the left, bank of the Indus.

During the night, March 18/19, a determined attack was made on an advanced post at Ghazikot, a place about three-quarters of a mile north of Kanar, which was held by a company of the 4th Sikhs. At about 3 a.m. the enemy charged up out of a nala on the north side of the village, and occupied the buildings, from which they opened a heavy fire on the Sikhs' bivouac. The troops, however, defended themselves with great spirit till dawn, when, having received reinforcements, they were able to take the offensive and give their assailants a rough handling.

On March 20 the weather cleared, and during the next two days Palosi, Ril, and Seri, were occupied. Roadmaking was pushed forward with all possible vigour, and on the 23rd a flying bridge was put in hand at Bakrai, under the protection of a detachment of the 4th Sikhs. Two companies of this regiment were posted in a breastwork about 500 yards north-west of Bakrai to cover the working parties, but at about 4.30 p.m. the tribesmen were seen to be assembling in some force on the high ground to the north. Lieutenant Harman, who was in command of the detachment, then decided to attack and disperse this gathering, which was done with great resolution and complete success at the cost of four wounded, including Lieutenant Harman himself. Just as the Sikhs were about to withdraw to their breastwork, Colonel Gaselee, commanding the regiment, who had been present earlier in the day, returned, and at about the same time reinforcements, consisting of two companies of the Guides Infantry and another company of the 4th Sikhs, arrived on the scene. Finding the tribesmen pressing forward in force as his men fell back, and being unwilling to allow the enemy to occupy a commanding position after darkness set in, Colonel Gaselee decided to make a counter-attack with one company of the Guides and one of his own regiment, supported by the covering fire of another company of the 4th Sikhs. The tribesmen did not await the attack, and at about 7 p.m. the village of Diliarai, one mile north-west of Bakrai, was occupied. Here Colonel Gaselee concentrated his three companies of Sikhs, and the Guides Infantry returned to Palosi. The enemy lost twenty-eight men killed or wounded during these encounters, but the British loss was only four wounded in all. Colonel Gaselee was reinforced at Diliarai the next day by three guns of No. 2 (Derajat) Mountain Battery.

On March 23 Seri was destroyed, and on the following day General Hammond arrived at Palosi, having left detachments at Tilli, Ril, and Makranai, in accordance with the plan of General Elles, which has already been described. The enemy were seen to be in some force in the valley to the north and in the hills about Baio, a village some three and a half miles south-west of Palosi.

On March 25 General Hammond, whose advance was covered to some extent by Colonel Gaselee's Sikhs at Diliarai, occupied Darbanai after a short fight, and on this day also the Reserve Brigade was moved north from Rawal Pindi. This brigade reached Darband on March 31, where it remained till April 7, when it left for Kohat to take part in the second Miranzai Expedition of 1891.

The next fortnight was devoted principally to further road-making, reconnaissances, and correspondence with Mian Gul, the leader of the tribesmen, who had assembled about Baio from Buner and the adjacent country. Eventually this gathering dispersed without complicating the situation, and on April 8 all the troops were moved across to the left bank of the Indus, with the exception of the 37th Dogras, who held the western end of the bridge of boats at Kotkai.

The weather in the Indus Valley was now beginning to get hot, and, as the inhabitants seemed submissive enough, arrangements were put in hand for abandoning the river posts except Bakrai, moving the troops higher up the mountain, dismantling the bridge of boats, and transferring the advanced depot of the force from Dar-band to Aghi. By the end of the first week of May all these measures were carried out; the Hassanzais had long ceased to offer any resistance, but occasional raids were necessary against Akazai villages, the inhabitants of which were still backward in making formal submission. At length, however, the submission of the Hassanzais and Akazais was complete, and on June 11 the main body of the Hazara Field Force started its return march to India, leaving the force named below, under General Hammond, to occupy the Black Mountain and Aghi until the British terms were fully complied with. The Black Mountain was held till the end of November, when, a settlement being finally made, the British force withdrew, leaving 200 Border Police to preserve order. The principal results of the expedition were—

1. The tribal leaders in the hostilities just brought to an end, as well as the Hindustani fanatics, were to be excluded from Hassanzai and Akazai territory.

2. The roads constructed were to be protected.

3. As the tribesmen were permitted to enter British territory at will the former were to accord a similar privilege to British subjects.

4. Representatives of the tribes were to accompany British troops marching along the frontier, and escorts were to be provided for officials whenever necessary.

5. Suitable redress was to be made for outrages against the person or property of British subjects, but the latter were not to be arrested nor their property detained by the tribesmen; in case of dispute or grievance the matter was to be referred to the Deputy-Commissioner of Hazara.

> No. 9 Mountain Battery, Royal Artillery.
> 1st Battalion Royal Welsh Fusiliers.
> 4th Sikhs.
> 28th Bengal Infantry.
> 1st Battalion 1st Gurkhas.*
> Four Companies, 32nd Pioneers.†
> No. 4 Company Bengal Sappers and Miners.

Within five months of the final withdrawal of the British troops from the Black Mountain the tribesmen violated their agreement by allowing Hashim Ali, the leading spirit in the disturbances of recent years, to return and settle with his family at Baio and Doba, a small village about one mile south of Baio. Efforts

---

* This battalion had replaced the 11th Bengal Infantry at the end of May.
† Till July 10, 1891.

having failed to procure peaceful compliance with the terms of the agreement, a force consisting of two brigades with divisional troops assembled at Darband in September, 1892, under the command of Major-General Sir W. S. A. Lockhart, K.C.B., C.S.I., with the object of expelling Hashim Ali and punishing the tribesmen who had allowed him to return.

The force was known as the Isazai Field Force, because the Hassanzais, Mada Khel, and Chagarzais, the clans now concerned, are termed collectively Isazais, being descendants of Isa, a son of Yusaf, the founder of the important tribe of Yusafzais, west of the River Indus. Sir William Lockhart began his advance from Darband on October 2, 1892, and halted three days later with the 1st Brigade at Wale, and the 2nd at Manja Kot. On the following morning both brigades marched on Baio, which was found to be deserted. Baio, Doba, and some other villages, were destroyed, and the force returned to Darband on October 11 without encountering any opposition. Since 1892 no further military expedition into the Black Mountain District has been found necessary.

THE FIRST MIRANZAI EXPEDITION, 1891. (*Map II.*)

When the Afghan War of 1878 broke out, the Orakzais, like so many of their neighbours, adopted a hostile attitude to the British Government, but the prompt and effectual punishment meted out to the Zaimukhts in 1879 had the effect of keeping them in check, and preventing any serious outbreak. During the next twelve years, however, the Orakzais became so defiant, and committed so many raids across the border, that in January, 1891, it was decided to send an expedition against them under the command of Brigadier-General Sir William Lockhart, K.C.B., C.S.I. The composition and starting-points of this force are shown in Table XIV.

After some delay through bad weather, the force concentrated at Gwada, in the Khanki Valley, on January 29, and from there reconnaissances and the destruction of hostile villages were carried out by flying columns, with the result that the Orakzais speedily came to terms and agreed to the construction of three fortified posts on the Samana Ridge, with roads connecting them with each other and the Miranzai Valley. Practically, no opposition was encountered during these operations, but the

TABLE XIV

MIRANZAI FIELD FORCE, 1891

FIRST EXPEDITION

BRIGADIER-GENERAL SIR W. S. A. LOCKHART, K.C.B., C.S.I.

FIRST COLUMN.	SECOND COLUMN.	THIRD COLUMN.
Colonel A. McC. Bruce.	*Lieutenant-Colonel A. H. Turner.*	*Lieutenant-Colonel C. C. Brownlow.*
5th Punjab Cavalry (25th Cavalry), 3 Troops. No. 4 (Hazara) Mountain Battery (24th Hazara Mountain Battery). Half Company Bengal Sappers and Miners (1st Sappers and Miners). 1st Punjab Infantry (55th Coke's Rifles). 4th Punjab Infantry (57th Wilde's Rifles). 23rd Bengal Infantry Pioneers (23rd Sikh Pioneers), 4 Companies. 29th Bengal Infantry (29th Punjabis). Starting-point : Shahu Khel.	No. 3 (Peshawar) Mountain Battery (23rd Peshawar Mountain Battery). Half Company Bengal Sappers and Miners. 2nd Punjab Infantry (56th Punjabi Rifles). 5th Punjab Infantry (58th Vaughan's Rifles). Starting-point : Togh.	3rd Sikh Infantry (53rd Sikhs). 23rd Bengal Infantry Pioneers, 4 Companies. Starting-point : Hangu.

troops suffered severely from the cold; the force was broken up at the end of February.

The Second Miranzai Expedition, 1891. (*Map II.*)

Reference has been made already to the second Miranzai Expedition of 1891 in the account of the operations of the Hazara Field Force in the Black Mountain District in the same year, for, it will be remembered, the 3rd Brigade, under the command of Sir William Lockhart, was withdrawn from the Indus Valley on April 7, and ordered to proceed to Kohat in consequence of a serious outbreak on the part of the Orakzais.

At the beginning of March, 1891, the work was taken in hand of improving the communications along the Samana Ridge, and of constructing fortified posts thereon for the protection of the Miranzai Frontier. At first the attitude of the tribesmen was to all appearances entirely friendly, but on April 24 the 29th Punjab Infantry, and four companies of the 3rd Sikhs, who were furnishing escorts for the working parties, were attacked at about 3 p.m., and became heavily engaged till dusk, but drove off their assailants, with the loss to themselves of fourteen killed and seven wounded. On the following day, however, the tribesmen succeeded in rushing the piquets posted at Sangar and Gulistan on the Samana Ridge, the latter of which incidents is described in the *Pioneer* of April 12, 1891, in the following terms:

"The villagers seemed on the best terms with our men, and drove their cattle amongst them, as though they were driving them to graze. While talking and laughing with our men, who were separated from each other, the Pathans suddenly drew knives from under their clothes and attacked them, killing and wounding ten or more; while the Sikhs,* being surprised, could not fire on their assailants, fearing lest they might kill some of the cows that had previously been driven amongst them. On hearing the firing and noise, Captain Fasken hurried up with sixty men of the 3rd Sikhs, and sixty Frontier Militia, and occupied the village of Islai, which was successfully held with gallantry against large masses of the enemy for over twenty-four hours, and

---

* The piquet was composed of Sikhs of the 29th Punjab Infantry. It should be explained, for the benefit of the reader who is not well acquainted with the peculiarities of Indian races, that the Sikhs are a people to whom the cow is an animal of great sanctity.

then abandoned, as the party had neither food nor water. The retreat was conducted most skilfully, and heavy losses were inflicted."

The reason ascribed to the outbreak just related was the fear on the part of the Orakzais that the occupation of the Samana Ridge was but a prelude to the annexation by the British Government of the whole of their territory, and they determined to strike before it was too late. The result was one more contribution to the crowded history of an eventful year. In addition to the Black Mountain Expedition just described, and that which follows immediately, there was trouble in the Chin Hills; but overshadowing all three was the massacre of British officers at Manipur in the early part of the year, which filled the whole Empire with horror, and called for speedy retribution. The closing months of the year witnessed the invasion of Hunza and Nagar, far away to the extreme north of India, and the independent States under British influence.

On April 5 reinforcements were hurriedly sent out from Kohat to Darband, but the garrison of Kohat itself was at this time much reduced, owing to the absence of many men on furlough, so that it was necessary to strengthen the force available in the district by the despatch of additional troops from Bannu and stations east of the Indus. These movements provided occasion for two of those remarkable performances which are the visible proof of genuine efficiency. The 3rd Mountain Battery Royal Artillery and the 15th Sikhs left Rawal Pindi by rail on April 6, detrained at Khushalgarh, crossed the Indus, and marched into Kohat, a distance of thirty-two miles, the same night. A few days later the 6th Punjab Infantry covered the eighty miles between Bannu and Kohat in eighty hours.

While the foregoing movements were taking place the gravity of the situation increased. The tribesmen had assembled in such force that the evacuation of the Samana Ridge and concentration at Darband had become necessary, sporadic firing was frequent, and a determined, but unsuccessful, attack was made on the British camp at Darband. On the Samana Ridge itself the enemy were busy destroying the roads that had been recently begun, and constructing sangars for the defence of the position. By April 16, however, the expeditionary force sanctioned by the Government of India, and ordered to concentrate at Darband and Hangu, was ready to begin operations.

TABLE XV

MIRANZAI FIELD FORCE, 1891

SECOND EXPEDITION

BRIGADIER-GENERAL SIR W. S. A. LOCKHART, K.C.B., C.S.I.

FIRST COLUMN.	SECOND COLUMN.	THIRD COLUMN.
Colonel Sym, 5th Gurkhas.	*Colonel Turner, 2nd Punjab Infantry.*	*Colonel C. C. Brownlow, 1st Punjab Infantry.*
No. 3 Mountain Battery Royal Artillery (No. 3 Mountain Battery Royal Garrison Artillery). 1st Battalion King's Royal Rifles. 1st Punjab Infantry (55th Coke's Rifles). 2nd Punjab Infantry (56th Punjabi Rifles). 27th Punjab Infantry (27th Punjabis). 1st Battalion 5th Gurkhas.	No. 2 (Derajat) Mountain Battery (22nd Derajat Mountain Battery), 3 guns. 3rd Sikhs (53rd Sikhs). 15th Sikhs.	No. 3 (Peshawar) Mountain Battery (23rd Peshawar Mountain Battery). 6th Punjab Infantry (59th Scinde Rifles). 19th Punjab Infantry (19th Punjabis). 29th Punjab Infantry (29th Punjabis).
	CAVALRY BRIGADE.	NOTE.—In addition to the above, the 5th Company Sappers and Miners and three Native Field Hospitals accompanied the force.
	Colonel Biscoe, 19th Bengal Lancers.	
	5th Punjab Cavalry (25th Cavalry). 19th Bengal Lancers (19th Lancers).	

The chief command was entrusted to Brigadier-General Sir William Lockhart, whose intimate knowledge of the district and influence among the neighbouring clans rendered him eminently suited for the appointment. Details regarding the composition of the force will be found in Table XV.*

On April 17 the whole force was engaged in a combined movement against the enemy's position on the Samana Ridge. Very little opposition was encountered, but the troops suffered severely from the absence of water before returning to camp in the evening. Some more desultory fighting took place on the next day, but the Samana Ridge was permanently occupied, and from there the destruction of the hostile villages was carried out on the two following days. No organized resistance was offered, but the heat and absence of water again proved to be most trying. On April 20 a small but successful fight took place at Gulistan, where the enemy had taken up a position. The 1st Column was sent against them, and the 60th Rifles and Gurkhas were detailed for the attack. At 2 p.m. the guns opened fire, under cover of which the infantry advanced, and in half an hour had closed with the enemy, inflicting a loss, estimated afterwards at 200 men, and putting the remainder to flight with the small loss of one man killed and four wounded.

During the remainder of April and the first week of May Orakzai territory was scoured in all directions by various detachments; the enemy were given no rest, and all opposition speedily came to an end. The final submission was made at Gulistan on May 9, and a fortnight later the force was broken up, one native mountain battery and three regiments of infantry† remaining on the Samana Ridge to insure the uninterrupted progress of the work, which had been begun in March.

* As the writer has been unable to get access, without restriction, to any published account of the Miranzai Campaign of 1891 to which reference can be suggested for such details, the names of the officers composing Sir William Lockhart's Staff are appended. They are taken from the files of the *Pioneer* for 1891:

Assistant Adjutant-General ...	Major Egerton, 3rd Punjab Cavalry.
Deputy-Assistant Adjutant-General	Captain Hickman, 34th Bengal Infantry.
Commanding Royal Engineer ...	Major Shone, R.E.
Assistant Superintendent of Army Signalling	Lieutenant C. D. Down, Wiltshire Regiment.
Principal Medical Officer	Brigade-Surgeon Harvey.
Chief Commissariat Officer ...	Captain E. C. C. Sandys.

† No. 3 (Peshawar) Mountain Battery, the 2nd and 29th Punjab Infantry and the 15th Sikhs.

CHAPTER IX

HUNZA AND NAGAR

(*Map I.*)

IN 1891 an entirely new portion of the North-West Frontier of India, and the territories under the direct influence of the Indian Government, claimed the attention of the British arms. Situated in the extreme north-west of Kashmir, literally at the point where three empires meet, were the practically independent states of Hunza and Nagar. Though nominally tributary to the Maharaja of Kashmir,* their rulers, thanks to the inaccessible nature of their country, enjoyed an almost complete immunity from interference, and the petty acts of oppression so commonly practised on subject races by a suzerain power. This immunity from the pains and penalties of a dependent position not unnaturally had the effect of imbuing the chiefs of Hunza and Nagar with an exaggerated sense of their military power and political importance,† which eventually led to a state of affairs so intolerable as to render British intervention necessary.

The district which became the theatre of war in 1891 comprises the upper portion of the basin of the Kanjut or Hunza River, which flows into the Gilgit River two miles below Gilgit Fort. It is a rugged, mountainous

---

* The annual tribute of Hunza was
$\begin{cases} \text{20 oz. gold-dust.} \\ \text{Two horses.} \\ \text{Two hounds.} \end{cases}$

The annual tribute of Nagar was
$\begin{cases} \text{Some gold-dust.} \\ \text{Two baskets of apricots.} \end{cases}$

† Mr. E. F. Knight gives the following illustration of this complacent attitude: "It is said that it was a point of etiquette in his savage court on certain occasions for a Wazir to ask in the Thum's presence, 'Who is the greatest King of the East?' and for another flatterer to reply: 'Surely the Thum of Hunza, unless perhaps it be the Khan of China; for these, without doubt, are the two greatest.'"

country, and was at the time in question most difficult of access from the outside world. This latter feature was due to the deliberate policy of the Thums of Hunza and Nagar*—as the rulers of these states were styled—of making communication with their territories from without so difficult as to secure their virtual independence, and leave them free to follow the lawless fancies of their rapacious hearts. Surrounded on all sides by the highest mountains of the world, and living in a country where snow in winter and swollen streams in summer, caused by the melting of the winter mantle of the hills, made the difficult routes that existed wellnigh impassable, the inhabitants of the Hunza Valley had some excuse for thinking themselves unassailable. Every strategical position, however, has a vulnerable point, and the Hunza Valley was the point of weakness, or rather diminished strength, in the Hunza-Nagar *enceinte*—the gorge of the vast natural redoubt whose parapets are the Himalayas and the Hindu Kush. The track which was the means of communication with Kashmir was, in 1891, unworthy of the name of road. It followed the Hunza River, crossing it by frail bridges of crude construction, and points, which became impassable when the river was in flood, were turned by narrow, dizzy tracks on the hillsides, overhanging appalling precipices. There were many places along this so-called road where a handful of men might have held a large army at bay, but, fortunately, the tribesmen contented themselves with merely destroying the road, and offered no resistance till their border fort of Nilt was reached. Within the borders of these two mountain states the means of communication improved, giving further proof of the strategical sagacity of the Thums in making easy any concentration of their forces to cover the natural obstacles guarding their defensive perimeter. Hunza and Nagar, the chief towns of the states of the same names, face one another on opposite banks of the Hunza River—Hunza on the right and Nagar on the left bank—but the two tribes, as is often the case with near neighbours, were often at daggers drawn, though they invariably sank all differences in the face of a common danger. The Kanjutis, as the inhabitants of the Hunza or Kanjut Valley were known to the outside world, are a hardy, warlike race professing the creed, but acknowledging few of the

* In 1891 their names were—of Hunza, Safdar Ali Khan; of Nagar, Zafar Khan.

obligations, of Muhammadanism. Of the two sections the Hunzas appear to have been predominant, and the Thum of Hunza boasted of descent from no less a personage than Alexander the Great.* The Kanjutis had been long known in Central Asia for their predatory proclivities; they had carried their raids not only into Kashmir, but into Afghanistan and Chinese Turkestan as well. Many a rich caravan on the Leh-Yarkand route had fallen into their hands, and certain of the neighbouring tribes to the north even found it economical in the long run to pay a yearly tribute in order to secure themselves and their property from molestation. In addition to this source of revenue the Kanjutis derived considerable profit from the practice of slave-dealing, and frequent gangs of captives from all quarters crossed the passes of the Hindu Kush, to perish by the way or find a ready sale in the markets of Turkestan.

The same intrigues, the same wholesale slaughter of relatives who might possibly become rivals for the throne, as has been so common in the history of Eastern nations, were prominent features of the court life of Hunza and Nagar. The rulers of these states acknowledged no authority except that of the sword, but were not gifted with sufficient penetration to read the signs of the times, and discern the Power to which conciliation, if not homage, could best be shown. Influenced, no doubt, by tradition, China was the Power most respected in this remote corner, Russia came next, and Great Britain third. The position of Russia in the order of merit is no doubt due to the contact of the Kanjutis with races inhabiting countries under Muscovite influence, and, shortly before the events about to be described took place, to direct contact with representatives of the Russian people in Hunza itself. Hunza and Nagar had seldom been visited by British officers—in fact, when active British intervention became necessary, Colonel Lockhart (in 1886), Colonel Durand (in 1889), and Captain Younghusband (in 1891), had alone penetrated the inhospitable mountain fastnesses of these robber states.

The result of Colonel Durand's visit in 1889 was the conclusion of a treaty by which the latter agreed to cease raiding on the Leh-Yarkand Road, and to allow properly

* When asked why he did not visit India, Safdar Ali Khan, the Thum of Hunza in 1891, is said to have replied: "It is not customary for great Kings like myself and my ancestor Alexander to leave their dominions" ("Where Three Empires Meet," p. 331).

accredited officers to visit their country when necessary. As a solatium for giving up a lucrative source of revenue, annual subsidies were to be paid by the British and Kashmir Governments. It was not long, however, before the Thums violated their treaty obligations, raiding recommenced, and demands were made for an increased subsidy. Not content with this, the Hunza - Nagaris assembled their forces, and in May, 1891, marched on Chalt, the Kashmir frontier post held by the Maharaja's troops. Fortunately, Colonel Durand, the British Agent at Gilgit, got timely warning of this movement, and by making forced marches, was able to throw a reinforcement of 200 men under a British officer into Chalt Fort before the tribesmen appeared. Disappointed in their expectation of an easy triumph over the inexperienced Kashmir troops, the invaders then withdrew to their own territory.

Matters had now taken so serious a turn that the intervention of the Indian Government became necessary. In the expectation that the Kanjutis would renew their attacks as soon as the passes on the road to India were closed by snow, important points on the road between Gilgit and Chalt were held by fortified posts with signalling communication right along the line, and steps were taken to accumulate a large store of grain at Gilgit. At the same time an ultimatum was sent to the Thums, offering to condone the infraction of the treaty of 1889, on condition that raiding was immediately stopped, and facilities were given for the construction of a mule road from Gilgit to Hunza and Nagar, and beyond if considered necessary ; moreover, a new fort was to be built at Chalt. In addition to those connected with the Hunza-Nagaris themselves, there was, however, another urgent reason for the strengthening of the British position in this quarter. Reference has already been made to the influence of Russia on the external policy of the Thums of Hunza and Nagar ; this attracted considerable attention in 1891, when great Russian activity was displayed on the Pamirs, followed by incursions into Chitral and Hunza territory. Two British officers were arrested by Russians on neutral ground, and, as was afterwards abundantly proved, the hostility shown by the Kanjutis to their rightful suzerain as well as their confident demeanour were due to an impression left at the court of Hunza that they would receive the moral and material support of Russia in repudiating their treaty obligations.

The military exploits of the Kanjutis, assisted by the natural difficulties of their country, against past invaders, undoubtedly encouraged them in anticipating yet another triumph over any troops that could be sent against them. In 1848 they had annihilated a Sikh army from Gilgit, in 1866 they had repelled a Dogra invasion, and in 1888 they had captured Chalt Fort from its Kashmiri garrison. Since the last Kanjuti success, however, a great reform had taken place in the military system of Kashmir. The wise and economical policy of substituting a small body of efficient troops trained under the supervision of British officers for large numbers (at least on paper) of undisciplined, ill-supplied, and unreliable men, had been introduced in all the important native states. The system of the raising of Imperial Service troops by the principal Indian Chiefs for objects indicated by their title had been successfully introduced; the system was now put to the supreme test of war, and for the first time Imperial Service troops stood shoulder to shoulder with the soldiers of the Crown in an imperial cause. The admirable fighting qualities of the troops of H.H. the Maharaja of Kashmir will be apparent in the course of the narrative of the Hunza-Nagar campaign; those that took part in the expedition came of the same stock as some of the most highly esteemed Indian troops, and they proved themselves fully worthy of their traditions.

From Gilgit to Hunza and Nagar the distance is sixty miles, divided into two equal sections by Chalt Fort. From Gilgit to Srinagar is 240 miles across the Burzil Pass, 13,800 feet above sea-level. The excellent military road, which now exists to Gilgit, was in 1891 in course of construction by Messrs. Spedding and Co., whose navvies, under the direction of Mr. Spedding himself, rendered invaluable assistance during the expedition.

During September, October, and the first half of November, 1891, preparations for the coming campaign were pushed forward unostentatiously, and with all possible despatch. It was particularly desired that these should be well advanced before news of them could reach Hunza and Nagar, or Chilas, the attitude of which state was considered doubtful. It was thought that, if warning of the British intentions reached the tribesmen prematurely, the latter would cause serious complications by attacking forthwith the Kashmiri garrisons at Gilgit and Chalt. Great difficulties were experienced in collecting at Gilgit the large quantities of supplies necessary to maintain even a small expeditionary force till the summer. An early winter soon began to set in, the Kamri Pass route was soon blocked by snow, and much labour attended with considerable loss of life had to be expended before the troops could leave Gilgit. It was impossible to postpone the concentration to the summer, for in the meantime, knowing that communication with India was, for military purposes, cut off, the Hunza-Nagaris would have gathered in strength,* and fallen upon the isolated garrisons with some prospect of success. Moreover, in summer the difficulties of the road into Hunza and Nagar would have been greatly increased when the waters of the Hunza River were swollen by the melting snows.

During September a contingent of 200 men of the 5th Gurkhas and two guns 24th (Hazara) Mountain Battery† were ordered up from Abbottabad, as a "strengthening of the Agent's bodyguard at Gilgit"; but even these were delayed on the road, first by an outbreak of cholera, and then by snow on the Burzil Pass. When crossing the pass many cases of frost-bite occurred, particularly among the transport followers, who, with the improvidence characteristic of this class of individual, had before the march began sold much of the warm clothing issued to them. Many of these men lost hands or feet, and several died on the pass or at Astor.

While supplies were being collected at Gilgit, the road to Chalt was improved by a party of seven men of the Bengal Sappers and Miners under Captain F. J. Aylmer, R.E., and 200 Pathan navvies, employed by Messrs. Spedding and Co. on the main Gilgit road, whose services were now patriotically offered by Mr. Spedding to the Government. All European civilians in the neighbourhood also took service with the force as members of the 1st Punjab Volunteers, among them being Mr. E. F. Knight, who was at this time in Kashmir gathering material for his interesting work, "Where Three Empires Meet." The narrative of the campaign which follows is virtually a *précis* of the account given by Mr. Knight.

At length all preparations were complete, and on November 16 the advance northwards began. The troops

---

* They are said to have been able to put 5,000 men in the field, more or less well armed.

† 7-pounder rifled muzzle-loader.

comprising the force now under the command of Colonel Durand consisted of—.

> 5th Gurkhas, 188.
> 24th (Hazara) Mountain Battery, 2 guns.
> 20th Punjab Infantry (Agent's Bodyguard), 30.
> Three Regiments Kashmir Imperial Service Troops.
> A Kashmir Mountain Battery.
> Bengal Sappers and Miners, 7.
> Spedding's Pathans, armed and organized in 6 Companies, 200.*

From this force garrisons had to be found for Chalt, Gilgit, Bunji, and Astor, on the line of communication with India, leaving about 1,000 men out of a total of 2,000 available for operations in the enemy's country. The natural difficulties of the country were known to be so great that the force had to be kept as small as possible, and to make up in efficiency for what it lacked in numbers.

Chalt was reached by the rear of the column without mishap on November 28, and there a reply, couched in insolent but somewhat amusing terms,† was received to the British ultimatum. It transpired later that the Nagaris were inclined to accede to the British demands, but they were overruled by the more warlike Hunzas.

Nothing now remained to be done but to advance into Hunza and Nagar and bring the tribesmen to reason at

---

* Mr. Knight commanded one of these companies.

† Some of these are so quaint that they are transcribed here from "Where Three Empires Meet," p. 361. In one the Thum of Hunza asks why the British had strayed into his country "like camels without nose-strings," and goes on to say that he cared nothing for the womanly English, as he hung on the skirts of the manly Russians ; also that he warned Colonel Durand that he had given orders to his followers to bring him the Gilgit Agent's head on a platter.

The bellicose spirit of the descendant of Alexander is betrayed by the following :

"I will withstand you if I have to use bullets of gold."

"If you venture here, be prepared to fight three nations—Hunza, China, and Russia."

"I have been tributary to China for hundreds of years. Trespass into China, if you dare."

Here is another, which somehow seems to carry one back to the shores of St. George's Channel at once : "We will cut your head off, Colonel Durand, and then report you to the Indian Government."

As a further illustration of the Hunza style of correspondence, the following must surely be awarded the prize for quaintness and originality. When demanding the surrender of the fort at Chalt, the Thum ingenuously states that "the fortress of Chalt is more precious to us than are the strings of our wives' pyjamas."

the point of the sword. The force which marched out of
Chalt Fort on December 1, 1891, consisted of—

> 5th Gurkhas, 188.
> 20th Punjab Infantry, 28.
> 24th (Hazara) Mountain Battery, 2 guns.
> Bengal Sappers and Miners, 7.
> Kashmir Imperial Service Infantry, 661.
> Spedding's Pathans, 200.
> Puniali levies.
>
> Total, about 1,000 fighting men.

Sixteen British officers accompanied the force. It was
decided to advance up the left (or Nagari) bank of the
Hunza River, the first day's march being directed to
the foot of a kotal or small pass, by which a point, where
the river-bank could be followed, had to be turned. The
baggage allowance of officers and men was cut down as
much as possible; * one coolie was allowed for each officer,
and no tents were taken. The kotal was occupied without opposition, though traces of its recent occupation by
the enemy were evident, the bivouac being formed at the
foot on the near side. An early start was made on the
following day, and preceded by fifty Gurkhas as advanced
guard, with twenty of Spedding's Pathans and the Sappers and Miners to do what they could to improve the
road, the force at length surmounted the arduous ascent
to the kotal, and descended on the far side. During the
advance up the Hunza Valley the heights were crowned
by parties of Gurkhas and the Puniali levies, who also
covered the passage by the main body of two difficult
nalas, where the road had been destroyed by the
enemy, and had to be made passable before the troops
could proceed. It was after one o'clock when the neighbourhood of the Nagari border fort of Nilt was reached.
It was known that the Nagaris had been engaged in
strengthening this fort for some time past, and it was
now a formidable obstacle to any further advance. The
fort was really a fortified village, surrounded by an inner
and an outer wall, the former 15 to 20 feet high and
12 feet thick, and the latter about 8 feet in height. Both
walls were loopholed for musketry, but the loopholes
were so small that they offered a very small target to
the marksmen of the British force. The smallness of the
loopholes, however, contributed in no small degree to

---

* Mr. Knight says he found room for his golf-clubs, he and another officer
attached to Spedding's Pathans being enthusiastic golfers. It would be
interesting to know if golf-clubs have been taken on an Indian frontier
expedition before or since.

the undoing of the Nagaris, for they were unable to use
their rifles with the freedom necessary to repel a determined assault. The roofs of the houses were covered
with rubble to such a thickness as to make them im-
pervious to the small 7-pounder shells of the mountain
guns, and the walls themselves would have been proof
against ordnance of considerably superior weight. The
defence of the inner wall was further strengthened by
large square towers constructed at intervals along the
perimeter. Such was the obstacle that now confronted
the British force. The troops had been without water
since leaving the bivouac; it was absolutely necessary to
capture the fort without delay, or retire.

The Nagaris were the first to open fire, but, though the
foreground had been well cleared, the Gurkhas, who led
the advance by the direct route, moved rapidly forward
and opened a brisk fire on the loopholes and walls. In
the meantime the Puniali levies, followed by the 20th
Punjab Infantry, succeeded in working their way round
the walls, and occupied the summit of a hill in rear of
the fort, whence they were able to fire down into the
interior of the place. The enemy were well protected,
however, and it is probable that little damage was done.
The Punjabis then pushed on down the hill and crept
close up to the walls. The 7-pounders and a Gatling
gun that accompanied the force also came into action, but
a satisfactory artillery position was hard to find, and
some exposed ground, only 150 yards distant from the
fort, had to be occupied. The Gatling gun, as machine
guns have often done on critical occasions, jammed several
times, and the 7-pounders were able to make little impression on the well-protected defenders, while several
casualties occurred among the gun detachments. About
this time Colonel Durand was wounded, and the command devolved on Captain L. J. E. Bradshaw. The
turning-point of the engagement, however, had been
reached, for Spedding's Pathans had been sent to reinforce the Puniali levies, and already the enemy were
beginning to abandon the position and make good their
escape up the Hunza Valley; some of these were shot
down by the troops that had worked round in rear of
the fort.

Now followed the brilliant decisive exploit of the
attack. Covered by the fire of the whole force in general,
and by a party of 100 Gurkhas under Lieutenant Boisragon in particular, who forced their way through the

outer wall, Captain Aylmer made his way up to the main gate of the fort, and, under heavy fire the whole time, laid a charge of guncotton slabs at the foot. The first attempt to detonate the charge failed, so Captain Aylmer went forward again to the gate and readjusted the fuze. A deafening report followed, and before the stones and other *débris* had stopped falling Captain Aylmer, Lieutenants Boisragon * and Badcock, and six men were inside the gate fighting hand to hand with the defenders. So thick was the smoke and dust caused by the explosion that the remainder of the covering party could not find the breach at first, so Lieutenant Boisragon went back to call them up. In a few moments the Gurkhas were inside and hunting the enemy all over the interior of the fort. Most of the Nagaris escaped at the back, running the gauntlet of the fire of the Punialis and Pathans on the hill commanding the interior of the place, but many were killed or taken prisoners inside. Attempt at pursuit so as to carry some sangars farther up the valley had to be abandoned, for it was found that the road had been destroyed, and the enemy were holding a very strong position in great force. Thus fell the cherished Nagari fort of Nilt, which was thought to be impregnable. The British loss was very small when the formidable character of the defences is considered ; six men were killed and twenty-seven wounded, five of whom were officers. As usual, the loss of the enemy could not be accurately determined, but it was estimated at over eighty killed ; nine prisoners were taken in the fort. Large quantities of ammunition of all kinds, miscellaneous arms, and grain, were discovered in Nilt. A small garrison was detailed to hold it, and the remainder of the force bivouacked outside the walls.

On the following day—December 3—Captain Bradshaw desired to repair the road, cross the Nilt nala, and attack the Nagari fort of Thol on the other side ; but the troops detailed to cover Spedding's Pathans while they were at work were fired on so heavily from Thol and the breastworks below it, only 80 yards distant, that several casualties occurred, and they had to be withdrawn. Spedding's men were protected at first by the configuration of the ground, but they also soon came under severe fire, and were recalled.

The position from which the British force was now

---

* For their gallantry on this occasion, Captain Aylmer and Lieutenant Boisragon were given the Victoria Cross.

obliged to recoil was an exceedingly strong one. At
this point the Hunza Valley is 1,500 yards broad, and the
river receives a tributary from either side, flowing into
the main stream nearly opposite one another. The
tributary on the left bank is called the Nilt (flowing past
the north side of the fort of the same name), and that on
the right bank is the Maiun. Built on plateaux overlooking the confluences of these streams, are the Hunza
fort of Maiun on the one side, and the Nagari fort of
Thol on the other. The slopes of the two plateaux down
to the Maiun and Nilt nalas are precipitous, and were
defended by breastworks constructed on the edge of the
cliffs. The flanks were protected by sangars reaching
up to glaciers on the sides of the hills. All the tracks
whereby access might be gained had been destroyed,
and immediately below Thol the slopes had been rendered
still more inaccessible by a glacis of ice, which the tribesmen had made by diverting a small watercourse, the
water from which had frozen. The range of Thol from
Nilt is about 2,000 yards. The hostile garrison was
estimated at not less than 400 men, well armed and
vigilant, and ready to impede assault by rolling down
rocks, each of which produced a small avalanche, or
illuminate the foreground at night with lighted balls of
resinous wood. Reconnaissance only served to reveal
fresh difficulties; the guns could make no impression on
the well-built sangars, and it seemed impossible to detect
a weak spot in the whole extended front of the position.
The situation was serious; no help could be expected
from India till the summer, and it was feared that the
check to the British advance would have a most unfortunate effect on the neighbouring tribes. However,
there was nothing to be done but settle down to a kind
of siege, and hope to find some opportunity of taking the
enemy by surprise. This it appeared impossible to do,
for, thanks probably to information received from the
British camp, the tribesmen were always ready at every
point, either by night or day. Spedding's men were
constantly employed in strengthening the British position; shots were exchanged every day, and individual
reconnaissances, both by day and night, were undertaken
by all ranks of the besieging force. As the possibility of
a prolonged halt became apparent, arrangements were
made to send the wounded back to Chalt and get up the
tents which were most acceptable in the cold weather
that now prevailed.

On December 7 it was decided to make an attempt to carry the position at the lower end of the Nilt nala at dawn the following day. Under cover of darkness troops were assembled in the gully where Spedding's men had been at work on the morning of the 3rd, and preparations were made to cover their advance by a heavy covering fire on the enemy's breastworks. Information of the British design, however, must have been conveyed to Maiun, for the hostile sangars were found to be so strongly held that the attempt had to be abandoned as likely to prove too costly. Moreover, the ground over which the troops had to retire was so swept with fire that they had to remain in the gully throughout the long cold day till darkness enabled them to withdraw in safety.

After an abortive parley on the 9th, the next week was passed in further reconnaissances, more unsuccessful attempts to gain a footing on the enemy's position, and in pushing forward sangars down to the Nilt nala under cover of darkness as posts of observation. This last proceeding had the effect of considerably disconcerting the enemy, who could not understand its object, and of making them weaken other parts of their line to reinforce their centre. About this time, too, symptoms were observed that the tribesmen were beginning to weary of the war, particularly the Nagaris, who had never been favourably disposed towards it, but had been drawn into it by the more truculent Hunzas. Notwithstanding these encouraging signs, some anxiety was caused by a report of intended movements against the British line of communication. The question of supply was becoming serious, so, as little work remained for Spedding's Pathans to do at the front, and there was much for them to do in rear, this excellent body of men, whose services had been invaluable, left on December 16 to resume their work on the Gilgit Road.

At last the continued reconnaissances of the approaches to the enemy's position were crowned with success. A Dogra sepoy,* belonging to the Kashmir contingent, succeeded in climbing the precipitous side of the Nilt nala on the far side under cover of darkness, and reported that the slope was so steep that the ground at the bottom could not be swept by the enemy's fire. Captain Bradshaw was away at Gilgit at the time conferring with Colonel Durand; but Captain Mackenzie, the senior officer on the spot, determined to lose no time

* Named Nagdu.

in profiting by the discovery. Great precautions were taken to prevent the plan of the intended attack being generally known in camp, and so reaching the enemy. Before the moon rose on the night December 19/20, fifty Gurkhas and fifty Dogras from the Kashmir troops left camp quietly under Lieutenants Manners-Smith and Taylor, and, crossing the Nilt nala unobserved, halted in the dead ground underneath four Nagari sangars on the hillside above Thol Fort. A further detachment of the force was moved up on to the high ground above Nilt before dawn, and divided into four sections to sweep the same four sangars with a rapid fire, and prevent the defenders from leaving them to reach the edge of the cliff and fire down on the assaulting troops. The range to the sangars was about 500 yards.

Lieutenant Manners-Smith had orders to wait half an hour after the covering fire had begun, and then to commence to scale the 1,200 feet of cliff above him. At dawn no suspicion of the presence of the troops in the nala had reached the Hunzas or Nagaris. A fierce fire was opened on the sangars, which had the effect of effectually pinning their garrisons to the cover of the walls, and after the interval ordered, Lieutenant Manners-Smith started, with the Gurkhas leading. The first attempt to reach the top ended in failure by reason of a precipice which barred the way, but another attempt was made without delay lower down the nala. It was not till the head of the assaulting infantry was within 60 yards of the top that the tribesmen became aware of their danger. The men climbing the cliffs were first seen from Maiun; the news was passed up rapidly along the position, but the defenders of the sangars, unable to show themselves outside the cover of the walls on account of the covering fire, could only impede the climbers by throwing rocks up out of the sangars over the edge of the cliff. Thanks to the steepness of the ascent, most of these passed harmlessly by, and the little attacking column pressed on unchecked. At last the summit was gained, and Lieutenant Manners-Smith,* followed by the foremost men, passing round to the rear of the first sangar, rushed in. Those of the Nagaris who were not killed in the sangar were shot down as they fled by the covering party and troops posted at Nilt Fort. The other sangars were cleared in a similar manner; the enemy's left flank was now completely

* Lieutenant Manners-Smith afterwards received the Victoria Cross.

rolled up, and in a few minutes Thol and Maiun were evacuated, and their garrisons in full flight up the Hunza Valley.

The road was quickly repaired, and the British force started in pursuit. The garrison of the first sangar on the road to Thol, unable to escape, laid down their arms, and ninety-two prisoners, their rifles (mostly Sniders), a quantity of Government Dum Dum ammunition, besides other miscellaneous arms, fell into the hands of the troops. The Puniali levies were sent to move up the right bank of the Hunza River, while the rest of the force pressed on up the left bank. A strong position at Pissan was found unoccupied, and there the troops halted for the night. So deadly had been the covering fire that the enemy could offer little effective resistance to the party under Lieutenant Manners-Smith, and the British casualties on December 20 only amounted to four men wounded. One hundred and fifteen Hunza and Nagari prisoners were taken and sent to Chalt, those that were wounded being kept at Nilt.

Early next morning the pursuit was resumed, and the troops, pressing on ahead of the baggage, occupied Nagar the same day. During the march the Nagaris and Hunzas tendered their submission; the Thum of Nagar awaited capture in his capital, but the Thum of Hunza, it appeared, had already fled, and left his subjects to their fate. The Hunzas were not unnaturally somewhat incensed at the action of their Chief, and informed the British officers that they had sent a party after him in pursuit. Hunza was occupied without opposition on the 22nd, and large quantities of arms and ammunition of British, Russian, French, and Belgian manufacture, besides considerable stores of native gunpowder, were found in the fort.

On the 25th a force of 100 Kashmir troops under three British officers started towards the Kilik Pass in pursuit of the fugitive Thum, who was reported to have 400 followers and all the valuables he could collect with him. The march was arduous; still, the inhabitants of the country were friendly. Numbers of the Thum's followers were met returning, but the Thum himself made good his escape across the frontier over the Kilik Pass. The British force reached the foot of the pass on December 30, and, being obliged to abandon the pursuit there, returned to Hunza on January 6, 1892. The whole force returned to Gilgit on January 11. Information was subsequently received that Safdar Ali was an unwelcome fugitive in Chinese territory, where he was soon in sore straits. His half-brother, Nazim Khan, was made chief of the Hunzas, and Zafar Khan, who had been against the war from the beginning, was reinstated as Thum of Nagar. The country has been opened up. Hunza and Nagar are still tributary to Kashmir, but enjoy almost complete control of their own domestic affairs. Both states have been perfectly loyal since, and, as will be seen presently, rendered valuable service to Colonel Kelly in his expedition to relieve Chitral three years later.

Before turning away from the historical survey of this distant corner of the vast territory controlled wholly or partially by the Indian Government, it is necessary to make a brief reference to events in Chilas during 1982 and 1893. There is no particular military interest attaching to what took place, but the fighting which occurred there furnishes an explanation of the anxiety felt at the beginning of the Chitral campaign as to the attitude of the inhabitants, and affords a good example of the lasting result of prompt and vigorous action.

The township of Chilas, the principal place in the district of the same name, stands on the left bank of the Indus roughly forty miles a little to the west of due south from Gilgit. The people are not of a warlike disposition, and were in 1891 tributary to Kashmir. During the Hunza-Nagar campaign there was some doubt as to the attitude of the people of Chilas, but no rupture occurred. In 1892, however, the demeanour of the Chilasis became so defiant that Surgeon - Major G. Robertson proceeded to the district in November with an escort of some 160 Kashmiri troops and levies to try and restore tranquillity. Near Chilas a determined attack was made on the British Agent's escort, in consequence of which the place was burnt and the fort there occupied. The tribesmen then professed repentance for their misdeeds, a garrison of 300 Kashmir troops under British officers was left in the fort, and a line of communication opened up with Bunji, forty miles higher up the river on the same bank.

For three months no further outbreak occurred, but during the night March 4/5, 1893, a large body of tribesmen opened fire on the fort from the village. At daybreak an enveloping attack was made on the enemy, who suffered severely; but, being greatly outnumbered, the Kashmir garrison were obliged to retire on the fort, with the loss of one British officer killed* and one wounded, besides some fifty casualties among the rank and file. Although the counter-attack on the tribes-men was only partially successful, it was delivered so promptly and with such determination that the moral effect on the Chilasis was even more important than the physical, great as the latter undoubtedly was. The enemy did not renew the attack, but withdrew from the village during the night March 5/6. Reinforcements were sent to Chilas from Gilgit and Bunji, but the tribesmen had learnt their lesson, and no further fighting took place. The peace of the district has been unbroken ever since.

* Major Daniell, who was in command, was killed, and Lieutenant Moberly wounded.

CHAPTER X

THERE are not a great many points of military interest to notice in this campaign, but what there are are valuable, because most of them are not brought out in the study of other Indian frontier campaigns. In the first place, this was a war of small parties; it might almost be said of individuals. After Captain Aylmer had blown in the gate of Nilt Fort, the place was rushed by a small handful of Gurkhas: the reconnaissances of the Maiun-Thol position were conducted by individuals, and a practicable path was discovered by a Dogra sepoy; and, finally, the enemy's position was eventually assaulted with success by another small handful of men. Military skill and personal gallantry brought victory where mere numbers would only have led to embarrassment and possible disaster.

British troops engaged in fighting the frontier tribes of India do not usually have to undertake what are virtually siege operations; yet, after the capture of Nilt, the opposing forces remained facing one another for eighteen days. Many features common to siege operations were present : there were the constant search for a vulnerable point, attempts at surprise by small parties, the creeping forward nearer to the enemy's position by means of sangars constructed at night, and small daily outbursts of fire. The hostile defences were strong by nature, but the engineering skill to take advantage of the ground was there too. It is seldom that the flanks of a defensive line can rest on glaciers, nor are there usually facilities for converting a steep slope into a sheet of slippery ice. The flanks of the Maiun-Thol position could not be turned ; penetration of the front was therefore compulsory. The absence of guns sufficiently powerful to be effective against the well-built sangars was seriously felt; even a light howitzer would have been invaluable.

One of the great principles of defensive warfare was totally neglected by the Hunzas and Nagaris. The initiative remained with the British during the whole campaign. Not a single instance is recorded throughout in which the enemy made any attempt to assume the tactical or strategical offensive. Possibly it may have been due to mutual distrust leading to indifferent combination; possibly the absence of a definite leader may have been the cause. That favourable opportunities occurred is unquestionable: between Chalt and Nilt alone there were three points—the kotal and two nalas —where the opposition of even a dozen well-posted men would have caused the greatest inconvenience; and before Thol, even if the tribesmen thought a general counter-attack inadvisable, small sorties might have greatly accentuated the gravity of the British situation. It would seem, however, that a great opportunity for dealing a counter-stroke was missed on December 8, when part of the British force had to remain all day in the gully between Nilt Fort and the nala of the same name. If the tribesmen had delivered a counter-stroke while these troops were pinned to the gully, they might have had a fair prospect of success; at any rate it was the best chance they had. Fortunately, neither Hunzas nor Nagaris were students of Wellington or Lee, and were unacquainted with the warning of Hamley that "purely passive defence, strategical or tactical, leaves an enemy free to complete his plans, lets his errors go unpunished, and invariably ends in failure."*

It has been mentioned in the narrative of the campaign that towards the end of what may be termed the siege fears were entertained of an intended attack on the British line of communication. Had this movement been carried out earlier, the consequences might have been most serious. Colonel Henderson says that "the strategic counter-stroke is the best weapon of the defence." If the attack had been made in sufficient strength the initiative would have passed at once to the enemy; the whole British force even might have had to retire to secure their chain of supply. With the help of reinforcements from Chilas —the attitude of which state was certainly not friendly— a descent on Gilgit might have cleared the Hunza Valley of invaders. The British troops could expect no help

* "Operations of War," p. 368.

from India. Washington would have been threatened, and Richmond relieved. But the Indian frontier tribesmen are happily not masters of great combinations; still, it is impossible not to think that under similar circumstances the Afridis would have exacted a heavy toll during the march to Nilt, and been far from allowing the British camp to remain undisturbed night after night. Every convoy from Gilgit would probably have had to fight its way up the Hunza Valley.

Reference has already been made to the probable presence of spies in the British camp at Nilt. The difficulty presents itself in all armies, but is particularly great when the non-combatants belong to an alien race similar in appearance to, if not in sympathy with, the enemy's fighting men. It is marvellous how information leaks out in spite of all precautions; yet without secrecy there will be no surprise, and without surprise there will be no decisive victory. In India—using the name as a general term—the people sometimes seem to know even the unspoken thoughts of their European masters; reports fly like magic through bazaar or camp, and are picked up without asking by interested persons. The camp-fire and the huqqa,* beloved of the classes from which Indian camp-followers are drawn, are redolent with gossip. Of course, it is not in India only that this difficulty is experienced; a study of wars in any other part of the world will reveal the same thing. The only remedy seems to be to carry out Marshal Bugeaud's injunction to his officers in Algeria, "parle comme si tu avais confiance en tout le monde et agis comme si tu ne pouvais t'en rapporter à personne." History affords many examples of the success of this policy. The name of Stonewall Jackson recalls at once one of its ablest exponents. Marshal Bugeaud himself ultimately wore down the resistance of the Arabs by adhering to it; and Lord Wolseley's descent on Ismailia in 1882 is another famous instance. The happy result of secrecy is illustrated in the Hunza-Nagar campaign itself. Before the successful attack of December 20, the officers concerned received their instructions quietly and in confidence; arrangements were made for the party, under Lieutenant Manners-Smith, to leave camp without attracting attention; and the result was no gossip in camp, no warning for the enemy, and complete success the following day.

The vigorous pursuit of the enemy after the Maiun-

* The native pipe.

Thol position had been carried deserves notice. Though no opportunity of inflicting actual material loss presented itself, still the Hunzas and Nagaris had no chance of gathering for further resistance. The pursuit never stopped till the hostile capitals were reached. "The strategic pursuit is the decisive operation in war."* One great tactical lesson must impress itself on anyone who reads an account of the capture of Nilt or the storming of the Thol position, and that is the great use made of covering fire. It is not too much to say that without it neither exploit could have succeeded. Under cover of the fire of the rest of the force, Lieutenant Boisragon's Gurkhas were able to reach the outer walls of the fort and maintain their ground, while Captain Aylmer did his work. On December 20 the well-directed fire of the troops on the high ground above the fort prevented the enemy from leaving their sangars to repel the advance of the party under Lieutenant Manners-Smith.

We are told that the covering force consisted of 135 rifles, so that, after deducting these and the 100 men who carried out the assault, there remained roughly 600 for employment elsewhere. The absence of cover, the strength of the enemy, and the large expenditure of ammunition entailed, no doubt prevented any demonstration by the troops not actively engaged at the decisive point; but, if any such demonstration had been possible, it is at least a matter for conjecture whether the advance of the assaulting column would have ever been discovered at all. As matters were the Gurkhas were not observed till they were within a comparatively few yards of the crest; reinforcements could not reach the enemy in time to save the situation, and the result could hardly have been more decisive nor the British casualties fewer.

* Colonel Henderson.

CHAPTER XI

WANA AND SEQUEL, 1894

(*Map III.*)

Before proceeding to describe the affair at Wana and the subsequent operations, it is necessary to record in a few words the events which led up to this outbreak. The cause was far-reaching in its effect, for it not only led up to the events about to be described, but lay at the root of the great frontier rising three years later.

Ever since the annexation of the Punjab brought the Government of India into contact with the Waziris, there had often been a difficulty in deciding the delicate question as to whether the Indian or the Afghan Government was responsible for the maintenance of good order in these parts. The Amir laid claim to suzerain rights over the country ; but the Waziris had always declared their absolute independence, and acknowledged no allegiance to the court of Kabul, except when it seemed to them that the Afghan claim to suzerainty might be used to the advantage of their own ends. In any case the control of the Amir in the affairs of Waziristan had always been of the most nominal description, and no attempt had been made to make it more effective.

In consequence of the lawless character of the Waziris, it had been felt for a long time that some definite line should be laid down which would determine clearly where the responsibility of the Government of India ceased, and that of the Amir began ; but nothing practical was done till 1893, when Sir Mortimer Durand proceeded on a mission to Kabul to come to a definite understanding on the subject. The Amir—Abdur Rahman—looked upon the proposed agreement with disfavour from the first, probably because he thought it would lower his influence and prestige among the frontier tribes, and be only the prelude to the ultimate annexation by the

British Government of all the tribal territory east of the new boundary line. It is improbable, however, that the Amir's concern for the affairs of the border tribes arose from purely unselfish motives, but rather from the fear that, if the buffer between him and India was swept away, the loss of a slice of his own territory would follow. Nevertheless, after prolonged negotiations, Abdur Rahman yielded, the agreement was signed, Sir Mortimer Durand returned to India, and the demarcation of the frontier was put in hand. The work of laying down the Durand line was begun in Southern Waziristan ; but, as the boundary pillars were put up, the tribesmen, who shared the apprehensions of the Amir, thought that the time had come for making their protest before it was too late, and the attack on the camp of the Delimitation Commission and its escort at Wana was the result.

When the British camp was pitched at Wana the work of delimitation had been in progress for some little time, and the tribesmen had shown so few signs of hostility that for the sake of better sanitation and greater comfort generally more ground was taken up than would have been occupied if the inhabitants had been known to be hostile. At the beginning of November, 1894, however, reports were received of a change in the attitude of the tribesmen, and these reports were confirmed on November 2 in so unmistakable a manner that preparations were made for an attack during the night, November 2/3, in the manner described in the *Pioneer* of November 9, 1894, as follows :

"At 4 a.m. all the troops were called in and warned, being ordered to be down in their tents wearing accoutrements. Guards, piquets, etc., had been strengthened the night before, owing to the report of an intended attack by the Mullah Powindah and his followers being partly confirmed. No sound was heard till 5.15 a.m. The camp faces north, and the Gurkhas lay on the west flank with one and a half companies in piquets and supports, three-quarters of one company guarding the hospital, one and a quarter companies at a detached post guarding a dangerous nala and the main approach on the east of the camp. The remaining four and a half companies were in their lines. At 5.15 the piquet on the northwest front heard crowds advancing, and immediately doubled back on their supports. As they did so three signal shots were fired consecutively by the enemy, and the first mob of from 800 to 1,000 Ghazis started amid a terrific discharge of firearms, the beating of drums, and wild yells and shrieks. They reached the Gurkhas' left flank in less than three minutes, having covered over 600 yards, giving no time to the Gurkhas to reach their alarm posts. The men fought their way out of the tents hand to hand, and eventually reached their appointed places. It was in this mêlée in the darkness that so many were killed and wounded. B and E Companies, detailed for the reserve, formed into a rallying square, and, being surrounded on all sides, fought magnificently, inflicting terrible loss on the enemy, whose main charge they succeeded in breaking through. A few succeeded in getting into camp, where they came dancing and yelling and waving swords down the main street, but were soon shot down. F Company, 2nd Battalion 1st Gurkhas, attached to the 1st Battalion, had in the meantime reached the alarm post to the north-west of the camp behind the breastwork, and they checked the advance of the crowds of fanatics down the nala running along the front of the camp. A company of the 1st Gurkhas formed up in an extended line on the front face of the camp, and materially assisted by a flanking fire to check the rush.

" A very few minutes later, and almost simultaneously, a second attack was delivered on the direct west flank of the camp, being met by the left supports to the piquets, twelve men of G Company 1st Gurkhas, who had just reached their alarm posts, and ten rifles of the regimental police—in all less than fifty men. These split this charge into two, the right portion of which swept down past the rear of the camp, here protected by a precipice. The left half passed between the two companies of Gurkhas, fighting in the centre of the camp, and the above-named fifty men hacked their way through the transport lines and the followers of the Gurkhas into the centre of the camp, from whence they were driven out by charging bodies of the 20th Punjab Infantry and 3rd Sikhs. Individual Gurkhas, trying to reach their alarm posts, killed over twenty Ghazis *en route.* The right portion of the second attack tried to rush the guards in the rear of the camp, but, being met by heavy fire and strong opposition, only a stray few succeeded in entering the camp, the remainder going down the nala in rear of the camp, trying to find a favourable point to effect an entry. The opposition being too continuous, they retired over the neighbouring hills. Immediately the second rush was broken, Colonel Meiklejohn and Lieu-

tenant Thompson, with two companies of the 20th Punjab
Infantry, advanced up through the camp in extended
order, bayoneting all the Ghazis they met *en route*
without firing any shots; and with one company of the
3rd Sikhs under Lieutenant Finnis they joined the
Gurkhas, and formed a line covering the left flank of
the camp. . . . When the line was formed, a third attack
took place, evidently in two distinct attempts; but both
failed to get within 50 yards of the line. During all this
time the front was threatened by crowds of men, but the
heavy firing and star shell prevented them from charging
home. A smaller number of the enemy fired into the
east of the camp, but after the third rush in, the dim and
most welcome light of breaking day began to show up
the camp and adjacent ground. The enemy then retreated. All the attacks were delivered during the great
darkness which preceded the dawn, and it was impossible
to tell friend from foe at ten paces. The enemy had
sufficient numbers to threaten the whole of the front and
east, and to attack the west flank in three distinct and
intact bodies of about 800 each, thus preventing the
troops being withdrawn in any numbers from the east
to reinforce the west. . . . No kind of panic was visible
anywhere, all the troops behaving admirably.

" As soon as one could see 20 yards General
Turner ordered Major O'Mealy, with a squadron of the
1st Punjab Cavalry, to cut off the enemy's retreat. The
squadron started in a few seconds, and, overtaking
several hundreds of the enemy, cut them down on all
sides."

In addition to those who took part in the assault the
enemy expected strong reinforcements to arrive, but, fortunately, these did not appear on the scene. Twenty-one
officers and men were killed and thirty-four wounded, in
addition to forty-three casualties among the followers,
before the attack was beaten off, but the enemy lost at
least 100 killed and some 50 more during the pursuit
by the 1st Punjab Cavalry, besides many more wounded,
The Mahsuds, it will be seen, succeeded in closing on
the camp without being discovered. Their plan was to
disregard the piquets and to attack in three distinct bodies.
The first and largest column was to assault the weakly
entrenched western face in successive waves; the second
column was to attack the northern and eastern faces so
as to prevent reinforcements being sent to the Gurkhas
from those sides; while the third column was to sweep

through the camp from the rear, or south side, and cut
loose the horses and do the looting.

The escort to the Delimitation Commission consisted
of the troops named below, under the command of
Brigadier-General A. H. Turner.

> 1st Punjab Cavalry, 1 Squadron.
> 3rd (Peshawar) Mountain Battery.
> One Company Bengal Sappers and Miners.
> 3rd Sikhs.
> 20th Punjab Infantry.
> 1st Battalion 1st Gurkhas.

As soon as news of this outbreak was received in
India, troops were moved up to the frontier and the
detached posts strengthened, pending the receipt of the
Mahsuds' reply to the ultimatum which was sent to them
at once, requiring them to make reparation before the
end of November. The time limit was extended into
December, but in the meantime preparations were made
for the despatch of an expedition into Mahsud territory
under Lieutenant-General Sir W. S. A. Lockhart, K.C.B.,
C.S.I. Details regarding the Staff and troops will be
found in Tables XVI. and XVII.* It is worthy of note
that the 2nd Battalion Border Regiment was armed with
the Lee-Metford rifle, which, together with cordite, was
used for the first time in Indian frontier warfare.

As no satisfactory reply was received from the Mahsuds,
the three columns were set in motion on December 18,
the Wana Column being directed on Kaniguram, that
from Jandola on Makin, and the Bannu Column on Raznak.
Practically no opposition was encountered by any of the
columns, and, in spite of the cold and the badness of the
roads, all three columns reached their destinations on
December 21, the Bannu Column moving on to Makin on
the 22nd. Parties were sent out at once to destroy the
hostile villages and fortifications, and on the 25th lightly
equipped columns, carrying food for three days but no
tents, went out and scoured the country in various directions. Only two met with any resistance, and all returned
to their starting-points on the 27th.

During the next fortnight all the Mahsud valleys were
overrun. Snow had fallen, and at times the cold was
intense,† as much as sixteen degrees of frost being reg-

---

* Details regarding the Staffs are given, because reference cannot be
suggested to any published work in which this information may be found.

† Makin is over 6,000 feet above sea-level, and Kaniguram nearly 9,000.

TABLE XVI

THE MAHSUD EXPEDITION, 1894-95

HEADQUARTERS STAFF

A.A.G.	Major Martin.	Chief Signalling Officer ...	Captain Browne, Border Regiment.
D.A.A.G.	Captain Grover.	Chief Commissariat Officer	Captain Wharry.
A.D.C.	Lieutenant A. Lockhart.	Chief Transport Officer ...	Captain Scudamore, Royal Scots Fusiliers.
Orderly Officers ...	{ Lieutenant Hon. F. Roberts. Lieutenant Barrow. }	P.M.O.	Brigade-Surgeon Lieutenant-Colonel Spencer.
Intelligence Officer	Lieutenant-Colonel Mason, D.S.O., R.E.		

STAFF OF COLUMNS

	WANA COLUMN.	JANDOLA COLUMN.	BANNU COLUMN.
D.A.A.G. ...	Captain Duff.	Major Mackenzie.	Captain Dillon.
D.A.Q.M.G. ...	Captain Stewart.	Captain Davison.	—
Orderly Officer	Lieutenant Maxwell, 2nd Bengal Lancers.	Lieutenant Fane, 2nd Punjab Cavalry.	Lieutenant Badcock, D.S.O., 5th Gurkhas.
Intelligence Officer ...	Captain McSwiney, D.S.O.	Captain Douglas.	Captain Egerton, Guides.
Signalling Officer ...	Lieutenant Evatt, 5th Gurkhas.	Lieutenant Baumgartner, East Lancashire Regiment.	Lieutenant Campbell, Gordon Highlanders.
Commissariat Officer	Captain Grey.	Lieutenant Sanders.	Captain Ewart.
Transport Officer ...	Lieutenant Pollard, Royal Scots Fusiliers.	Lieutenant Pryor, 13th Bengal Lancers.	Lieutenant Finlay.
Senior Medical Officer	Brigade-Surgeon Lieutenant-Colonel Davies.	Surgeon-Major Shearer.	Surgeon-Major Sykes.

TABLE XVII

THE MAHSUD EXPEDITION, 1894-95

LIEUTENANT-GENERAL SIR W. S. A. LOCKHART, K.C.B., C.S.I.

WANA COLUMN.	JANDOLA COLUMN.	BANNU COLUMN.
Brigadier-General A. H. Turner.	*Brigadier-General W. P. Symons, C.B.*	*Lieutenant-Colonel Egerton, D.S.O., 3rd Punjab Cavalry.*
2nd Battalion Border Regiment.	14th Sikhs.	3rd Punjab Cavalry (23rd Cavalry), 300.
3rd Sikhs (53rd Sikhs).	33rd Punjab Infantry (33rd Punjabis).	No. 1 (Kohat) Mountain Battery (21st Kohat Mountain Battery).
1st Battalion 1st Gurkhas.	38th Dogras.	1st Sikhs (51st Sikhs).
1st Battalion 4th Gurkhas.	1st Battalion 5th Gurkhas.	2nd Punjab Infantry (56th Punjabi Rifles).
1st Punjab Cavalry, 1 Squadron less 35.	GARRISON LEFT AT WANA.	6th Punjab Infantry (59th Scinde Rifles).
3rd (Peshawar) Mountain Battery (23rd Peshawar Mountain Battery), 4 guns.	1st Punjab Cavalry, 35.	
	3rd (Peshawar) Mountain Battery.	
	20th Punjab Infantry.	

istered; but the task of dealing out retribution for the attack of November 3 went on just the same, and at the same time much valuable survey work was accomplished.

On January 9, 1895, all three columns concentrated at Jandola. The scouring of the neighbouring country was resumed, often necessitating long marches ; but large captures of cattle were made, and on the 21st representatives of the tribe met before Sir William Lockhart to hear the terms of peace, which were accepted eventually, and the operations came to an end. The terms imposed were :

1. The surrender of loot carried off from Wana.

2. The expulsion of the Mullah Powindah till the demarcation of the frontier was complete.

3. A fine of Rs. 1,200 (£800), 50 breech-loading rifles, 200 matchlocks, and 200 swords or daggers.

4. The surrender of hostages to be kept at Dera Ismail Khan till the terms were complied with.

5. The construction of frontier posts and their occupation by levies.

6. The safety of roads and telegraph lines, with a fine of Rs. 200 for each time the wire was cut.

After some little reorganization of the troops available, a column, under the command of Colonel Gaselee, explored the Tochi Valley for a distance of seventy miles, and on March 17 the whole force was finally broken up.

It only remains to add that the demarcation of the frontier was then carried out without interruption up to the Khaibar Pass. The boundary north of the Khaibar was then taken in hand, but progress was very slow owing to the necessity for frequent references to the Indian and Afghan Governments, and finally matters were brought to a standstill by the outbreak in Chitral, and have been left incomplete ever since. Before leaving the narrative of events connected with the demarcation of the Durand line, however, it may be permitted to anticipate a little, and indicate the far-reaching effect of this undertaking. The apprehension of the tribesmen as to their independence only increased as time went on, and it must be confessed that the establishment of military posts at Wana, in the Tochi and Kurram Valleys, in Chitral, on the Malakand Pass, and on the Samana Ridge, gave undeniable colour to their fears. The mullahs were not slow to make the most of the opportunity for proclaiming a jehad or holy war, and the series of outbreaks that occurred in 1897 was the result.

The Mahsud Campaign, 1894-95 : Review.

The operations of 1894-95 deserve a separate review on account of the many valuable lessons contained in the story of the affair at Wana, just before dawn on November 3. Practically all the principles laid down in "Field Service Regulations," part I., section 147, which deals with "protection when at rest," are illustrated by this memorable little episode. There is one consolation to be derived from anything which may be called a regrettable incident, and that is the practical warning given of what may happen if any of the principles governing the class of operation in question are disregarded, or not given their proper value. This may be cold comfort to those immediately concerned with the cause or effect of some such error of judgment, but it is only human, and indeed necessary from a military point of view, to profit by the misfortunes of others. But, before proceeding to suggest the weak points of the situation and dispositions of the British camp at Wana, it is necessary to draw attention to the fact that, within a few hours of the sudden attack which was made, the attitude of the tribesmen had been, to all appearances, perfectly friendly, and this impression had considerable influence on the military situation at the time of the outbreak.

The time-honoured characteristic of the Mahsuds of shunning combat in the open, but seizing any opportunity, such as that which occurred at Wana,* must have been well known. Military precautions were not neglected, but they were incomplete, for which reason it would appear that, to leave weak places in the defence in the presence of a population like the Mahsuds, however friendly they might appear, was to throw out a bait of a tempting and insidious character. The bait, as we know now, was promptly taken, and in the light of our present knowledge it would have been surprising if the result had been otherwise.

On the one hand was a people, whose independence had long been their boast, being approached by the same influence as was sufficient, three years later, to set the whole frontier in a blaze from Malakand to Maizar. Within four years this people had seen the outposts of the British Army in India posted on the crest of the Samana Ridge to the north, and in the Zhob Valley to the south ; it needed no great strategical

* Compare the attack on the camp at Palosin on April 23, 1860.

sagacity to see that both flanks of their jealously guarded mountain fastnesses were now threatened. They had seen their neighbours the Orakzais and the Shiranis both compelled to withdraw their protests; what more natural than to think that their turn had now come, and what more natural to a freedom-loving people than to be reluctant to abandon that which they prized most without a blow? In the line of boundary pillars, slowly but surely advancing from the south, they could see no purpose save as a mark of the advance of the all-absorbing power to the east, whose forces they could see deployed before them from their native hills.

On the other hand was a comparatively small force of unwelcome invaders, whose camp lay in a situation, the tactical weakness of which was accentuated by the dispositions adopted; it was certain that loot would be found there in plenty. A British defeat would have the effect of calling forth all the neighbouring tribes to join in the pursuit.

Proceeding to deal categorically with the many points of interest presented by the story of Wana, the tactical weakness of the general situation first attracts attention. In the first place we are told that there were nalas on two sides of the camp. Now, the obvious disadvantage of having a nala in close proximity to a camp is that it affords an avenue by which an enterprising assailant can approach unseen, and points of assembly within a short distance of the objective. One of the principal features of the Wana Plain, however, is the number of nalas which intersect it; since therefore the camp had to be pitched somewhere in the neighbourhood, there was no alternative but to make the best of the situation and trust to the friendly disposition of the tribesmen to prevent hostilities, and to the efficiency of the troops to beat off any attack that might be made.

In view of the complacent attitude of the inhabitants, moreover, tactical considerations were allowed to give way to the claims of general comfort, and the area covered by the camp was somewhat out of proportion to the number of troops available for its defence. Breastworks were thrown up on the northern and eastern faces, but as attack was not expected from the west * there were practically no entrenchments of any kind

---

* It will be remembered that this was the side on which the main attack was delivered. The south side was protected by the precipitous bank of a nala.

on that side. The clearly defined defensive perimeter advocated nowadays only existed partially at Wana, no obstacles or means of illuminating the foreground appear to have been provided, and there was no general reserve from which to reinforce the hard-pressed Gurkhas. The position of the men in camp was at some distance from their alarm posts, so that when required for action it took them some time to reach their appointed places. Even on the night November 2/3, when attack was expected, and the troops were ordered to be ready to turn out at a moment's notice, they were not moved up closer to their alarm posts. The result was that the tribesmen were inside the camp before the majority of the Gurkhas could do anything to stop them. We are told that "the men fought their way out of the tents hand to hand," and that the darkness was such that "it was impossible to tell friend from foe at ten paces."

The piqueting arrangements also appear to be open to adverse comment. The teaching of the present day is that piquets composing an outer line of defence in uncivilized warfare "must be of sufficient strength to maintain themselves if attacked," and that in case of attack they "must hold on to their positions, and on no account fall back on the camp."* Now, the piquets fell back at the first alarm; no doubt the defensive capabilities of the ground were not great, and the troops available were not sufficiently numerous to furnish strong piquets round the widely extended camp; but if this was so, it strengthens the case for the necessity for a strong defensive perimeter at Wana, with the troops at hand to man it at a moment's notice. It is stated that the attacking tribesmen pressed forward, ignoring the piquets. This gives colour to the idea that the latter were too extended to be of much use for defence, and that it would have been better to have had no troops at all outside the defensive area, but to have trusted to the vigilance of sentries posted along a well-entrenched perimeter, with the remainder of the troops ready to hand. The dangers of masking the fire of the defenders, or of being mistaken for the enemy, are possibilities which it is sought to avoid by forbidding piquets to fall back on camp. Again and again a few men well posted and prepared for an all-round defence have had no difficulty in maintaining their position against superior numbers, who must achieve success quickly or not at all.

* "Field Service Regulations," Part I., section 147 (3).

Two more points to which attention is drawn in the tactical manual of the present time are :

(*a*) " Men should be told off in each unit to stand to all animals."

(*b*) " Special places should be allotted to the followers in the camping-grounds of units."*

Many of the cavalry horses were cut loose and lost for the time being or disabled by the enemy's swordsmen, but the number of the latter who found their way into the lines was small, so the indication is that the arrangements connected with the horses left something to be desired. At any rate, it should not have been possible for a few individuals to do so much damage that a squadron of cavalry could only turn out sixty sabres to take up the pursuit.

Camp - followers have always been recognized as a necessary evil in any class of warfare, but their presence is particularly unavoidable in campaigns undertaken by the Army in India, where social differences and questions of caste cannot be disregarded. Camp-followers are not as a rule remarkable for their bravery, but at the same time it must not be forgotten that they are unarmed, and are therefore entitled to the protection of the combatant troops. A few armed men can easily keep a large number of followers under control if the latter are assembled at some suitable place ; there will then be no chance of desertion and, more important still, of treachery.

Surveying the dispositions of the camp at Wana as a whole, the impression left on the mind is that they amounted to a compromise between the rigors of active service on the one hand and the comforts of peace on the other. Half-measures are seldom judicious, and may often be fatal, particularly when anything in the shape of military operations is concerned. Taking the particular instance under discussion as typical, it is undeniable that, if it is worth while to make arrangements for the defence of a locality at all, it is necessary to make those arrangements as complete as circumstances will permit. If attack is possible, the threatened point can never be foretold with absolute certainty, and a weak point in the defence may be an irresistible provocation to an enemy whose prudence and resolution are about equally matched.

Although the lessons drawn from the fight at Wana

* " Field Service Regulations," Part I., section 147 (3).

have been hitherto of a negative character, there were
also those of an opposite kind. In spite of the sudden-
ness of the onslaught and intense darkness, there was
never the slightest loss of discipline on the part of the
troops. They belonged to some of the most famous
regiments of the Indian Army, and in a situation certainly
as trying as any recorded even in their extended history
they proved themselves worthy upholders of their traditions. When reading the story of the grim struggle in
the darkness, however baldly it may be told, it is impossible not to admire the gallant conduct of the Gurkhas,
on whom the brunt of the attack fell, the irresistible
march of the 20th Punjabis in extended order across the
camp, sweeping back the intruders with their bayonets
"as a housemaid disturbs black beetles with a broom,"*
or the dauntless pursuit of some 3,000 cut-throats by
sixty men of the 1st Punjab Cavalry.†

Turning to the enemy, the well-devised plan of attack,
the precautions taken, the silent approach, the well-timed
assault, and the rapidity of the final charge, deserve
special notice. The plan of containing the northern and
eastern faces while the main attack was delivered on the
unentrenched western side was carried out to the letter.
The assaulting waves came on exactly as had been
planned, and had the reinforcements which were expected put in an appearance, the situation of the British
force might have been most critical. Fires were lit to
guide the attacking columns, but even so, it is no small
feat for some 3,000 men to arrive before the objective
and deploy correctly in pitch darkness without being
detected. Those who have tried to do it know how
difficult such an operation is even with regular troops,
but how much greater does that difficulty become with
a force of undisciplined bandits! The tribesmen are
said to have covered the last 600 yards separating them
from the Gurkha camp in three minutes—that is to say,
a speed of nearly nine miles per hour across broken
ground in the dark.

Regarding the subsequent operations under Sir
William Lockhart, the most noteworthy points are the
time of year at which the expedition took place, and the
successful employment of three distinct columns converging on one objective. The troops were not set in
motion till December 18, and ten days later were ex-

* " The Indian Borderland," p. 236 (Sir T. H. Holdich).
† Now the 21st Cavalry.

periencing a climate in which the thermometer registered sixteen degrees of frost. Contrary to the expectation of the tribesmen, however, the severity of the cold proved no deterrent to Sir William Lockhart's columns—indeed, it made their task easier, for the Mahsuds, unable to take refuge in the mountains, were compelled to remain in the valleys, where the troops could reach them. Their chief place—Kaniguram—is situated at an altitude of nearly 9,000 feet above sea-level, but it was reached without delay in the depth of winter, and held till the expeditionary force withdrew. The use of converging lines of operation in Indian frontier warfare is so common as to call for nothing more than just a passing notice.

CHAPTER XII

THE CHITRAL CAMPAIGN, 1895

(Map I.)

THE first negotiations of the British Government with the State of Chitral took place in 1877, when Major Biddulph was sent thither to promote friendly relations with the Mehtar, and to establish British influence in this region with a view to the better protection of our frontier. No very definite arrangements were made, and it was not till 1885, when war with Russia seemed probable, that attention was again drawn to this quarter, and political negotiations were resumed. At this time the Mehtar of Chitral was one Aman-ul-Mulk, a man of considerable force of character, who had succeeded in consolidating his power by amalgamating a number of small neighbouring states with his own, and ruling them with the firmness so essential for securing the obedience of these wild Eastern races. Colonel Lockhart* was deputed by Lord Dufferin, the Governor-General at the time, to visit Chitral, to report upon the country, and to put relations with Aman-ul-Mulk on a satisfactory footing. This was duly done, and, after an absence of about a year, Colonel Lockhart returned to India.

In August, 1892, Aman-ul-Mulk died, leaving seventeen sons, only two of whom, however, were of high birth, to wrangle for the vacant Mehtarship. Just as on many other occasions in Eastern history, when the death of a strong ruler has been the signal for a period of anarchy and an internecine struggle for the throne on the part of the various claimants, so it was now in Chitral. At the time of Aman-ul-Mulk's death only one of his two legitimate sons was present in Chitral. He was the younger, and his name was Afzul-ul-Mulk, the elder, Nizam-ul-Mulk, being some 160 miles.

* Afterwards General Sir William Lockhart, G.C.B., K.C.S.I.

164

distant, carrying on the duties of Governor of the Province of Yasin. Afzul promptly seized the arms and treasure in the fort, murdered several of his half-brothers, and, collecting a large following, marched against his brother Nizam, who fled at his approach to Gilgit, and placed himself under the protection of the British authorities at that place. Afzul was now recognized as Mehtar of Chitral, but he was not allowed to remain long in undisputed possession of the position he had usurped.

Living in watchful retirement in Afghanistan was Sher Afzul, a brother of the late Mehtar, who, as soon as news of the events just related reached him, gathered together what adherents he could and appeared one night at a gate of the fort at Chitral. He succeeded in inducing Afzul-ul-Mulk to come to the gate, and shot him dead. The people, anxious to be on the winning side, then accepted Sher Afzul as their ruler.

It was now Nizam-ul-Mulk's turn to make his bid for the throne, and, securing the concurrence of the British authorities at Gilgit, he advanced towards Chitral, won over the people to his side, and caused the flight of his uncle back into Afghanistan. This was in December, 1892. In order to strengthen his position as Mehtar, Nizam-ul-Mulk at once applied for the moral support of the British Government in the person of an officer deputed to reside at his capital. Accordingly Surgeon-Major G. S. Robertson was sent to Chitral with an escort of fifty men of the 14th Sikhs, and, after suffering considerable hardship from the cold while on the march, arrived there on January 25, 1893. The mission remained at Chitral till September, when, as Nizam-ul-Mulk seemed to have established his power sufficiently to render its presence at the capital no longer necessary, it was withdrawn to Mastuj.

The inhabitants seemed to have settled down to a well-ordered existence when the country was again plunged in strife by the murder, on January 1, 1895, of Nizam, by a half-brother, Amir-ul-Mulk, whom the former, against his better judgment, had permitted to survive in deference to the dislike he knew the British Government entertained for the usual summary method of removing a possible rival. Amir-ul-Mulk was not the class of man likely to secure peace and prosperity for his country, so Lieutenant B. E. M. Gurdon, who was now in charge of the British Mission at Mastuj, and happened to be at Chitral with eight men at the time of the murder, antici-

pating trouble ahead, called up fifty more of his escort
from Mastuj. Further reinforcements were hurried up
to Mastuj and the neighbourhood, and Surgeon-Major
Robertson, Political Agent at Gilgit, started for Chitral,
which he reached after an arduous march on January 31,
1895.

It was not long before the consequences of Amir-ul-
Mulk's unfortunate act developed. To the south of
Chitral lay the Pathan State of Jandol, whose ruler, Umra
Khan, had lately gained several military successes over
neighbouring tribes, and now thought he saw in the disturbed condition of Chitral an opportunity for adding
that important state to his dominions. Accordingly
Umra Khan invaded Chitral with 3,000 men, in spite of
the severe weather, and occupied Kila Drosh, twenty-
four miles from the capital, with the connivance of the
leading men of the place, where he was joined by Sher
Afzul, who reappeared from Afghanistan at the end of
February. A demand was then sent to Surgeon-Major
Robertson, who had arrived at Chitral, that he should
return to Mastuj. The latter reproved Umra Khan for
the manner in which the demand had been made, and
answered that he had applied to the Government of India
for instructions. At the same time Surgeon-Major
Robertson thought it advisable to occupy the fort with
the force he now had with him, amounting to 400 men.
Amir-ul-Mulk was deposed, and Shuja-ul-Mulk,* a boy
of ten, recognized provisionally as Mehtar.

In consequence of the invasion of Chitral by Umra
Khan, decisive action by the Indian Government became
necessary, and on March 14 Umra Khan was ordered to
withdraw to his own territory before April 1. Orders
were given for the mobilization at Peshawar of the First
Division of the field army under Major-General Sir
Robert Low, and the following proclamation was issued
to the people of Swat and Bajaur:

" To all the people of Swat and the people in Bajaur
who do not side with Umra Khan.

" Umra Khan, the Chief of Jandol, in spite of his often
repeated assurances of friendship to the British Government, and regardless of frequent warnings to refrain from
interfering with the affairs of Chitral, which is a protected state under the suzerainty of Kashmir, has forcibly
entered the Chitral Valley and attacked the Chitrali people.

---

* Afterwards known to the British soldiers of Sir Robert Low's force as
" Sugar and Milk."

"The Government of India have now given Umra Khan full warning that, unless he retires from Chitral by April 1, corresponding with the fifth day of Shawal, 1312 H., they will use force to compel him to do so. In order to carry out this purpose they have arranged to assemble on the Peshawar border a force of sufficient strength to overcome all resistance and to march this force through Umra Khan's territory toward Chitral.

"The sole object of the Government of India is to put an end to the present, and prevent any future unlawful aggression on Chitral territory; and, as soon as this object has been attained, the force will be withdrawn. The Government of India have no intention of permanently occupying any territory through which Umra Khan's misconduct may now force them to pass, or interfering with the independence of the tribes; and they will scrupulously avoid any acts of hostility towards the tribesmen as long as they on their part refrain from attacking or impeding in any way the march of the troops. Supplies and transport will be paid for, and all persons are at liberty to pursue their ordinary avocations in perfect security."

Before the time given to Umra Khan had expired, however, news was received that the Chitralis had thrown in their lot with Umra Khan, and that two bodies of British troops had been attacked between Mastuj and Chitral, and considerable loss sustained. Immediate action was therefore deemed necessary, and instructions were sent to Colonel Kelly, the senior officer in the Gilgit District, to co-operate with a force marching on Chitral by the direct road from India. Some account must now be given of the two incidents which caused the Government to realize the gravity of the situation—the dangerous position of the Political Agent and his small force suddenly isolated in the midst of a hostile population, and the necessity for expediting as much as possible the military measures to be taken.

MISHAP TO PARTY UNDER LIEUTENANT EDWARDES.

On March 5 Lieutenant S. M. Edwardes, 2nd Bombay Grenadiers, left Mastuj for Chitral with a convoy of ammunition and engineering stores, escorted by twenty Bengal Sappers and Miners and forty-two Kashmir Infantry. At that time no news of any outbreak at Chitral had been received, but on the 7th, at a defile about thirty miles from Mastuj and two miles beyond a village called Reshun, the road was found to be blocked by a large body of armed men. The British force, therefore, retired to Reshun, suffering several casualties on the way, and occupied a small group of houses for the night, which they prepared for defence as well as the materials at hand allowed. Here they were surrounded and besieged till the 13th, when the enemy showed a white flag, and a conversation ensued between Edwardes and Mahomed Isa, the leading spirit of the besiegers, during which the British officer was assured that all was quiet at Chitral, and that he need be under no apprehension for the safety of his party. Lieutenant Edwardes was unwilling to place too much confidence in this unexpected protestation of friendship, and the vigilance of the British force was not relaxed. The Chitralis, however, sent supplies into the fort, and refrained from molesting men going down to the river to fetch water.

The position occupied by the garrison was 100 yards from the river, but owing to the severity of the enemy's fire it had only been possible hitherto to fetch water at night, and, even in order to do this a sortie, had to be made to clear the tribesmen out of two sangars which had been built in positions whence the track down to the river could be commanded. The sortie was rapidly and effectively carried out by Lieutenant J. S. Fowler, R.E., the only other British officer with the force, and twenty men, who surprised the occupants of the first sangar at dusk on March 10, and then fell upon the occupants of the other from behind. The attacks were delivered with such resolution that the enemy had no time to defend themselves, and those that escaped death took to precipitate flight ; not a man of Fowler's party was scratched.

Further assurances of friendliness and of tranquillity at Chitral were given on the two following days. No act of hostility occurred; and when on March 15 Mahomed Isa asked if his men might play polo on a piece of ground just outside the fort, the British officers thought there could be no objection, particularly as the ground was within close range of the garrison. At the request of Mahomed Isa, Edwardes and Fowler, moreover, went down to the ground to look on, thinking that a refusal might give a bad impression. What followed is described in the book written by Captains G. J. and F. E. Younghusband as follows :

The polo-ground at Reshun is about 50 yards broad

and 120 yards long, and slopes away from the post occupied by the British, the farther side of the ground not being covered by the fire of the British garrison. Lieutenant Edwardes asked Mahomed Isa to order the men, who numbered about 150, and who were armed with rifles and swords, to go to the farther side of the ground. The officers had some tea made, and brought out for the Chitralis to drink. After the polo was over, Mahomed Isa asked if the men might dance, as is the custom of the country at the conclusion of a game. The British officers consented, and the dance began. Then, under the excuse that there was a wet place in front of the officers, the bedstead on which they were seated was moved to the right, bringing it under cover of the end of the wall and the polo-ground. The officers found it difficult to object to this, as it seemed that any attempt at treachery could not be unattended by heavy loss to the Chitralis. As the dance proceeded, more men began to collect and to press forward in a ring round the dancers, and the officers observed that a number had come over to the wall side of the polo-ground. At a pause in the dance the officers stood up and said that they were tired, and would now go back to their post. On this Mahomed Isa himself suddenly seized the British officers, and a rush of men was made upon them, and they were dragged under cover of the wall. A volley was immediately fired by the British garrison; but the Chitralis kept under the wall, and none of them seemed to have been hit. Firing then became general for a short time, till it gradually died down into single shots fired at intervals. The officers in the meantime had their feet and hands bound, and were dragged by the legs along the ground away from the gap. All their buttons, badges, etc., were violently torn off and their pockets rifled, and Fowler's boots and stockings were taken off. The officers were then taken to Mahomed Isa's house, and the Chitralis rushed the fort, killing many and taking twelve prisoners. The ammunition which the British force had been escorting fell into the hands of the tribesmen. It had been planned to destroy it at the last moment in the event of extremities, but in the meantime the boxes were used to form a parapet as protection against the enemy's fire, and owing to the scarcity of material efficient substitutes could not readily be found.

"On March 19 the British officers and twelve men were taken to Chitral and brought before Sher Afzul, who expressed regret at the treachery which had been shown, and promised that they should be well treated. The officers were allowed to communicate with the garrison in the fort at Chitral through a native clerk, but were not allowed to visit the defenders. On March 24 the British prisoners were sent to Umra Khan at Kila Drosh, who treated them well, and gave them the choice of returning to Chitral (but without the twelve men), or going with him to Jandol. Unwilling to desert their men, Edwardes and Fowler accepted the latter alternative. On the way the prisoners were very carefully guarded, as much to prevent injury being done to them by any of the many hundreds of evil-looking tribesmen who came daily and at all times to look at them as to prevent their escape. The food provided was scanty in the extreme, and of very inferior quality; but when Dir was reached in safety on March 28, after crossing the Lowarai Pass—10,000 feet high and then deep in snow— the officers received better quarters and better food. They remained a day at Dir, and were taken on March 30 to Barwa, Umra Khan's chief fort on the south side of the Janbatai Pass. On April 1 the Mussulman soldiers were released, and great excitement prevailed among Umra Khan's following at the approach of Sir Robert Low's column. As the relieving army drew near the officers received greater consideration, and finally, after an interview on the 12th between Umra Khan and a native political officer sent by Major Deane, Political Officer with Sir Robert Low, Lieutenant Edwardes was released, and given two letters to deliver to the British General. Lieutenant Fowler was released two days later."[*]

Mishap to party under Captain Ross.

The day after Lieutenant Edwardes left Mastuj for Chitral with his party a letter was received from that officer saying that he expected to be attacked near Reshun. Accordingly Captain Ross, who had just arrived at Mastuj, started to the assistance of Edwardes, with one other British officer (Lieutenant Jones) and ninety-four rank and file, carrying supplies for nine days and 140 rounds per man. Buni was reached at 11 p.m. on March 7, and there a connecting-post was left, consisting of one native

* "The Relief of Chitral," pp. 40-42.

officer and thirty-three rank and file. Resuming the march
the next day, all went well with the party under Captain
Ross till the afternoon, when the road was found to be
blocked at a narrow defile close to the Chitral River,
about half a mile beyond a place called Koragh. The
tribesmen, posted on the hills in considerable force,
opened fire on the British troops, and began rolling
rocks down the precipitous sides of the mountains in
such numbers as to render the road at the bottom impassable; the baggage coolies immediately took to flight.
Captain Ross tried to make his way back to Koragh, but
his force suffered so severely in its exposed situation
that he withdrew the survivors to the shelter of two
caves in the river bank, where they waited till darkness
set in, when another unsuccessful attempt was made to
return to Koragh. The party then tried to gain the
hills, and so avoid the road on which so many casualties
had already occurred; but, being ignorant of the locality,
and finding further progress completely cut off by a
precipice, Captain Ross made his way back to the caves,
arriving there at 3 a.m., with his men in an exhausted
condition. The caves were held during the whole of
the 9th, and at 2 a.m. on the 10th another attempt was
made to force a way to Koragh. The enemy were driven
out of the sangars they had thrown up to block the road,
and the retirement was slowly but successfully carried
out. Lieutenant Jones and fourteen men, nine of whom
were wounded, reached Buni at 6 a.m., where, owing to
the want of transport and the crippled condition of the
detachment, they were obliged to take up a defensive
position till relieved by Lieutenant Moberly from Mastuj
on March 17. Regarding the fate of the remainder of
the men under Captain Ross Sir George Robertson
says :

"An uncertain number of Sikhs, between twenty and
thirty, failed to follow Jones, and fell back once more to
their old hiding-place, where they were closely invested,
small sangars being even built on the top edge of the
mouths of the caves. For seven or eight days they
lived there without food or water, sustained, Harley
conjectures, by the opium which Sikhs usually have
about them. Then three chiefs, Mahomed Isa, Yadgar
Beg, and the latter's nephew, came on from Reshun,
where they had treacherously seized Edwardes and
Fowler and slaughtered their following. During a
parley they swore to spare the imprisoned soldiers in

return for immediate surrender. These terms were
accepted, and the emaciated Sikhs came slowly out,
broken in spirit and with faltering steps. All those
unable to walk were at once slaughtered—a terrible
commentary on the trust to be placed in the word of
a Chitrali. The others were shut up in a house at
Kalak. Next morning, by order of the infamous trio
(two of them blood-relations and the third a foster-
brother of Sher Afzul), the helpless Sikhs were brought
out singly and hacked to death, one man only escaping.
This man was reserved that he might be slain by a
headman at a distance, who was supposed to desire
the honour of murdering an infidel in cold blood, but
who relented. Many Chitralis refused to participate in
the butchery, for even their lax consciences were shocked
at the perfidy of the chiefs. The killing was done by
Broz men."*

The two foregoing incidents have been related in some
detail, for, though their importance as military operations
is insignificant, yet their consequences had a distinct
influence on the strategical situation in the whole theatre
of war. This will be apparent presently, and will also
be commented upon in the general review of the campaign. Moreover, they present two very fair examples
of situations young officers may suddenly be called upon
to face ; they afford some valuable lessons ; and they
emphasize the vital necessity, which really amounts to
a sacred duty owed to their superiors and men alike,
for officers to do all in their power in peace to take to
heart the lessons which history teaches, that they may be
the better prepared to act with sound judgment when
the hour of trial arrives.

THE DEFENCE OF CHITRAL.

On arrival at Chitral Surgeon-Major Robertson found
affairs there in a very disturbed state, so much so that,
"under the excuse of carefully guarding certain stores
which were in the fort,"† he sent a guard of 100 Kashmir
troops to hold the main gate, and steps were taken at
once to lay in as large a stock of supplies as possible.
Great efforts were made by the Chitralis on various
pretexts to induce the British Agent to break up the force

---

* " Chitral : The Story of a Minor Siege," p. 117.   † *Ibid.*, p. 83.

at his disposal, but the latter not only firmly refused to listen to these suggestions, but, on hearing of the surrender of Kila Drosh, moved the whole of his escort into the fort. Further preparations for defence were then made; ranges were taken, a covered way was made down to the river, and the troops were practised in the duties they were required to perform in the event of an alarm. In response to the urgent appeal of some of the inhabitants who were hostile to Umra Khan, and expressed friendliness to the British Government, a detachment was sent to Gairat, a fort sixteen miles from Chitral in the direction of Kila Drosh, to stiffen the defence; but, when Sher Afzul joined Umra Khan, this detachment had to be withdrawn hurriedly to Chitral in consequence of the following incident:

"A few headmen, who wanted to show Sher Afzul how energetic they were in his service, by a clever intrigue convinced the defenders of Gairat that the British officers there had no objection to their leaving their posts to go and salaam to Sher Afzul, and then bring him to me [Surgeon-Major Robertson] at Chitral. So they trooped away, and this invaluable military position was left to the care of a few Khushwaktis and Campbell's troops — a force insufficient for its defence."*

Surgeon-Major Robertson had barely concentrated his force in the fort at Chitral, when news was received at 4.30 p.m. on March 3 that Sher Afzul was approaching with a large gathering. To clear up the situation, Captain Campbell, who was the senior combatant officer present, decided to make a reconnaissance down the valley with a party of 200 Kashmir Infantry. All the officers accompanied the reconnaissance except Lieutenant Harley, who remained with his detachment of Sikhs in the fort. The troops were divided into two parties, one of whom, about fifty strong, ascended the hills on the right bank under Captain Baird and Lieutenant Gurdon, and the other advanced down the valley under Captains Campbell and Townshend. The enemy were met in considerable numbers about two miles from the fort by both parties, and firing began at once, with the result that in a very short time Captains Campbell and Baird were wounded, as well as several of the rank and file, and some of the latter killed. The Kashmir Infantry soon lost two of their own officers, and this, in addition

* "Chitral: The Story of a Minor Siege," p. 93.

to numerous other casualties, had a bad effect on their *moral*.   Finding himself opposed to an overwhelming force of the enemy with darkness setting in, Captain Campbell, who was still able to mount a pony and exercise command, then commenced to retire on the fort; but the Chitralis, elated at their success, pressed the retirement with great determination.   The British troops slowly fought their way back to the fort, covered to some extent by the darkness, being greatly assisted as they drew near by a party of fifty Sikhs, who succeeded in checking the advance of the pursuers.   The Chitralis then closed round the fort, and for forty-seven days the little British garrison was completely cut off from communication with the outside world.   The loss sustained in this encounter was two officers wounded (one of whom—Captain Baird—afterwards died), besides twenty-three killed and thirty-three wounded among the rank and file.

Here it will be well to quote the description of the fort given by Captains G. J. and F. E. Younghusband to see what manner of place it was that our troops were now called upon to defend:

"The Chitral Fort is 80 yards square, with walls 25 feet high, and about 8 feet thick.   At each corner there is a tower some 20 feet higher than the wall, and outside the north face on the edge of the river is a fifth tower to guard the waterway.   On the east face a garden runs out for a distance of 140 yards, and 40 yards from the south-east tower is a summer-house.   On the north and west faces were stables and other outhouses.

"The fort is built of rude masonry, kept together, not by cement or mortar of any description, but by cradle-work of beams of wood placed longitudinally and transversely, so as to keep the masonry together.   Without this framework of wood the walls would fall to pieces.

"The fort is situated on the right bank of the Chitral River* some 40 or 50 yards from the water's edge.   It is commanded from nearly all sides for Martini-Henry or Snider rifle fire, for mountains close by the river rise above the valley bottom.   The fort is so situated for the purpose of maintaining water, and at the time of its construction breech-loading rifles were not in possession of

* The river flowed past the north face.

the people of the country, so that the fort could not then be fired into." *

The garrison consisted of :

> Surgeon-Major G. S. Robertson, Political Agent.
> Captain C. Campbell, Central India Horse, Inspecting Officer Kashmir Imperial Service Troops (incapacitated from duty by reason of the wound received during the reconnaissance on March 3).
> Captain C. V. F. Townshend, Central India Horse, commanding British Agent's escort, and now Commandant of the fort.
> Lieutenant B. E. M. Gurdon, Assistant to the British Agent.
> Surgeon-Captain Whitchurch, 24th Punjab Infantry.†
> 14th Sikhs, under Lieutenant H. K. Harley, 99.
> Kashmir Infantry, 301.

In addition there were 109 non-combatants, including 52 Chitralis, inside the fort. The ammunition available was 300 rounds per Martini-Henry rifle for the Sikhs, and 280 rounds per Snider rifle for the Kashmiris, and supplies were calculated to last for two and a half months by putting everyone on half-rations.

Captain Townshend at once set to work to organize the defence, and to give increased protection against the severe fire which the enemy constantly opened on the garrison. As the interior of the fort could be commanded from outside, cover from reverse fire had to be provided for men lining the parapets; but this so exhausted the very limited supply of available material, that little beyond cover from view could be provided for men moving about inside the fort. The ground round the fort was cleared as much as was possible with the means at hand in spite of the enemy's fire, and a covered way was built along the 30 yards that intervened between the water-gate and the edge of the river.

On the night March 7/8 a determined attack was made on the covered waterway, as well as an attempt to set fire to the tower commanding it, but both were frustrated by the steady fire of the defenders. Independent firing at night was prohibited; only volleys were allowed. The difficulties of the defence were much increased by the fact that many of the rifles in the possession of the troops soon became unserviceable, also the *moral* of

---

* " The Relief of Chitral," pp. 108, 109.
† Afterwards decorated with the Victoria Cross for gallantry displayed in bringing Captain Baird into the fort after he had been wounded.

the Kashmir troops was much shaken by their experiences on March 3, and it was only by the utmost exertions and personal example of the officers that their spirits could be kept up at all; moreover, the Chitralis inside the fort had to be carefully watched to prevent them communicating with their friends outside.

As the material used in the construction of the fort consisted so largely of wood, special precautions had to be taken against fire. The water-carriers were told to sleep with their skins filled, and any other vessels that were to hand were ordered to be kept filled in readiness. Patrols were detailed to give warning of the outbreak of fire both by day and night. The non-combatants were organized into parties for carrying water, putting out fire, and work on the defences, so as to relieve the troops as far as possible of these duties. The three combatant officers* divided each twenty-four hours into watches of four hours on duty and eight off, but always held themselves in readiness to turn out at a moment's notice. To cause him annoyance thirty rounds per day were fired at the house occupied by Sher Afzul, and to light up the foreground at night fires were lit on platforms built out from the walls.

Attacks were frequently delivered on the east face of the fort and on the waterway, especially the latter, which was constantly strengthened, but they were repulsed successfully in every case. On March 15, in the hope of creating despondency, the Chitralis informed the defenders of the mishaps to the parties under Captain Ross and Lieutenant Edwardes; but the news was not credited till on the 20th a native clerk was allowed to go outside the fort and hold a conversation with Lieutenant Edwardes. Various attempts were made to communicate with the outside world, but without success; and the situation began to look grave when, at the end of March, the officers had begun to eat horseflesh, only 343 rifles in all remained fit for use,† and provisions for the men began to run short.‡ At this time

* Captain Townshend and Lieutenants Gurdon and Harley.
† Number of rounds left on March 30 for 82 Martini-Henry rifles, 29,224, or 356 each ; number of rounds left on March 30 for 261 Snider rifles, 68,587, or 262 each.
‡ Forty-five thousand pounds of grain left, being issued at 540 pounds per day, but only 36 pounds of ghi, which was kept for sick and wounded. A ration of 1 drachm of rum was given to the Sikhs every four days, and a tea ration to the Kashmiris every third day.

the guards and piquets in the fort were arranged
thus :

	Men.
Main gate	10
Parapet (10 to each parapet)	40
Water piquet	20
Water tower	25
Stable piquet	20
Water-gate guard	10
Guard over Amir-ul-Mulk	6
Guard over Chitralis at night	4
Guard over ammunition	6
Guard over garden-gate	6
Guard over four towers	24
	171
Available for sortie	172
Rifles available	343*

April 7 was a critical day for the garrison, for the
enemy succeeded in setting fire to the south-east tower,
apparently through want of sufficient vigilance on the
part of the Kashmiri guard. The large amount of wood
used in the construction of the fort has already been
mentioned, and for this reason the fire soon assumed
alarming proportions, especially as the men were greatly
impeded by the severe and accurate fire the Chitralis
opened on anyone who ventured to give them a target.
While superintending the extinguishing of the flames,
the British Agent, who had been handicapped by bad
health throughout the siege, had the further misfortune
to receive a bullet-wound in the shoulder; but, though
the injury was severe, he was still able to assist in the
defence. At length, however, the fire was got under,
thanks to a liberal supply of water; but the Chitralis
renewed their attempt the next day, when the attention of
the sentries was momentarily relaxed at the time of relief.
As further precautions against similar enterprises, Sikh
sentries, being better disciplined, were placed to watch
the ground under the walls instead of the Kashmiris,
and were relieved at a different time from day to day :
also the means of bringing a flanking fire to bear along
the foot of the walls were greatly improved. At this
time the number of sick was eighty-five, composed of
eleven Sikhs, nineteen Kashmir Infantry, six non-
combatants, and forty-nine out-patients.

* "The Relief of Chitral," p. 120.

On April 10 and 11 the last assaults on the waterway were unsuccessfully delivered, and on the next day many of the enemy were seen moving off towards Mastuj to oppose Colonel Kelly, but others occupied the summer-house near the south-east tower, where they made a terrific noise at night, singing and beating tomtoms till daylight. This was repeated for the next three nights, and then suspicions were aroused that the enemy were constructing a mine, and that the noise thus made was to drown the sounds of their work. At midnight on April 16 a sentry reported that he could hear the noise of picks; the noise became unmistakable the next morning, and it was then evident that the mine was within 12 feet of the walls. A sortie was now absolutely necessary to rush the summer-house and destroy the mine, so Lieutenant Harley was placed in command of a party of forty Sikhs and sixty Kashmiris, and given the following instructions:

" No firing; bayonet only. Forty rounds in pouch. Take a prisoner or two if possible. Take three powder-bags, 110 pounds powder, 40 feet powder hose, picks and spades. To go straight for the gap in the wall of house; no dividing up the party; no support. Having rushed the place, to hold the house on front towards Fateh Ali Shah's house, and with the remaining men destroy the mine by pulling down the uprights and wooden supports, if any, or blow it in as he saw fit. No hurry. If the sangar in front of the garden-gate annoyed, he should send some men round it, first sounding the ' Cease fire' and let us know what he was going to do, and we would cease firing from the parapets on the sangar in question." *

All the native officers as well as Harley carried matches, and were made acquainted with what was required. At 4 p.m. the party issued quietly from the east gate, and rushed the summer-house, taking its occupants completely by surprise. Covered by the fire of a portion of his force, Lieutenant Harley then destroyed the mine, and in one hour was back inside the fort, with the loss of eight killed and thirteen wounded. Thirty-five Chitralis were bayoneted as they ran out of the mine, two prisoners were taken, and at least twenty-five more of the enemy were shot down.

On the next day (April 18) information was received that the siege had been raised, and that Colonel Kelly

* Captain Townshend's report.

was only two marches distant. The news was received
with caution, and vigilance was in no way relaxed ; but
patrols were sent out, who confirmed the welcome intelligence, and reported the neighbourhood completely
deserted by the enemy. On the 20th Colonel Kelly
arrived, having successfully accomplished one of the
most remarkable marches in history, and after forty-
seven days of confinement and anxiety the siege of
Chitral was at an end.

The casualties to the British force during the siege,
including the reconnaissance on March 3, were :

	Killed.	Wounded.
British officers	1	2
Native rank and file	35	54
Levies	—	2
Non-combatants	6	4
Total	42	62

COLONEL KELLY'S MARCH.

In the middle of March, when news of the events at
Chitral was received, the British forces in the district
consisted of—

32nd Pioneers (commanded by Colonel Kelly, senior
military officer in the district), 800.
14th Sikhs, 200.
Three Battalions Kashmir Infantry, each 660 strong.
1st Battery Kashmir Mountain Artillery.*

These were distributed as under :

At Chitral (besieged), 100 Sikhs, 300 Kashmir
Infantry.
At Mastuj (also besieged), 100 Sikhs, 150 Kashmir
Infantry.
Between Gilgit and Mastuj, 240 Kashmir Infantry.
At Gilgit, 690 Kashmir Infantry.
Between Hunza and Gilgit, 200 Kashmir Infantry.
At Chilas, 400 Kashmir Infantry.
At Bunji, 800 Pioneers.

Great anxiety was felt as to the attitude of the small
neighbouring states, particularly Hunza and Nagar,

* " Relief of Chitral," p. 135.

which had only been brought under subjection three years previously. The latter, however, at once gave proof of their loyalty by sending a contingent of 900 men to reinforce the British arms; but Yasin and Chilas caused some misgiving, particularly the former, situated as it is on the line of advance to Mastuj and Chitral. It was felt that the smallest reverse would have a most unfortunate effect on the attitude of the people, but that any show of irresolution would at once be construed into weakness.

The road from Gilgit to Chitral is 220 miles long, and, 130 miles from Gilgit, crosses the Shandur Pass, 12,000 feet high, and at this season of the year deep in snow. West of the Shandur Pass the whole country was known to be in arms, but there it was also known that two British garrisons were cut off, and their safety and British prestige alike demanded that a column should start to their relief with the least possible delay. Accordingly a force consisting of 400 men, 32nd Pioneers, organized in two detachments of 200 men each, and accompanied by two guns Kashmir Mountain Artillery, moved out from Gilgit on March 23 and 24. It was decided to take the guns, in spite of the well-known difficulties of the road, on account of the excellent moral effect they were expected to produce on the Chitralis, now elated with their unexpected initial successes. The greatest difficulty was experienced in the matter of transport, as everything had to be carried by coolies. It was therefore decided to take no tents, to limit each man to 15 pounds of baggage, and that each man should carry his greatcoat and pushtin, as well as eighty rounds of ammunition.

Ghizr was reached without mishap on March 31, and here reinforcements were received, consisting of forty Kashmir Sappers and Miners, and 100 Hunza and Nagar levies. On resuming the march the next day the snow was found to be so deep as to make progress so slow that it was evident that the whole force would not be able to cross the formidable Shandur Pass (now a little way ahead) in one day. Moreover, the gun-mules were quite helpless in the deep snow, and it seemed probable that they would have to be left behind, when the men came forward and volunteered to carry them over themselves, rather than lose the moral and physical effect of their presence. If the enterprise was not to be abandoned, Colonel Kelly had now to make up his mind to incur the risk of descending into the midst of a possibly hostile population with his force divided into two detachments, separated by a snow-bound pass 12,000 feet high. Colonel Kelly, therefore, returned to Ghizr with half his force, leaving the other half, under Captain Borradaile, at a place called Teeru, four miles nearer the Shandur Pass. Owing to a heavy snowstorm Captain Borradaile was unable to make any progress on April 2, but a start was made the next day, and, after a most toilsome march, his party reached the foot of the pass late in the evening. The account of the struggle of Captain Borradaile's detachment on April 3 and the following day is best told in detail in the words of Captains G. J. and F. E. Younghusband:

"All day long the men struggled through the snow with the guns, till, between nine and ten o'clock in the evening, it was so dark that the track could scarcely be seen, and it was then decided that, if the men were to get in at all, those behind would have to drop their loads. This was accordingly done, ammunition-boxes, etc., were stacked in the snow, and the troops marched on to Langar, the camping-spot at the foot of the pass. Here at Langar there was only one small hut in which the more exhausted men were placed, and the remainder, being without tents, had to remain in the open for the whole night. The men with Captain Borradaile were Sikhs from the plains of the Punjab, brought up for generations in one of the hottest climates in the world, and they were now called upon, after the severe struggles of this and previous days, to spend a night on the snow at nearly 12,000 feet above sea-level, with the thermometer somewhere about zero (Fahrenheit). Sleep for most of them was out of the question. The men, as far as possible, gathered round small fires, which had been made up from the brushwood to be obtained near the camping-spot, and wearily awaited the dawn and final struggle of the coming day. On the following morning Captain Borradaile set off for the pass; but as it had now become clear to him that, if his men were to attempt to carry over the guns as well as their own kit, they would inevitably break down altogether, he decided to leave Lieutenants Stewart and Gough* behind, and directed these two officers to employ that day in bringing the remaining loads into camp, and storing them

---

* Lieutenant Stewart was the officer in charge of the guns, and Lieutenant Gough in command of the forty Kashmir Sappers and Miners.

there till Captain Borradaile could send back assistance
from the opposite side of the pass, or until aid could
come from Ghizr. Captain Borradaile's men found the
task of crossing the pass just heart-breaking ; every few
steps they would sink in through the snow, although
some sort of a track had been beaten out by the levies
going on in front. At times they would fall in almost up
to their arm-pits, so that they had to be pulled out by
their comrades. This was fearfully trying to men loaded
as they were, to men, too, who had passed an almost
sleepless night, and started for this, the crisis of the
enterprise, thoroughly exhausted. By the time the party
had reached the middle of the pass men were falling out
in twos and threes, sitting down in the snow as if they
were on the point of giving up the struggle. The heavy
loads which they had to carry — rifles, ammunition,
haversacks, greatcoats, etc.—were weighing them down
and utterly exhausting them. The snow was from 3 to
5 feet deep, and quite 18 inches of it were soft and fresh,
at the same time the sun was pouring down upon the
men and adding to their discomfort by the glare which
it produced from the white surface of the snow; and,
although all the men were provided with blue spectacles,
many cases of snow-blindness occurred. The absence
of water, too, caused the men additional suffering. Little
relief was afforded them from sucking snow, and many
were afraid to do that, thinking that there must be some
bad influence from it. So exhausted were the men that
it seemed at one time to the British officers that it would
be necessary to spend another night on the snow, but at
about 5.30 the advance guard came to the end of the flat
part of the top of the pass, and the descent was at last
commenced. News was at once passed along the line,
and fresh spirit came into the men. They pulled themselves together for a final effort, and, when a little farther
on some water was obtained, they began to step out
quite briskly. A critical time had now been reached ;
the party were descending the western side of the pass
into the heart of the country which had for a month now
been up in open arms against the British. It was known
that there was a village at the foot of the pass, and it
was quite possible that Captain Borradaile's exhausted
troops might find resistance offered them here at the
very culminating point of their troubles. Captain Borradaile had, therefore, to send on his few levies to scout
and discover if the enemy were in any force in the

village of Laspur at the foot of the pass, and to report on the state of affairs there. Fortunately, no opposition was met with, for the Chitralis had scarcely expected that the troops would be able to cross the pass in its then condition, and at about 7.30, nearly twelve hours after the first start had been made from Langar, Laspur was reached."

The remainder of Captain Borradaile's party reached Laspur the next day (April 5), with assistance sent back to them from the western side of the pass, when it was found that there had been twenty-five cases of frost-bite and thirty of snow-blindness, fortunately none of them severe. Reconnaissances were pushed along the Mastuj road, and on the 8th, sufficient baggage coolies having been collected, the advance was resumed for eleven miles to Gasht, accompanied by Colonel Kelly, who had arrived at Laspur two days before with an escort of fifty levies. The relief column now came into touch with the enemy, who were found occupying a strong position across the valley at Chokalwat. This position is described in the official report thus :

" The road from the river, after leaving Gasht, brought us on to an alluvial fan, the ascent of which was short and steep. It was covered with boulders, and intersected with nullahs.* The road led across this fan and then along the foot of steep shale slopes and shoots within 500 yards of the line of sangars crowning the opposite side of the river bank, and totally devoid of any sort or description of cover for some two miles ; it could also be swept by avalanches of stones set in motion by a few men placed on the heights above for that purpose. The enemy's position consisted of a line of sangars blocking the roads from the river up to the alluvial fan on which they were placed. The right of the position was protected by a snow glacier, which descended into the river bed, and furthermore by sangars which extended into the snow-line up the spur of the hills."

In order not to give the tribesmen time to gather strength to oppose him, Colonel Kelly decided to attack the Chokalwat position without waiting for the arrival of his second detachment from the other side of the Shandur Pass. Accordingly, on the morning of April 9 the little British force, which, all told, only mustered 190 32nd Pioneers, 40 Kashmir Sappers and Miners, 50 levies, and

* The Hindustani word for a watercourse is *nala*, the first "a" being long.

2 guns, advanced against this formidable position. The levies were sent up the hills to turn the enemy's flanks, while Colonel Kelly delivered the frontal attack with the remainder of his force. One and a half companies of the Pioneers, with the guns in the centre, formed the first line ; half a company of Pioneers and the Kashmir Sappers and Miners were in reserve. Fire was opened by the guns at a range of 825 yards across the river from the alluvial fan on the right bank at the first sangar on the opposite side, while the infantry, beginning with volleys at 800 yards, advanced to within 200 yards as the action progressed. The first sangar was soon vacated, and, just as the second was being cleared in the same way, the tribesmen driven off the hills by the levies began streaming down into the valley and took to their heels, together with the defenders of the sangars. The British force followed, and, crossing the river, covered by the fire of the reserves, occupied the first two sangars. Thus easily in the space of one hour was the first attempt to check Colonel Kelly's advance brushed aside by a force of less than 300 men. The enemy's strength was computed at some 400 men armed with Martini-Henry and Snider rifles, of whom they were estimated to have lost 50, while the casualties on the British side numbered only 4 wounded. The advance on Mastuj was then continued, and, when nearing the place, Colonel Kelly's force joined hands with the garrison, who, seeing the Chitralis moving off towards Chokalwat, had left their fort to follow them up.

Events at Mastuj since the beginning of the outbreak may be summarized in a few words. When Captain Ross left on March 6 to go to the assistance of Lieutenant Edwardes, Lieutenant Moberly was left in charge of the fort with 70 Kashmir Infantry, a number which was increased a week later to 230 by reinforcements arriving from Ghizr. Failing to hear any news either of Ross or Edwardes, Lieutenant Moberly started on the 16th with 150 Kashmir Infantry to ascertain the fate of the missing officers. No coolies were available, so the men carried their blankets, ammunition, and supplies themselves.* Buni was reached at 5 p.m. on the 17th, and here Lieutenant Jones was found with fifty men who survived of Captain Ross's party. As the tribesmen were reported to be gathering in the neighbourhood, and there were

---

* One hundred and twenty rounds per man and three days' cooked rations were carried.

some awkward defiles to be crossed on the road back to Mastuj, Moberly decided to begin his march back to Mastuj the same evening. The defiles were secured in advance, and the whole party reached Mastuj without mishap on the evening of the 18th. Lieutenant Moberly immediately started to make all possible preparations for meeting the attacks that now appeared inevitable; the fort was surrounded on March 22.

"Mastuj Fort is about 90 yards square, and is built of masonry and woodwork in the same manner as are all the forts in these parts. The walls are about 25 feet high, but at the time of the siege were in a dilapidated condition, for the place had only been temporarily occupied by the British as a residence for the Political Agent and his escort pending the decision of the Government as regards our permanent policy towards Chitral. The fort is situated on the edge of a sloping plain running down from the hillside, which at one point approaches to within about 400 yards of the fort." *

The enemy fired from behind the cover of houses and sangars some 300 yards from the walls, and on one occasion Lieutenant Moberly, taking with him a party of eighty men, delivered a successful sortie against one of the latter. The Chitralis made the same assurance of the absence of any hostile intentions on the part of Sher Afzul as they had given to Lieutenant Edwardes, and offered a safe conduct to Gilgit; but Moberly was not to be beguiled, and on April 9, seeing the enemy moving off towards Gilgit, he followed them up, and met the relief column under Colonel Kelly fresh from their success at Chokalwat, as has already been narrated.

On reaching Mastuj Colonel Kelly's column made a halt of three days to organize the transport and supply arrangements for the final stages to Chitral, to allow time for the second detachment to arrive, and to reconnoitre a formidable position that the enemy were said to have taken up at a place called Nisa Gol, which seems to have been the stock defensive position in this part of Chitral. It was reported to be held by 1,500 Chitralis under Mahomed Isa, whose name is already familiar from the prominent part he took in the treacherous capture of Lieutenants Edwardes and Fowler at Reshun nearly a month before. Quoting again from the interesting and most lucid account of Captains G. J. and F. E. Younghusband:

* " The Relief of Chitral," p. 157.

"The valley of the Chitral River at the Nisa Gol position is about a mile wide, and is bounded on either hand by steep rocky mountains, rising for several feet above the river. On the left bank especially the mountain-sides are very precipitous, and up against these the Chitral River runs. On first looking down the valley it appears as if in between the mountains there was nothing but a smooth plain running down from the right-hand side, and it is not till one is actually on it that it is discovered that the seemingly open plain is cleft by a nullah between 200 and 300 feet deep, and with absolutely perpendicular sides. This nullah is the Nisa Gol, and only one path leads across it, that of the road to Chitral, and this path the enemy had now cut away. There had been a small goat-track across this nullah at another point, but the enemy had now entirely obliterated it. Sangars had also been erected at the head of these paths and along the right bank of the nullah. These sangars were sunk into the ground, and head-cover was provided by a covering of timber and stones. On the left of their position they had sangars on the spur of the hill in a general line with the sangars on the plain, and on the hill parties of men were stationed to throw down stones. On the right of their position across the Chitral River, and slightly in advance of the general line, they had another line of sangars on a spur stretching away high up into the snow-line."[*]

After a careful reconnaissance the previous day, Colonel Kelly left Mastuj to attack this position at 7.30 a.m. on April 13. His plan was for the levies and advanced guard to take ground to their right on reaching the plain across which the enemy were posted, where it would be able to advance under cover to within 500 yards of the ravine. The advanced guard was then to silence the sangars on the enemy's left, which commanded the main advance across the plain. This having been accomplished, the main body was to engage the main sangars, while the levies ascended the hills on the British right so as to turn the enemy's left. The force at Colonel Kelly's disposal now consisted of—

32nd Pioneers, 382.
Kashmir Infantry, 100.
Kashmir Sappers and Miners, 34.
Kashmir Mountain Artillery, 2 guns.
Hunza and Punial levies, 100.

---

[*] "The Relief of Chitral," pp. 161, 162.

The instructions given to the advanced guard were duly carried out, supported by the effective fire of the guns, at first at a range of 500 yards and then at 275 yards. The guns then moved to their left, and turned their fire on to the main sangars at from 875 to 1,200 yards, while the infantry engaged the enemy posted in front and on the hills on the British left at about 300 yards' range.

When the Chitralis abandoned the sangars on their extreme left, they had to cross a belt of open ground within 400 yards of the British firing-line; although they tried to give as small a target as possible by trying to make their escape in driblets, many of them fell to the deadly volleys before they could gain a place of safety. Search was now made for a way across the Nisa Gol, and at length three officers and twelve men managed to cross with the help of some scaling-ladders brought from Mastuj. The officers were under the impression that a company of Kashmir Infantry were following; but, as the latter were about to descend into the nala, a bullet struck some cakes of guncotton, which had been left on the bank by the Sappers and Miners while they were fixing the scaling-ladders. The bullet ignited the gun-cotton, so the men were withdrawn for fear of an explosion. The enemy, thinking our men were retreating, left their sangars in pursuit, but were speedily driven back by the fire of the covering infantry. The flank attack of the levies now developed, and the Chitralis, finding their retreat threatened not only by the levies, but by the small party which had already crossed, began evacuating the main sangars, and streamed away down the valley pursued by the fire of the guns and infantry. There was now no need for the troops to use the slow and somewhat perilous point of passage where the scaling-ladders had been placed; the goat-track mentioned in the description of the position was now open, so the men got across there. An attempt at pursuit was made, but the enemy's flight was so rapid that all thought of catching them had soon to be abandoned. The fight lasted about two hours altogether. Besides 12 prisoners taken, the Chitralis were estimated to have lost 60 killed and 160 wounded; while on the British side 8 men were killed and 16 wounded. The latter were sent back under escort to Mastuj.

Besides the actual physical result of the victory, the moral effect of the summary manner in which they had been turned out of their most cherished position was so profound as to take all heart out of the tribesmen, and went far towards causing them to realize the utter futility of prolonging the struggle. Colonel Kelly continued his advance without delay, and, turning the formidable defiles which had proved so fatal to the parties under Captain Ross and Lieutenant Edwardes by marching along the side of the hills, he finally reached Chitral on April 20, and found that the enemy had already raised the siege and melted away into the mountains. Thus ended one of the most remarkable marches in history. In twenty-eight days a force of some 500 men, most of whom were not accustomed to severe cold, marched 220 miles through a mountainous country practically without transport, crossed a pass 12,000 feet high with snow 3 to 5 feet deep, fought two successful actions, and brought relief to two hard-pressed British garrisons. British prestige in the district was firmly restored; but, had Colonel Kelly met with the slightest reverse, it is probable that instead of finding enemies only in front, he would have found a swarm of determined foes in rear anxious to be on what they would have taken to be the winning side. As things were, the advance was continued with such resolution, and took the tribesmen so completely by surprise, that no untimely complications arose, and those who were seated on the fence at the beginning of April had no difficulty in discerning quickly the best side on which to alight. The levies from the States of Hunza, Nagar, and Punial were of the greatest assistance throughout, for they were familiar with the country, inured to its climate, and expert at overcoming the difficulties of the road. Lieutenant Beynon says of them: "We always got our earliest and most reliable information from the levies, as most of them had blood-relations among the Chitralis. They also knew just where to look for hidden grain and supplies of all sorts. As a rule there was generally a cache under or near the fireplace in the main room; but I have also seen the levies find them in the most unlikely places, and very queer odds and ends they sometimes pulled out of these underground store-rooms."*

Sir Robert Low's Advance.

While Colonel Kelly was covering the first stages of his way from Gilgit to Chitral, the main British army

* "With Kelly to Chitral," p. 56.

was mobilizing at Peshawar. It consisted of some 15,000 men, organized in three brigades, under the command of Major-General Sir Robert Low, K.C.B., with Brigadier-General Bindon Blood, C.B., R.E., as his Chief of the Staff, and Major Deane as Political Officer. The troops that took part in this expedition are shown in Table XVIII.

Brigadier-General A. G. Hammond, V.C., commanded troops on the line of communication with the base at Nowshera, consisting of a mountain battery and three battalions of infantry.* Two lofty passes lay on the line of operations—the Janbatai, 6,000 feet, and the Lowarai, 10,000 feet, above sea-level—and only pack transport was possible. Baggage had therefore to be reduced to the absolute minimum. Each officer was allowed 40 pounds and each man 10 pounds, but, in spite of this very modest allowance, 30,669 pack-animals had to be collected to supply the force with the necessary military stores and the absolute necessities of life. The concentration of the troops at Nowshera was effected without a hitch, and the force was ready to move off in seventeen days from the date of the order to mobilize.

There were three points at which the British frontier might be crossed—the Malakand, Shakot, and Morah Passes—each about 3,500 feet high, and at intervals of about seven miles. It was desired to disturb the frontier tribes as little as possible, and for this reason the Government of India issued the proclamation already mentioned to the people of Swat and Bajaur, and it was decided to make no use of the Morah Pass. Moreover, time was of the greatest consideration. Not only had no news been received from Chitral since the commencement of the outbreak, but it was known that the whole population, elated with two initial successes, was up in arms. It was calculated that the garrison at Chitral had provisions to last them only up to the end of April, and Lieutenants Edwardes and Fowler were known to be prisoners in the hands of Umra Khan. In spite of the Government's proclamation, all three passes were reported strongly held, so it was decided to threaten Morah and Shakot, and make the main attack on the Malakand.

Sir Robert Low's force left Nowshera on April 1. The 1st Brigade were detailed to threaten Shakot, and then

---

* No. 4 (Hazara) Mountain Battery, 1st Battalion East Lancashire Regiment, 29th and 30th Punjab Infantry.

TABLE XVIII

CHITRAL RELIEF FORCE

Major-General Sir R. C. Low, K.C.B.

First Brigade.	Second Brigade.	Third Brigade.	Divisional Troops.
Brigadier-General A. A. Kinloch, C.B.	*Brigadier-General H. G. Waterfield.*	*Brigadier-General W. F. Gatacre, D.S.O.*	11th Bengal Lancers (11th Lancers). Guides Cavalry. 15th Field Battery Royal Artillery (15th Battery Royal Field Artillery). 3rd Mountain Battery Royal Artillery (3rd Mountain Battery Royal Garrison Artillery). 8th Mountain Battery Royal Artillery (8th Mountain Battery Royal Garrison Artillery). No. 2 (Derajat) Mountain Battery (22nd Derajat Mountain Battery). Three Companies Sappers and Miners. Engineer Field Park. Half British Field Hospital. Two Native Field Hospitals. No. 1 Veterinary Field Hospital. Maxim Gun Detachment 1st Battalion Devonshire Regiment.
1st Battalion Bedfordshire Regiment. 1st Battalion King's Royal Rifles. 15th Sikhs. 37th Dogras.	2nd Battalion King's Own Scottish Borderers. 1st Battalion Gordon Highlanders. 4th Sikhs (54th Sikhs). Guides Infantry.	1st Battalion East Kent Regiment. 2nd Battalion Seaforth Highlanders. 25th Punjab Infantry (25th Punjabis). 2nd Battalion 4th Gurkhas.	

NOTES.—One British and one Native Field Hospital was attached to each Brigade.

In addition to the above, troops were detailed for the line of communication, a reserve brigade at Rawal Pindi, and a movable column at Abbottabad.

The 15th Field Battery Royal Artillery did not go farther north than Dargai.

close on the main body opposite the Malakand, while the cavalry demonstrated against the Morah Pass. On April 3 the Malakand was carried by the 2nd Brigade, supported by the 1st, with the 3rd in reserve.

"The enemy's position extended along the crest of the pass, holding the heights on either flank, while a series of breastworks built of stone, each commanding the one below, were pushed down the main spurs. The position was of extraordinary strength, and one which in the hands of an organized enemy would have taken a week to capture. The enemy's numbers were afterwards found to be about 12,000, about half of whom were occupied in carrying off the killed and wounded, fetching water, and bowling down huge rocks on the assaulting columns. The extent of the position may be put down at one and a half miles."*

The Guides and 4th Sikhs were ordered to ascend the hills and turn the enemy's right, but owing to the precipitous nature of the ground and the determined opposition of the enemy their progress was slower than was expected, and ultimately the frontal attack had to be begun before the effect of the turning movement on the British left had fully developed. Covered by the fire of the guns, the Gordons on the right and the King's Own Scottish Borderers on the left advanced up two parallel spurs, supported by the King's Royal Rifles and the 15th Sikhs, who made their way up a water-course between the King's Own Scottish Borderers and the Guides. The Bedfords and the 37th Dogras carried out a turning movement against the enemy's left, and, when the position was carried, pursued the retreating tribesmen down to the Swat River. The crest of the hills was from 1,000 to 1,500 feet above the plain and the slope very steep, which may have accounted for the small loss sustained by the British force.

The advance was made without a check, and near the crest the whole line halted to gather strength for the final rush; the assault followed, and in five hours from the commencement of the engagement the position was won. The enemy were well protected by the rocks, and defended themselves with great gallantry; but finding their retreat threatened and pressed in front by the resolute British advance, they were compelled to give way, and streamed away down the hills towards the

* "The Relief of Chitral," p. 64.

Swat River. Their loss was estimated at from 1,200 to 1,500 men, while the casualties on the British side numbered only 70 killed and wounded. Following up his victory, Sir Robert Low sent on two battalions of the 1st Brigade to Khar, on the Swat River, while the remaining two battalions bivouacked on the crest of the pass, with the 2nd Brigade at the foot on the south side. Less than seven rounds per man were fired by the British troops, and only two men were killed and eighteen wounded.

April 4 was spent in passing the transport over the pass, but the operation would not have been completed then had not a disused track, used by the King's Royal Rifles the day before in their advance, been improved and utilized to supplement the ordinary road. The whole of the 1st Brigade was concentrated in the Swat Valley, but, being threatened by a body of 2,000 tribesmen who came down into the plains towards evening, after hovering about all day in the hills in the direction of the other two passes, it was joined by a small body of fifty of the Guides Cavalry.* The cavalry at once manoeuvred to catch the enemy in the open, and, seizing a favourable opportunity, were in among the astonished tribesmen before they could gain the hills. The charge was most effective, and the moral effect immense. At least 250 of the enemy are said to have been killed, while the losses on our side did not reach double figures. Accounts of the terrible prowess of the cavalry were spread far and wide across the hills, and the fear of being caught at close quarters by that arm was a veritable sword of Damocles to the tribesmen for the rest of the campaign.

On the two following days reconnaissances were made for fords across the Swat River and to keep touch with the enemy. No enemy were seen on the 5th, but on the 6th a force of about 4,500 were found in a strong position defending the river. The Guides Cavalry and 11th Bengal Lancers, supported by the 14th Sikhs, were then sent up-stream to cross higher up, and turn the enemy's flank, while the guns and infantry opened a long-range fire on the position in front. The cavalry charged and pursued the fugitives, cutting down about 100 of them, while the guns and infantry accounted for 300 more. Crossing the swollen river armpit deep, the infantry seized the strongly constructed fort of Chak-

---

* Under Captain Adams.

dara, while the sappers set to work to construct a bridge, and cavalry patrols pushed on to the Panjkora River.

The Panjkora River was found to be in flood, and impassable for infantry; but on the night April 12/13 the Guides Infantry succeeded in getting across by a foot-bridge, constructed during the day with logs of wood and telegraph wire. Before further troops could cross, however, the bridge was washed away, and the Guides were left isolated on the far bank in the presence of some 9,000 of the enemy, who were reported to be in the neighbourhood. The instructions given to Colonel Battye, commanding the Guides, were to clear the enemy off the hills overlooking the place where the bridge had been, whence they were able to fire on working parties. This Colonel Battye proceeded to do in the morning with his battalion single-handed. The hills were cleared and some hostile villages burnt without difficulty; but when the retirement to the river began, the tribes-men adopted the tactics of which they are so fond—closing in and harassing the flanks and rear of the troops. To reach their entrenched position the Guides had to retire down a mountain-side and cross the Jandol River, which flows into the Panjkora River close by. They were attacked by the enemy in two strong columns on both banks of the Jandol River, that on the right pressing them directly, while that on the left endeavoured to cut off their retreat. The retirement was conducted in the way all such operations should be conducted in this class of warfare. It was extremely deliberate, and the fire discipline perfect. To check the advance of the enemy on the left bank and secure the line of retreat, two companies, who had been guarding the remains of the bridge, moved to the assistance of their comrades, while the whole of the 2nd Brigade, a battery of artillery, and a maxim, lined the east bank of the Panjkora River to cover the retirement of the Guides. Between the foot of the hills and the Jandol River was a strip of level ground where the enemy pressed forward with great daring, but were invariably repulsed with heavy loss by the steady fire of the Guides. Some of the tribesmen even tried to cross the Jandol River, but, encountering the flank fire of the 2nd Brigade, none of them succeeded in reaching the far bank.

"During the day the enemy, who numbered 5,000, lost from 500 to 600 men; the Guides' total loss was

13

only about 20, a result due to the skilful manner in which the retirement was effected, as well as to the fine cover afforded by the broken ground on the mountain-side."*

In this operation, however, the Guides unfortunately sustained the loss of their commanding officer, Lieutenant-Colonel F. D. Battye, who was killed just as his regiment reached the level ground bordering the Jandol River. A night attack was expected, and preparations were made accordingly; but, though contemplated, no disturbance took place, owing, it is said, to the terrifying effect produced by a star-shell.

A halt of two days had to be made at the Panjkora River to give time for the construction of a suspension bridge,† during which time Major Deane, Political Officer to the force, entered into negotiations with Umra Khan, as the result of which Lieutenants Edwardes and Fowler were set at liberty, thus removing a grave source of anxiety. No news, however, was obtained of the beleaguered garrison at Chitral, and in the hope of relieving pressure there it was arranged that the Khan of Dir, who was loyal to the British cause, should push on with 1,000 levies in that direction. On April 17 the enemy made their last show of resistance near Umra Khan's fort at Munda. The 3rd Brigade was engaged in this skirmish, but it was of very short duration, for Umra Khan soon abandoned the fort, and he and his following rapidly disappeared across the hills in the direction of Nawagai. Munda was occupied, and in it among other things of interest was found " a letter from a Scotch firm in Bombay, offering to provide Umra Khan with every luxury in the way of arms and ammunition, from maxim guns at Rs. 3,700 each, down to revolvers at Rs. 34 apiece. Luckily, the benevolent intentions of this patriotic firm had been frustrated by the astute intervention of Major Deane, at that time Deputy-Commissioner of Peshawar. The firm in question has found it expedient to transfer itself and the blessings to humanity which it provides to Cairo."‡

All opposition was now at an end, and nothing remained but to march on Chitral and congratulate the gallant little garrison on their successful defence.

---

* " The Relief of Chitral," p. 82.

† Made in forty-eight hours by Major Aylmer, V.C., R.E., out of logs and telegraph-wire.

‡ " The Relief of Chitral," p. 94.

The Buffs, a company of the 4th Gurkhas, and No. 2 (Derajat) Mountain Battery, were deputed to push on over the Lowarai Pass to Chitral under General Gatacre with ten days' supplies, while the remainder of the force guarded the line of communication. In spite of the snow on the pass and the difficulties of the road, General Gatacre reached Chitral on May 15, and the subjects of Shuja-ul-Mulk saw European troops for the first time. On the morning of the 16th Sir Robert Low arrived at Chitral with a company of the Seaforth Highlanders, and at a parade of the British Agent's escort and the two relief columns, complimented the gallant defenders of the fort and Colonel Kelly's men on their brilliant achievements.

Sher Afzul was captured shortly afterwards with 1,500 of his followers, and marched down into India under escort. As for the Chitralis, they seemed to have no spirit left in them ; they were heartily sick of fighting, and bitterly regretted having been led astray by the misrepresentations of the British power made to them by Umra Khan's Pathans. As has already been stated, the inhabitants of Dir had been loyal throughout. The Swatis opposed our advance through their territory, but, being at heart men of peace, found no difficulty in submitting to the new *régime* and turning their swords into ploughshares. Some three months later the future policy of the Government of India with regard to Chitral was decided and approved by the Secretary of State. It was determined to hold Chitral for three reasons : firstly, because the people were clearly unable to stand alone ; secondly, to watch the frontier ; and, thirdly, to establish British prestige in the district, a most important consideration in dealing with these impressionable Eastern tribes. The British garrison in the country was fixed at two battalions of Indian infantry, two mountain guns, and one company of sappers, stationed at Kila Drosh, 24 miles from Chitral, and 130 miles distant from the Punjab frontier, with a detachment of half a battalion at Chitral. The Malakand Pass was to be held by two Indian infantry battalions, a mountain battery, and a company of sappers; the bridge over the Swat River was to be guarded by another battalion of Indian infantry, and the road from the Swat River to Kila Drosh was to be kept open by 250 Swat and 500 Dir levies. Since then it has been found possible to reduce this garrison, and the Indian Army List for July, 1911,

gives the following as the present force maintained
between Malakand and Chitral :

> Detachment Indian Cavalry.
> Detachment Frontier Garrison Artillery.
> One Section of a Mountain Battery.
> One Section Sappers and Miners.
> Three Battalions Indian Infantry.

Thus within six weeks of the first outbreak peace was
firmly restored once more. In this short space of time
were included a memorable defence, a brilliant march
through some of the most difficult country in the world,
and some of the most decisive actions as regards actual
physical effect in the history of Indian frontier warfare.
The campaign is rich in valuable examples, from the
teaching of which many of the precepts of the present
day are derived. No account, however, would be complete without some tribute to the loyalty and devotion
displayed by the troops of His Highness the Maharaja
of Kashmir. Most of them had not been in action before,
and if the ordeal of their baptism of fire was trying, it is
all the more to their credit that they never swerved from
their loyalty for one instant, and emerged triumphant in
the end.

CHAPTER XIII

THE CHITRAL CAMPAIGN : REVIEW

In reviewing the Chitral campaign in search of lessons for the future, there is one point which stands forth pre-eminent. Whether, figuratively speaking, we are accompanying Colonel Kelly across the snows of the Shandur Pass, and through the defiles of the Chitral Valley, whether for the time being we are fighting for our lives with a mob of desperate foes on every side, or whether we are following Sir Robert Low upwards from the plains of India, nothing is more striking than the influence of moral considerations in this campaign. The effect of this dominating factor has been noticed before, and it will be noticed again ; but nothing can be lost, and much may be gained, by making the emphasis laid upon it as strong as possible. In India the three great lessons which have been taught in the past from our constant wars in that country have been : " Never refuse battle," " Never show a sign of hesitation," and " When you get the enemy on the run, keep him there." All three precepts are well illustrated in the operations under consideration. At Chokalwat Colonel Kelly lost no time in launching his 300 men to the attack of a strong position, nor was the slightest hesitation displayed in proving the futility of the formidable Nisa Gol as an obstacle to determined men. Careful reconnaissance was followed in both cases by resolute and well-directed attack. The advance of our infantry to the assault of the Malakand Pass, and the action of the Guides at the Panjkora River, are further illustrations of the happy results of this absence of hesitation. The principle has been the same, whatever the period and whatever the surroundings ; and if as a set-off to our Plassys, our Delhis, or our Charasias, we have an occasional Maiwand, the result will generally be found to be due not to any hesitation on the part of the commander or his troops, but to other causes.

During the advance of Sir Robert Low the cavalry were always to the fore following up the flying enemy, and the immense moral effect they produced (to say nothing of the physical) was abundantly shown in the Swat Valley. After the Malakand Pass had been carried, our infantry were pushed on to prevent the tribesmen gathering in strength to oppose the passage of the Swat River, and Colonel Kelly gave the Chitralis no time to rally for a stand after crossing the Nisa Gol.

In his instructions to his officers Skobeleff said : "Do not forget that in Asia he is the master who seizes the people pitilessly by the throat and imposes upon their imagination." Whatever may be said of the first sentiment, there can be no two opinions about the latter. It is well known that rumours travel like magic among uncivilized races. One has only to notice from the events at Chitral following the death of Aman-ul-Mulk, for instance, how readily these Eastern people transfer their allegiance from one ruler to another. They are children who need the firm hand of a master, not only to protect them from outside enemies, but to save them from themselves, and, above all, they require that behind the firm hand there must be a strong arm. They are swift to respect power, but equally swift to perceive the least sign of weakness ; a desire to be on the winning side is, after all, only human nature, and these men are familiar with many terrible examples from past history of the consequences of being on the wrong side. Mahmud of Ghazni, Timurlane, and Nadir Shah did not cross the passes of North-Western India without leaving their mark behind them.

The initial successes of the Chitralis at Koragh over Captain Ross, at Reshun over Lieutenant Edwardes, and at Chitral during the reconnaissance on March 3, only seemed to them to confirm the statements of Umra Khan's men that the British power was no longer paramount ; the result was that the whole country west of the Shandur Pass was against us. Mention has already been made of Colonel Kelly's anxiety as to the attitude of the small states in the neighbourhood of Gilgit, and we have seen how his resolute advance and skilful avoidance of any contretemps—moral effect alone—was sufficient to reassure any waverers that the British power was as great as ever.

The converging lines of the relief columns undoubtedly had the effect of relieving the pressure round Chitral.

Neither Umra Khan nor Sher Afzul were strategists of sufficient merit to appreciate the possibilities of acting on interior lines, and even if they had been so, their followers were certainly not sufficiently trustworthy to undertake operations requiring a high order of discipline and power of combination. The hostile forces were therefore scattered over the whole theatre of war, and were strong enough nowhere to achieve success. The success of convergent lines of operation in this class of warfare is also illustrated in the three invasions of Afghanistan, and in the Bazar Valley Expedition of 1878.

As regards armament, the enemy were almost as well armed as ourselves. In Chitral Martini-Henry and Snider rifles were opposed by precisely similar weapons. The question naturally arises how these arms came to be there. No doubt some had been stolen from India, but possibly the letter found at Munda by Sir Robert Low's force may furnish another explanation. It is deeply to be regretted that as long as customers can be found willing to pay a sufficiently remunerative price, there will be firms willing to supply munitions of war that they know may, in all probability, be used even against their own countrymen.

In addition to whatever moral effect they may have produced, the guns with Colonel Kelly's column were undoubtedly of great practical value. They were only 7-pounder R.M.L. guns—antiquated even in 1895—but they were used with great effect on the enemy's sangars. The ranges at which they were used were short—even as little as 275 yards—but 1,200 yards is about the limit of effective range of this gun. They were handled with boldness, and gave the closest support to the infantry, so they seem to have fully justified the labour of transporting them across the Shandur Pass.

As regards the infantry, volleys were used almost to the exclusion of independent firing, at any rate by the defenders of Chitral and by Colonel Kelly's force. Apart from any question of the fire discipline of the day, the reason probably was that a considerable portion of the troops were not experienced soldiers. It is well known that men of this kind will sometimes fire away large quantities of ammunition in the excitement of the moment if left to themselves. Transport, as we have seen, was almost unobtainable, and consequently the expenditure of ammunition had to be carefully controlled. We know that independent firing at night was forbidden at Chitral; moreover, there was another serious objection to the unnecessary use of the rifles. This was apparent during the siege of Chitral ; for three weeks before relief came 14 per cent. of the rifles in the fort were useless. These rifles may have been old before hostilities began, but, if so, it points very clearly to the necessity of having nothing but sound serviceable weapons in the hands of troops in exposed situations who may be called upon to make use of their arms in deadly earnest at any moment.

Just as the Tyrolese caused great embarrassment to the French in 1809, the showers of stones that the Chitralis were able to roll down the hillsides in selected places on to troops passing along the road below proved a most formidable obstacle. The only way to overcome the difficulty is to detach flankers up the hillsides to get above the enemy and cause their withdrawal, as was done with success at Chokalwat.

The difficulties of both relief columns in the matter of transport, owing to the execrable roads, have already been noticed. Colonel Kelly was able to live on the country to some extent, but that, of course, was impossible for the much larger force under Sir Robert Low. North of Chitral coolies were always scarce and sometimes unobtainable. Lieutenant Moberly had to march from Mastuj to the relief of the survivors of Captain Ross's party without transport at all. Until he got to Mastuj Colonel Kelly could only collect sufficient coolies to move half his force at a time. Many escaped at Ghizr, and throughout those that were secured had to be carefully guarded. The coolies with Captain Ross apparently were not guarded, and fled at the first shots.

With both columns baggage had to be cut down to an absolute minimum, and the weight of the kit they had to carry told heavily on the 32nd Pioneers when battling with the snow of the Shandur Pass. The moral is plain : History will repeat itself. In peace men must gain experience in carrying heavy loads under unfavourable conditions. An order to this effect is no doubt unpopular to some, but what of that ? It is a steep climb to Parnassus ; all experience that is of real value is more or less painful. Everyone knows that there is a distinct art in the arrangement and method of securing a load that a man has to carry ; the lightest article will be a burden if it is not suitably placed. The nature of the country to be traversed is not the least important consideration in the problem as to how weight is to be distributed. The coolie of the plains, where the ground is flat, carries his load on his head ; but the man of the hills has to throw his body forward to help him in ascending the steep slopes he meets, consequently he puts his load on his back. Some say that a man very soon learns to accommodate himself to circumstances, and that practice makes him cunning. Doubtless this is true enough, but it must be remembered that the first few marches, when the marching power of men is seldom at its best, may easily be the critical time of a campaign. We have seen in this instance what effect initial success has on imaginative tribesmen ; it will, therefore, always be of the utmost importance to leave no stone unturned to remove every possible risk of initial failure. On the North - West Frontier of India transport and supply difficulties make it imperative that no larger force be employed than is absolutely necessary for the attainment of the object in view. Consequently, every available man must be at the decisive point at the appointed time ; moreover, he must arrive fit for anything he may be called upon to do. If, then, he has already wasted energy in finding out what he might have learnt in time of peace, when called upon to carry his own kit, is not that giving a gratuitous handicap to fortune ? The nature of transport employed on the line of communication of Sir Robert Low's force is most interesting, and has been considered so instructive that it is given in Lieutenant-Colonel Brunker's " Notes on Organization and Equipment " as a typical example of the various kinds of animals that may be used on a North-West Frontier expedition. The plate given in Lieutenant-Colonel Brunker's book is reproduced on page 202.

Turning to the defence of Chitral for any special points brought out there, in addition to those already mentioned, the first thing that comes to mind is the reconnaissance on March 3, at the very beginning of the crisis. It will be remembered that half the whole force, and four out of five combatant officers, took part in this operation ; that it resulted certainly in gaining unmistakable evidence of the attitude and numbers of the people, but at the cost of two officers, one of whom died, and the other was incapacitated for the whole siege, besides no less than fifty-six other casualties. Moreover, the losses sustained by the Kashmir Infantry had a most unfortunate effect on their *moral* for the greater part of the siege. These facts point to the conclusion that the strength of the reconnoitring force was unnecessarily

LINE OF COMMUNICATION, CHITRAL CAMPAIGN
1895

Scale of Miles

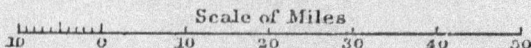

L. of C. Naushera
to Chitral, 1895

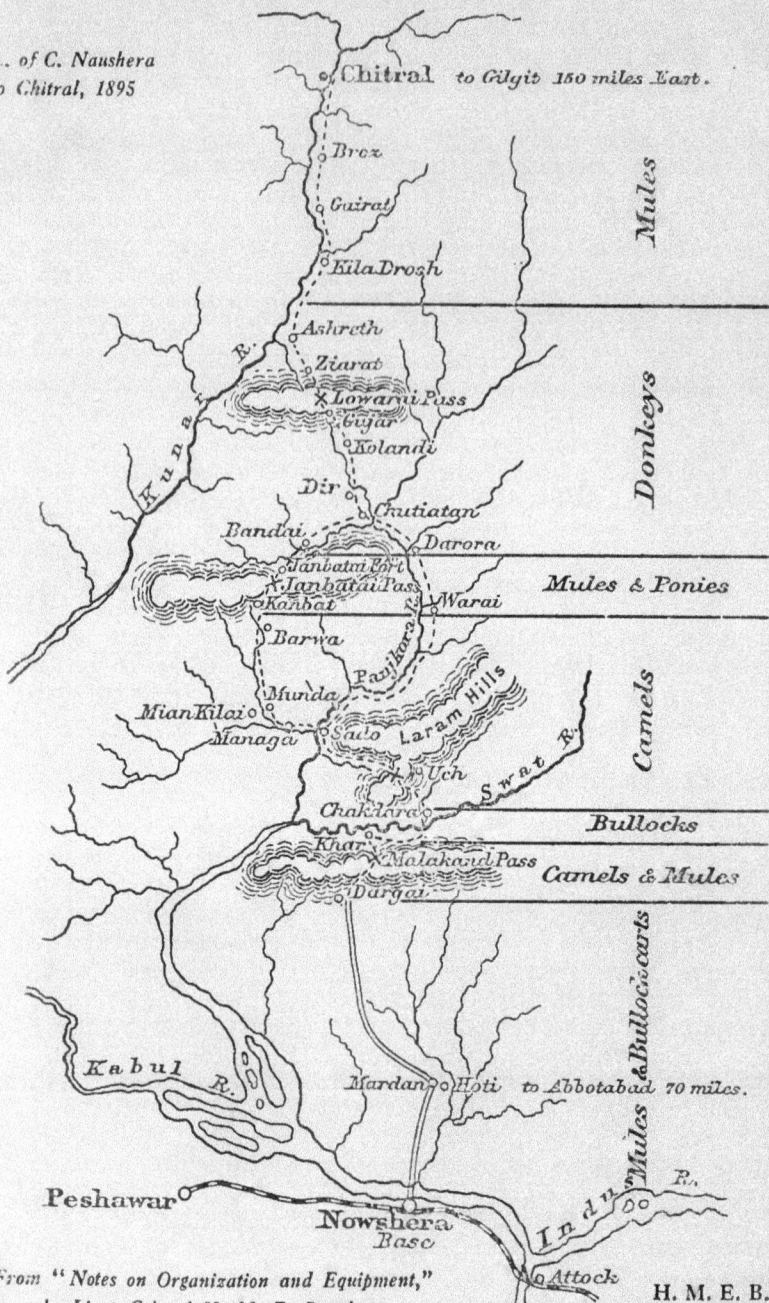

Chitral   to Gilgit 150 miles East.

Brez

Gairat

Kila Drosh

Ashreth

Ziarat

Lowarai Pass

Gujar

Kolandi

Dir

Chutiatan

Bandai   Darora

Janbatai Fort

Janbatai Pass

Kanbat   Warai

Barwa

Panjkora

Munda

Mian Kilai

Managa   Sado   Laram Hills

Uch

Chakdara

Khar   Malakand Pass

Dargai

Mules

Donkeys

Mules & Ponies

Camels

Bullocks

Camels & Mules

Mules & Bullock-carts

Kabul R.

Mardan   Hoti   to Abbotabad 70 miles.

Indus R.

Peshawar

Nowshera
Base

Attock

From " Notes on Organization and Equipment,"
by Lieut.-Colonel H. M. E. Brunker

H. M. E. B.
1907

strong for the purpose of obtaining information, and dangerously weak to attack an enemy of unknown strength. One of our handbooks, published exactly ten years after the Chitral Campaign, says, on the subject of strong reconnoitring parties :

"When it is uncertain whether a position is occupied in strength or not, and it is impossible to determine the fact by any other means, recourse may be had to a reconnaissance in force. But this method of clearing up the situation involves so many disadvantages that it should never be employed unless the necessity is urgent. If only a portion of the force is used, it may be exposed to the counter-attack of far superior numbers, and in open country might find it most difficult to withdraw."*

This is exactly what happened at Chitral. In the same volume, from which the above quotation is taken, it says also, under the head of the composition of reconnoitring parties : "Not a man or horse more than is required should be employed. It should be remembered that a few bold men can often bring back information which a larger body of men would find it impossible to obtain."†

In the case under discussion there seems no reason to suppose that a patrol or two could not have gained all the information required, without incurring any loss of either life or *moral*. As it was, when the enemy was met, the British force was too large to withdraw without fighting. To refuse battle would probably have had precisely the same effect on the esteem in which the Chitralis held the garrison as the subsequent costly retirement. From this incident, then, we may deduce the maxim in dealing with hill-tribes—beware of the risk of having to give battle unless you are prepared to face any conditions likely to arise. A reverse or loss of *moral* incurred by a detachment of more than one-eighth of the total force will probably affect the *moral* of the whole.

Besides the construction of cover and clearing of the foreground, the extremely systematic way in which the defence of the Chitral Fort was conducted is deserving of notice. Every man had his duties assigned to him, whether he was a soldier or non-combatant ; the most was made of a limited supply of material, and the officers did

* "Combined Training, 1905," section 112 (8). In "Field Service Regulations," Part I., 1909, the successor to the 1905 manual, reconnaissances in force are not even mentioned.
† "Combined Training, 1905," section 97 (1).

all they could by personal example to prevent depression among the troops. The water-supply was naturally the most vulnerable point of the defence, and both at Chitral and with Lieutenant Edwardes at Reshun the enemy were not slow to perceive it. The food and ammunition supply was carefully husbanded from the first, and due precautions were taken against treachery within. The danger of posting inexperienced troops in responsible positions is exemplified in the dangerous situation on April 7, when the south-east tower was set on fire, presumably through want of vigilance ; also the repetition of the attempt the following day brings out how no opening should be left to an observant enemy of profiting by a too regular system of patrols and reliefs.

We now come to the sorties of small parties of the various besieged detachments. Of course, the most important was Lieutenant Harley's at Chitral, but there were also two others which should be noticed—Lieutenant Fowler's at Reshun, to clear the road to the river, and Lieutenant Moberly's at Mastuj, to clear the enemy out of a sangar whence they were annoying the garrison. All three in their different degrees are happy examples of how such operations should be conducted. The force employed was kept as small as possible, thus surprise was made easier ; all three were delivered with the greatest resolution, hence the small loss sustained and the decisive effect upon the enemy ; the bayonet—the weapon of such enterprises—was well *en évidence*.

Every frontier war brings out the sensitiveness of these hill-tribes to movements threatening their line of retreat, and their dislike of having an enemy above them. Every offensive engagement fought by our troops in this campaign illustrates this fact to a greater or less degree —in fact, the strategical plan of campaign was on this principle. While Sir Robert Low engaged the main body in front, Colonel Kelly came in from a flank and completed the discomfiture of the enemy. The engagement of the Guides at the Panjkora River on April 13 furnishes yet another instance of a well-conducted and successful retirement, and illustrates the daring shown by these frontier warriors in the pursuit of their favourite tactics ; but the question of retirements will be discussed more fully in the study of the 1897 campaigns.

The hardships, the difficulties, and the brilliant ultimate success of Colonel Kelly's march will already have been fully appreciated ; it only remains to draw our lesson from it as a whole as distinct from the lessons it has been sought to draw from separate incidents. It adds another to the long list of achievements that History records which make it rash to say that in a military sense anything is impossible. Where there is the will there is almost invariably a way. The Chitralis thought it impossible for troops to cross the Shandur Pass in its condition at the beginning of April, but they were mistaken; the mutineers thought it impossible for European troops to march hundreds of miles through the plains of India in the middle of the hot weather, yet this was what General Havelock, Sir Colin Campbell, and Sir Hugh Rose actually did. Napoleon crossed the St. Bernard Pass in the winter of 1800, and Moncey the St. Gothard, to concentrate for Marengo ; General San Martin crossed the Andes from east to west in thirteen days in 1817, to fall on the rear of the Spaniards and secure the independence of Chili ; in 1813, when Napoleon was in Bohemia, and the allies threatened to cut him off from Dresden, he marched ninety miles in three days with 80,000 men, and saved his army; in 1880 General Kuropatkin, marching from Khiva to take part in General Skobeleff's siege of Geok Tepe, covered 266 miles of sandy, waterless desert in eighteen days. These are only a few of the memorable achievements History records ; but it is not only in the matter of marching that the apparently impossible has been accomplished. The possibility of coming under artillery fire from the top of Coleskop was a contingency not contemplated by the Boers in 1899; the German transport and supply arrangements proved equal to the sudden change of direction when the great strategic wheel of the 3rd and 4th Armies was made towards Sedan ; the Dutch Fleet in the Texel was charged across the ice by French cavalrymen mounted. Other feats will occur to the mind of the student of military history, but these are sufficient to justify the assertion that the word "impossible" is one that should be received by military men with the greatest caution. Another dictum of Skobeleff's was—"To conquer you must know how to surprise."

It is always difficult to criticize operations which for one reason or another have ended in misfortune ; the more recent they are the greater does that difficulty become. Yet it often happens that more is to be learnt by trying to investigate the causes of failure, so as to take warning for the future, than by applauding the apparent ease with which success has been achieved. It is very easy to be wise after the event when the fog of war has lifted, and the whole theatre of war is bathed in the fierce light of posthumous knowledge. Anyone who has ever commanded the smallest military unit, even at a field day, will be able to appreciate the position of a commander who, in war, has to decide on the spur of the moment what his course of action is to be when lives, and not marks or men temporarily out of action, are at stake. Experience undoubtedly makes men swift to applaud, but slow to condemn. On more than one occasion the writer has heard the late Major-General Clements,* who always commanded the respect and confidence of those under him both in peace and war, say, when criticizing a point of minor tactics, "I never like to say anyone is wrong." There are certain principles which must be duly considered in war, but no hard-and-fast rules ; though we think we may feel quite sure, still it is really impossible to do more than conjecture whether a certain course of action would or would not have succeeded under a particular set of circumstances.

Having thus, it is hoped, successfully repudiated all but the very best motives in seeming to sit in judgment on the actions of brave men who did their best in a most difficult situation, it is now possible to proceed to try and draw what lessons we can from the mishap to the party under Captain Ross at the Koragh defile. It was an ideal place for an ambuscade—a narrow gorge flanked by lofty mountains and commanded at both ends by steep cliffs. The enemy were holding the farther end of the defile, and directly the party was fairly inside, they came down the hills and threw up sangars, closing the rear end. Had the main body waited to enter the gorge until the advanced guard had passed through, and reported the way clear and themselves in position at the far end, the advanced guard probably would still have suffered some loss from the fire of the ambushed tribesmen, but the main body might not have been involved. The force might have fallen back on Mastuj, and, having got reinforcements and recruited their transport, found and tried the way taken by Colonel Kelly five weeks later. The fact, then, that the whole force entered the defile before it had been traversed from end to end by troops

* Major-General R. A. P. Clements, C.B., D.S.O., late commanding 4th (Quetta) Division.

in advance seems to have been the primary cause of the disaster. As matters were, it is, at any rate, a matter for conjecture whether it would not have been better to have persevered in the attempt to break out on the night of the 8th ; the loss could not well have been greater than that which was eventually incurred. Each hour's delay gave time for fresh enemies to arrive, enabled them to strengthen their position, and last, but not least, increased their confidence of victory. The surmise is supported by the fact that when a desperate attempt to escape was made on the night of April 9/10, it met with success, though at terrible cost. In spite of the heavy fire and avalanches of stones rolled down the side of the hill, the sangars were cleared with great gallantry at the point of the bayonet, Captain Ross himself killing four men with his revolver before meeting his end.

The position taken up by the survivors at Buni was unsatisfactory for defence, but we are told that no transport was available for the wounded, all the coolies having disappeared ; still, if the force had been able to reach Mastuj unassisted, it would have obviated the necessity for a relief expedition, with all the risks attendant to small parties in the state the country was in then. We know, however, that Lieutenant Moberly's emissaries failed to get news of the fate of Lieutenant Edwardes and Captain Ross ; therefore any men sent out by Lieutenant Jones to communicate with Mastuj must also have been compelled to turn back. That the Chitralis entertained a very profound respect for the fighting qualities of Lieutenant Jones and his fifty men is shown by the fact that they never ventured to attack the little British force, crippled though it was.

One other point deserves notice. The attempt to find a way of escape by the hills raises the question whether it would not have been better to have sent out one or two men to reconnoitre and report, before committing the whole party to one chance. No doubt it was thought that valuable time would be saved if a path were found, and that all the men would be close together ; but still one or two men always have a better chance of carrying out an object undiscovered than a large number.

In all such operations as those under review the British officers are the heart and soul of the enterprise. The more critical the situation, the scarcer they always seem to be, and therefore the more valuable do their lives become. Of course, it is not meant to suggest that

British officers should be unwilling to accept any necessary risk, or be backward in showing a good example to their men; none would entertain the idea for a moment. But in great crises the lives of officers and men are not their own; they have no right to expose them to unnecessary risk without reasonable prospect of furthering the general cause. There are times, no doubt, when officers must expose themselves freely to steady their men, but these occasions are happily very rare. The man in the ranks, whether he be British or Indian, seldom has need of such example; ninety-nine times out of a hundred he would probably resent any such attempt as being tantamount to an aspersion on his courage. In the Chitral campaign there is a very good instance of the embarrassing consequences of the undue exposure of British officers. At Reshun, directly Lieutenants Edwardes and Fowler were captured, the little fort they had made was immediately rushed, though it had already held out successfully for eight days; the moral encouragement to the Chitralis was immense, and the precarious position of the two officers after they became prisoners was a matter for grave anxiety to Sir Robert Low. Lieutenants Edwardes and Fowler had their suspicions that the honey only concealed the poison in the cup, so it does not seem to have been worth while to sacrifice the very practical effect of their continuous presence in the midst of their men for any Quixotic considerations for the feelings of Mahomed Isa and his followers. Two-thirds of the British force were men who could never be expected to stand alone, and these were the first to suffer from the consequences of the sudden removal of a guiding hand.

CHAPTER XIV

1897—1898

In 1897 occurred the most formidable outbreak the British arms have ever been called upon to suppress on the North-West Frontier of India. Various causes more or less probable have been attributed to this outburst, but the one which seems to be at the root of the whole matter was a misunderstanding on the part of the tribes-men of the object of the Durand Mission to Kabul in 1893, and the subsequent demarcation of the frontier. In the chapter devoted to the account of the attack on the British camp at Wana and subsequent operations it has been explained that, owing to the absence of any definite line dividing the spheres of British and Afghan in-fluence, considerable difficulty had arisen in the past in determining which Government was responsible for the infliction of punishment and restoration of order when raids, or other outbreaks, occurred. After some show of reluctance, the Boundary Agreement was at length signed by the Amir Abdur Rahman, and the actual demarcation of the frontier by pillars began. In all probability the Amir was opposed to the conclusion of the agreement, because he feared that the formal recog-nition of a sphere of British influence among the frontier tribes would be only a prelude to permanent annexation, and ultimately cause the removal of the only buffer between his country and India. The tribesmen, also considering the matter from their own point of view, foresaw no result from the agreement but the eventual loss of their jealously guarded independence, and opposed the demarcation of the boundary-line from the very beginning.

The soil was now ready for the sowing of the seed of fanaticism—the second cause of the outbreaks of 1897—and the opportunity was not neglected. From the earliest times political agitators have found that the surest way

to gain the support of wild impressionable tribes is
through the medium of their religious beliefs, but
European nations have little reason to affect superiority
on this score. The Pathan tribesmen are only behind
the times, and the lapse of only a single decade finds
them considerably less so. Before the high-minded citizen
of the civilized West lifts up his hands in righteous
horror at the tales which recent History unfolds before
him, let him turn back the pages a few centuries, and see
whether the record therein of iniquities committed in the
name of religion do not bring him at once to familiar
ground. One has only to look ahead ten years from the
time of which the following pages treat to see that the
tree of knowledge had taken root among the mountain
fastnesses of the Indian borderland. In 1908 great efforts
were made by the spiritual leaders of the frontier tribes
to encompass what would have been the temporal undoing of their flock ; their failure to secure the support
or even the welcome of the Afridis, who are by far the
most powerful section, is a matter of recent memory.

In 1897, however, great success rewarded the exertions
of the mullahs. They made capital out of the result of
the Turco-Greek War ; they announced that the subsidies paid by the Indian Government to the various
tribes were the price of that peace which force of arms
was powerless to insure ; but the prospect of annexation
was a trump-card that they knew well was bound to win
a trick. A good illustration of the kind of story the
tribesmen were asked to believe is afforded by the following translation of a letter which was found with others
in the house of a prominent man during General Kempster's visit to the Waran Valley in November, 1897.

*Translation of a Letter from Kazi Mira Khan and other
Adam Khels composing the Afridi Jirga at Kabul, to
Mullah Saiyid Akbar Aka Khel, dated the 28th Jamadi-
ul-Awal, 1315 A.H. (October 25, 1897).*

"AFTER COMPLIMENTS.—Let it be known to you that
having been appointed by you and other Mussulman
brethren as Jirga to attend on His Highness the Amir,
we arrived here, and held an interview with His Highness, who advised us not to fight with the British Government, and this was and has been his advice ever since.
We said we accepted his advice, but that our wishes
ought to be met by the British Government. We were

ordered to record them in detail, when His Highness said he would, after consideration, submit them to the British Government, and see what reply they would give. We put down our wishes in detail, and presented them to His Highness, who submitted them to the British Government, but no reply has yet been received. We shall see what reply comes.

"There is a British Agent at Kabul who has on his establishment many Hindustani Mussulmans. One of these became our acquaintance. This man is a good Mussulman, and a well-wisher of his co-religionists. He has given us a piece of good and correct news, which is to the following effect :

"'You, Muhammadans, must take care lest you be deceived by the British, who are at present in distressed circumstances. For instance, Aden, a seaport, which was in possession of the British, has been taken from them by the Sultan. The Suez Canal, through which the British forces could easily reach India in twenty days, has also been taken possession of by the Sultan, and has now been granted on lease to Russia. The British forces now require six months to reach India. The friendly alliance between the British and the Germans has also been disturbed on account of some disagreement about trade, which must result in the two nations rising in arms against each other. The Sultan, the Germans, the Russians, and the French, are all in arms against the British at all seaports, and fighting is going on in Egypt against them. In short, the British are disheartened nowadays. The Viceroy and the Generals who are to advance against you have received distinct orders from London that the operations in the Khaibar and Tirah must be brought to an end in two weeks' time, as the troops are required in Egypt and at other seaports. In the case of the Mohmands and people of Gandab, who had killed ten thousand British troops, and had inflicted a heavy loss of rifles and property on them, the British, in their great dismay, concluded a settlement with them for twenty-four rifles only, whereas thousands of rifles and lakhs of rupees should have been demanded. This peace with the Mohmands is by way of deceit, and when the British get rid of their other difficulties, they will turn back and demand from the Mohmands the remaining rifles and compensation for their losses. They will say that as the Mohmands have become British subjects by surrendering twenty-five rifles, they must make good the

remaining loss too. The British are always giving out
that their troops will enter the Khaibar and Tirah on
such and such dates, but they do not march on those
dates, and remain where they are. This is deceitful on
the part of the English, who wish to mislead Mussulmans
by a payment of five rupees, and seek for an opportunity
to make an attack by surprise. I have thus informed
you of the deeds and perplexities of the English.'"

Moreover, a pamphlet issued by the Amir of Afghanistan* about this time did not improve the situation. In
it he says : "The need of those persons who defend the
frontier of Muhammadan territories for one prayer is
equivalent to five hundred prayers of those who stay at
home and do not proceed to the frontier for keeping
watch ;" and, "O true believers, when ye meet a party of
infidels stand firm, and remember God frequently, that
ye may prosper. . . . When ye meet the unbelievers
marching in great numbers against you, turn not your
backs on them, for whoso shall turn his back unto them
on that day, unless he turneth aside to fight or retreateth
to another party of the faithful, shall draw on himself the
indignation of God, and his abode shall be hell : an ill-
journey shall it be thither !"

The attitude of the Amir eventually became so questionable as to call forth a strong remonstrance from the
Government of India, which had the effect of inducing
him to deny all sympathy with the revolting tribesmen,
and to order that his subjects should give neither assistance of any kind to our enemies nor asylum to any armed
refugees.

It is only fair to add that during the operations of 1897
Abdur Rahman preserved a strictly neutral attitude ; he
refused to recognize the religious character of the outbreak, and in warning the tribesmen of their folly said :
"In short, I have nothing to do with your affairs, and no
concern with you, because I have no trust in you. Do
not be led to think that like Sher Ali I am such a fool as
to annoy and offend others for your sake. Your real
object is to make me fight with the British Government,
and if I were to do such a foolish thing, I am sure you
would assume the position of simple spectators."

By the end of July, 1897, the mullahs had done their
work, and the whole frontier rapidly burst into a blaze.
On July 29 the British garrison at Malakand was attacked
and Chakdara invested. The conflagration moved from

* Entitled "Takwim-ud-din."

north to south; Shankargarh was raided by the Mohmands, the Samana forts were beseiged by the Afridis
and Orakzais, and control of the Khaibar Pass was completely lost. The story of each outbreak will now have
to be told separately.

THE TOCHI VALLEY EXPEDITION. (*Map II.*)

In order to get a clear idea of the events that led up to
the Tochi Expedition of 1897 it is necessary to survey
briefly the events of some eight years before. The
Tochi Valley, it will be remembered, is the drainage
channel of the northern portion of the territory of the
Darwesh Khel Waziris. The waters of this river flow
down from the border-hills in an easterly direction, and,
passing Bannu on the left bank, at a point some sixty
miles distant from the Afghan frontier, pour themselves
into the mighty Indus. Following the Indian border-
line southwards from the Kurram, the Tochi Valley is
the next important avenue of approach into India from
the west, and to the south again lies the Gomal Pass,
with Dera Ismail Khan as its *point d'appui.* In October,
1895, the territory of the Dawaris, through which the
Tochi River runs, was annexed by the British Government at the request of the inhabitants, and arrangements
were put in hand at once for the effective government of
the country. A readjustment of the annual allowances
paid to neighbouring clans took place, as well as a
revision of the services for which they were paid, and by
the end of 1896 the following military dispositions had
been made :

"In Southern Waziristan a cantonment had been built
at Wana, held by a battalion of Native Infantry, one
squadron of Native Cavalry, two mountain guns, and
two maxims ; while military posts had been established
at Sarwakai and Jandola, on the Shahar line of communications with Tank. The object of this force was to
safeguard the Gomal and protect Zhob from Waziri
raids by watching the Mahsuds and the Ahmadzai
Darwesh Khels of Wana and Shakai. In Northern
Waziristan the Tochi was held by a military force, with
headquarters at Miram Shah and posts at Idak and
Saiadgi. In the autumn of 1896 both the civil and
military headquarters were transferred from Miram Shah
to Datta Khel, and in the following spring the permanent
strength of the troops was reduced to four guns of a

mountain battery, two maxims, one squadron of Native
Cavalry, and two battalions of Native Infantry."*

In spite of this occupation of the country, however,
the Waziri outrages continued unabated, until finally a
dispute arose over the payment of a fine of Rs. 2,000,
which had been imposed for the murder of a Hindu
writer attached to the levy post at Sheranni, which led
to the famous Maizar outrage, and the subsequent military
expedition. The inhabitants of the group of villages
known as Maizar objected to the payment of their share
of the fine, on the ground that the whole burden should
be borne by the guilty parties, so Mr. H. A. Gee, the
Political Officer of Tochi, arranged to visit the scene of
the dispute and endeavour to obtain a settlement of the
difficulty. With this object in view Mr. Gee, accompanied by the escort shown below, left Datta Khel for
Maizar on June 10, 1897. The description of the locality
and events which took place given in the official account
of the operations of the Tochi Field Force is so clear,
and of so interesting a nature, that it is quoted here
verbatim :

> No. 6 Bombay Mountain Battery, 2 guns.
> 1st Punjab Cavalry, 12 sabres.
> 1st Sikh Infantry, 200.
> 1st Punjab Infantry, 100.
> *Commander* Lieutenant-Colonel A. C. Bunny,
>   1st Sikhs.

"After leaving Datta Khel camp the road traverses for
some eight miles a fairly open valley, till it reaches the
large Madda Khel village of Sheranni, after which it
passes for two and a half miles through low stony hills,
intersected with watercourses running down to the Tochi,
until the low ridge overlooking Maizar is reached. Looking back eastwards from this point, where the road crosses
the ridge (spoken of hereafter as the kotal) the camp at
Datta Khel can be seen in the distance. On the western
side of the kotal, and between it and the right bank of
the Shawal stream, lies the cultivated tract known as
Maizar, a plateau which extends some 2,500 yards from
north to south, and 1,200 yards from east to west, and
has an elevation of 4,600 feet above sea-level. Maizar
consists really of an upper and lower plateau; along
both sides of the former are scattered about a dozen
walled hamlets, or 'kots,' belonging to the Madda Khel,

---

* " Operations of the Tochi Field Force," p. 4.

while the central portion consists of open, terraced fields. The Shawal stream skirts the western edge of the lower plateau, joining the Tochi at the northern end of Maizar Between the two plateaux there is a steep descent of 20 or 30 feet.

"The Bannu-Ghazni Road, after crossing the kotal, skirts the Maizar Plateau for about a quarter of a mile in a northerly direction, and then descends to the Shawal stream, which it crosses by a ford. It continues westward up the right bank of the Tochi, fording the river twice before Dotoi, about four miles above Maizar, is reached. . . . Mr. Gee and his escort reached Maizar at 9.30 a.m. There was no sign of intended hostility ; on the contrary, women and children were seen about the villages. The Maizar maliks appeared to be perfectly friendly, and pointed out a spot under some trees on the edge of the upper plateau where they suggested the troops should halt, while they partook of a meal that was being prepared for the Mussulman sepoys of the escort. This food had, as a matter of fact, been provided by Sadda Khan,* but its proffer was taken at the time as a token of spontaneous hospitality on the part of the Maizarwals. All these circumstances combined to lull the party into a false feeling of security. It is, indeed, doubtful whether Sadda Khan himself at all realized the irritation that existed. He was, of course, aware that the Maizarwals had defied his authority as regards the distribution of the fine, but he seems to have expected that they would be cowed by the appearance of the troops, and to have had no misgivings whatever as to the possibility of an outbreak until some time after the troops reached Maizar.

"The spot selected by the Maizarwals for the troops was close to the walls of a Dreplari village,† and was commanded by several other villages from 200 to 400 yards distant. Colonel Bunny ordered the mountain guns to unlimber close to the garden-wall of the Dreplari village, and drew up the infantry on the outer flank of the guns. As a precaution guards were posted facing outwards, the men were not allowed to pile arms, and each sepoy retained his rifle.

"Directly after the arrival of the troops at Maizar Mr. Gee, with Captain Browne, Royal Artillery, and Lieutenant Higginson, visited Dotoi with an escort of sowars, and in company with the maliks. They returned

---

* Chief of the Madda Khel.
† The Dreplaris are a subsection of the Madda Khel.

at 11.30 to Maizar, at about which hour the promised meal was produced from a neighbouring kot for the Mussulman sepoys; and the whole escort had breakfast, while a jirga was being held on the lower plateau. Suddenly a hubbub began in the village; the villagers who had been listening to the pipes drew off; a man was observed to wave a sword from the top of a tower, and two shots were fired in quick succession from the village, the second of which wounded Lieutenant Seton Browne in the thigh. Firing now commenced from the villages to the south and east, and a hot fire was opened from the Dreplari village on the north. This was directed on the British officers, and Colonel Bunny was almost immediately mortally wounded by a shot in the stomach, but, supported by two sepoys, he continued for some time to direct the operations.

"The guns had first to open with case at 100 yards range on a large number of men who were firing from the entrance of the Dreplari village, and were moving forward to charge the guns. They had not been long in action before Captain Browne, Royal Artillery, was wounded in the upper arm by a bullet which severed the artery, and Lieutenant Cruickshank, Royal Artillery, was twice shot in the right arm. Both officers still continued fighting their guns, and, when the case-shot were expended, shrapnel was fired reversed, thus driving the enemy back into the village. But, as only sixteen rounds per gun had been brought, the ammunition soon began to run short, and Colonel Bunny accordingly gave orders for a retirement to the ridge.

"At the commencement of the firing there had been a general stampede among the baggage-mules, so that when the retirement was ordered most of the reserve ammunition, and much other equipment, had to be abandoned. The enemy now appeared on all sides in great force, but the retirement, which now commenced under such very trying conditions, was carried out with great deliberation, and in the most stubborn and gallant manner. At its commencement Lieutenant Higginson was shot through the arm, and Surgeon-Captain Cassidy in the knee, so that all the British military officers were now wounded, two of them mortally; but they all continued to carry out their duties and lead their men. These circumstances were trying in the extreme for the troops, and their staunchness is worthy of the highest praise. Subadars Narain Singh, 1st Sikhs, Sundar

Singh, 1st Punjab Infantry, and Jemadar Sherzad, 1st Sikhs, behaved with the greatest gallantry. Getting together a party of their men, they made a most determined stand by the wall of a garden, whence they covered the first withdrawal, remaining themselves under hot fire till the enemy closed with them. It was at this spot that Subadar Sundar Singh, 1st Punjab Infantry, was killed, and that by far the greater number of the casualties of the day occurred.

"Under cover of this stand the wounded men were carried and helped away, the guns withdrawing along a lane to a low kotal 300 yards distant, where a fresh position was occupied, and the survivors of the party at the garden-wall then withdrew. At this kotal a fresh stand was made, the guns firing blank to check the enemy, as the service ammunition had been all expended. Here Lieutenant Cruickshank received a third wound, which was instantly fatal. Captain Browne also, who had remained in command of the guns, supported by two men until he fainted from loss of blood, and who had been fastened on to Mr. Gee's pony when the retirement from the village was made, was found to be dead on arrival at the kotal. A further retirement from this kotal now became necessary, and it was carried out by successive units very deliberately, and with complete regularity, positions being held on the ridges stretching from south to north, until the Sheranni Plain was reached about two miles farther east. All this time the enemy was constantly enveloping the flanks, and the main road along which the troops had marched in the morning had to be abandoned, as it was commanded on both sides, and as parties of the enemy were advancing from Sheranni. . . . Eventually, about 5.30 p.m.,* a good position was found about a mile from the last of the above-mentioned ridges; reinforcements began to appear at sight, and the enemy was beaten off. These reinforcements, which had been summoned from the camp at Datta Khel by sowars sent back from the kotal, reached the force about 6.15 p.m. They consisted of two companies of the 1st Sikhs under Lieutenant de Brett, Royal Artillery, accompaned by Lieutenant Stockley, Royal Engineers, bringing up extra ammunition. They had covered the distance from camp (nine miles) in less than an hour and a half.

"With the ammunition now received the heights around

---

* The fact that the retreat over a distance of three miles occupied three and a half hours shows how stubbornly the enemy was resisted.

and the village of Sheranni were shelled, with the result
that the enemy finally retired, and the village was partially
set on fire. The further withdrawal was then unmolested,
and the rear-guard reached camp at 12.30 a.m. . . . The
numbers of the enemy at first were estimated at 500; but
constant reinforcements during the retirement raised the
eventual numbers to probably much over 1,000. They
lost 100 killed and many wounded."*

As soon as news of the Maizar outrage reached the
Government of India, it was decided that a force consisting of two brigades under the command of Major-
General G. Corrie Bird, C.B., should be despatched with
as little delay as possible into the Tochi Valley, to exact
punishment from the treacherous tribesmen. There were
three formidable difficulties in the way of the assembly
of a force of this size west of the Indus at this time of
year. The first was the Indus itself, which in June
becomes greatly swollen by the large volume of water
caused by the melting of the snows among the mountains
to the north. The bridge of boats at Khushalgarh, however, on the Khushalgarh-Kohat route to Bannu had
fortunately not been dismantled, so this route, though
the longest, was selected as the line of communication
with India, and orders were given that the bridge should
be maintained as long as possible. There is no doubt
that "had the outbreak at Maizar occurred a few days
later the bridge at Khushalgarh would have been dismantled as the river rose, and once dismantled its
re-establishment would have been practically impossible
till the month of September. Fortunately, the orders
were issued in time, and the bridge was maintained
throughout the hot weather, and proved of the greatest
value, not only for the Tochi Field Force, but also for the
subsequent operations in Tirah beyond Kohat."†

The other difficulties were the heat and the scarcity of
good water, especially between Kohat and Bannu, a distance of eighty-four miles, which necessitated special
arrangements being made along the line of march for the
protection of the British troops from the sun, and for
the provision of pure water. Owing to the heat by day
the marches were accomplished by night, but tents had
to be provided (and suitably guarded) at the points where
the troops halted. These preparations were made in
eleven days from the date on which the despatch of the
expedition was ordered, and on June 28 the first British

* ' Operations of the Tochi Field Force," pp. 5, 6.   † *Ibid*, p. 11.

unit left Khushalgarh. In the meantime supplies and transport were being collected at Bannu; but much had to be done before the force could move forward, as "at the time of the outbreak there were only one month's supplies in the Tochi for the ordinary garrison of the valley."* Difficulties also arose from the hostility of the tribesmen who infested the Tochi Valley, and made the passage of small parties along the road most unsafe; but at length all preparations were made, and the concentration of the force at Datta Khel was completed by July 19. The composition of the Tochi Field Force is given in Table XIX.

On July 20 the 1st Brigade occupied Sheranni, and the cavalry attached to it went on to Maizar. Both were found deserted, and the next sixteen days were spent destroying the towers and hamlets in the neighbourhood. The only fighting that took place consisted of sniping at night and some attacks on convoys by small parties of the enemy. Strenuous efforts were made by the Madda Khel, in whose territory the British force was operating, to procure assistance from without, but in this they met with little response. Nevertheless, the news of events in the Swat Valley induced the tribesmen to prevaricate over the terms of the inevitable surrender to such an extent that the whole of the Tochi Valley right up to the Afghan frontier had to be overrun systematically before the Madda Khel came to terms on November 15. In the meantime the troops had been suffering severely from the heat and inferior quality of the water at Sheranni—in fact, the number of men in the 3rd Battalion Rifle Brigade incapacitated by sickness became so serious that it was considered advisable in October to order the return of the battalion to India. During the various small expeditions that took place to all parts of the Tochi Valley much useful survey work was done, opportunities being afforded of exploring a large extent of new country before the troops withdrew. The Tochi Field Force was broken up in January, 1898.

THE TOCHI VALLEY EXPEDITION : REVIEW.

The chief moral of the events in the Tochi Valley in 1897 is obvious. From times even earlier than the days of Hector and the siege of Troy the bearers of

* "Operations of the Tochi Field Force," p. 11.

TABLE XIX

TOCHI FIELD FORCE, 1897

Major-General G. Corrie Bird, C.B.

First Brigade.	Second Brigade.
Brigadier-General C. C. Egerton, C.B., D.S.O., A.D.C.	*Brigadier-General W. P. Symons, C.B.*
1st Punjab Cavalry (21st Cavalry), 1 Squadron.	1st Punjab Cavalry (21st Cavalry), 1 Squadron.
No. 3 (Peshawar) Mountain Battery (23rd Peshawar Mountain Battery).	No. 6 (Bombay) Mountain Battery (26th Mountain Battery), 4 guns.
No. 2 Company Bengal Sappers and Miners (2nd Company 1st Sappers and Miners).	3rd Battalion Rifle Brigade.
2nd Battalion Argyll and Sutherland Highlanders.	6th Jat Light Infantry.
1st Sikh Infantry (51st Sikhs).	14th Bengal Infantry (14th Sikhs).
1st Punjab Infantry (55th Coke's Rifles).	25th Bengal Infantry (25th Punjabis).
33rd Bengal Infantry (33rd Punjabis).	

Note.—One British and three Native Field Hospitals were divided between the two Brigades.

gifts have been deserving more of suspicion than un-qualified gratitude. It may seem a cynical suggestion, but it is none the less true, that uncalled-for generosity from unexpected quarters seldom springs from the purest motives. In the East few axes are ground with-out careful preparation, but Asiatic races are not peculiar in this respect; the process is familiar enough in the moral West to put its representatives on their guard. Nevertheless, the number of successful conspiracies re-corded by History, whether against an individual or against a class, points to the conclusion that man is an unsuspecting creature whatever the colour of his skin may be. Society always finds excuses for simplicity, but finds nothing but condemnation for guile. So in the case of the Maizar outrage, it is instructive to investigate the cause of success of the plot; treachery certainly was suspected, but the precautions against it do not appear to have gone farther than a warning to the troops to be on the alert. The position taken up by the escort was, tactically speaking, unsound; the attractions of shady trees for breakfast seem to have overridden more important considerations. The troops had arrived in Maizar nominally as an escort to the Political Officer, but practically to compel the payment of a fine which the tribesmen had resisted for a long time as, in their opinion, unjust; consequently, the most hospitable of welcomes was hardly to be expected, and there must be a reason or motive for a phenomenon or action of an unnatural kind.

The retirement of the troops was conducted with admirable steadiness, but the failure of ammunition for the guns was a serious matter. It is stated that only sixteen rounds were available for each of the two guns which accompanied the escort. This small quantity is soon expended in quite an ordinary situation even by muzzle-loading guns, and what occurred supports the statement that if it is considered worth while to take guns into an exposed situation at all, they should go out fully equipped.

In a supplementary despatch to that describing the Maizar outrage it is stated that "after the two Royal Artillery officers had fallen—that is, almost immediately after the attack began—the gunners continued to fire under the orders of their non-commissioned officers until their ammunition was expended, No. 3 Subdivision firing blank by the Havildar's orders until the mules were ready."* It is not explained how it happened that no shell were available for use with the surplus cartridges; but, passing that by, the use of blank on service is certainly a point which catches the mental eye. It is probable from the wording of the despatch that only quite a few rounds of blank were fired; nevertheless, the same despatch goes on to say that the range at which the guns were firing was only about 100 yards, so the tribesmen could hardly have failed to realize the state of affairs. There is, then, nothing in this incident to cause any qualification of the assertion that if guns are fired at all their fire should be effective. Artillery fire may be ineffective from a variety of causes, but when the cause is the use of blank, as in the example in question, it is almost certain that, so far from frightening the enemy, the only result will be to advertise the otherwise possibly unrecognized fact that the supply of shell is exhausted, or nearly so, and all the moral effect of the guns—their most valuable asset—will be lost.

The record of the operations of the Tochi Field Force, under Major-General Corrie Bird, is one of struggles against climate and Nature rather than a human enemy. The swollen Indus, the heat, and the scarcity of water, are typical of the chief difficulties to be overcome by regular troops in small wars, and the Tochi Valley Campaign of 1897 furnishes an interesting example of how such difficulties may be overcome.

* Supplementary despatch by Lieutenant-Colonel Gray, commanding Tochi Valley troops, to Assistant Adjutant-General Punjab Frontier Force.

CHAPTER XV

THE RISING IN THE SWAT VALLEY

THE DEFENCE OF MALAKAND. (*Map I.*)

AFTER the conclusion of the Chitral Campaign, the arrangements made with the tribes inhabiting the Swat Basin were of so satisfactory a character, and the indications of a new era of unprecedented prosperity were so full of promise, that the gathering of a wave of fanaticism in this quarter was as unexpected as it was to be deplored. Little importance was attached at first to the growth of the new movement, but, towards the end of July, 1897, the gravity of the situation could no longer be ignored, and it was considered necessary to warn the troops stationed in the neighbourhood to hold themselves in readiness for action at the shortest notice. At this time the garrisons of Malakand and Chakdara—both posts on the line of communication with Chitral—were as stated below:

MALAKAND BRIGADE.

Colonel W. H. Meiklejohn, C.B., C.M.G.

MALAKAND.	CHAKDARA.
11th Bengal Lancers, 1 Squadron.	45th (Rattray's) Sikhs, 180.
No. 8 (Bengal) Mountain Battery.	11th Bengal Lancers, 20.
No. 5 Company Madras Sappers and Miners.	
24th Punjab Infantry.	
31st Punjab Infantry.	
45th (Rattray's) Sikhs.	

The Malakand position is described thus in the official account of the Malakand Field Force:

"The Malakand position (see accompanying plan) was somewhat extended: the fort itself had been erected about 600 yards west of the kotal, on a narrow spur running up towards the high hill known as Guides Hill.

223

MALAKAND POSITION

1897

Scale of Yards

200 0 500 1000

North Camp

to Chakdara

1st Position of
X 45th Sikhs
26.VII.97

2nd Position
of 45th Sikhs
26.VII.97

Bazar Serai

The Crater

1

2

3

Political Officer's
House

Road

Malakand Kotal

Signalling
Tower

FORT

Buddhist

Guides
Hill

from Dargai

●● *Piquets*
1 24th Punjab Infantry.
2 Sappers & Miners and Supplies.
3 45th Sikhs

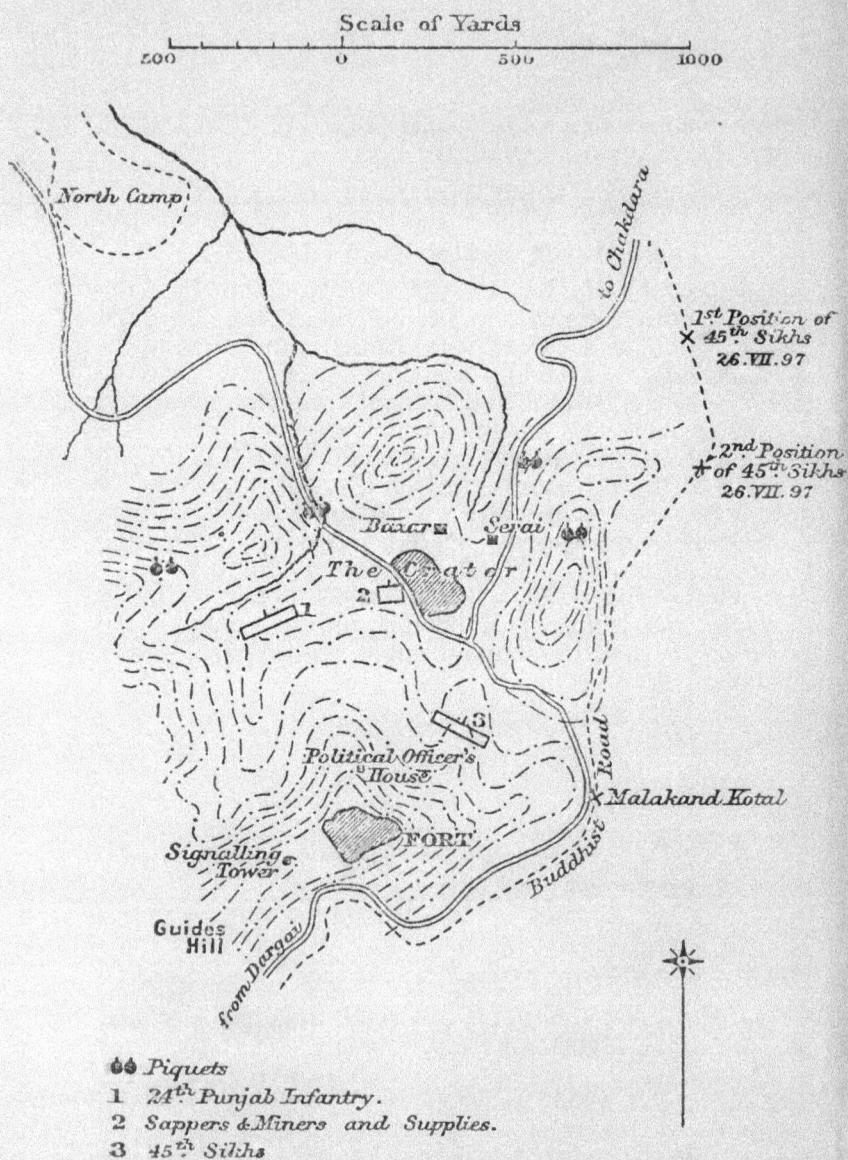

from ' The Operations of the Malakand F.F.

This fort was held by 200 men of the 24th Punjab Infantry, with two 9-pounder smooth-bore guns. Still farther south-west of this fort, at a distance of 1,100 yards from it, on the summit of Guides Hill, was a small one-storied tower with a defensible roof, from whence signalling was maintained with Chakdara signalling tower, nine miles distant in a direct line to the north-east. Immediately in front of the Malakand Fort to the north is an irregular cup-shaped hollow, of about 600 yards in diameter, called the Crater, in and around which were located the camps of the 24th Punjab Infantry, 45th Sikhs, No. 5 Company Queen's Own Madras Sappers and Miners, as well as the Engineer park, Commissariat stores, and bazar. The northern slopes of the spur on which the fort was located were covered with trees and scrub jungle. The central position of this camp was a low, rugged, irregular-shaped mound, around which were located the Sappers and Miners' camp, the Engineer park, and the Commissariat godown and office, the whole being surrounded by a line of abatis and wire entanglement. The remainder of the troops with the transport were encamped on a flat open piece of ground, some 1,300 yards to the north-west outside this hollow. This camp, which was called the North Camp, was protected by low breastworks and by abatis. Communication between the two camps was by means of a broad road, passing through a narrow dip in the spur which lay between the two camps. Both positions were overlooked by the high hills on the east and west."*

On July 26 the situation assumed so grave an aspect that the Guides were summoned from Mardan, and preparations were made for despatching a column to hold the Amandara Pass on the road to Chakdara. Before the latter movement could be carried out, however, news was received at 10 p.m. on July 26 of the approach of the tribesmen from the north, and a detachment of the 45th Sikhs was sent out to delay their advance. The enemy approached from the north and east, compelling the Sikhs to fall back ; but the latter were then reinforced by the rest of the regiment, and succeeded in maintaining their position till 2 a.m., when the tribesmen withdrew. In the meantime a determined attack had been made on the north and centre camps, particularly the latter, during which a detached post at the serai, close to the Chakdara road, which was held by levies, was carried without

* "Operations of the Malakand Field Force," p. 14.

resistance. The night was very dark, and the enemy succeeded in entering the camp occupied by the sappers and miners, and carrying off a considerable quantity of ammunition before they could be ejected. The engagement lasted till 4 a.m., but the tribesmen met with no further success.

At daybreak the troops occupying the north camp, who had been only lightly engaged, were ordered to follow up the line of retreat taken by the enemy, but they met the latter in such force that they were obliged to fall back on the position without committing themselves to an engagement. At the same time forty men of the 11th Bengal Lancers were ordered to proceed to Chakdara by way of the Amandara Pass, but, finding the direct road blocked, they were obliged to make a wide *détour* to the north, and succeeded in reaching the Swat River by a difficult path. Under a hot fire they followed the river-bed for some little way, until an island was reached; when this had been traversed, they took to the river again, and, using their carbines to cover one another's advance, eventually reached Chakdara in safety.

The enemy were now increasing rapidly in strength, so the troops were concentrated at the crater and kotal, the tents and heavy baggage at the north camp being perforce abandoned, owing to the necessity for the rapid occupation of a less extended front. The Guides arrived at Malakand on July 27, having accomplished a remarkable march under trying conditions of intense heat. The order calling up the Guides from Mardan—a distance of thirty-two miles—was received at 9 p.m. on the 26th; both the cavalry and infantry left between 2 a.m. and 2.30 a.m., the former arriving at Malakand at 8.30 a.m. on the 27th, and the latter at 7.30 p.m.

The dispositions made for the defence of the post were now as follows: the 45th Sikhs, supported by two guns and 100 Guides Infantry, held the interval between the crater and the fort; the 24th Punjab Infantry were posted to the west of the crater, and the remainder of the force guarded the camp in the centre. The serai was garrisoned by twenty-five men of the 31st Punjab Infantry. At 8.30 p.m. on the 27th the tribesmen attacked all along the line, but were repulsed everywhere except at the serai, which was held with great gallantry till 3 a.m., when the enemy succeeded in setting it on fire, and so compelled the garrison to fall back on the main position. At dawn on the 28th a most successful counter-attack was made by the 24th Punjab Infantry, which not only inflicted a loss of about 100 men on the enemy, but produced a most salutary moral effect. During the day the defences of the post were strengthened, but all telegraphic communication was severed. Between 10 p.m. and 3 a.m. the enemy again attacked, directing their efforts chiefly against the centre, but failed to pierce the defence at any point, though the troops were now becoming exhausted with their long-continued exertions.

On the 29th further improvements were made in the fortification of the position, signal communication was opened with Chakdara, and a squadron of the 11th Bengal Lancers arrived with 12,000 welcome rounds of ammunition. During the night the enemy attacked again, the objective this time being the flanks, more especially the left, where the 24th Punjab Infantry were stationed. Bonfires were used to illuminate the foreground, by the light of which it was found possible to make use of the 9-pounder guns in the fort. The fighting was of a most desperate character, but the Punjabis stood firm in spite of efforts to undermine their loyalty, for it is related that " during an interval in the fighting the enemy lying opposed to the Punjab Infantry opened parley with the Afridis of that regiment, urging them to join their ranks and take part with them in the sacking of the Malakand, which, they stated, must inevitably fall into their hands. The Afridis pretended to consent to this arrangement, and thereby put the tribesmen off their guard, whereupon they instantly shot those who were foolish enough to expose themselves."*

On July 30 news was received of the approach of the relief column under Colonel A. J. Reid, and 200 men of the 31st Punjab Infantry actually arrived at Malakand from Dargai, where the remainder of the relieving force camped for the night. The enemy delivered another attack during the night, but with far less determination than they had shown on the four previous occasions, and again the bonfires were found to be of the greatest assistance. The relief of the Malakand garrison was accomplished the next day by the arrival of Colonel Reid with 700 men of the 35th Sikhs, 38th Dogras, and Guides, and 190,000 rounds of ammunition. The laconic but appealing message, "Help us!" was received by signal from Chakdara, but the troops were so exhausted after their long exertions that it was decided to postpone the advance in

* " Operations of the Malakand Field Force," p. 22.

force on the beleaguered fort till August 2. An effort was made by a small detachment to relieve Chakdara on August 1, but the enemy were met in considerable strength, and, in spite of a successful charge over bad ground by the Guides Cavalry, the attempt failed. No night attack was made on July 31 or August 1. Sir Bindon Blood, who had been appointed to the command of the expeditionary force now being assembled for the chastisement of the hostile tribes, arrived at Malakand on August 1, and assumed the direction of operations.

At 5 a.m. on August 2 a relief column left Malakand for Chakdara. The infantry met with some strenuous opposition in clearing the heights on the north of the position, but at length the enemy gave way, and, as they crossed the open ground below, presented a fine opportunity to the cavalry, which the latter promptly seized. Two squadrons of the 11th Bengal Lancers and two squadrons of the Guides dashed rapidly forward and did great execution among the defeated tribesmen. The cavalry soon seized the Amandara defile, and, pressing on in spite of the difficulties of the road, reached the Swat bridge at 9 a.m., and Chakdara was relieved. The cavalry then crossed the river in pursuit till their horses showed signs of exhaustion. Chakdara was burned, and, after reinforcing the garrison of the fort and replenishing ammunition and supplies, the relieving force returned to Amandara.

THE DEFENCE OF CHAKDARA.

The *raison d'être* of Chakdara Fort was the protection of the suspension bridge over the Swat River, which had been constructed during the Chitral Campaign. It is situated on the right bank of the river about three-quarters of a mile south-west of the village from which its name is derived. The defences of the fort are described thus in the official account of the operations of the Malakand Field Force:

" This work was of stone and was erected around a small, isolated, rocky, conical-shaped mound on the river bank, and about 150 yards distant from the end of a spur running down from the main ridge of the hills on the west. On the north-west and west the faces of this work consisted of double-storied barracks 25 feet high, with rows of loopholes, and with flank defence in which were located the garrison. The north-east end of the mound, which was very steep and rocky, was scarped and protected by barbed-wire entanglement and a low stone wall. On the south of the mound was a small hornwork protected by a stone wall, near approach to which was prevented by high barbed-wire entanglement Five hundred yards to the west on the summit of a small knoll on the spur above mentioned there was a small, square, one-storied blockhouse with a defensible roof, held by ten men of the 45th Sikhs, from whence signalling with the Malakand was maintained. The bridge on the left bank was closed by a pair of strongly constructed one-storied blockhouses, with defensible roofs with a double-hung, loopholed iron gate between them. The armament of the fort consisted of one 9-pounder smooth-bore muzzle-loading gun (placed on the summit of the mound) and two maxims, one of the latter, in July, 1897, being placed in the blockhouse on the left bank."*

At the time of the outbreak about to be described the garrison consisted of 20 men of the 11th Bengal Lancers and 180 men 45th Sikhs, under Lieutenant H. B. Rattray of the latter regiment. On July 23, 1897, Lieutenant Rattray was warned of the possibility of a rising of the tribesmen, and three days later a large number of men appeared in the vicinity of the post, showing unmistakable signs of hostile intent. The news was transmitted immediately to Malakand, and arrangements were made with the Dir levies for the latter to give warning of impending attack during the night by lighting a fire on a neighbouring hilltop. At 10.15 p.m. the prearranged signal was given, and a few minutes later a determined attack was made on the west side of the fort, which was beaten off. Fighting was continued at intervals till dawn, the eastern and southern faces being also assaulted in turn.

On July 27 the welcome reinforcement of forty men of the 11th Bengal Lancers arrived from Malakand, as already narrated, under Captain Wright, who now assumed command, and another desperate attack made by the enemy on the northern and eastern faces was repulsed with great loss. During the day the defences were greatly improved by the provision of head-cover, and the supply of water in the signalling tower was renewed, in spite of the enemy's fire. This tower was provided with a tank capable of holding 1,220 gallons of water; but it had not been kept filled, so water had to be taken up daily under

* "Operations of the Malakand Field Force," p. 28.

the fire of the assailants. The telegraph wire with Malakand was cut early in the outbreak, and signal communication could not be carried on without great risk of life. During the night the post was attacked again on all sides, but some assistance was derived from the gun, which was trained by daylight on likely avenues of approach, and, apparently, did considerable execution. Further improvements were made to the defences during the daytime on the 28th, and at dusk the enemy again advanced to the attack, directing their chief efforts during the night against the hornwork held by the cavalry.

As further protection to the garrison traverses were constructed on the 29th, and between 3 p.m. and 8 p.m. a desperate, but unavailing, attack was made on the signal tower. The enemy's loss on this occasion, as on others, was enormous; but they had been worked up to such a pitch of religious frenzy as literally to court death at the muzzles of the British rifles. More attacks were delivered during the 30th and 31st, and during the night July 31/August 1 the tribesmen loopholed the walls of the hospital, which was situated between the fort and the signal tower, and were enabled to command the interior of the fort.

At 5 a.m. on August 2 the enemy made one last bid for victory, and the situation was becoming most critical when the flash of a heliograph from Amandara told the hard-pressed and exhausted defenders that help was at hand. The relieving cavalry appeared in sight at 7.20, and an hour later Chakdara was relieved. Directly the enemy began to withdraw the garrison sallied out, and delivered a counter-attack in conjunction with the cavalry of the relief column. So confident had the tribesmen been of success that they had done no damage to the bridge over the river, and had abstained from firing on the horses and mules within the defensive area, though these had been exposed to fire throughout.

The enemy's loss during the attacks on Chakdara had been enormous—the number of killed alone was estimated at 2,000—but so well had the garrison been protected, and so perfect was their discipline, that their casualties were only five killed and ten wounded. Such figures must always be regarded with suspicion, but the tribesmen themselves computed their losses before Malakand and Chakdara at 3,700 killed besides wounded.

THE OPERATIONS OF THE MALAKAND FIELD FORCE.

As soon as the serious nature of the outbreak was realized by the Government of India, orders were issued for the mobilization of an expeditionary force, under the command of Sir Bindon Blood, for the punishment of the tribes involved. This force was constituted as shown in Table XX., and, concentrating rapidly, in spite of the heat, between Malakand and Chakdara, was ready for action on August 7. On the following day reconnaissances were pushed up the Swat Valley, and the unconditional surrender of the lower Swatis was received, but, as a set-off to this clearing of the political situation, news was received also of the Mohmand attack on Shabkadr, which will be related presently. Sir Bindon Blood's advance was delayed for some days by rain, but on August 16 Thana was occupied, and the road to Landakai reconnoitred.

Continuing his advance up the Swat Valley the next day, Sir Bindon Blood found his way barred by the enemy, who were holding a strong position at right angles to the line of advance. General Meiklejohn was deputed at once to make a turning movement to the south, with a battery and three battalions, so as to threaten the enemy's line of retreat into Buner. The effect of this movement was soon apparent, for the tribesmen abandoned their position and took to flight in the direction of the Buner hills, pursued by three squadrons of the Guides. In spite of the difficulties of the ground, the cavalry pressed on to Nawakila, whence parties of the enemy were seen making their escape as rapidly as possible to the south. Pursuit offered little chance of success, so the Guides dismounted and opened fire on the retreating tribesmen, but a party of five British officers and five men pressed on. These soon came under a heavy fire, two officers were killed, two were wounded, and even more serious loss would have occurred but for the bravery of the surviving officers and men.* Before returning to camp at Landakai the Guides reconnoitred farther up the road to Barikot, which was the intended direction of Sir Bindon Blood the next day.

On August 18 the Malakand Field Force advanced to Barikot, and reached Mingaora the following day, where

---

* Lieutenant-Colonel R. B. Adams, Queen's Own Corps of Guides, and Lieutenant A. E. Viscount Fincastle, 16th Lancers, received the Victoria Cross, and the men with them the Order of Merit.

TABLE XX

MALAKAND FIELD FORCE, 1897

Brigadier-General Sir Bindon Blood, K.C.B.

First Brigade.*	Second Brigade.*	Third Brigade.*	Divisional Troops.
Brigadier-General W. H. Meiklejohn, C.B., C.M.G.	*Brigadier-General P. D. Jeffreys, C.B.*	*Brigadier-General J. H. Wodehouse, C.B., C.M.G.*	10th Bengal Lancers (10th Lancers), 1 Squadron. 11th Bengal Lancers (11th Lancers), 1 Squadron. Guides Cavalry. 10th Field Battery Royal Artillery (10th Battery Royal Field Artillery). No. 1 Mountain Battery Royal Artillery (1st Mountain Battery Royal Garrison Artillery). No. 7 Mountain Battery Royal Artillery (7th Mountain Battery Royal Garrison Artillery). No. 8 (Bengal) Mountain Battery (28th Mountain Battery). No. 3 Company Bombay Sappers and Miners (19th Company 3rd Sappers and Miners). No. 4 Company Bengal Sappers and Miners (4th Company 1st Sappers and Miners). No. 5 Company Madras Sappers and Miners (13th Company 2nd Sappers and Miners). 21st Punjab Infantry (21st Punjabis). One Section British and two Sections Native Field Hospital.
1st Battalion Royal West Kent Regiment.† 24th Punjab Infantry (24th Punjabis). 31st Punjab Infantry (31st Punjabis).† 24th Sikhs.	1st Battalion East Kent Regiment.† 35th Sikhs.† 38th Dogras. Guides Infantry.	1st Battalion West Surrey Regiment. 2nd Battalion Highland Light Infantry.‡ 22nd Punjab Infantry (22nd Punjabis). 39th Garhwal Rifles.	

* To each Brigade were attached half a British and one and a half Native Field Hospitals.
† Exchanged Brigades in September.   ‡ Detained on line of communication.

a halt was made till the 24th, to enable the Swat Valley tribes to tender their submission. Sir Bindon Blood then returned to Barikot, and on the 25th reconnoitred the Karakar Pass leading into Buner. During the advance into Upper Swat the 3rd Brigade was despatched to Rustam to hold the Bunerwals in check, and prevent any hostile movement from the south; this brigade shortly after-wards was moved up to Uch to support the Nawab of Dir in his efforts to restore order north of the Swat River.

Sir Bindon Blood's first proposal was that he should advance into Buner and deal with the tribes inhabiting that district, before turning his attention to the north and west. The Government of India, however, preferred that, in view of the political situation in the neighbour-hood of Peshawar, any forward movement should be in a westerly rather than an easterly direction. Accord-ingly preparations were made for an expedition into the territory of the Utman Khel, living on the left bank of the Swat River, and this movement was actually in pro-gress when Sir Bindon Blood was ordered to advance into Bajaur against the followers of the Hadda Mullah and co-operate with the Mohmand Field Force under General Elles. In pursuance of these orders General Wodehouse was ordered to proceed from Uch to Sado on September 4, and seize the bridge over the Panjkora River at that place. This movement was carried out just in time to forestall a similar move by the tribesmen of Bajaur and Dir, which would have aggravated the diffi-culties of the situation considerably.

On September 8 the 2nd Brigade and Divisional Head-quarters arrived at the Panjkora River, General Meikle-john's Brigade being detailed for the protection of the line of communication. Reconnoitring the country care-fully in all directions without opposition as he advanced, Sir Bindon Blood halted on September 13, with the 2nd Brigade at Khar and the 3rd at Shamshak. While the 3rd Brigade pushed on to Nawagai, General Jeffreys was ordered to cross the Rambat Pass and invade the territory of the Utman Khel, living on the right bank of the Swat River. On September 14 Sir Bindon Blood and General Wodehouse reached Nawagai, and General Jeffreys occupied the summit of the Rambat Pass with part of his force, while the main body camped at Mark-hanai. During the same night a sudden attack, pressed more or less vigorously till 2 a.m., was made on General Jeffreys' camp, and at daybreak the next morning the

cavalry went out in pursuit. After going a little way
the cavalry came across a body of armed men, who said
they were vassals of the Khan of Khar, and had come to
the assistance of the British force. At first they professed
complete ignorance of the movements of the enemy, but,
on being pressed, pointed towards the Mamund Valley,
in which direction the cavalry at once proceeded. After
going about six miles, a small party of men was seen
making its way up the valley, and a prolonged chase
ensued, which was only terminated by the inaccessible
nature of the ground, but, before the enemy could gain a
position of safety, twenty-one of their number had been
cut down by the pursuing sowars. The tribesmen, however, were not disheartened, for, directly the retirement
of the cavalry began, they pressed forward in pursuit to
within three miles of camp, where the withdrawal of the
mounted men was covered by the Guides Infantry.
During this retirement the cavalry found themselves
at a considerable disadvantage, owing to the inferiority
of the carbines, with which they were armed, to the long-
range rifles in the hands of the enemy.

Owing to the unfavourable reports regarding the
Mamund Valley for the encampment of troops, and to
the scarcity of water, General Jeffreys decided to establish
his camp at Inayat Kila, and to carry out punitive operations from there. In accordance with this plan the
2nd Brigade was divided into three columns, composed
as under, for the work of September 16.

LEFT COLUMN.	CENTRE COLUMN.	RIGHT COLUMN.
Major Campbell.	*Colonel Goldney.*	*Colonel Vivian.*
The Guides.	11th Bengal Lancers, 1 Squadron. The Buffs. No. 8 (Bengal) Mountain Battery, 4 guns. 35th Sikhs.	38th Dogras. No. 8 Mountain Battery, 2 guns. Sappers and Miners, 1 Section.

Moving up the Mamund Valley the cavalry of the
Centre Column soon gained touch with the enemy, who
retreated in a northerly direction, followed by the
35th Sikhs. Several hostile villages were destroyed
without difficulty, but, when the retirement began, the

tribesmen pursued their favourite tactics with great effect. To relieve the pressure the Sikhs made a counter-attack with the bayonet, the cavalry charged a body of Mamunds who were pressing the Sikhs, and a company of the Buffs came up to cover the withdrawal. The charge delivered by the 11th Bengal Lancers deserves something more than merely a passing mention, because its object was achieved by moral influence alone. The cavalry were prevented from closing with the enemy by a nala, but the cheer and resolute air with which they approached were quite sufficient to put the tribesmen to flight.

The Guides Infantry now arrived on the scene, and checked the pursuit. General Jeffreys also came up, and ordered an attack on Shahi Tangi to be made by the Buffs and the 35th Sikhs as a punishment for the molestation of the retirement, and to restore *moral*. Covered by the fire of the guns, and a company of the 35th Sikhs under Captain Ryder on the British right, the Buffs and the remainder of the 35th Sikhs cleared the enemy out of the village, and destroyed it. At 3.45 p.m. a general retirement was ordered, which was again hotly pressed by the Mamunds, and Captain Ryder's detached company was soon in a very critical position. This officer had received no orders to retire, but he conformed on his own initiative to the movements of the remainder of the force as soon as he became aware of them. Seeing their advantage, the tribesmen swarmed around the small isolated party as it retired slowly down the hill which it had been occupying. Several casualties occurred, and progress was very slow. Captain Ryder's situation now became known to the General, who ordered the brigade to halt while the hard-pressed Sikhs were extricated by a half-company of the Guides. This assistance was received in the nick of time, for Captain Ryder's men were becoming exhausted with the heavy fighting in which they were engaged at the close of a long day.

As soon as it was seen that the Sikhs were near the bottom of the hill down which they were retiring, General Jeffreys ordered the brigade to march on towards camp, but, being still anxious about the safety of the troops in rear, delayed the retirement of a party consisting of four guns, No. 8 Bengal Mountain Artillery, thirty-five sappers and miners, and a section of twelve men of the Buffs, with the result that these troops became detached from the main body in the darkness, and a thunderstorm which came on at the same time. General Jeffreys, who was himself present with the guns and their escort, then decided to take up a position for the night at a neighbouring village called Bilot. The Mamunds, however, anticipated this move, and when the British force reached the village it was not strong enough to clear the enemy out in spite of several gallant attempts on the part of the sappers and infantry.* The guns fired a few rounds of case-shot into the village, which had the effect of preventing the enemy from becoming too bold, but firing was going on at ranges varying from 5 to 20 yards, and stones and bundles of lighted grass were showered on the troops from the adjoining walls. The night was very dark, and rain was falling heavily, but the tribesmen continued their attacks till about midnight, when they took to flight at the approach of four companies of the 35th Sikhs under Major Worledge, who, like the guns, had been benighted in their efforts to cover the retirement of the brigade. These companies also had taken up a position in the neighbourhood of Bilot, and, as soon as the moon rose, had gone to the assistance of the party in the village. The rest of the night passed undisturbed, and early the next morning the party under General Jeffreys reached camp in safety, covered by the cavalry and 38th Dogras.

Between September 18 and 23 systematic operations were conducted in the Mamund Valley for the punishment of the clan. The villages were destroyed, and supplies found in such abundance that the whole of the transport animals of the 2nd Brigade, numbering 1,265, were able to live free of cost for nearly a month. Little opposition was offered to the work of destruction and spoliation, but the retirements were usually harassed, though never with any success.

It will be convenient now to record the doings of the 3rd Brigade under General Wodehouse, which, it will be remembered, reached Nawagai on September 14, accompanied by Sir Bindon Blood. When the news of General Jeffreys' fighting in the Mamund Valley reached the Government of India, Sir Bindon Blood was ordered to retire on Inayat Kila, and concentrate the two brigades operating in Bajaur for the punishment of the Mamunds. For political reasons, however, Sir Bindon Blood con-

* Lieutenants T. C. Watson and J. M. C. Colvin, both of the Royal Engineers, and Corporal Smith of the Buffs, received the Victoria Cross for gallantry on this occasion.

BILOT

SEPTEMBER 16, 1897

Scale   1 inch = 20 yards.

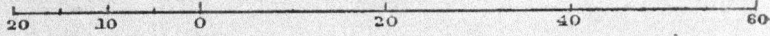

Yards

| 20 | 10 | 0 | 20 | 40 | 60 |

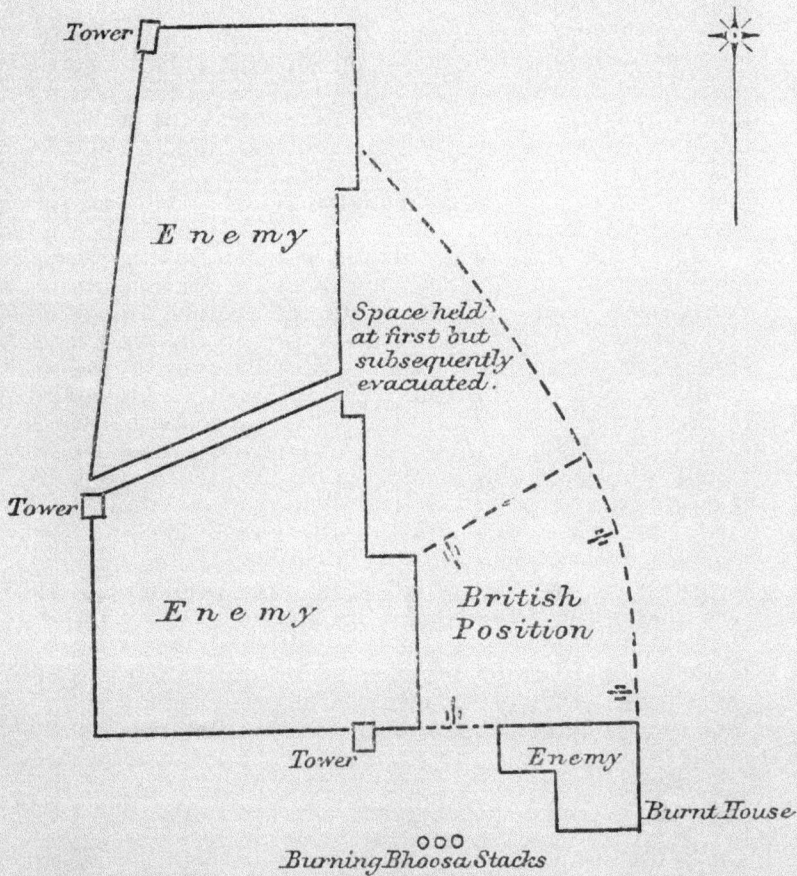

Tower

Enemy

Space held
at first but
subsequently
evacuated.

Tower

Enemy

British
Position

Tower

Enemy

Burnt House

○○○ Burning Bhoosa Stacks

Breastworks — — — — —

from 'The Operations of the Malakand Field Force'

sidered this course inadvisable, owing to the necessity
for exerting moral pressure on the Khan of Nawagai,
whose attitude at this juncture was somewhat doubtful.
Moreover, he considered that the force at the disposal of
General Jeffreys was sufficient for present needs, and
therefore decided to remain at Nawagai till General
Elles arrived with the Mohmand Field Force, when combined operations could be undertaken against the Hadda
and Safi Mullahs, who were the two chief religious
zealots of the district.

From Nawagai reconnaissances of the surrounding
country were carried out in all directions, and efforts
made to open communication with General Elles, which,
however, were not rewarded with success till September 18. At 11.30 p.m. on the following night an attack
was made on the camp at Nawagai, the plan of which
was as shown in the accompanying sketch. The terrain
was as follows:

"The camp itself was situated on open stony ground,
sloping gently to the south, and prepared for cultivation
in terraced fields. To the north the ground was level
and bare for a considerable distance; on the west face
successive terraces gave 4 or 5 feet of cover to within
30 or 40 yards of the camp entrenchments, while 150
to 200 yards away was a dry stony nullah with banks
8 to 10 feet high, in which the enemy subsequently collected in considerable numbers; on the east the ground
was much broken with deep nullahs, and the slope was
steep."* The enemy attacked the corner held by the
Queen's in two lines, the first about 150 strong (mostly
swordsmen), and the second about 1,000 in number. It
was intended that the second line should be in readiness
to confirm any success gained, but, although the first succeeded in approaching unperceived to within fifty yards of
the parapet, they were received with so steady a fire
that the attempt failed, and the second line was never
engaged.

Another attack was made on the camp occupied by
General Wodehouse's Brigade on the night September 20/21. At 9 p.m. a volley was poured into camp,
which was followed by a rush of swordsmen from
several directions, covered by the fire of others in rear.
The position of the headquarters had evidently been
marked down, for it was soon subjected to a heavy fire,
during which General Wodehouse was wounded. The

* "Operations of the Malakand Field Force," p. 62.

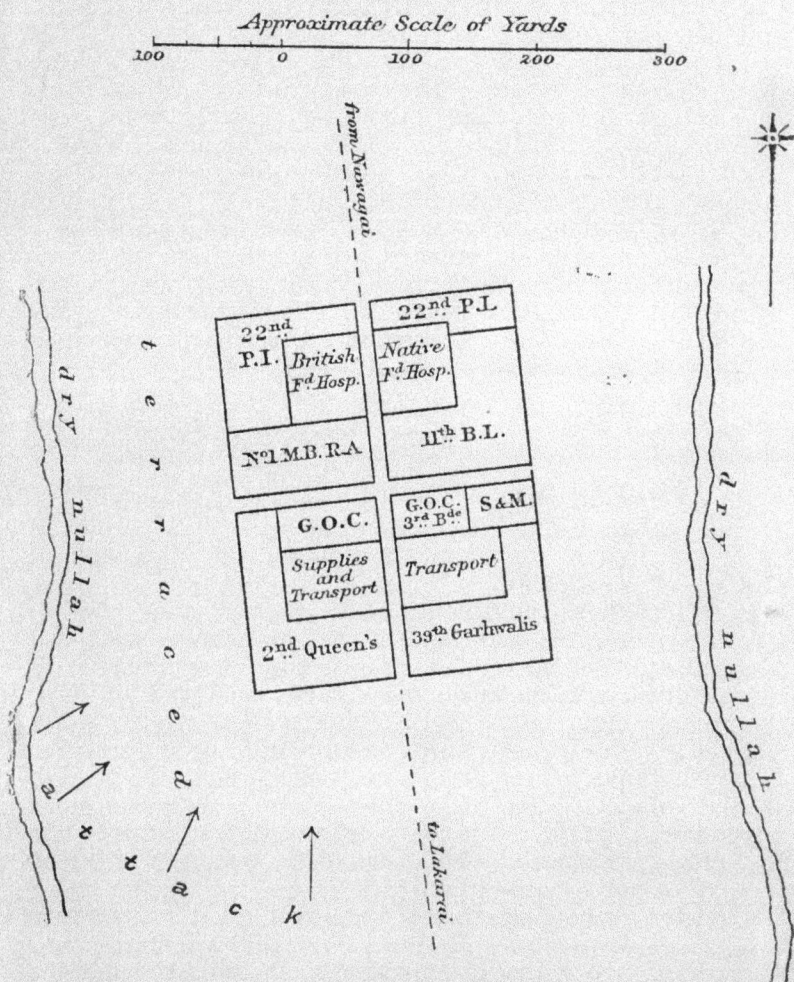

CAMP OF 3RD BRIGADE
MALAKAND FIELD FORCE AT NAWAGAI

SEPTEMBER, 1897

From "The Operations of the Malakand Field Force"

The following points should be noted:

1. *The means of communication as afforded by the main roads*
2. *Central position of headquarters*
3. *Non-combatant units surrounded by fighting troops*
4. *Both arms of each corner of the camp held by men of the same corps*

engagement lasted till 2 a.m., when the moon rose, and the enemy withdrew; the discipline and efficiency of the defensive arrangements proved most satisfactory, but 32 casualties were sustained, and no less than 133 animals killed and wounded.

On September 21 General Elles arrived, and General Wodehouse's brigade, the command of which now devolved on Lieutenant-Colonel B. C. Graves, 39th Garhwalis, was attached to the Mohmand Field Force. An account of its doings will be found in the narrative of the operations under General Elles.

After handing over his 3rd Brigade to General Elles, Sir Bindon Blood returned to Inayat Kila with two squadrons of the 11th Bengal Lancers, and, owing to the numerous casualties sustained, ordered the reorganization of General Jeffreys' brigade. The following changes were made in the allotment of troops:

No. 8 Mountain Battery ...	Replaced by No. 7 Mountain Battery.
The Buffs	Replaced by Royal West Kent Regiment.
35th Sikhs	Replaced by 31st Punjab Infantry.

In addition two squadrons of Guides were despatched to Inayat Kila. The troops relieved were then employed on the line of communication under the command of General Meiklejohn.

When these movements had been carried out, operations were resumed against the Mamunds, who still hesitated to tender their submission. On September 30 an attack was made on the villages of Agrah and Gat, situated eight miles north of Inayat Kila, which "occupied a very strong position in a re-entering angle on the lower slopes of the great spur which divides the head of the valley. Long rocky spurs, strewn with enormous boulders, guarded the flanks of the two villages, while between them is a small rugged spur with precipitous sides covered with large rocks."*

After a reconnaissance of the position General Jeffreys decided to attack Agrah first. The Guides Infantry were ordered to occupy the spur west of the village, while the West Kent Regiment attacked it in front, and ascended the hills to the north for a short distance. The 31st Punjab Infantry were deputed to seize the ridge between Agrah and Gat, and the 38th Dogras formed a reserve in rear of the guns, which opened fire in the first instance on the enemy opposed to the Guides Infantry. The

---

* "Operations of the Malakand Field Force," p. 66.

ATTACK ON AGRAH AND GAT

September 30, 1897

Scale 2 inches = 1 mile
Scale of Yards

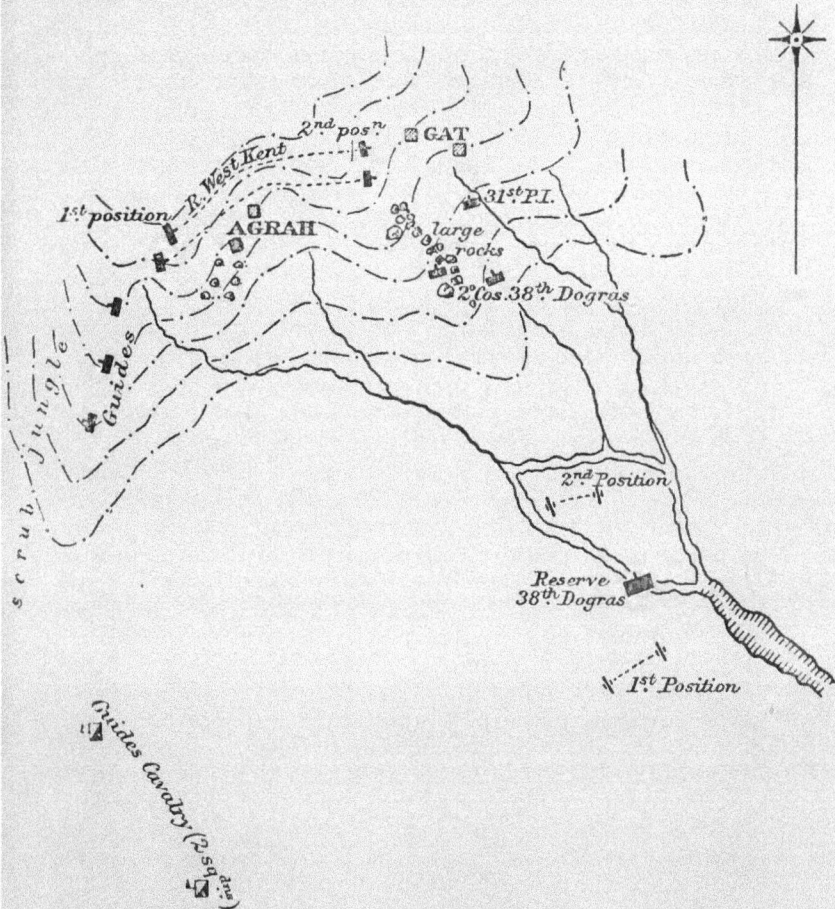

From "Operations of the Malakand Field Force," p. 66

16

31st Punjab Infantry, however, met with the most opposition, for, as they advanced, "it soon became apparent
that large numbers of the enemy were concealed amongst
the crags on the spur between the two villages. The
artillery accordingly brought a searching fire to bear on
that point, but, in spite of it, the enemy, ensconced among
the large boulders, held on to the position, which they
had considerably strengthened by a number of sangars.
After a most stubborn resistance the 31st Punjab Infantry
advanced, and, having with great gallantry driven the
enemy out at the point of the bayonet, occupied the position. . . . An order was thereupon sent to the 31st
Punjab Infantry to retain their position on the spur, and
not to enter Gat village until reinforced by the West
Kent Regiment. As soon as it became evident that the
31st Punjab Infantry were being stubbornly opposed,
two companies of the 38th Dogras were despatched to
occupy a low rocky mound on the right rear, and the
guns were also advanced to a second position, whence
they could shell the ground on the east of Gat. Meanwhile the Guides Infantry had gained the spur on the
west under a heavy fire, but without loss, and the Royal
West Kent Regiment then occupied the slopes of the
hills above Agrah, which was now completely destroyed
by No. 4 Company Bengal Sappers and Miners. As the
enemy still continued to oppose the 31st Punjab Infantry,
the Royal West Kent Regiment were directed to wheel
to their right towards the north-east against the village
of Gat, so as to support the left flank of the 31st Punjab
Infantry. The Guides Infantry remained in their position on the spur on the left, where they held in check
large numbers of the enemy who were in front of them
and on their left flank. . . . The Royal West Kent
Regiment, in moving across to its right, soon became
hotly engaged with the enemy at close quarters. The
ground was exceedingly difficult to move over, and the
high-standing crops in the terraced fields, with their
stone-faced revetments, 3 to 10 feet high, considerably
favoured the enemy's tactics. Their sangars were also
cunningly constructed, and each one appeared to be
covered by the fire of some other sangar situated still
farther up on the hills above. As at Zagai, where the
Buffs had several casualties after capturing and occupying
one of the sangars, so in a similar manner at Gat the
Royal West Kent Regiment lost Second Lieutenant
W. C. Browne-Clayton, killed, and several men wounded.

The wounded men were quickly moved towards the rear by their comrades. This, however, very considerably reduced the number of men holding the sangar. Noting this, a large number of swordsmen charged the four or five men left in the sangar with Second Lieutenant Browne-Clayton's body and forced them to retire. Thereupon Major Weston directed a spirited counter-attack, and quickly recovered the sangar at the point of the bayonet. Part of the village of Gat was then destroyed, but by this time large numbers of the enemy, with two or three white standards, had arrived from the eastern villages of the valley, and were streaming over the spurs from the Zagai direction." *

As the troops withdrew the enemy followed, but the retirement was conducted with great steadiness, and camp was reached without mishap at 4 p.m. The casualties during the day had been twelve officers and men killed and forty-nine wounded.

On October 3 the village of Badalai was destroyed, near which Captain Ryder's company had suffered severely on September 16, and on the following day re-inforcements arrived, consisting of four guns of the 10th Field Battery Royal Artillery, the 2nd Battalion Highland Light Infantry, and No. 5 Company Queen's Own Madras Sappers and Miners. Regarding these re-inforcements the official account says :

" The advance of the 10th Field Battery from the Panjkora Bridge is worthy of notice. After having successfully hauled his six guns over the ford of the Panjkora River just above the bridge without mishap, the Officer Commanding † took four of the guns on to Inayat Kila, over ground destitute of any road of even the roughest description. Overcoming all obstacles—man-hauling the guns frequently—the battery without a single casualty arrived at the Watelai Valley, and thus reached a point in the hills fifty miles farther than any other wheeled traffic had ever proceeded." ‡

After the destruction of Badalai, active operations against the Mamunds came to an end ; but a settlement was not made with the clan till October 18, after which the troops were withdrawn, the 1st Brigade to Jalala and the 2nd to Malakand, the Guides returning to Mardan. Between November 23 and December 6 an

* " Operations of the Malakand Field Force," p. 67.
† Major (Major-General) C. A. Anderson.
‡ " Operations of the Malakand Field Force," p. 69.

expedition was made against the Utman Khel, living on
the left bank of the Swat River, and the surrender of the
clan was received without a shot being fired.

THE BUNER EXPEDITION.

After the peaceful submission of the Utman Khel to
Colonel Reid in November and December, 1897, the
only tribes inhabiting the country adjacent to the
frontier line north of Nowshera, who had not been
brought to book, were the Bunerwals and those whose
territory lay between Buner and the Indus. Sir Bindon
Blood was now free to turn his attention once more to
this quarter, so, while the organization of the Buner
Field Force was being carried out, an opportunity was
given to the tribesmen of saving their country from the
penalties of invasion by timely surrender. Impelled
thereto, in all probability, by the recollection or traditions of the expeditions under Sir Sydney Cotton and
Sir Neville Chamberlain, the tribes between Buner and
the Indus forthwith tendered their submission; but the
Bunerwals, whose military reputation in the district had
stood high since the Ambela Campaign in consequence
of the prominent part they had taken therein, refused
compliance with the British terms.

The reorganization of the force and its concentration
at Kunda having been completed on January 1, 1898, as
shown in Table XXI., the march east was begun on the
following day, and on January 6 the division concentrated at Sanghao on the Buner border with an infantry
detachment of two battalions at Pirsai and five squadrons
of cavalry at Rustam, threatening the lines of approach
from those points. Reconnaissance of the Buner border
revealed the fact that all the passes were held by the
enemy, so Sir Bindon Blood decided that "the troops at
Sanghao should force the Tanga Pass, the mouth of
which is one mile north of Sanghao, while the Pirsai
detachment was to force the pass of that name early the
same day; and the cavalry from Rustam were then to
cross the Pirsai Pass, working thence onwards towards
the enemy's line of retreat from the Tanga Pass."[*]

In execution of this plan the 20th Punjabis were
ordered to carry out a turning movement against the
enemy's right flank on the morning of January 7, while

* "Operations of the Buner Field Force," p. 81.

TABLE XXI

THE BUNER FIELD FORCE, 1897

Major-General Sir Bindon Blood, K.C.B.

First Brigade.	Second Brigade.	Divisional Troops.
Brigadier-General W. H. Meiklejohn, C.B., C.M.G.	*Brigadier-General P. D. Jeffreys, C.B.*	10th Bengal Lancers (10th Lancers), 1 Squadron.
1st Battalion Royal West Kent Regiment.	1st Battalion East Kent Regiment.	Guides Cavalry.
16th Bengal Infantry (16th Rajputs).	21st Punjab Infantry (21st Punjabis).	10th Field Battery Royal Artillery (10th Battery Royal Field Artillery).
20th Punjab Infantry (20th Punjabis).	Guides Infantry.	No. 7 Mountain Battery Royal Artillery (7th Mountain Battery Royal Garrison Artillery).
31st Punjab Infantry (31st Punjabis).		No. 8 (Bengal) Mountain Battery (28th Mountain Battery).
		No. 4 Company Bengal Sappers and Miners (1st Sappers and Miners).
		No. 5 Company Madras Sappers and Miners (13th Company 2nd Sappers and Miners).
		2nd Battalion Highland Light Infantry.
		3rd Bombay Light Infantry (103rd Mahratta Light Infantry).
		Two and a half British Field Hospitals.
		Four Native Field Hospitals.

the Buffs and 3rd Bombay Light Infantry, supported by
the guns and a squadron of the 10th Bengal Lancers,
covered the frontal attack, which was to be delivered
by the 1st Brigade.   Under cover of the fire of the
10th Field Battery, the Buffs and 3rd Bombay Light
Infantry extended about 1,500 yards from the crest of
the pass, and opened fire with long range volleys, under
cover of which the two mountain batteries then advanced
to a position about 300 yards in rear of the line of extended infantry, and likewise opened fire on the enemy's
position. The 1st Brigade now formed up for the assault
in the following order from the right: 16th Bengal
Infantry, Royal West Kent Regiment, 31st Punjab Infantry, Highland Light Infantry ; and at noon, when the
turning movement against the enemy's right had developed, the brigade advanced to the assault.   The
slopes were steep, and the tribesmen endeavoured to
impede progress still further by fire and by rolling
large rocks down the side of the hill; but they were so
demoralized by the steady and accurate fire maintained
by the covering troops that the issue was never in doubt,
and at 2 p.m., when the final assault was made, it was
found that the enemy were already in full flight.

The retreat of the tribesmen was so rapid that pursuit,
tactically speaking, was useless; but some loss was inflicted by means of long range volleys, and the Royal
West Kent Regiment was sent forward to occupy
Kingargali, two miles from the top of the pass on a well-
cultivated plain.   Great difficulty was experienced in
supplying the advanced troops with the barest necessaries on account of the impracticable nature of the
track, and, until this could be made passable for mules,
everything had to be carried over the pass by a corps of
500 coolies, collected for the purpose at Sanghao.

While the main body of the division was engaged in
the attack on the Tanga Pass, the detachments at Pirsai
and Rustam concentrated at the former place, carried
the Pirsai Pass with little opposition, and crossed over
the same day.   The cavalry, who had some trouble in
surmounting the difficulties of the road, reconnoitred as
far as Tursak, and then joined the troops occupying
Kingargali, the infantry of the detached force remaining
at Chorbanda.

On January 8 the headmen of the villages in the
neighbourhood of Kingargali tendered their submission,
and Sir Bindon Blood made them responsible for the

protection of the camp from the attentions of marauders, informing them that "if any firing into camp took place their villages would be immediately destroyed."[*] This intimation was attended with the most happy results, for it is recorded that "throughout the time that the troops were across the border not a single shot was fired into camp at night."[†]

A halt lasting ten days was made at Kingargali to enable the road over the Tanga Pass to be made practicable for mules, and to collect sufficient supplies for a further advance into Buner. While the main body halted at Kingargali, a portion of General Jeffreys' Brigade, accompanied by the 10th Field Battery, was sent to occupy the Ambela Pass, being joined later by three squadrons of the 10th Bengal Lancers. It took three days of heavy labour to make the road over the Tanga Pass fit for mule traffic; but at length the work was accomplished, and mules were able to pass over at the rate of 200 per hour. As soon as he had replenished his supplies, Sir Bindon Blood resumed his advance, and operating in two columns, one commanded by himself in person, and the other by General Meiklejohn, traversed the whole of Buner from end to end, meeting with no opposition and receiving the submission of the tribesmen at all points.

On January 17 General Jeffreys crossed the Ambela Pass and occupied Kogah in the Chamla Valley, during which march the sites of the British camp and piquets of 1863 were clearly visible. On the same day the submission of the Bunerwals and Chamlawals was complete, and on the 19th the entire force withdrew over the Ambela Pass into British territory, having surveyed the whole of Buner and completely discredited the military reputation of the tribe. Mardan was reached on January 20, and there the force was broken up with the exception of one mountain battery, three squadrons, six battalions, and two companies of sappers and miners, who were retained in the district to keep open the road to Chitral. Also the defences of Malakand and Chakdara were considerably strengthened.

The operations of the Malakand and Buner Field Forces thus came to an end. Including the defences of Malakand and Chakdara, the experiences of the troops engaged had been of a most varied and extended character. An area of nearly 300 square miles had been

[*] "Operations of the Buner Field Force," p. 84.   [†] *Ibid.*

completely pacified, and the history of mountain warfare enriched by many striking incidents. The art of the defence of camps and fortified posts against the assaults of a greatly superior number of fanatical foes, in addition to the tactics of pursuit, retirements, and combined attack, are all admirably illustrated by this interesting and instructive campaign.

CHAPTER XVI

THE MALAKAND AND BUNER FIELD FORCES
REVIEW

It has been thought better to keep the review of the operations of the Malakand and Buner Field Forces separate from that of the Mohmand and Tirah Campaigns for two reasons. Firstly, because the story of the critical situations, the desperate fighting, and the complete eventual triumph which fell to the lot of the troops is rather apt to be overshadowed by the account of the larger and more generally familiar Tirah Campaign which commenced three months later; and, secondly, because the salient features of Sir Bindon Blood's expeditions differ considerably from those that took place farther to the south.

The wave of fanatical feeling which travelled from north to south along the western border of British India had its origin in the Swat Valley; the locality had been for a long time a recognized religious centre, and consequently it is not a matter for surprise that this fact had a distinct influence on the methods of warfare of the people. At Malakand and Chakdara, and in a minor degree at Nawagai, the same reckless impulse is to be seen which hurled the Mahdists against the British squares at Abu Klea, El Teb, and Omdurman, for the sake of a martyr's crown. To some extent the North-West Frontier tribes of India present an anomaly to the world in their methods of warfare. At times they show all the characteristics of well-armed but unorganized adversaries, at others the latent fire of the untamed barbarian blazes forth, and no epithet but savage can be applied to the class of warfare which is the result. The desperate and repeated attacks on the garrisons of Malakand and Chakdara are conspicuous examples of the savage side of the methods of war practised by the Muhammadan tribes inhabiting the north-western borderland of India. It is true that the attacks were delivered at night and not in broad daylight as in the Sudan, but they were renewed with greater persistency. There is no instance in the military history of the Egyptians or Sudanese in which temporary insanity brought on by religious fervour has lasted more than twenty-four hours. Before Malakand and Chakdara the tribesmen were religious maniacs for eight days, and advanced to the attack with a bravery which fully entitled those that fell to any reward that such a death may bring. The vigour of the assaults no doubt diminished towards the end of this time, but every bodily or mental affliction must run its course. A man is not on his back, or a raving lunatic, one moment and in robust health, or sane, the next without some intermediate period of convalescence. It is not, however, as affording examples of courage, whether natural or artificial, that the operations of the Malakand and Buner Field Forces are chiefly remarkable; both types are common enough in the military history of the world, but the time at which much of the fighting took place was unusual. It is a well-known fact that night operations are not generally popular among irregular warriors, probably because this class of warfare requires a high standard of discipline and combination, which is the prerogative of well-trained troops. Nevertheless, the record of events in 1897, in or near the Swat Valley, affords numerous instances in which night attacks on a considerable scale were planned and carried out by men possessing neither organization nor recognized leader. At the same time the results of these same night attacks are instructive, for without exception they are all examples of the reward for vigilance and discipline on the part of regular troops in face of superior numbers.

Occasions on which success has not rewarded the efforts of the British arms, or has been achieved only after considerable difficulty, are always more fruitful of useful military lessons than victories won without any period of serious anxiety. The operations in the Mamund Valley are a case in point. Like the unsuccessful attack on the Bizoti section of the Orakzais at the Ublan Pass in 1868, and the indecisive expedition against the Jowakis in August, 1877, the events in the Mamund Valley prove that it is useless to attempt to carry out punitive operations in a hurried or perfunctory manner. In all three instances it was sought to accomplish in one day work which eventually occupied (in the last two examples) two months and one month respectively before it could be brought to a satisfactory termination. No doubt the absence of any initial discouragement to the tribesmen contributed to some extent to the prolongation of the subsequent operations in 1877 and twenty years later, but this cannot be the entire cause. In both cases the British troops invaded what was, in a military sense, absolutely virgin territory, consequently it was highly desirable to make the impression left of British prowess as marked as possible with a view to the maintenance of peace in the future.

It is too much to expect that untamed barbarians will submit with a good grace to the terms dictated by an invader without some practical demonstration of the latter's superiority. A decisive battle is, of course, by far the best means to this end, but in irregular warfare, particularly among mountains, decisive battles are the exception rather than the rule, and the destruction of property of some form or other has to take their place. The destruction of property must be done thoroughly, or it is not worth doing at all, for the people will be merely exasperated without suffering any real injury. While a portion of the force is levelling a village to the ground the men have to be protected from molestation by the enemy, who is usually in the vicinity; the destruction of each village, therefore, may involve a fight for the possession of the tactical points in the neighbourhood, and, beyond the North-West Frontier of India, will entail more often than not a stubborn rear-guard action directly the withdrawal begins.

The time required to carry out a special task depends far more on the enterprise of the enemy than on the actual distance or nature of ground involved. In arranging, therefore, the programme of a day's operations during an Indian frontier campaign when opposition is possible, either an ample margin must be allowed for variations of that all-important factor in war called time, or a commander must be prepared to abandon a portion of his designs rather than expose himself and his troops to the danger of being benighted on possibly unfavourable ground in the midst of a bloodthirsty enemy. The last-named misfortune is, of course, what actually befell the party who were isolated at Bilot on September 16, after the first expedition up the Watelai Valley. In illustration of the happy results attendant on the operations of regular troops, when conducted with the cohesion born of thoughtful preparation and a common purpose, the attacks on Agrah and Gat, and the storming of the Tanga Pass, will be readily called to mind. In both cases the troops were launched to the attack in suitable numbers, in accordance with a well-laid scheme; confidence and resolution were the result, and victory was never in doubt.

As regards the action of individual arms, the Malakand and Buner Expeditions furnish some points of special interest to cavalry and artillery. Once more the moral and physical effect of cavalry, even in hill warfare, is clearly brought out. One of the most successful charges in the history of Indian frontier wars took place on August 2, 1897, between Malakand and Chakdara, when two squadrons of the 11th Bengal Lancers and a similar force of the Guides played havoc with the retreating tribesmen. Again, at the commencement of the retirement of the 2nd Brigade after the first expedition up the Watelai Valley, the sight of the approach of the 11th Bengal Lancers, and the sound of their cheer, were sufficient to relieve the pressure on the rear-guard, in spite of the fact that a nala prevented the cavalry from getting to close quarters; the fruit of previous exploits was reaped at a most opportune season.

The operations of the single squadron engaged in the Watelai Valley furnish yet another important point of interest to the cavalry arm, and that is in the matter of their equipment. The question as to what are the best weapons for cavalry for general use, and how they should be carried, always has been, and always will be, a matter for controversy; but there can be no question on one point, which is that, if a certain weapon is worth carrying at all, it should be the very best of its kind procurable. A man who finds that his arms are outclassed by those of his enemy is never likely to be effective on the battlefield; he may fight with courage, and make the best possible use of what he has got, but he is handicapped from the beginning, and the knowledge of this fact is bound to tell on his *moral* in the end.

Without turning the pages back at all far, History is full of warning to those whose duty it is to place weapons of war in the hands of those who will have to use them. The Mexicans in 1847, the Confederate artillery (1861-1865), the Austrian infantry in 1866, and the Russians in 1877, were all severely, if not fatally, handicapped by the inferiority of their equipment to that in the possession of the opposing troops. It is said that coming events cast their shadows before, and, with the wisdom of after-events at command, it certainly does look like a warning when we read that even the uncivilized hillman of North-Western India was able to put the trained troopers of a regular Indian cavalry regiment at a disadvantage by the possession of arms of superior range and precision. When the 11th Bengal Lancers took up the pursuit of the Mamunds after the attack on General Jeffreys' camp at Markhanai on the night of September 14/15, they found their carbines quite outclassed by the long-range rifles opposed to them. But warnings whispered by a handful of men in a remote mountain-valley are almost certain to pass unheeded; sometimes they are repeated, but more frequently the penalty for their neglect has to be paid without further caution. It was so with the British cavalry in South Africa. As in the Watelai Valley in 1897, so in the basin of the Orange River in 1899, the value of a fine body of men was discounted greatly by their possession of an inferior weapon.

From an artilleryman's point of view, also, the operations of Sir Bindon Blood present some points of interest. In the first place the 10th Field Battery Royal Artillery, by reaching Inayat Kila, established a record which still remains unbeaten for the penetration of the Indian border hills by wheeled carriages, and, later on, did useful work during the storming of the Tanga Pass at the commencement of the invasion of Buner. That guns can be employed with advantage in defence by night, when well protected and preparations for directing their fire have been made by day, is shown by their use in the defence of Chakdara. Like the guns near the Crag Piquet in the Ambela Campaign, the 9-pounders in the fort at Chakdara could be trained on likely avenues of approach, and their fire is said to have been effective. Nevertheless, the occasions on which artillery fire can be usefully employed in defence at night must be very rare. In the first place, all firing at night is to be deprecated, as tending to disturb rest; secondly, an attack must be of formidable character when it is considered advisable to order guns to be fired, and, as has been noticed already in this review, night attacks on a large scale are not popular with ill-organized warriors; and, thirdly, even if guns can be trained with accuracy in the dark, the smallness of the flash produced by the bursting charge of the man-killing projectile of mobile, and especially mountain, artillery must always render the observation of fire difficult, in spite of the probable shortness of the range. In exposed situations, such as Bilot on September 16, guns are merely an encumbrance after darkness sets in, except, perhaps, for the purpose of firing star-shell; so, as a general rule, it will be better to make some sacrifice of their fire rather than run the risk of incurring the consequences involved if they are benighted. The value of artillery fire in a rear-guard action is not overlooked, but, even if they could be easily replaced, the moral effect of the loss or capture of guns, particularly in Asiatic warfare, cannot be disregarded. The strong sentiment which prevails about guns among soldiers and civilians alike has drawbacks as well as advantages; in a class of warfare where all the enemy, and two-thirds of one's own troops, are imaginative Asiatics, the moral effect of the loss of a gun would be most serious. The capture of a British gun by the frontier tribesmen would be instantly proclaimed in every village, and construed as a decisive success, with the result that every waverer would at once hasten to the scene to reap, as he would expect, the fruits of victory.

CHAPTER XVII

OPERATIONS IN MOHMAND TERRITORY AND THE KHAIBAR PASS

THE MOHMAND EXPEDITION. (*Map I.*)

IN the first week of August the banias * of Shankargarh, a small village on the British side of the border adjoining Mohmand territory, made good their escape from the place in consequence of the warnings received of what was about to happen. The Peshawar Movable Column† was sent out at once under Colonel Woon, but it was too late to save the bazar from the flames, and found the enemy occupying what may now be called the Shabkadr position‡ on a plateau one and a half miles from the fort. The following is a description of the place :

"Shabkadr Fort itself was built by the Sikhs. It stands on a mound, and has walls 50 feet high, so is practically impregnable to any force without artillery. Shankargarh was an old Sikh cantonment bazar, and it is inhabited chiefly by rich Hindu moneylenders who have had very profitable dealings with the tribesmen on both sides of the border distant only three miles away."§

After destroying Shankargarh the Mohmands had made a determined attempt to capture Shabkadr, but its garrison of forty Border Police held out for twelve hours, till the approach of the Peshawar column on August 7 caused the enemy to withdraw. On the

---

* Hindu corn-merchants. These men are usually moneylenders as well, and in time of famine, especially, derive much profit from the unthrifty peasantry.

† Consisting of—

> 51st Field Battery Royal Artillery, 4 guns.
> 13th Bengal Lancers, 2 squadrons.
> 20th Punjab Infantry.
> 1st Battalion Somerset Light Infantry, 2 companies.

‡ Compare events here in 1852 (Sir Colin Campbell) and 1864 (Colonel A. Macdonell), *q.v.*

§ " The Indian Frontier War," p. 16 (Lionel James).

same day the cavalry pushed the tribesmen back farther towards the hills, and on August 8 Colonel Woon moved out his force against them. The cavalry and guns were delayed by the difficulties of the ground in reaching the plateau close to the fort, and, while the infantry waited there, the Mohmands, to the number of about 7,000, tried to creep down, aided by the broken ground, and cut off the Somersets and Punjabis from Shabkadr. At this juncture General Elles arrived from Peshawar and assumed the direction of operations, the infantry retiring on the fort covered by the guns, but hard pressed by the enemy. An opportunity then occurred of repeating the success achieved by the squadron of the 7th Hussars under Colonel Macdonell in 1864. The two squadrons of the 13th Bengal Lancers, who at the beginning of the day had been acting as escort to the guns, were sent to work round the enemy's flank. They succeeded in taking the confidently advancing tribesmen by surprise, and added another effective charge to the record of cavalry achievements in Indian frontier warfare. The enemy broke and fled in disorder to the hills, pursued by the Lancers as fast as the nature of the ground would permit.

The next few days were spent in patrolling the surrounding country up to a distance of five miles from Shabkadr, reconnoitring the roads leading into Mohmand territory, and in watching the movements of the enemy. In the meanwhile the Government of India had decided to send a division under Brigadier-General Elles against the Mohmands, with instructions to co-operate with another division under Brigadier-General Blood to the north, known as the Malakand Field Force. The constitution of the Mohmand Field Force will be found in Table XXII.

On September 14 preparations for the advance were complete, so on the following day the advance up the Gandab Valley began at 5.30 a.m. The path led up a stony nala, passing through country the barrenness of which was relieved at rare intervals only by houses or vegetation. Throughout a stretch of ten miles not a drop of water was to be found; the heat was intense, and it was soon manifest that previous information regarding the state of the road, and the distance to the proposed camping-place, was totally inaccurate. The 1st Brigade led the advance, but, except for a little desultory firing near a place called Dand, no opposition was

TABLE XXII

THE MOHMAND FIELD FORCE, 1897

Brigadier-General E. R. Elles, C.B.

First Brigade.	Second Brigade.	Divisional Troops.
Brigadier-General R. Westmacott, C.B., D.S.O.	*Brigadier-General C. R. Macgregor, D.S.O.*	13th Bengal Lancers (13th Lancers).
1st Battalion Somerset Light Infantry.	2nd Battalion Oxfordshire Light Infantry.	No. 3 Mountain Battery Royal Artillery (No. 3 Mountain Battery Royal Garrison Artillery).
20th Punjabis.	37th Dogras, 6 Companies.	No. 5 (Bombay) Mountain Battery (25th Mountain Battery).
2nd Battalion 1st Gurkhas.	9th Gurkhas.	No. 5 Company Bengal Sappers and Miners (1st Sappers and Miners).
		28th Bombay Infantry (128th Pioneers).
		A detachment of Jodhpur Lancers.
		1st Patiala Infantry.
		Three maxims.
		Three Sections Native Field Hospital.

NOTE.—Half a British and one Native Field Hospital accompanied each Brigade.

17

encountered. The absence of the enemy was a most
fortunate and unexpected circumstance, for the passage
of the Karapa Pass proved most trying to the troops.
The path was "nothing but a stairway of boulders, up
which the transport literally had to be hauled—great
stepping-stones more like the ascent of the Egyptian
pyramids than anything else."* The steep ascent and
the heat induced a thirst among the men which could
not be assuaged till camp was reached at Gandab, twenty
miles distant from Shabkadr, instead of twelve, as had
been reported. It was dusk before the head of the
column reached Gandab, and very little of the transport
arrived that night; most of it spent the night on the
Karapa Pass. That no opposition to speak of was
encountered is probably due to the fact that the Mohmands never expected the British force to get so far the
first day, and were engaged to the north in opposing
General Jeffreys, as has been described in the account
of the operations of General Blood.

From September 10 to 19 reconnaissances were conducted towards the Nahaki Pass, and touch gained by
heliograph with General Blood. Many villages and
fortified posts were found, also more cultivation; but
water was scarce everywhere, rain-water collected in
tanks being the sole source of supply. At Gandab the
lower and more peaceable Mohmands tendered their submission,† telegraphic communication was opened with
Shabkadr and Peshawar on the 18th,‡ and the roads over
the Karapa and Nahaki Passes were greatly improved.

On September 20 the 1st Brigade, accompanied by
General Elles, moved forward over the Nahaki Pass, and
reconnoitred to the north in search of the enemy, who
were reported to be opposing the junction of the Mohmand Field Force with General Blood. The next day
General Westmacott's brigade, with the divisional troops,
advancing in the direction of Nawagai, joined hands with
Colonel Graves' brigade§ at Lakarai, five miles from
Nawagai, and Generals Elles and Blood met. The two
brigades then marched up the Badmanai Valley, under

---

* " The Indian Frontier War," p. 26 (Lionel James).
† The terms imposed were a fine of Rs. 500 and 2,400 maunds of grain, free
forage as long as the troops occupied the country, the surrender of all breech-
loading and Enfield rifles, 300 firelocks, and 300 swords.
‡ This was at the rate of seven and a half miles a day over a very bad road.
§ Colonel Graves, it will be remembered, had succeeded to the command
of General Wodehouse's Brigade, when the latter was wounded on the night
September 20/21.

the direction of General Elles, through country of greater fertility, for a combined movement against Jarobi, the stronghold of one of the principal religious leaders of the district, and camped for the night two miles from the Badmanai Pass. The pass was held by the enemy, and some sniping occurred during the night.

For the attack on the Badmanai Pass, which took place on September 22, General Westmacott's brigade advanced on the left, Colonel Graves' brigade on the right, and the three mountain batteries* with the column (No. 1 and 3 British, and No. 5 Native) were massed in the centre. The road over the pass, though comparatively easy, was protected by a fortified village at the foot, and a conical hill, crowned with a small fort, on the British left. Two companies of the Somerset Light Infantry were detached against the conical hill, while the remainder acted as escort to the guns. The enemy had prepared a series of positions on successive ridges between the foot and the summit of the pass, and it looked as if some severe fighting was in store. As matters were, however, opposition was not prolonged, though determined enough while it lasted. General Westmacott's brigade, on whom the brunt of the engagement fell, became engaged at 7.45, when the 20th Punjab Infantry came in contact with the first of the series of hostile positions.

The Mohmands held out gallantly at first, and did not evacuate their first line of defence till the Punjabis were within 40 yards. The tribesmen tried then to take ground to their right, but, coming under the fire of a maxim, which had taken up a commanding position after a stiff climb, were forced to retire straight towards their rear. Supported by the guns and Gurkhas, the 20th Punjab Infantry were launched against the second line of defence. Utilizing all the cover afforded by the ground, General Westmacott's infantry climbed steadily on, undaunted by a heavy fire, but the Mohmands did not wait for them to close, and the engagement was brought to an end by the precipitate flight of the enemy down the far side of the pass. General Elles complimented the 1st Brigade and maxim on the way in which the attack had been carried through, but the work of the Afridi company of the 20th Punjabis deserves special mention. Mr. James says: "They were a detached piquet the night

* No. 1 (British) Mountain Battery was attached to Colonel Graves' brigade.

previous to the assault, and they joined their regiment without food or water, and fought through the battle, being fourteen hours under arms without water, as they were too eager for the front to wait for the water mules";* and that they " with the maxims took the lower spurs, and had an engagement to themselves. A party of forty of the enemy ensconced themselves in a ziarat, and declared defiance by beat of drum and well-sustained fire. A detachment of Afridis of the 20th worked up to them, in spite of the Martini fire by which they were received, and, collecting under a pathway, rushed the position with the greatest pluck."† In view of the state of affairs on the North-West Frontier the loyalty and devotion shown by these Afridis on all occasions, but at Landi Kotal and Badmanai in particular, were especially remarkable. The British casualties during the day were only one killed and six wounded ; the enemy's loss is unknown. By two o'clock the engagement was over, and camp was formed at Badmanai Fort.

On September 23 and 24 the advance on Jarobi, the stronghold of the Hadda Mullah, was continued without opposition by the enemy, who, nevertheless, were close by, and on the 25th Jarobi was burned. The place is approached through a narrow gorge, which broadens out into a cultivated valley of great fertility. A company of the 20th Punjab Infantry and four companies of Gurkhas crowned the heights on the right and left of the line of advance, while two more companies of the 20th Punjab Infantry and the Sappers went forward to destroy Jarobi. The slight opposition offered was soon overcome, but, when the retirement began, the tribesmen immediately adopted their favourite tactics of harassing the flanks and rear of the retreating troops. The Bombay Pioneers and mountain batteries covered the retirement, and camp was formed without mishap at the mouth of the gorge on the Badmanai side. Some sniping took place at night, but the total casualties since the fight of the 22nd only numbered eighteen.

It was now decided that the column should circle round left handed back to Nahaki, and that a detachment of the 2nd Brigade should be sent out from that place (where it had remained during the operations just described) to co-operate in the Bohai Dag. Several Mohmand villages were destroyed on the 26th, which

---

* "The Indian Frontier War," p. 61.   † *Ibid.*, p. 59.

had the effect of producing some signs of a desire on the part of the tribesmen to come to terms, and on the next day a movement, supported by the Oxfordshire Light Infantry from Nahaki, was made against the Khuda Khel. Little opposition was encountered; the work of destruction was done with the protection of the usual flanking parties, and the retirement carried out without loss under the cover of artillery fire, which effectually stopped all attempts at pursuit.

September 28 was devoted to the discussion of terms of peace with representatives of the various sections of the Mohmand tribe, the result of which was that proportionate fines of money and arms were imposed, which had to be paid within a week. The work of the expedition was now done, and, while part of the force remained in the country till the fines had been paid, the remainder left for India in compliance with a new scheme of distribution of the troops to the Malakand and Tirah Field Forces. The total casualties to the Mohmand Field Force only amounted to four killed and twenty-five wounded. Though no decisive action had been fought, owing to the reluctance of the tribesmen to make any determined stand, a large tract of territory was overrun which had never been visited before by a British force, and sufficient proof was given that depredations across the border could not be carried on with impunity.

THE ATTACK ON THE KHAIBAR FORTS. (*Map II.*)

In the middle of August, 1897, reports reached the ears of the British authorities of negotiations between the Afridis and Orakzais for simultaneous attacks on the British posts in the Khaibar Pass on the one hand, and in the Kurram Valley and on the Samana Ridge on the other. Accordingly, the garrisons of the forts at Jamrud and Bara were strengthened, the troops at Kohat were reinforced, and Brigadier-General A. G. Yeatman-Biggs was sent to command the troops in the Kohat District. There was some difficulty in arranging details connected with the simultaneous rising of the Afridis and Orakzais, and the delay thus caused afforded valuable time for strengthening the British position along the border. At length the first blow was struck on August 23, when an overwhelming attack was made on Ali Masjid and Fort Maude, a small fort three miles on the Khaibar Pass side of Jamrud, both of which were garrisoned by detachments of the Khaibar Rifles. Ali Masjid was abandoned without a struggle, but the little garrison of about forty men at Fort Maude held out bravely for a time till they, too, fell back on a force sent out from Jamrud to the mouth of the Khaibar Pass;* both forts were burnt to the ground.

Flushed with their initial success, the tribesmen then retraced their steps up the pass, and appeared before Landi Kotal at noon the next day. The garrison of Landi Kotal, which consisted of 370 men of the Khaibar Rifles drawn from various clans, defended themselves with bravery and success, in spite of some defections, till about 10 a.m. on August 25, when the gate of the fort was treacherously opened and the assailants rushed in. Some of the garrison at once joined in the looting and destruction of the fort, some were allowed to escape after giving up their arms, but others succeeded in fighting their way through, and reached Jamrud in safety, bringing their rifles with them. As soon as the fort had been looted, and the quarters of the troops set on fire, the tribesmen dispersed to their homes; their losses were estimated at 12 at Ali Masjid, 34 at Fort Maude, and 200 at Landi Kotal.

The road through the Khaibar Pass remained closed till reopened by General Hammond's column at the end of December. After the conclusion of the expedition into the Bazar Valley, the reconstruction of the forts was put in hand at once.† These were not found to be so damaged as had been supposed, for, although the interior had been gutted in each case, the walls were intact, and the water-tanks about a mile and a half below Landi Kotal were untouched. Before peace was restored, small skirmishes were of frequent occurrence, during one of which the 2nd Battalion Oxfordshire Light Infantry lost three killed and fourteen wounded, and the troops in the Khaibar Pass had to be reinforced by the despatch of two additional battalions to Landi Kotal, and the 1st Brigade from Jamrud to Ali Masjid. The road connecting Landi Kotal with the Bazar Valley by way of the Bori Pass was reconnoitred by General Hammond on December 27, but was found to be impracticable for military purposes.

---

* With the Khaibar Pass full of Afridis, it was not considered safe for this force to enter the defile; the withdrawal of the Khaibar Rifles was, however, covered by a few rounds from the guns.

† They were constructed at a cost of 3 lakhs of rupees (£20,000).

CHAPTER XVIII

EVENTS IN THE KOHAT DISTRICT

(*Map II.*)

ON August 20, 1897, it was considered advisable to send out to Hangu from Kohat a support to the troops stationed in the Kurram Valley and on the Samana Ridge. This force consisted of the troops named below, under the command of Colonel G. L. R. Richardson, C.I.E.

> 18th Bengal Lancers.
> 3rd Punjab Cavalry, 1 squadron.
> No. 2 Derajat Mountain Battery, 4 guns.
> 5th Punjab Infantry.
> Reinforced on August 28 by—
> 9th Field Battery Royal Artillery.
> 2nd Battalion Royal Irish Regiment.

From Hangu reconnaissances were made in various directions, and the supply of ammunition at Forts Lockhart and Gulistan was replenished. It was not, however, till August 26, the day after the withdrawal of the Afridis from Landi Kotal, that the Orakzais plucked up courage to assume the offensive. On that day they seized the Ublan Pass, some six miles north-west of Kohat, and threatened the British post of Muhammadzai, situated near the foot. Accordingly, the force named below moved out from Kohat at dawn on the 27th, under General Yeatman-Biggs, and, in spite of a heavy fire from the enemy's marksmen posted on the inaccessible crags overlooking the pass, gained the summit about 8 a.m.

> 3rd Punjab Cavalry, 1 squadron.
> 9th Field Battery Royal Artillery.
> 2nd Battalion Royal Scots Fusiliers, 2 companies.
> 2nd Punjab Infantry.

The majority of the enemy fled down the northern slopes of the pass, but, as soon as the withdrawal began, the snipers concealed among the rocks, whom neither the guns nor the infantry had been able to dislodge, proceeded to harass the retirement, and several casualties occurred. The troops were handicapped greatly throughout by the absence of cover, the heat, and the scarcity of water, but the whole force returned to Kohat the same day without mishap. It will be remembered that the Ublan Pass was the scene of an unsuccessful attack from Kohat in March, 1868, but was crossed without opposition after a sudden advance by a force under Colonel Keyes in the following February.

While the operations just related were taking place in the Ublan Pass, the force at Hangu made an expedition to the crest of the Samana Ridge to relieve the police posts at Lakha and Saifaldara, which were being hard pressed by the Orakzais. This was accomplished without much fighting, except during the retirement, which was persistently, but not seriously, harassed, and the troops returned to Hangu, after a fatiguing day, at 11 p.m. On August 30 the following incident occurred :

"It was noticed that several men were lurking about on the near hills above camp, whence the firing had come, evidently a refuge whence to snipe safely into camp. Accordingly one of the 12-pounders was trained on to the cave, and about 9 a.m. a shrapnel shell was fired into it. As may be easily imagined, no more sniping occurred, and five or six bodies were being buried the following day."*

On August 30, also, in consequence of reports of a threatened attack on the Kurram Valley post, the force named below started for Sadda, under Colonel Richardson, arriving there on September 5 after a rapid march, in spite of trying conditions due to heat and rain, and some opposition on the part of the enemy.

> 18th Bengal Lancers.
> No. 2 Derajat Mountain Battery, 4 guns.
> No. 4 Company Bombay Sappers and Miners.
> 5th Punjab Infantry.
> 15th Sikhs.

In the meantime things had begun to look serious in the Kurram Valley, for a force of some 3,000 Afridis and Orakzais was in the neighbourhood, more were expected to arrive, and on September 1 nothing had been heard of the approach of Colonel Richardson's column from Hangu. On September 1 the post of Balish Khel, three miles

---

* The *Pioneer*, "The Risings on the North-West Frontier," p. 123.

north-west of Sadda, was attacked as a preliminary to an assault on the latter, the incident being described as follows in the account of the risings on the North-West Frontier published by the *Pioneer* Press :

" The firing began in broad daylight, and increased as twilight deepened into darkness, when a continuous fusillade was kept up on every side till midnight. The Balish Khel post consists of a small tower, with a courtyard on the south side, in which are the huts inhabited by the garrison, which amounted at the time of the attack to twenty men of the Kurram Militia, under a havildar. No doubt the Afridis expected to make small work of this mere handful of men ; but the fire kept up from the ramparts was so severe that for a long time none of the attackers dared venture near the walls. About midnight ammunition began to run short; the Afridis crept up to the courtyard gate and began to hew it in pieces with axes. This they soon succeeded in doing, but the fire from the tower still kept them, almost literally, at arm's length. They tried, but failed, to set the huts on fire. Matters were getting serious for the little garrison, and they made signals of distress by throwing up bundles of burning grass from the top of the tower. The enemy were now closing in when help at last arrived from two directions. Fifty men (Malik Khel) arrived from Sadda, and charged right up to the fort walls, losing two of their number in doing so. The Afridis drew off, leaving two bodies in the gateway of the courtyard. Fifty Kurram Militia also arrived from Hassan Ali, but they were just too late to get into touch with the enemy. Only one of our men in the fort was wounded." *

The news received on September 2 of the approach of reinforcements was a pleasant surprise to the garrison of Sadda, and a great blow to the Afridis, who dispersed at once without further attack. In this connection it should be mentioned that the Turis—a Kurram Valley tribe— proved their loyalty to the British cause by sending a contingent to the assistance of the garrison of Sadda, but, with the arrival of Colonel Richardson's column, no occasion arose for the use of their services. An attack was made on Sadda during the night, September 16/17, but the discipline of the troops, and their allotment to the defensive perimeter, was so good that, though some casualties occurred, particularly among the animals, there was never the slightest doubt as to the result.

* The *Pioneer*, " The Risings on the North-West Frontier," p. 128.

The organization and part played by the Kurram Movable Column during the expedition against the Chamkannis will be found recorded in the account of the Tirah Campaign which follows, but, to save a digression then, it will be well to narrate here the circumstances which led up to a mishap to the Kapurthala Infantry, which points its own moral.

On November 6 Colonel Hill, commanding the Kurram Movable Column, made a reconnaissance from Sadda of a defile leading to Chamkanni territory. Esor was reached at 11 a.m. without opposition, and the retirement began two hours later, when the tribesmen pressed forward with some determination, but, being severely checked at the outset, allowed Colonel Hill's force to complete the last five miles to Sadda without molestation. In the meantime, however, a mishap occurred to a piquet of thirty-five men of the Kapurthala Infantry, who had been assisting to guard the heights flanking the line of march, which is related thus:

"When the piquet was signalled to withdraw and join the main body, the message was acknowledged; but, unfortunately, the withdrawal was not begun forthwith, though the route by which the piquet had ascended was a perfectly safe one, as none of the enemy were near it, having, in fact, begun to retire up the defile. What was worse, the delay made in executing the order of withdrawal entirely escaped attention, and, indeed, it was eventually reported to Colonel Hill that all units of his column were present. Thereafter the march of the column to Sadda was resumed, and the five miles were covered in ignorance of the absence of the piquet. Stranger still, 'All present' was again reported to the officer commanding the force in camp the next morning, and it was actually not until late in the day that Colonel Hill was informed that a subadar and thirty-five men of the Kapurthala Infantry were missing. Search parties were sent out, but no trace of the party could be found, and all too late it was discovered that only a few members of it had actually rejoined the column when it started back. What really happened to the ill-fated piquet was only discovered later. The subadar in command had apparently watched the running fight in the defile with the closest attention, and conceived the idea of sharing in it. The sepoys were equally keen, and it is perhaps not to be wondered at that a body of brave men, whose discipline is not of the hard-and-fast kind which obtains in our own regiments,

Plate IV

A FRONTIER HOUSE : GURKHA PIQUET

To face p. 266

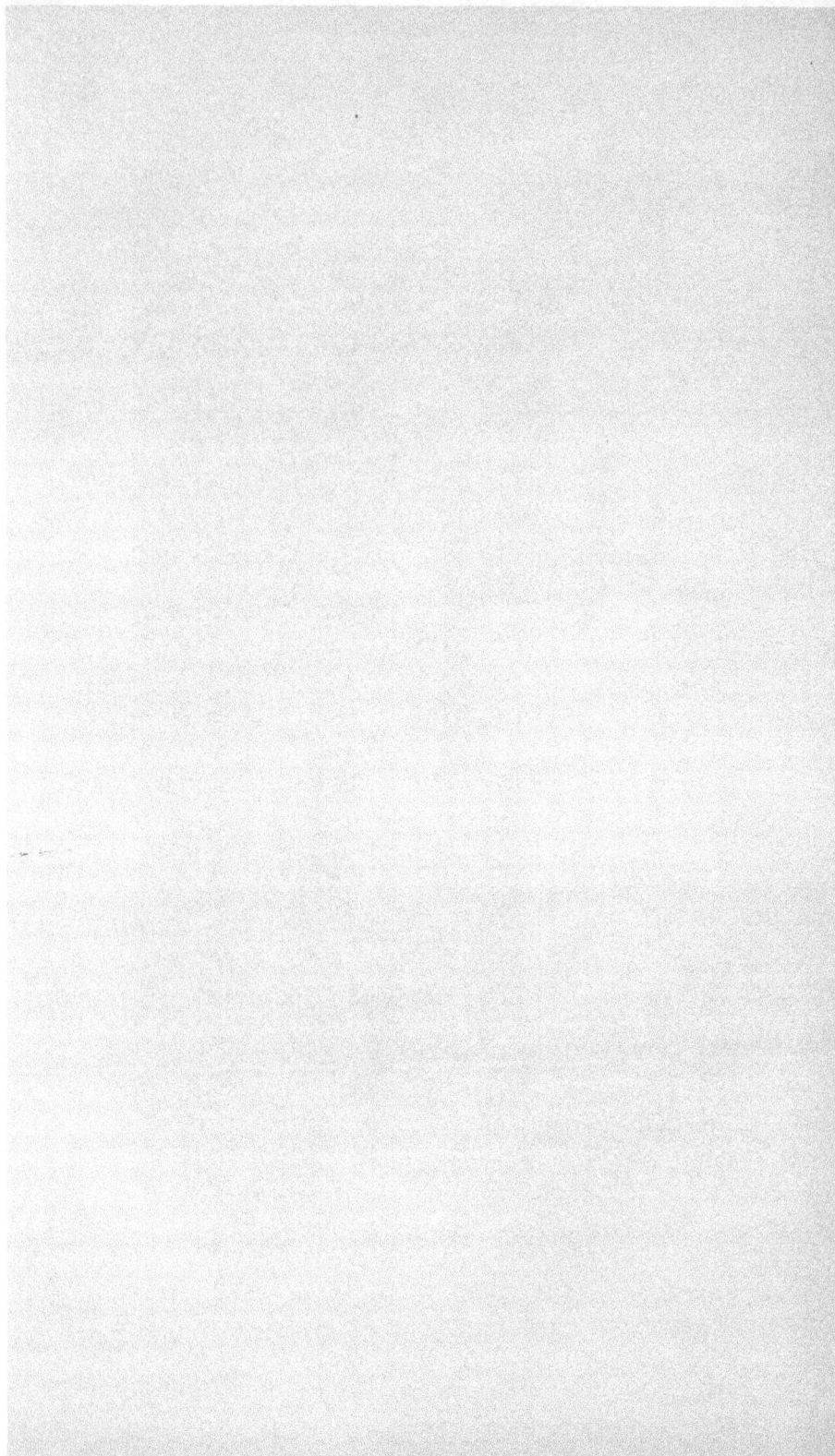

should have been excited when they saw an action taking place only a couple of miles or so away in which they had no prospect of participating.

"When the signal to retire was received, the last hope of the piquet of even a chance skirmish disappeared. Very reluctantly they began to descend. The route by which they ascended was taken at first; but after it had been followed for some distance the subadar and the more impetuous spirits decided to disobey the order signalled to them, and to move down the ridge in a direction which would bring them into the defile considerably higher up. The signallers and five men went on in the original direction, and reached the main column in safety. So far as could be made out, the subadar's party soon got into very broken ground among cliffs and nalas, and eventually dropped into a narrow and difficult ravine. If they had been able to follow this to its junction with the defile they would have come out above the Gurkha rear-guard, and would even then have been in a highly dangerous position. But as they moved down the ravine they discovered that the way was barred, the jungle being on fire. Finding themselves trapped, they endeavoured to retrace their steps, and were observed by some of the tribesmen. The lashkar thereupon halted in its retirement, and, the enemy turning back, swarmed about the nala, effectually cutting off all retreat. As heavy firing might have attracted the attention of the main body of the troops, the Massuzais and Chamkannis contented themselves by sitting on guard, and it was not until the moon rose that they made their attack, rolling stones into the ravine and shooting down the whole party."[*]

THE ATTACKS ON THE SAMANA FORTS.

The story of the attack and defence of the Samana Forts must now be narrated. On September 10 General Yeatman-Biggs, who had assumed command of the troops at Hangu, heard that a large force of Afridis and Orakzais was marching down the Khanki Valley towards the eastern end of the Samana Ridge. He therefore marched out on the following day to intercept this movement, and succeeded in turning the tribesmen back, but had to return to Hangu for want of water. Here he remained

---

[*] The *Pioneer*, "The Risings on the North-West Frontier," p. 184.

on September 12 and 13, ready to move in any required direction ; but in the meantime a grim tragedy was being enacted at Saragarhi, a small post on the Samana Ridge between Forts Lockhart and Gulistan. The story is told in the account published by the *Pioneer* Press in the following words :

"After repeated assaults the tribesmen succeeded in capturing, on September 12, under circumstances that will long be remembered, the small post of Saragarhi on the road between the two forts. The garrison, which consisted of only twenty-one men of the 36th Sikhs, made a gallant defence, holding out from nine o'clock in the morning till 4.30 in the afternoon against odds which from the first were clearly overwhelming. Two determined assaults were brilliantly repulsed ; but at the third rush the enemy succeeded in breaking down the door, and, when the plucky Sikhs manning the walls rushed down from their posts to defend the doorway, the swarming tribesmen scaled the walls and all was over. But not a sepoy even then thought of surrendering while life remained, and eventually the whole of the gallant defenders fell victims to their heroism. One stout-hearted soldier in the guard-room killed twenty of the enemy without hurt to himself, and lost his life by refusing to budge when the Afridis, unable to get at him, finally set the room on fire. The signaller, as brave as the rest, coolly kept up communication with Fort Lockhart up till the very last moment. The entire garrison, in fact, behaved with splendid courage, and there is perhaps no more touching instance of inflexible devotion to duty than this in the whole narrative of frontier fighting."[*]

It must not be overlooked that the only accounts available of the defence of Saragarhi are those furnished by the enemy. Not a single defender escaped to tell the tale, so it is impossible to be quite sure of all the details of this desperate fight. Another account says :

"After the second assault on Saragarhi two of the enemy had been left behind in a dead angle of the flanking tower. These, working with some instrument, had speedily removed a stone, and then mass after mass of the masonry fell. Soon a practicable breach was made, and in less time than it takes to write all was over.

---

[*] The *Pioneer*, "The Risings on the North-West Frontier," p. 133. In this and other extracts the modern spelling, "Saragarhi," has been substituted for "Saragheri."

Hundreds swarmed in through the breach and over the walls. The little garrison — twenty-one rifles only in all before the fight began—retreated to their sleeping quarters and fought it out grimly to the bitter end." *

The whole attack had been visible to the garrisons of Forts Lockhart and Gulistan, but the enemy were in such force that it was quite impossible to do anything to save the situation. *À propos* of Saragarhi in particular, and frontier posts in general, the following comment appeared in the *Pioneer :*

" Some of them are certain death-traps in case of attack by large bodies of tribesmen, and in the interests of those who have to defend them something should be done to give the garrisons some chance of holding out until help can reach them. In more than one instance we read of wooden doors having been forced open. Is there any good reason why those doors should not be so placed as to be out of the reach of anyone who has not a scaling ladder? All along the borderland and in Afghanistan are towers which might be well taken as patterns for our very small posts. The lower portions of these are of rocks and stones ; the door is 10 or 15 feet above the ground, and access to the tower is gained by a ladder, which is pushed up when there is an alarm of an enemy approaching. At Saragarhi, and at Sadda also, the doors seem to have been flush with the ground, and the tribesmen could thus get at them with pickaxes, and, in the case of Saragarhi, force an entrance   The fact seems to be that our smaller posts are built for occupation by levies, and the men ordinarily occupying them can generally arrange to make terms with their assailants and so escape with their lives. But when war breaks out and there is a great rush of hostile bodies across our frontier, some of the posts have to be taken over by regular troops and held at all costs. They are hastily provisioned, a scanty supply of water is given to the garrison, and only in the matter of abundant ammunition are our sepoys made happy. They cheerfully face the danger into which they are thus thrust, and they die fighting to the last. There must be something very wrong in a system which thus makes the fate of a small party of soldiers a foregone conclusion. We are told that it was essential to hold Saragarhi in order to maintain communication by signalling between Forts Lockhart and Gulistan. If that were so, the little post should

---

* The *Pioneer*, " The Risings on the North-West Frontier," p. 139.

have been originally made so strong that it could hold out for at least three or four days."

Another account states that "there was much dead ground round the fort, and that 100 men would have been required to defend it successfully."

While Saragarhi was being attacked, Fort Gulistan was also closely invested; but, as soon as the former fell, and the reinforcements thus set free had arrived, the tribesmen pressed forward with great daring to within 20 yards of an enclosure 80 yards long by 30 broad on the west side of the fort. As it was feared that, in order to breach the wall, the enemy might make use of the dead ground which existed near the bastions, it was decided to make a sortie and drive the assailants to a more respectful distance. The garrison of Fort Gulistan consisted of 165 men of the 36th Sikhs, under Major C. H. Des Vœux, assisted by Lieutenant H. R. E. Pratt and Surgeon-Captain C. B. Pratt, in addition to whom there were the wife and family of Major Des Vœux. Havildar Kala Singh volunteered to carry out the sortie with his section, numbering sixteen men, and the exploit which followed is described thus :

"The enemy at the immediate point to be attacked numbered at least 200. The little party with bayonets fixed crept out of the south-east gateway and along the south wall of the hornwork ;* then, when within 20 yards or so of the enemy, made a rush. They were met with such a fire that they could not get up to the enemy, but, though sadly reduced, they had no thought of retreat, but lay down at a distance of only six paces from the enemy's sangar and returned the fire. At this juncture Colour-Havildar Sunder Singh and twelve men posted in the hornwork at the nearest point to the sangar, without waiting for orders, and of their own initiative, scrambled over the wall and joined Kala Singh's section ; and the combined party then charged the enemy, killed and wounded a great number, drove the remainder out, and captured three of their standards, which they brought back to the fort, amidst ringing cheers from their comrades. It was then discovered that two wounded men had been left behind. Three sepoys, two of whom had taken part in the sortie, at once of their own initiative again got over the wall and brought the two wounded men in. During the sortie a hot fire was kept up from every effective rifle in the fort and hornwork, and thanks

* The enclosure already mentioned.

partly to this the casualties were not greater, though twelve of the first party and four of the second were wounded, and several afterwards died."*

The moral effect of this counterstroke was excellent, for not only were the spirits of the garrison greatly raised, but a large number of the enemy at once returned to their homes. On the same day (September 13) Major Des Vœux managed to send a letter to Fort Lockhart to ask for help, but by evening the tribesmen had surrounded the post, and kept up a fire on the defenders all through the night. The garrison, however, were much encouraged by the sight, at 7 p.m., of the 9th Field Battery in action in the Miranzai Valley, the presence of which will be explained presently; but it was not till 8 a.m. on September 15 that the jaded garrison, who had never been able to relax their vigilance for an instant, heard the welcome sound of the firing of the relief column. The enemy then made a supreme bid for victory, but at noon Saragarhi was recaptured by General Yeatman-Biggs, and the tribesmen round Gulistan melted away. The total loss during the siege was two killed and forty wounded. Major Des Vœux, and indeed the entire garrison, spoke in terms of the warmest praise of the bravery and devotion shown by Miss Teresa McGrath, Mrs. Des Vœux's nurse, who was indefatigable in her care of the wounded throughout the siege.†

It has been mentioned already that on September 11 General Yeatman-Biggs visited the Samana Ridge, and drove back up the Khanki Valley a large force of Afridis and Orakzais; but owing to want of water was obliged to return to Hangu the same day. The events which followed are best described in the graphic words of the special correspondent of the *Pioneer*:

"At 3.30 p.m.,‡ just as we had started on our return to Hangu, we received news by helio that the greater part of the lashkar we had been hunting had doubled on its tracks, and was at that moment investing the posts we had left the day before, Saragarhi and Gulistan being hard pressed. There was not a drop of water to drink nearer than Hangu, and to fight our way back in the

---

* The *Pioneer*, " The Risings on the North-West Frontier," p. 135.
† Miss McGrath was afterwards awarded the Indian Frontier Medal, with clasps for 1897 and Samana, and the Royal Red Cross was bestowed on her by Her Majesty Queen Victoria. She died at Peshawar in 1907. Mrs. Des Vœux also assisted as far as she was able, but her physical condition at this time prevented her from undergoing any exertion.
‡ September 11, 1897.

dark without it was, in view of the condition of men and animals, a physical impossibility. Very reluctantly the General, not daring to leave Hangu unprotected, followed the convoy, and we toiled painfully down the path, much harassed by the tribesmen, and at 6.30 p.m. arrived in camp dead beat. All next day we rested as well as we could after receiving the news of the fall of Saragarhi, which reached us that evening, haunted by the fear that we should be too late to relieve Gulistan, which, be it remembered, contained English women and children. As a diversion, five squadrons and four field guns were sent off under Major Middleton, 3rd Bengal Cavalry, to get as near as possible under Gulistan, and do what they could. As it turned out this was a good deal, for though their fire at that range could not be very effective, their appearance not only cheered the beleaguered garrison, but misled the enemy, by suggesting to them that our advance would be by Doaba. This they showed by breaking up the roads and planting sangars against us.

"At midnight the relieving force started from Hangu, carrying only great-coats, waterproof sheets, and one day's provisions, with every pakhal we could muster. The whole force was concentrated at Lakha at 4.30 a.m., and at daybreak we advanced to Gogra Hill. As we anticipated, the enemy, though taken by surprise, soon took possession of an ideal position on the hill, with advanced posts at Tsalai, with eleven standards and about 4,000 men. They opened a hot and fairly accurate fire on our advance, but the guns, which were brought up quickly into the front line, soon produced an effect, and the 3rd Gurkhas, supported by the 2nd Gurkhas, stormed the hill. The enemy's retreat was pounded by the guns and long-range fire of the Royal Irish, and Colonel Haughton on the west, hurrying down from Fort Lockhart with all of the 36th Sikhs and signallers and sick of the Royal Irish that could be spared, materially quickened their pace.

"Our force rapidly pushed on for Fort Lockhart, passing on its way the little post of Sangar, besieged for the last twenty-four hours. Its garrison of forty-one men of the 36th Sikhs were drawn up as we passed, proudly displaying a standard which they had captured in a smart little sortie the night before. On we pushed to Fort Lockhart, and the General, mounting the fort tower, could see Saragarhi Hill, on which the captured post stood, covered with masses of the enemy. . . . Still there was no news of Fort Gulistan, so the General, ordering up the guns, soon had the hill so swept by shrapnel that on the advance of the infantry not a soul was found. It was a thousand pities, for, had we but known it, Gulistan was safe for some hours yet, and, had we but had the time, we might have inflicted heavy loss on an enemy whose line of retreat would have been open to our fire. However, so far as we knew, no time was to be lost; so, limbering up, we pushed on another two miles, and there, on the opposite hill, stood Gulistan Fort, still bravely holding out. The slopes above and beyond were literally packed with swarms of the enemy, now warned by the sound of our guns that the time for their departure was at hand. At the sight of our skirmishers on the sky-line, every man of the beleaguered garrison who could stand, wounded or whole, sprang to the parapets, and opened a heavy fire on the now wavering foe. Our guns hurried up, and, unlimbering, poured in their shrapnel, while the infantry, racing down the steep hillside, did their best with long-range volleys to persuade some at least of the tribesmen to stay behind.

"Saragarhi was a piteous sight. The fort which only two days before we had deemed impregnable unless reduced by want of ammunition, water, or food, was almost levelled to the ground, while the bodies of its gallant garrison lay stripped and horribly mutilated amid the ruins of the post they had so bravely held."

After the relief of Gulistan, the enemy evacuated the neighbourhood of the Samana Forts, and the opportunity was seized for improving the defences and communications. The water-supply, however, was a great difficulty, for though sufficient for the ordinary garrison of six companies, it was not sufficient for the requirements of a whole brigade. Very little further fighting took place, for preparations were begun at once for the despatch of the Tirah Field Force into Orakzai and Afridi territory, and just over a month later the first capture of Dargai was made.

CHAPTER XIX

TIRAH

(Map II.)

THE Afridis are by far the most powerful of the Indian frontier tribes ; the fertility of their valleys is sufficient not only to support a numerous population,* but to be a considerable source of wealth. Afridi territory covers a tract of country some 900 square miles in extent, which is nearly the size of the county of Essex. The Afridi character has been described thus : "Ruthless, cowardly robbery, cold-blooded, treacherous murder are to an Afridi the salt of life. Brought up from his earliest childhood amid scenes of appalling treachery and merciless revenge, nothing can change him ; as he has lived a shameless, cruel savage, so he dies." But Sir Robert Warburton, who gained the respect and confidence of the tribes adjoining the Khaibar Pass to an extent which is unique, says in his "Eighteen Years in the Khyber"†:—

"The Afridi lad from his earliest childhood is taught by the circumstances of his existence and life to distrust all mankind, and very often his near relations, heirs to his small plot of land by right of inheritance, are his deadliest enemies. Distrust of all mankind and readiness to strike the first blow for the safety of his own life have therefore become the maxims of the Afridi. If you can overcome this mistrust, and be kind in words to him, he will repay you by great devotion, and he will put up with any punishment you like to give him except abuse. It took me years to get through this thick crust of mistrust, but what was the after-result ? For upwards of fifteen years I went about unarmed amongst these people. My camp, wherever it happened to be pitched, was always guarded and protected by them. The deadliest enemies of the Khyber Range, with a long record of blood-feuds,

---

* They are said to be able to put a force of 30,000 men in the field.
† The modern spelling of the name is Khaibar.

dropped those feuds for the time being when in my camp. Property was always safe, and the only record of anything being ever removed was the gear belonging to the trooper of the Khyber Rifles, taken away from the serai at Landi Kotal, which was a case of enmity; but every item was brought back and placed at Malik Wali Muhammad Khan's Gateway in the Khyber."

The Afridi method of assembling the tribal forces and maintaining them in the field is interesting. Colonel Paget, in his "Record of the Expeditions against the North-West Frontier Tribes," says that councils are elected among the tribesmen, who "arrange all the plans of the campaign and the number of men required from each branch of the tribe, which are furnished in quotas from villages in proportion to their numerical strength, and each party is headed by its own malik. On taking the field each man brings with him a sheepskin full of flour, and the amount of ammunition that he can manage to collect; but should hostilities be protracted beyond the time that the supply of provisions will last, the tribes are either kept together and fed by contributions from villages in the neighbourhood, or disperse for a few days to make ammunition and to replenish their commissariat; but, should the latter contingency be adopted, it frequently happens that mistrust in each other and the fear of treachery in their neighbours prevent their again uniting."

The Afridis are essentially a fighting race; many of them have taken service under the British flag, and returned to their native land at the conclusion of their term of service to enjoy their pensions. It would appear at first sight that the only result of allowing these men to enlist in Imperial regiments is to teach them the art of war, to their great advantage in any subsequent fighting against us. No doubt this is true to a certain extent, but, as a matter of fact, the actual results of enlisting trans-frontier men in regiments of the Indian Army have been so far from proving undesirable, that in 1911 eight infantry regiments have fifteen companies composed entirely of Afridis, Orakzais, Mahsuds, or Waziris.* In the only class of fighting in which

* There are also seven companies of Khattaks in five regiments, the Khattaks being a Pathan clan living between Kohat and the River Indus.

In addition to these class companies, forty-seven companies of men, called broadly Pathans, are distributed among twenty regiments of the Indian Army. These companies are recruited mainly in British territory, but many transfrontier Pathans are included in them.

they are ever likely to be our enemies, we have little to
teach them in the tactics best suited to their conditions of
organization and *terrain*. It is only in the higher branches
of the art of war—the domain of strategy rather than
tactics—that they have much to learn. On the authority
of Napoleon, " in war men are nothing—the man is everything "; discipline and combination have always been the
foundation of the success of civilized armies against
irregular foes, and both require the presence of a master-
hand. Moreover, it is by no means certain, even if he
could acquire the principles of strategy during his service
in the ranks, or even as a native officer, that the frontier
tribesmen would put them into practice with advantage
to his race. Lack of organization has always been the
keynote of those guerilla tactics which have baffled again
and again the armies of civilized nations.

Politically speaking, the spread of the knowledge of
British power, of the real British attitude towards them,
and of education generally among the border tribes, has
undoubtedly been greatly furthered by the return of
Indian army pensioners to their homes among the north-
western hills. As was proved in 1908, they are no longer
the ready tools of misguided religious maniacs ; they
know the value of British friendship, and are able to
count the cost of losing it.

One of the greatest difficulties felt at the outset of the
Tirah Campaign was the lack of topographical information. Many of the parts about to be invaded had never
been visited before by Europeans, and native sources of
intelligence have always to be looked upon with suspicion.
Various lines of operations were possible, but it was
expected that the Orakzais would tender their submission as soon as their country was occupied, thus securing
the comparative safety of a long stretch of the line of communication. This advantage, and the greater defensive
facilities of the route, decided the question in favour of
penetration from the south. It was resolved to enter
Afridi territory by a single line of advance on account
of the difficulty of maintaining more than one line of
communication, the formidable combined strength of
the Orakzais and Afridis which was estimated at between
40,000 and 50,000 men, and the necessity for striking a
prompt and decisive blow.

The concentration, which took place at Kohat, thirty-
two miles by road from rail-head at Khushalgarh, on the
banks of the Indus, was greatly delayed by the necessity

for awaiting the arrival of troops from the Mohmand
and Malakand Field Forces, and the great strain
thrown on the resources of the department concerned with the provision of transport and supplies,
owing to the simultaneous progress of so many different
expeditions. At length, however, on October 10, all was
ready for an advance. In view of the known numerical
strength and warlike character of the Orakzais and
Afridis, the large force of two divisions was mobilized
so as to run no risk of failure. The composition of the
force is given in Table XXIII., and the troops detailed
for the lines of communication, movable columns, and
Rawal Pindi Reserve Brigade in Tables XXIV. and
XXV. In addition to the troops enumerated, two companies of Gurkhas were attached to each brigade for
scouting duties.

On October 11 the four days' march to Shinawari was
begun, with the 2nd Division leading; and on the 18th
a reconnaissance was made of the road to the Khanki
Valley through Dargai, with the object of finding an
alternative route for the transport, which included no
less than 42,810 animals.* On this day the 1st Division
was some sixteen miles in rear along the road to Kohat.

The Dargai Ridge is very steep—in fact, in many places
precipitous—and the road leading up it to the village of
the same name, situated on the top, was at this time
extremely bad. The crest was lined with sangars, from

* The number of transport animals employed with the different columns
was:

	Two-Maund Animals.	Five-Maund Animals.	Total.
Tirah Field Force	29,440	13,370	42,810
Peshawar Column	3,220	980	4,200
Kurram Column	280	2,390	2,670
Rawal Pindi Reserve Brigade ...	460	670	1,130
Malakand Field Force ...	2 950	3,320	6,270
Tochi Field Force	2,300	4,200	6,500
Kohat Garrison	180	750	930
Peshawar Garrison	500	790	1,290
Reserve	3,000	3,000	6,000
Totals	42,330	29,470	71,800

Two-maund animals include mules, ponies, and pack-bullocks; camels
are 5-maund animals; donkeys are 1½-maund animals. A maund equals
80 pounds ("The Indian Frontier War," p. 134).

TABLE XXIII

TIRAH FIELD FORCE, 1897

LIEUTENANT-GENERAL SIR W. S. A. LOCKHART, K.C.B., K.C.S.I.

FIRST DIVISION.

MAJOR-GENERAL W. P. SYMONS, C.B.

FIRST BRIGADE.	SECOND BRIGADE.	DIVISIONAL TROOPS.
Colonel I. S. M. Hamilton, C.B., D.S.O., succeeded by Brigadier-General R. Hart, V.C., C.B.	*Brigadier-General A. Gaselee, C.B.*	18th Bengal Lancers, 2 squadrons.
		No. 1 Mountain Battery Royal Artillery (1st Mountain Battery Royal Garrison Artillery).
2nd Battalion Derbyshire Regiment.	2nd Battalion Yorkshire Regiment.	No. 1 (Kohat) Mountain Battery (21st Kohat Mountain Battery).
1st Battalion Devonshire Regiment.	1st Battalion Royal West Surrey Regiment.	No. 2 (Derajat) Mountain Battery (22nd Derajat Mountain Battery).
30th Punjab Infantry (30th Punjabis).	3rd Sikhs (53rd Sikhs).	Two companies Bombay Sappers and Miners (3rd Sappers and Miners).
2nd Battalion 1st Gurkhas.	2nd Battalion 4th Gurkhas.	One Printing Section Bombay Sappers and Miners.
		28th Bombay Infantry (Pioneers).
		Nabha Regiment Imperial Service Infantry.
		Mala Kotla Imperial Service Sappers.
		One Section British Field Hospital.
		One Native Field Hospital.

SECOND DIVISION

Major-General A. G. Yeatman-Biggs, C.B.

Third Brigade.	Fourth Brigade.	Divisional Troops.
Brigadier-General F. J. Kempster, D.S.O.	*Brigadier-General R. Westmacott, C.B., D.S.O.*	18th Bengal Lancers, 2 squadrons.
1st Battalion Gordon Highlanders.	2nd Battalion King's Own Scottish Borderers.	No. 8 Mountain Battery Royal Artillery (8th Mountain Battery Royal Garrison Artillery).
1st Battalion Dorsetshire Regiment.	1st Battalion Northamptonshire Regiment.	No. 9 Mountain Battery Royal Artillery (9th Mountain Battery Royal Garrison Artillery).
15th Sikhs.	36th Sikhs.	No. 5 (Bombay) Mountain Battery (25th Mountain Battery).
1st Battalion 2nd Gurkhas.	1st Battalion 3rd Gurkhas.	Machine Gun Detachment 16th Lancers.
		No. 4 Company Madras Sappers and Miners (12th Company 2nd Sappers and Miners).
		One Printing Section Madras Sappers and Miners.
		21st Madras Infantry Pioneers (81st Pioneers).
		Jhind Regiment Imperial Service Infantry.
		Sirmur Imperial Service Sappers.
		One Section British Field Hospital.
		One Native Field Hospital.

NOTE.—One British and one Native Field Hospital were attached to each Brigade.

TABLE XXIV

LINES OF COMMUNICATION.	RAWAL PINDI RESERVE BRIGADE.
Lieutenant-General Sir A. P. Palmer, K.C.B.	*Brigadier-General C. R. Macgregor, D.S.O.*
3rd Bengal Cavalry (3rd Skinner's Horse).	2nd Battalion King's Own Yorkshire Light Infantry.
18th Bengal Lancers (18th Lancers).	1st Battalion Duke of Cornwall's Light Infantry.
One company Bengal Sappers and Miners (1st Sappers and Miners).	37th Bombay Light Infantry (127th Baluch Light Infantry).
2nd Punjab Infantry (56th Punjabi Rifles).	2nd Regiment of Infantry Hyderabad Contingent (95th Russell's Infantry).
22nd Punjab Infantry (22nd Punjabis).	One British and one Native Field Hospital.
39th Garhwal Infantry (39th Garhwal Rifles).	Jodhpur Imperial Service Lancers.
2nd Battalion 2nd Gurkhas.	
Ordnance and Engineer Field Parks.	
Two Native Field Hospitals.	
One British and one Native General Hospital, with 500 beds at Rawal Pindi.	
Two Field Medical Store Depots.	
Two British and two Native Field Hospitals for sick and wounded from front.	
One Veterinary Field Hospital.	
One Kashmir Mountain Battery.	
Jaipur Imperial Service Transport Corps.	
Gwalior Imperial Service Transport Corps.	

TABLE XXV

PESHAWAR COLUMN.	KURRAM MOVABLE COLUMN.
Brigadier-General A. G. Hammond, V.C., C.B., D.S,O., A.D.C.	*Colonel W. Hill.*
9th Bengal Lancers (9th Hodson's Horse).	6th Bengal Cavalry (6th Cavalry).
57th Field Battery Royal Artillery (57th Battery Royal Field Artillery).	One Regiment Central Indian Horse.
No. 3 Mountain Battery Royal Artillery (3rd Mountain Battery Royal Garrison Artillery).	3rd Field Battery Royal Artillery (3rd Battery Royal Field Artillery).
One company Bengal Sappers and Miners (1st Sappers and Miners).	12th Bengal Infantry (12th Pioneers).
2nd Battalion Royal Inniskilling Fusiliers.	1st Battalion 5th Gurkhas.
2nd Battalion Oxfordshire Light Infantry.	Kapurthala Regiment Imperial Service Infantry.
34th Pioneers (34th Sikh Pioneers).	One section British Field Hospital.
45th Sikhs.	One Native Field Hospital, with an additional section.
9th Gurkhas.	One Native General Hospital at Kohat, 200 beds.
One British and one Native Field Hospital.	
One British General Hospital at Nowshera, 250 beds.	
One Native General Hospital at Nowshera, 500 beds.	

TOTAL STRENGTH.

British officers	... ...	... ...	1,010
British troops ...	... ...	... ...	10,882
Indian troops ...	... ...	... ...	22,614
			34,506
Non combatants	... ...	... ...	19,934

which the enemy were able to bring a heavy cross fire to bear on attacking troops. The reconnaissance of October 18 was conducted by General Westmacott's brigade, supported by No. 9 (British) and No. 5 (Bombay) Mountain Batteries. The King's Own Scottish Borderers and the Gurkhas were detailed for the attack of the position, and, in spite of the enemy's fire, climbed to within 200 yards of the crest, when the Gurkhas again pushed on, covered by the fire of the King's Own Scottish Borderers. The enemy did not wait for the assault, but disappeared down the far side of the hill out of reach of pursuit. General Westmacott's brigade waited for two hours on the summit, during which time General Kempster's Brigade, which had been detailed to make a turning movement, but had been greatly delayed by the difficulties of the road, arrived on the scene. It was decided, however, not to hold Dargai, so the force withdrew to Shinawari the same day, covered by the 3rd Brigade, and closely pressed by the enemy.

The British loss at the first taking of Dargai was ten killed and fifty-three wounded, and the reasons ascribed to the evacuation are—

1. The force required to hold the position and guard the communications with Shinawari Camp could not safely be spared from the one division which had then arrived.

2. There was no water between Dargai and Shinawari.

3. It was sought to mystify the enemy as to the intended line of advance, and the occupation of Dargai would have made this impossible.

4. There were about sixteen miles of road between the two divisions in addition to the distance from Shinawari to Dargai.

At 4.30 a.m. on the 20th the 2nd Division was again ordered to move forward along the road to the Khanki Valley through Dargai. General Kempster's brigade, with the 2nd Battalion Derbyshire Regiment and 3rd Sikhs attached, led the advance; but, soon after the summit of the Chagru Pass was reached, it was discovered that the Dargai position was held by the enemy in increased strength. The leading brigade was ordered to clear the ridge, so the Gurkhas were ordered to lead the attack, supported by the Derbys and Dorsets, and covered by the guns of the 2nd Division, reinforced by a battery*

* No. 1 (Kohat) Mountain Battery.

THE DARGAI HEIGHTS

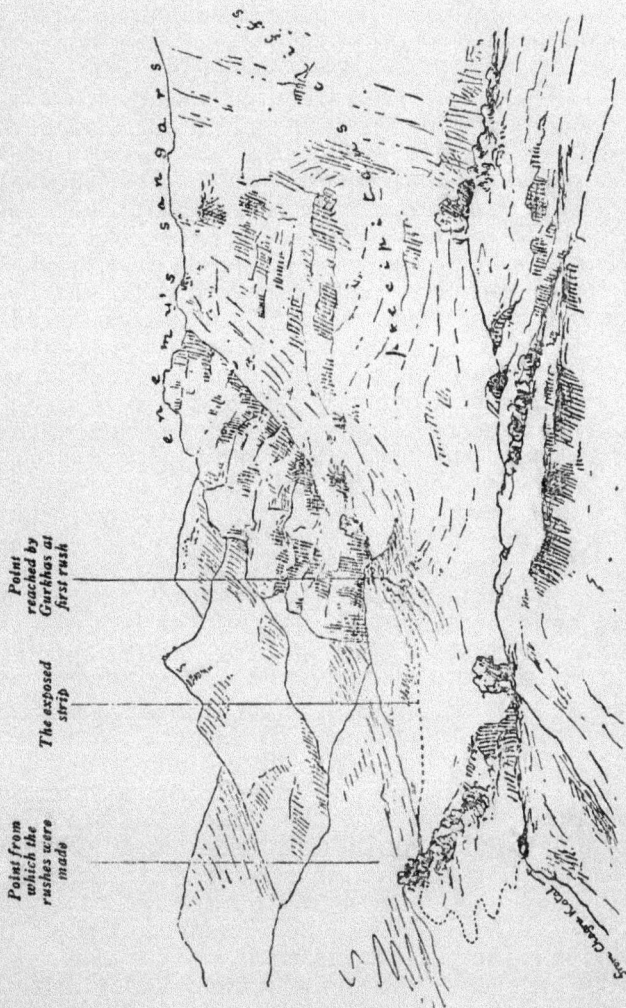

From "The Campaign in Tirah"

from the 1st, and the long-range fire of the Gordons. The 3rd Sikhs acted as escort to the guns. Owing to the precipitous nature of the slopes of the ridge, a frontal attack alone was possible, and the hostile defences had been so strengthened that an exposed stretch of 50 yards along the line of approach was swept by a severe cross fire. At 9.50 the enemy opened fire on the Gurkhas, who suffered so severely from the concentrated fire from the sangars on the crest, that only three companies succeeded in crossing the critical 50 yards of exposed ground, and reaching cover beyond. The Gurkhas and supporting battalions made other gallant, but fruitless attempts to reach the cover where the three companies of Gurkhas lay. The guns posted on the Chagru Kotal supported each rush with a concentrated fire, but the tribesmen were so well protected that they suffered little loss.

As the possession of Dargai was necessary to secure the road to the Khanki Valley, and it was now about noon, the Division Commander ordered General Kempster to make one more effort with the assistance of the two fresh battalions, who had hitherto taken no part in the actual assault. Accordingly, the Gordons and the 3rd Sikhs moved forward and formed up in echelon on the right of the Derbys, Dorsets, and Gurkhas, but only slightly in advance. When all was ready, the guns again opened a rapid fire on the crest, and, led by the Gordons, the five battalions dashed forward into the open by the path which had already proved so fatal earlier in the morning, and by another 100 yards lower down, which had been the route taken by General Westmacott's brigade two days before. Officers and men fell fast, but the cover halfway was gained, and with one more effort the position was reached, where the three Gurkha companies had lain for the past three hours. The enemy waited no longer, and, abandoning their sangars, fled rapidly down the hill; the narrow zigzag path up to the summit of the bluff was not defended, and at three o'clock the Dargai Heights were won. It was too late for the baggage to reach the Khanki Valley that night, so the troops passed a cold, cheerless night, bivouacking on the scene of the fight. The enemy were so well protected that their loss could not have been heavy, but the second capture of Dargai cost the British force 36 killed, and 159 wounded.

In the morning (October 21) General Westmacott's

Brigade led the advance of the 2nd Division down a bad road into the Khanki Valley. A small skirmish took place near the village of Kharappa,* where the camp was formed; but the Afridis soon took to flight, affording a fine opportunity for cavalry, if any had been available. The next week was spent in reconnoitring the road over the Sampagha Pass, leading into the Mastura Valley, improving communications and scouring the country for supplies, while the 1st Division and transport closed up. The pause in active operations caused by the delay in the arrival of the baggage and supplies, owing to the bad roads, was felt to be most unfortunate on account of the encouragement which the tribesmen always gain by such periods of inaction. Sniping was a matter of nightly occurrence. On the 23rd a night attack was repulsed,† and on the 25th a foraging party had to fight quite a severe rearguard action before camp was reached. In order to cope with the great inconvenience and serious loss of life caused by the harassing night tactics of the Afridis, small parties of thirty Gurkhas, under two officers, were organized to compete with the enemy at their own game. The Gurkhas soon proved themselves as adept at night stalking as their enemies, whose audacity thus received a decided check. In addition, a new system of piqueting was introduced shortly afterwards, which also had a most salutary effect. It was noticed that no sniping took place during the night following the arrival at a new camping-ground, but that subsequent nights were always disturbed more or less by petty annoyances. From this it was concluded that the enemy based their movements by night on observations by day of the lie of the camp and the positions of the surrounding piquets. Trading on the well-known dislike of the tribesmen to having an enemy above them, strong piquets were sent out to occupy peaks within range of camp, with instructions to maintain their position without attempting to fall back on camp or expecting reinforcements. So well was this duty performed that no instance occurred of any piquet being rushed throughout the campaign.

* Some accounts substitute Khangarbar for Kharappa.
† Of this night attack the following incident is recorded : "In front of the Gordons' lines was found an Orakzai, who had 80 yards of string trailing behind him. Evidently the object of this pioneer was to sneak into camp, and, if successful in finding a weak spot, to signal to his main attacking body at the end of the string " ("The Indian Frontier War," p. 127).

When the 1st Division arrived at Kharappa the force assembled in the Khanki Valley consisted of—

British troops	...	...	...	... 6,400
Native troops	...	...	...	... 11,200
Followers	...	...	...	... 17,000

On October 28 the advance towards the Sampagha Pass was begun, with the 1st Division leading. The pass was soon found to be held by the enemy, and the attack was made the next day. General Gaselee's brigade was detailed for the assault, supported by the 2nd Division and the fire of the massed guns, with battalions of General Hart's Brigade detached to operate on the flanks. The start was made before dawn, but some delay was caused by mistakes of the road by the guns and one of the infantry brigades, owing to the darkness and intricate nature of the ground.

The road over the Sampagha Pass (6,700 feet) is four miles long, surmounting three successive ridges before the main kotal is reached. The ridges were strengthened with sangars, and many parts of the road were commanded by hills, wooded in some places, but rocky and precipitous in others. The first shots were fired at 6.35 a.m., and in a few minutes the enemy were driven off the first ridge by the fire of the guns, which was then occupied by No. 5 Mountain Battery in order to cover the attack of the infantry on the second ridge. Assisted by detachments of the Gurkhas and the Queen's on the left flank, and reinforced by the two leading battalions of the 2nd Division, the 2nd Brigade pressed steadily on in spite of a heavy fire; but the Afridis, showing no disposition to allow the attacking infantry to get to close quarters, soon took to flight, leaving the pass in the hands of the British troops after four hours' fighting. When the heights had been crowned, the two divisions pushed on down a comparatively easy descent into the Mastura Valley, which was now visited by Europeans for the first time. Little of the transport reached camp that night; in fact, it was five days before the transport of the whole force could cross the Sampagha Pass, a distance of only seven miles. The British casualties on October 29 were two killed and twenty-two wounded.

Leaving the 1st Brigade (General Hart) in camp at Mastura, the advance of the remainder of the force was resumed on October 31 over the Arhanga Pass, out of Orakzai territory, into Tirah Maidan. Mr. James describes the pass as follows:

"The road to the pass lay . . . up a nullah, which was flanked by low hills, culminating in a conical eminence which exactly fronted the pass. The hill . . . had a walled village on the summit. This, consequently, was the first position that the main attack proceeded to hold. The pass was a low kotal connecting higher ridges, in no way like the Sampagha, which was a series of ridges. On either flank of the Arhanga were higher peaks, the right ones being wooded. Half-way between the village on the knoll and the pass stood a square blockhouse."*

Covered by the massed guns of the two divisions, General Westmacott's brigade occupied the village, but several casualties were caused by the enemy's marksmen stationed in the blockhouse before it was cleared and set on fire by the guns. The 2nd and 3rd Brigades were detached to the right and left respectively, but no further resistance was encountered, and the pass was won by 11 a.m. The troops then descended into Tirah Maidan, the summer home of the Afridis, a beautiful valley of remarkable fertility, thickly populated and dotted with numerous fortified houses, but now quite deserted. On the same day a reconnaissance was made four miles westward up the valley to Bagh, the great Afridi tribal centre, and a small skirmish took place. The baggage was late getting into camp, having been attacked with some success on the way under cover of darkness.

The next eight days were devoted to survey operations and the collection of ten days' supplies for the whole force by means of convoys and foraging parties in the valley itself. Attacks instigated, it is said, by the Zakha Khel were frequent, and intermittent firing into camp was indulged in by the enemy with such persistency that the Zakha Khel villages to the east of the valley were destroyed by General Westmacott on November 8, to exact punishment for these annoyances. On November 9 the first reconnaissance was made to Saran Sar—a peak commanding the eastern end of the Tirah Maidan—with a composite brigade, consisting of two batteries, a company of Madras Sappers, the 1st Dorsets, 1st Northamptons, 15th and 36th Sikhs, under the orders of General Westmacott.

As the events of this day afford some valuable lessons,

* "The Indian Frontier War," p. 144 (Lionel James).

a detailed description of the ground and of what took place is necessary. The main nala, which is the roadway from Tirah Maidan to the Saran Sar Pass, runs upward from west to east through a very broken country intersected by numerous subsidiary nalas. The total distance from camp to the Saran Sar Kotal is only four miles, but these four miles present extraordinary difficulties from a military point of view. About a mile and a half from the kotal the path leaves the main nala, which bends to the south, past the eastern face of a conical hill. Still working upwards, the path follows a bare spur, flanked on the left by another spur, which is wooded up to the summit. About half-way between the point where the path leaves the nala bed and the kotal is a knoll on which stood a solitary tree, and above the kotal to the north the Saran Sar Peak rises about 1,000 feet above the top of the pass. Before reaching the kotal the road traverses two ridges, passing the western face of Saran Sar, which is accessible on the north and east, but precipitous on the other sides. The slopes of the hills on the reverse or eastern side of the kotal are wooded, and lead down to a wooded valley flanked by high hills.

The advance was begun at 7.30 a.m., with the Northamptons in the centre following the nala, the Dorsets on the left, and the 36th Sikhs on the right; one battery and the 15th Sikhs occupied the conical hill in the bend of the nala, with the other battery a short distance in rear. The enemy first opened fire one mile out of camp, but the Northamptons and 36th Sikhs reached the point where the path leaves the nala, and the real ascent begins, without difficulty. Here it was found that the tribesmen had constructed some sangars to command the nala bed, and two men of the Northamptons were wounded. The main body of the Northamptons, however, avoided the nala and skirted the base of the conical hill on their right. The movements of the Dorsets now caused some anxiety, for desultory firing had been heard from their direction; no news had been received from them, and it was feared that they were making little progress. The enemy did not hold the sangars guarding the path to the kotal, so at about 9.45 the Northamptons and 36th Sikhs began the ascent. Further slight opposition was encountered at the knoll with the single tree and when nearing the summit, but the advance was made with such resolution that at 11.15 Saran Sar

SARAN SAR

RECONNAISSANCE OF NOVEMBER 9, 1897

Scale 1 inch = 1 mile

Scale of Yards

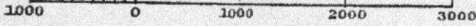

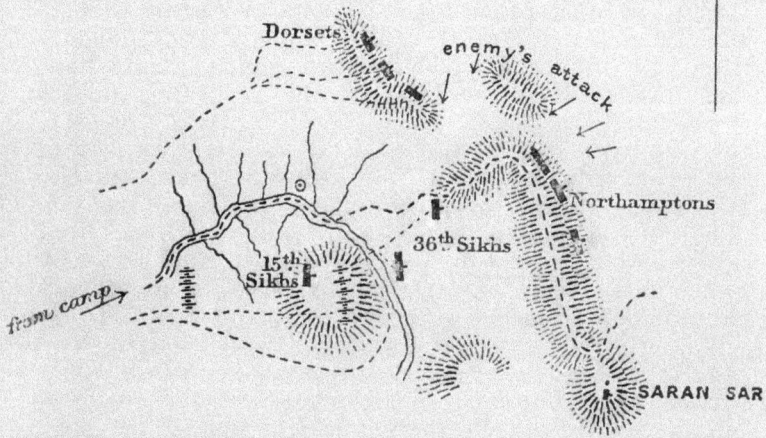

1000   0   1000   2000   3000

Dorsets

enemy's attack

from camp

15th Sikhs

36th Sikhs

Northamptons

SARAN SAR

------- *Path up Pass*

⊙   *Point where the party of the Northamptonshire Reg? was annihilated.*

From "The Indian Frontier War," p. 165

19

was won. Still no news had been received of the Dorsets, who had been delayed by the difficulties of the broken ground on their line of advance, so, to secure his left, General Westmacott sent five companies of the Northamptons to cross the northern slopes of Saran Sar, and watch the wooded slopes on the east side of the main ridge. Though the enemy could not be seen, they could be heard calling to one another among the trees.

The information required was soon collected, and at 12.15 General Westmacott ordered the 36th Sikhs to occupy the knoll with the single tree, and cover the retirement of the Northamptons; the retirement, however, was delayed till 2 p.m. by the arrival of Sir William Lockhart, who wished to examine the country himself. As the Northamptons retired from the eastern side of the Saran Sar Ridge, the rear company was suddenly fired into from the wooded spurs, which should have been occupied by the Dorsets, and several casualties immediately occurred. Encumbered by their wounded, this company had little choice but to retire by way of the main nala, which at first afforded cover; but the tribesmen, seeing their advantage, quickly closed in, aided by the broken ground and failing light, and fired down on the retreating troops from the high banks on either side. Men fell fast, and the fighting strength of the company became so reduced by the necessity for detailing men to carry the wounded away, that the two Sikh regiments were sent to the assistance of the hard-pressed Northamptons. The Dorsets were also engaged, but eventually the Northamptons got out of the nala, and at 7.30 the rear-guard, accompanied by General Westmacott, reached camp. A party of the Northamptons, however, under a second lieutenant, was found to be missing; their bodies were found the next day in the fatal nala, the detachment having been cut off, it was presumed, while trying to protect the wounded.

The casualties on November 9 amounted to nineteen killed and forty-three wounded, of whom eighteen and twenty-nine belonged to the Northamptons. With regard to the use of the ravine as the line of retreat, Colonel Hutchinson says: " It must be said that this was the route that the regiment had advanced by; that it was therefore known to them all, and was the most direct road back to camp; and that with a number of wounded to protect, and, believing probably that it was flanked on the right and left by other corps, it was natural perhaps that it should be chosen to retire by."* All accounts are full of praise of the gallant way in which the Northamptons fought their way back to camp; but it was an unfortunate affair, and another expedition to Saran Sar was necessary to restore *moral.*

On November 11 — two days after the events just recorded — another reconnaissance to Saran Sar was made by General Gaselee with his brigade, assisted by two batteries and the scouts of the 3rd and 5th Gurkhas. The same route was followed as that taken by General Westmacott on the 9th; very little opposition was met on the way up, but when the retirement began and the tribesmen sought to repeat their recent success, they met with a severe check through a ruse practised by the scouts of the 3rd Gurkhas. These men were the last to leave the Saran Sar position, and, having warned the battalion covering their retirement at the one-tree knoll of their intention, they retreated down the hill with such rapidity that the enemy thought they were in full flight, and, following up without caution, came under a heavy cross-fire from the covering battalion. The Afridi ardour was so damped by this unexpected reverse that the rear-guard suffered little further molestation for the rest of the day. The time taken to retire over the short space of four miles between Saran Sar and Maidan Camp after the reconnaissances is instructive: five and a half hours were taken on November 9, and four hours and a half on the 11th.

Following these reconnaissances General Kempster's Brigade marched *via* the Tseri Pass on November 13 into the Waran Valley inhabited by the Aka Khel, while the 36th Sikhs remained on the kotal to maintain communication. The foraging parties which went out were generally fired on, and on one occasion a smart rear-guard action was fought, in which the Dorsets repeated with success the Gurkha ruse of the 11th. While in the Aka Khel Valley a night attack was made on the side of General Kempster's camp, which was held by the Dorsets, but repelled without difficulty with the assistance of the star-shells of No. 5 (Bombay) Mountain Battery.

On November 16 General Kempster began his return march to Tirah Maidan, and another memorable rear-

* "The Campaign in Tirah," p. 124.

guard action ensued. The withdrawal from the Waran Valley was covered by No. 8 Mountain Battery and the 1st Battalion 2nd Gurkhas, supported by the 15th Sikhs at the Tseri Pass. From the very beginning the Gurkhas were so harassed that they were greatly delayed in reaching the kotal, at which point the 15th Sikhs took up the duty of covering the retirement. It was then 4 p.m., and little more daylight remained. The 15th Sikhs were soon heavily engaged; two companies were charged by about 200 tribesmen, who were beaten off with severe loss, but the officer commanding the regiment was wounded. The position of the rear-guard at this juncture was so serious that reinforcements were asked for, with the result that the 36th Sikhs, under Colonel Haughton, and two companies of Dorsets arrived. The withdrawal continued, but by this time the force was encumbered by many wounded men; darkness was drawing on, and the enemy, taking advantage of the ravines, were gathering in increasing strength on all sides. Recognizing the impossibility of reaching camp before darkness set in, Colonel Haughton, who had assumed command of the rear-guard, decided to take up a position for the night while daylight still remained. Selecting a cluster of houses close by which were already occupied by the enemy, he ordered his men to fix bayonets and charge; the place was successfully carried, and at the same time Major Des Vœux, with three companies of Sikhs and half a company of the Dorsets, seized another house about 400 yards distant. Colonel Haughton and Major Des Vœux immediately threw up sangars, under cover of which they both held out successfully till relieved by General Gaselee the next morning. Another party of eight men of the 36th Sikhs also took up a position for the night in a house, where they remained quite undisturbed. The wounded were collected in Colonel Haughton's group of buildings, and those of the Dorsets, who attached themselves to the Sikhs, also passed the night in safety; but a party who tried to make their way into camp were cut off, like the Northamptons on the 9th, and annihilated. On the morning of the 17th General Gaselee took his brigade out and brought in the benighted rear-guard.

On the 18th the camp of the three brigades was moved to Bagh. The next important series of operations began on November 22, when a reconnaissance was made in a north-easterly direction to Dwatoi, on the road into the

Bara Valley, with a force under General Westmacott, accompanied by Sir William Lockhart. The troops at General Westmacott's disposal left camp in the following order : the Yorkshires and 2nd Gurkhas,* starting at daybreak, crowned the heights on the right and left respectively of the line of advance ; the 3rd Gurkhas, forming the advanced guard, left at 9 a.m. ; then followed the 28th Bombay Pioneers, two companies Sappers and Miners, No. 5 Mountain Battery, King's Own Scottish Borderers, baggage, and the 36th Sikhs as rear-guard. The road, if it could be called a road at all, lay along the stony bed of a stream running through a defile commanded by high ground on both sides, the steep slopes of which were covered in many places with scrub. In spite of the good work of the flanking battalions, the main body was fired on every now and then by small parties of the enemy, who had to be dislodged by detachments furnished by the advanced guard. In this way the whole of the 3rd Gurkhas were gradually employed, so that the Bombay Pioneers, supported by the King's Own Scottish Borderers, were called upon to take up the duties of advanced guard. In one place, where the line of advance was enfiladed, several casualties occurred among the Borderers, but at length, after passing some more difficult country and a little further fighting, the head of the Bara Valley was reached at Dwatoi. Here camp was formed at 5 p.m., and the heights piqueted, but the baggage was still so far behind, owing to the difficulties of the road, that the troops were obliged to pass a cold night without blankets or food, except what they carried themselves, though unmolested by the enemy. As the next morning began to wear on, and no signs of the transport appeared, the Sappers and Pioneers were sent out to try and improve the road, but, in spite of this, the baggage was not in till 5 p.m., during which time some more fighting took place, followed after dark by the customary sniping.

On November 24 the return to Bagh began. The retirement was very skilfully conducted, for the baggage was loaded up before daybreak, and moved off quickly without confusion ; half the men furnishing piquets on the surrounding hills brought down the blankets of the

---

* The Yorkshires and 2nd Gurkhas were lent for the occasion. They held the heights on either side of the Dwatoi defile until the whole of General Westmacott's brigade had passed through on its return march to Bagh.

whole covered by the remainder, who withdrew so
rapidly when the proper time came, that the retiring
column had gone some distance before a shot was
fired, or the enemy realized what was happening. The
3rd Gurkhas supplied the flanking parties, the King's
Own Scottish Borderers the advanced guard and escorts
for wounded and baggage, and the 36th Sikhs were
again the rear-guard. As soon as the enemy discovered
the movement they closed round rapidly, and pressed
the Sikhs so severely that two companies of the Borderers
were detached to their assistance from the baggage-guard,
and some parties had to be sent back to carry away the
wounded. Some of the Afridis then tried to rush the
ponies ; the native drivers fled, but the Sikhs succeeded
in cutting off and practically annihilating the venturesome raiders. This severe lesson had a most salutary
effect, for the tribesmen displayed much greater caution
for the rest of the day, though they still hung on the
skirts of the column till close to Bagh. The British
casualties during the three days from November 22 to 24
were six killed and thirty-three wounded.

After the return of General Westmacott from Dwatoi
a combined movement was carried out with the Kurram
Column against the tribes living on the extreme west
of Afridi territory. On November 26 General Gaselee
started for the Kahu Pass, with his brigade reinforced
by a wing of the Royal Scots Fusiliers (lately arrived),
1st Battalion 2nd Gurkhas, 28th Bombay Pioneers, two
companies Sappers and Miners, and No 1 (Kohat), and
No. 2 (Derajat) Mountain Batteries, but, owing to opposition and the bad road, progress was somewhat slow. Less
opposition was encountered by the leading troops the
next day, but the road was still so bad that, although the
head of the column reached camp at Dargai,* in the
Massuzai Valley, the same afternoon, the whole of the
transport and rear-guard were not in till two days afterwards. During this time great discomfort was felt on
account of the cold, and the rear-guard was continually
harassed by the enemy, who also made an unsuccessful
attack on the baggage ; sniping at night was again the
rule.

Touch having been gained by heliograph with the
Kurram Column on November 29, General Gaselee
moved forward the next day to Esor, and there the two

* This is a common name on the North-West Frontier.

columns joined hands. The Kurram Column, under
Colonel Hill, consisted of—

Central India Horse and 6th Bengal Cavalry,
   100 mounted and 300 dismounted men.
12th Bengal Infantry, 400 men.
5th Gurkhas, 200 men.
Kapurthala Regiment, 200 men.

On December 1 Colonel Hill moved out with his
column, reinforced by the 1st (Kohat) Mountain Battery
and 4th Gurkhas, against the Chamkannis, a small
Orakzai clan living on the western border. From Esor
two roads lead into the Chamkanni Valley; that
on the west follows the banks of a stream, which
enters the valley through a narrow gorge, while that
on the east passes over a kotal before it drops
down and joins the other route. Colonel Hill, taking
with him the Mountain Battery and 4th Gurkhas, went
by the road over the kotal; the rest of the force marched
by the western route, the intention being to concentrate
in the Chamkanni Valley at about 11 a.m. Colonel Hill
executed his march without difficulty, but it was different
with the column in the gorge. The latter met with some
opposition, besides having a more difficult road to traverse,
with the result that, when the concentration was effected,
it was too late in the day to think of proceeding to carry
out the object of the expedition, which was to destroy
the chief Chamkanni village of Thabai. It was then
decided that the whole force should withdraw by the
kotal route back to Esor, but the enemy at once proceeded to harass the retirement to such purpose that the
troops returned to camp with a casualty list of seven
killed and eighteen wounded.

The next day a change was made in the composition
of the force entrusted to Colonel Hill with which to
chastise the Chamkannis. This now consisted of the
Kohat Mountain Battery, part of the Queen's, the 3rd
Sikhs, and 4th and 5th Gurkhas, besides the Gurkha
scouts. Taking the kotal route, the Chamkanni Valley
was reached soon after 9 a.m., and the Gurkhas were
ordered to hold the neighbouring hills while the work of
destruction was done by the 3rd Sikhs. Some opposition was met by the Gurkhas, during which a particularly
smart piece of work was done by the scouts under
Lieutenant Lucas.* After a climb so steep that in places

* This is described in Colonel Callwell's "Small Wars," p. 305, and in
"The Indian Frontier War," pp. 227, 228.

his men had to help each other up, Lieutenant Lucas found the enemy holding a sangared position on three successive spurs, whence his men were under fire from three sides. Lieutenant Lucas waited until the leading company of the 5th Gurkhas approached, then ordered half his force of eighty men to sweep the sangar on the first spur with a heavy fire, while he moved round to a flank and rushed the position. At first the Chamkannis showed signs of standing to meet the charge, but, suffering loss both of numbers and *moral* from the severe covering fire, they turned and fled back to the second sangar. Lieutenant Lucas repeated his tactics on the second and third spur, and, rapidly gaining the crest of the last, was able to shoot down several of the tribesmen as they fled down the reverse slope. So skilfully had the men been handled, and so resolute had been the attacks, that not a single Gurkha was touched, while some twenty-five Chamkannis were accounted for.

Other gatherings of the tribesmen were dispersed by the guns, and eventually the withdrawal was carried out without interference. The British casualties on this day were only two killed and four wounded.

On December 3 the Kurram Column retraced its steps to its headquarters at Sadda, while General Gaselee set out two days later to return to Tirah Maidan *viâ* the Khanki Valley. General Gaselee encountered no opposition, in fact the tribesmen whose territory he traversed themselves piqueted the heights to save their villages from the flames. Bagh was reached on December 6.

Every Afridi valley having been laid waste, and winter drawing on, it was now decided to evacuate Tirah. The withdrawal began on December 7, a day earlier than had been originally intended, and none too soon, for the troops had no sooner left than snow fell in Bagh. The decision to make the start on the 7th instead of the 8th may also have had something to do with the good fortune of the 2nd Division in not finding the Dwatoi defile on the Bara Valley route held by the enemy. Sir William Lockhart marched his two divisions out of the country by different routes, converging near the Indian frontier at Barkai; the 1st Division withdrew by the Waran and Mastura Valleys, while the second (accompanied by Sir William Lockhart) took the road that follows the Bara River. The former, destroying villages *en route*, met with only slight resistance; but the story of the march of the 2nd Division is one of desperate fighting by day

and night for five consecutive days against a numerous
and relentless foe. Moreover, the difficulties presented
by the climate and the ground were so incessant, that the
record of this march is unparalleled in Indian warfare
since the disastrous retreat from Kabul in 1842.

General Westmacott's brigade led the advance of the
2nd Division on December 7 from Tirah Maidan to
Dwatoi, with flanking parties found by the Gurkhas and
2nd Punjab Infantry* belonging to the 3rd Brigade. No
opposition was encountered at the defile, possibly owing
to the friendly offices of the clan inhabiting this part of
the country in their own interests, or possibly to the
change of the date of departure finding the Afridis unprepared. The King's Own Scottish Borderers had a
skirmish on reaching the Bara River, but Dwatoi was
reached by the leading troops at 3 p.m. General Westmacott's transport continued coming in unmolested far
on into the night, though the piquets all round the camp
were often heavily engaged; but the last of General
Kempster's Brigade was not in till the 9th. The first
night at Dwatoi was one of great discomfort; the men
were wet through from having to wade through the
streams, and food was very scarce. On the afternoon of
December 8 a company of the 36th Sikhs, under Lieutenant van Someren, was sent out to occupy a peak
commanding the line of advance into the Rajgul Valley,
the villages in which were to be destroyed the next day.
Lieutenant van Someren, finding the peak held in
strength by the enemy, signalled down for reinforcements, so a company of the 3rd Gurkhas, with another
company of the 36th Sikhs in support, was sent to his
assistance. Covered by the fire of No. 5 Mountain
Battery, the Sikhs and Gurkhas then made alternate
rushes, covering each other with fire, and carried the
position. While the 3rd Brigade was coming in on the
9th General Westmacott destroyed the villages in the
Rajgul Valley, and on the 10th the eventful march down
the Bara Valley was begun.

Below Dwatoi the Bara Valley opens out, but is commanded on the right (or south) by high wooded hills,
precipitous in many places, and on the left by bare but
gentler slopes. The width of the valley varies consider-

---

* This regiment had joined General Gaselee when returning from Esor,
and was now attached to the 3rd Brigade *vice* the 15th Sikhs, whose fighting
strength had become so reduced by the continuous fighting in which they
had been engaged for four months that they had to be sent back to the base.

ably, but the river-banks are never out of rifle-range from the hills on either bank. General Westmacott again led the advance of the division on December 10, with the 36th Sikhs and 3rd Gurkhas acting as advanced guard and watching the flanks. The advanced guard was soon engaged in driving the enemy from the hills, and a short skirmish took place at a village, causing a check to the progress of the baggage, which gave an opportunity to a few daring individuals to creep down and cause several casualties before they could be dislodged. On reaching the camping-ground a little farther on firing continued to be general all round while the transport was coming in; the 3rd Brigade, which had been continuously harassed ever since leaving Dwatoi, bivouacked three miles higher up the valley, being unable to close up to General Westmacott before dark. Rain fell during the night, it was very cold, and intermittent sniping also tended to increase the general discomfort.

It was sleeting and bitterly cold when the march into Zakha Khel territory was resumed in the same order the next day, December 11. The leading brigade met with practically no resistance, for the Afridis concentrated all their energies on trying to cut off General Kempster's rear-guard, consisting of the Gordons, 2nd Punjab Infantry, and 2nd Gurkhas. These troops were engaged incessantly the whole day and part of the night, with an enemy continually increasing in numbers and daring. Three miles from the new camp at Sher Khel the transport took a wrong road, and, becoming involved in swampy ground, a delay ensued, of which the tribesmen were swift to take advantage. The escorts had been already much weakened by having to furnish flanking parties, so the enemy were able to outflank the baggage and open a heavy fire on it. The native drivers and *duli* bearers immediately fled, and in a short time the rear-guard was completely surrounded. Darkness was approaching, the guns had pushed on into camp so as not to be benighted, there were many men wounded, and the fighting strength was still further reduced by the necessity for detailing men to carrry the *dulis* deserted by their regular carriers. Under these circumstances there was no alternative but to take up the best possible position for the night before darkness caused a serious disaster. Captain Uniacke of the Gordons, therefore, covered by the darkness, dashed up to the doorway of a house standing in a small village close by, which was occupied by the enemy, and, though he had only four men of his regiment with him, succeeded in giving the tribesmen such an exaggerated idea of his strength by shouting words of command, blowing his whistle, and other devices, that they hurriedly evacuated the place. Here the wounded men were collected, and the whole rear-guard gradually assembled. Preparations for defence were quickly made, but the enemy had begun to loot the baggage, and no attack was made.

Great anxiety was naturally felt in camp for the safety of the rear-guard, so a company of the King's Own Scottish Borderers* went up the valley, where, though it met no enemy and heard no firing, it succeeded in saving and bringing in many followers and baggage animals. In the morning, December 12, a company of the 2nd Punjab Infantry went out early and got into touch with the missing rear-guard, which was unable to move owing to the presence of the enemy all round, and the absence of means of transporting the wounded. The King's Own Scottish Borderers, Dorsets, and a mountain battery then went out under General Kempster and brought the whole force in. The total casualties sustained by the 3rd Brigade on the 11th were 41 combatants, 100 non-combatants, and 150 baggage animals. The division remained at Sher Khel all day on the 12th, improving the road and collecting much of the missing baggage ; the piquets were constantly engaged, and more sniping occurred during the night.

December 13 was the most anxious day of this memorable withdrawal. The order of march was changed, General Westmacott taking up the task of keeping the tribesmen at bay while the other brigade destroyed the Zakha Khel villages *en route*. The critical points of the day's march were at two narrow gorges through which the Bara River runs. The first was passed by the baggage without deviation, but at the second the stream was so swollen by the recent rain that a *détour* had to be made to avoid it. After their recent painful experiences, the transport followers were so eager to press on that at each gorge, where the front had perforce to be reduced, there was considerable delay and confusion, but at the point where the *détour* began the check and crowding caused thereby were most serious.

As on the 11th, the leading brigade met with little

* This was the first occasion on which any troops other than Gurkha Scouts had been sent out after dark.

opposition, and was further assisted by meeting the 2nd Battalion Oxfordshire Light Infantry, which had been sent out by General Hammond from Barkai. As happened also on the 11th, the case of the rear brigade was very different : it was fired on, and casualties occurred, even before it had moved out of Sher Khel Camp. The last regiments, covered by the guns of the division, did not get off till 11 a.m. Sher Khel was burned before leaving, but the smoke of the burning village caused some embarrassment by rendering it difficult to distinguish friend from foe. In a very short time General Westmacott was heavily engaged on all sides with a daring and numerous enemy. The 3rd Gurkhas, supported by the King's Own Scottish Borderers and 36th Sikhs,* formed the rear-guard. The heights were held with great difficulty while the baggage moved off, and within an hour the 3rd Gurkhas had expended all their pouch ammunition— in fact by 2 p.m. all three rear-guard regiments had been obliged to replenish ammunition from the reserve.

All went as well as could be expected till the second gorge was reached, when the Afridis tried to cut General Westmacott off from the *détour* round the defile, and drive him into the gorge, where they would have had him at their mercy. The Gurkhas especially were heavily engaged, one company being so closely pressed that, having exhausted its ammunition, it was obliged to retire with fixed bayonets on a company of the King's Own Scottish Borderers. By 4 p.m. all the rear-guard regiments were in line fighting in support of one another ; many casualties had occurred, but the march of the baggage was so successfully covered that not a single mule or article of baggage was lost. About this time the country became so much more enclosed that the flanking parties had to be drawn in, and, the fighting strength of the original rear-guard having been reduced to 450 men, reinforced by two weak companies of the Scots Fusiliers and four of the Northamptons, General Westmacott decided to take up a position for the night on a neighbouring ridge. The troops were scarcely assembled there when the Afridis made a most determined charge, a supreme effort for the victory that had seemed so near all day, one last bid for revenge before the hated invaders passed beyond their reach. The crisis, how-

---

* The wing of the Royal Scots Fusiliers that had accompanied General Gaselee to Esor was attached to the 4th Brigade, and formed part of the main body on this day.

Plate V

BARA VALLEY : GENERAL HAMMOND'S CAMP AT SWAIKOT

To face p. 30>

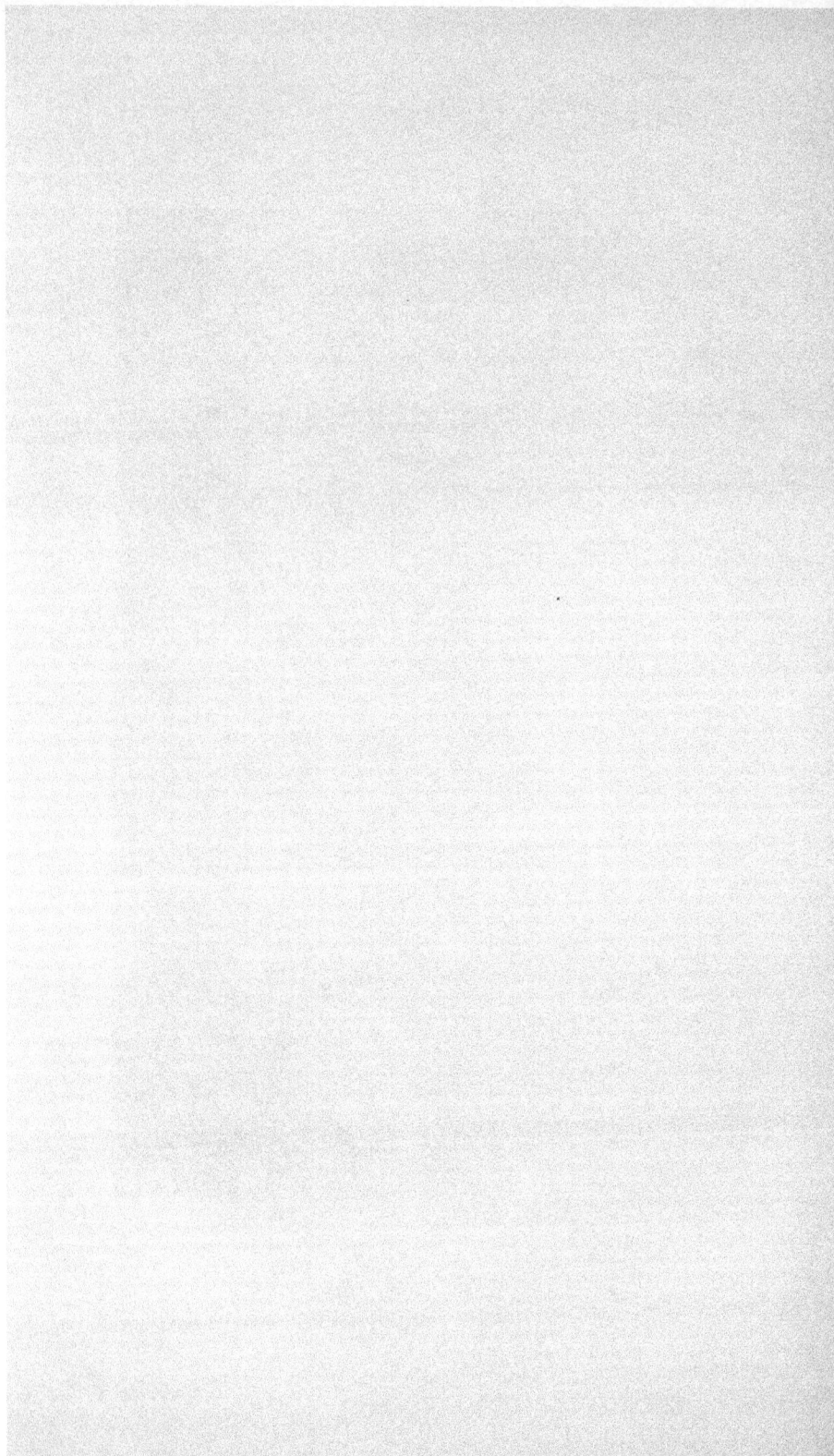

ever, was soon over, and no other attack was attempted. The British force remained all night on the ridge without food, water, blankets, or sufficient appliances with which to attend the wounded.

At daybreak the rear-guard again slowly fell back, still closely followed by the enemy, till near Barkai, where the 9th Gurkhas from the Peshawar Column were met, and Barkai itself, where the 3rd Brigade had already arrived after a quiet night, was reached about noon. General Westmacott's loss during December 13 amounted to 19 killed and 86 wounded, bringing the total casualties during the withdrawal from Tirah up to 164 killed and wounded, of whom 111 belonged to the 4th Brigade, and the total of the campaign to over 1,100.* At Barkai the following order was issued by General Sir William Lockhart to the General Officer Commanding the 2nd Division :†

"General Lockhart will be obliged if you will convey to the Officer Commanding the 4th Brigade his appreciation of the excellent work done by himself, his staff, and the troops under his command on December 13 and 14, when a very difficult operation was most successfully carried out. Sir William Lockhart regrets the many hardships to which the troops covering the withdrawal from Tirah were exposed, but they were unavoidable."

When the 2nd Division reached Barkai, the 1st Division was already assembled in the neighbourhood of Bara. The march down the Mastura Valley, though arduous, was uneventful as far as fighting was concerned. The destruction of property in the Waran Valley was entrusted to General Hart's brigade, which had remained at its post between the Arhanga and Sampagha Passes on the line of communication during the operations in Tirah and the neighbourhood.

THE BAZAR VALLEY EXPEDITION. 1897-98.

Sir William Lockhart was still determined that none of the Afridi valleys should remain unvisited by the troops under his command, so immediately after the return of

---

* From October 12, 1897, to conclusion of peace, the casualties were—

Killed	...	...	...	...	287
Wounded	...	...	...	...	853
Missing	...	...	...	...	10
					1,150

† General Yeatman-Biggs, who had been in poor health throughout the campaign, died at Peshawar on January 4, 1898.

both divisions from Tirah, preparations were made to complete the work, already so thoroughly done, by sending a division into the Zakha Khel valley of Bazar, and another column up the Khaibar Pass. While, therefore, the 2nd Divison held the Bara Valley from Bara to Barkai, the 1st Divison and Peshawar Column, under General Hammond, concentrated at Jamrud. On December 22 everything was ready. The Peshawar Column was to march up the Khaibar Pass to Landi Kotal and commence the restoration of the forts, while the 1st Division, accompanied by Sir William Lockhart, penetrated the Bazar Valley.* The next day General Hammond reached Ali Masjid unopposed, and on the 24th the 1st Division arrived at Lala China. It was arranged that, while General Hammond pushed on to Landi Kotal, Sir William Lockhart should take the Chora route into the Bazar Valley with General Gaselee's Brigade, and Generals Symons and Hart the road through Alachi and Karamna, with a detachment from the Peshawar Column to cover the right or northern flank of the advance.

The advance of both columns was begun on Christmas Day, but the Chora route proved so much the easier that, when General Gaselee arrived in the Bazar Valley the next day, practically without opposition, no news of the other brigade was forthcoming.

Mr. James thus describes his impressions of the Bazar Valley from a ridge overlooking it :

"Once on this sky-line and you are in the Bazar Valley proper—a huge rolling plain lies before you. As far as the eye can reach it stretches away to the Afghan border, while to right and left its boundaries must lie ten miles apart. This was the home of the Zakha Khel. Once in the Bazar Valley it is easy to appreciate the causes which have outlawed the Zakha Khel, even among their own tribes, for their valley is a fit type of the 'desolation of desolation.' It is one arid, bare, rocky wilderness, and as you stood at the entrance not a vestige of human habita-

---

* Sir William Lockhart was accompanied by General Sir Havelock Allan, V.C., M.P., who had come to India in order to visit the North-West Frontier. The latter, however, was killed on December 30, near Ali Masjid, under circumstances described by Sir William Lockhart in his despatches thus : "He left me at Lala China (on the 28th), and, with my permission, proceeded to Landi Kotal, arrangements being made to provide him with a sufficient escort. . . . As he was returning to Jamrud, he unfortunately left his escort near Ali Masjid, and, riding down a ravine by himself, was shot by the enemy. Every precaution had been taken to secure his safety, and, on bidding him good-bye at Lala China, I had impressed upon him the necessity of invariably remaining with the troops detailed for his protection."

tion or existence could be seen, save for the weary track
which faltered its way among the rocks and boulders.
But for occasional nullahs it is an absolute rolling plain,
much more so than Maidan or any of the Tirah valleys—
in fact the Bazar Plain is the first ground that cavalry
could usefully operate over that we have seen since the
Mohmand plateaux. Down the middle of the valley runs
a solitary spur, perhaps a thousand feet high, and the
Guides pointed out this as the covering hill to China, the
principal Zakha Khel centre."*

Camp was formed near China, which was quite deserted,
on the spot where General Maude camped in 1878, and a
quiet night ensued. On December 27, after China had
been destroyed, General Gaselee began his return march
to India, and touch was gained with the 1st Brigade, which
had been delayed at Karamna by the difficulties of the
road and some slight opposition. General Hart was
ordered to halt at Karamna for the night, and follow the
2nd Brigade next day, after destroying Karamna and
Burg. Except for a little skirmishing on the part of
General Gaselee's rear-guard, the withdrawal from
Bazar was affected without any fighting, thus bringing
the eventful year of 1897 to an end.

The tribesmen were known to have been reduced to
great straits by the British occupation of their country;
their houses had been destroyed, for, although there is
much to be said against this method of making war, the
Afridis were too elusive to suffer punishment in any
other way, and the tillage of their fields had been absolutely suspended. Every valley had been visited, and
the country satisfactorily surveyed; moreover, the
closure of the Khaibar Pass had brought discouraging
messages from the Amir to say that the war was not
looked upon with approval across the western border.
The dawn of the New Year found three British brigades
holding the Khaibar Pass from Jamrud to Landi Kotal, and
two more echeloned along the north-eastern boundary
of Afridi territory, but it was not until the blockade of
their country had continued till April, 1898, that the
last of the clans tendered their submission.

In the meantime another sharp fight took place, which
added materially to the already lengthy list of casualties,
and caused the death of one of the most distinguished
soldiers of the campaign, in the person of Colonel
Haughton, of the 36th Sikhs. In consequence of a

* " The Indian Frontier War," p. 279.

report that the Afridi cattle were brought down daily to graze in the Kajurai plain, due west of Bara, a combined movement of columns from Ali Masjid, Jamrud, Bara, and Mamanai was arranged for January 29th, 1898, with a view to effecting the capture of the entire herd and the attendant guards. Somehow or other the Afridis must have got warning of the plan, for the first three columns returned to their stations, after a tiring march, without seeing anything of the enemy or their cattle. It was different, however, with the Mamanai column, which consisted of the 2nd Battalion King's Own Yorkshire Light Infantry,* four companies 36th Sikhs, and two guns No. 5 (Bombay) Mountain Battery. The top of the Shin Kamar Pass was reached without opposition, and Colonel Haughton, with his Sikhs, visited some caves on the far side, but no cattle were to be seen. As soon as the retirement began the enemy pressed forward with great boldness, and seized a commanding knoll on the west of the pass, which had been evacuated prematurely through a misunderstanding. As this knoll commanded Colonel Haughton's line of retreat from the far side of the pass, it was retaken by two companies of the Yorkshire Light Infantry. These two companies, however, at once came under heavy fire from high ground to the north-west at a range of about 150 yards, and had great difficulty in holding their ground.

As soon as Colonel Haughton arrived on the scene he sent on three of his companies down the pass, and remained on the crest himself, with the other between the two companies of the Yorkshire Light Infantry on the knoll just mentioned, and another company of the same regiment, which was on the east of the road leading down through the pass. All three detachments were now so fiercely attacked, and were so encumbered by wounded, that retirement was almost impossible. An urgent message for help was sent back to the main body at the foot of the pass, but, before reinforcements arrived, four officers had been killed, including the gallant Colonel Haughton, and many of their men. Several more casualties occurred during the almost hand-to-hand fighting which ensued before the end of the pass was reached, but "the Yorkshires in this trying situation showed the utmost resolution and courage; and though they had to

---

* This battalion had taken the place of the 1st Battalion Northamptonshire Regiment in the 4th Brigade.

abandon their dead, they eventually brought away their wounded, and held the savage foe successfully at bay until all had been safely sent to the rear." *

The death of Colonel Haughton was a great loss to the army. His regiment had distinguished itself again and again throughout the campaign, and, after he had survived all the many desperate fights in which he had been engaged, it was indeed a cruel fate which claimed him in the end as a victim in the last encounter of the war. The losses at the Shin Kamar Pass amounted to twenty-seven killed and thirty-two wounded. It was the first engagement in which the Yorkshire Light Infantry had taken part during the campaign; it was a high trial, but they were not found wanting, and "they came out of it well. They were kept together, and well handled by their officers, and fought like men."† On January 31 General Westmacott again visited the Shin Kamar Pass and recovered twenty-two dead bodies; no opposition was offered to the advance, but five more casualties occurred during the retirement.

Happily, the unfortunate affair at Shin Kamar did not necessitate any further military operations. Thanks largely to Sir William Lockhart's personal influence among the tribesmen, one after another the Afridi clans recognized the futility of further resistance, and complied with the British demands. The Zakha Khel were the last to give up the struggle, but for all that they were not backward in joining a remarkable demonstration by our late enemies, which bore eloquent testimony to the influence and popularity of Sir William Lockhart among the frontier tribes. Colonel Hutchinson says: "When released at last from duty on April 5, and about to start from Peshawar for England to enjoy a much-needed change and some well-earned repose, crowds of Afridis, four or five hundred at least, with Zakha Khel in numbers amongst them (*mirabile dictu!*), surrounded his house in cantonments, wanted to hoist him on their shoulders, and drag his carriage to the station, and finally sent him off with shouts and cheers that made the welkin ring, vowing that in future they would be the friends of the English and fight on their side." *

Thus, in the presence of the performers and amid

---

* "The Campaign in the Tirah," p. 218 (Colonel Hutchinson).
† Letter from an officer who was present to Colonel Hutchinson ("The Campaign in the Tirah," p. 219).
‡ "The Campaign in the Tirah," p. 221.

happy surroundings fell the curtain on the great tragedy of 1897-98. The plot abounded with incident; interest was sustained from start to finish, and the scenery amidst which each act was set was varied enough to arrest the attention of the audience without confusing the mind with too frequent change. From the first volley at Maizar on June 10, 1897, to the last sad scene on the heights of Shin Kamar, when one of the principal heroes of the great drama is claimed by the God of Battles, every line is full of human interest, every incident contains a lesson of particular value to the soldier, and the campaign as a whole is pregnant with lessons in courage, devotion, and endurance for the entire British nation.

CHAPTER XX

TIRAH: REVIEW

NOT the least remarkable thing about Indian frontier warfare as a whole is that each campaign has some special distinguishing feature of its own. At first sight it would appear that within a comparatively circumscribed area, including a topography and population of little real diversity, there could hardly be room for much originality in the leading points attaching to the principal operations of war within its boundaries. But little reflection is needed to show that this is not so in reality. It has been shown already how the Hunza-Nagar Expedition owed its successful termination largely to acts of individual gallantry; how the influence of moral considerations predominated in the defence and relief of Chitral; and now in 1897 it is rear-guard actions that make the Afridi campaign a valuable study to the military reader. In fact, it is not too much to say that, included in the pages of history which deal with events on the north-west Hinterland of India in 1897 are to be found the law and the prophets concerning that most difficult of all operations which civilized troops have to carry out in savage warfare—namely, that of withdrawing before a well-armed, numerous, and, for the time being, exultant enemy through broken, mountainous country. Even in the short Mohmand Expedition, where the circular route taken by General Elles really constituted an advance throughout, instances of retirements and the advantage taken of them by the enemy are to be found on August 8 at Shabkadr, on September 25 at Jarobi, and two days later after the burning of the Khuda Khel villages.

But the Tirah Campaign is *par excellence* the one in which the most famous and most instructive examples of rear-guard actions are to be found. From the concrete

facts presented by these, practically all the abstract
principles governing such operations are to be deduced,
whatever the size of the force concerned may be. Some
of the lessons about to be discussed will have been
drawn already from past campaigns, but many are new,
and those that are not will lose nothing by repetition, if
only for the sake of corroboration. In the short space of
five weeks no less than six important rear-guard actions
occurred, which it may be useful to tabulate here :

    1. Nov. 9 : From Saran Sar (General Westmacott).
    2.   „   11 :   „   „   „   (General Gaselee).
    3.   „   16 :   „   Waran Valley (General Kempster).
    4.   „   24 :   „   Dwatoi (General Westmacott).
    5. Dec. 11 : Down Bara Valley (General Kempster).
    6.   „   13 :   „   „   „   (General Westmacott).

The principles governing the conduct of retirements in
mountain warfare are enunciated thus in the official textbook of the British Army on the subject of tactics :
    1. "Skilfully laid ambushes will cause the enemy to
move with caution in pursuit." *
    Now, ambushes constitute a species of counterstroke
which, as Colonel Henderson says, is the best weapon of
the defence, and rear-guard actions are really operations
of a defensive character. For illustration of the effect of
such a counterstroke the same six rear-guards supply
ample material ; the result was always the same—the
immediate check to the ardour of the pursuit. In the
second retirement from Saran Sar the Gurkha ruse was
a species of counterstroke ; the capture by General
Kempster's rear-guard on November 16 and December 11
of the houses, in which they passed the night, were
happily conceived and brilliantly executed feats of arms,
which served to warn the Afridis that attack during the
night offered little chance of success; and the annihilation by the 36th Sikhs of a party of the enemy who tried
to rush the ambulance ponies during General Westmacott's withdrawal from Dwatoi on November 24 took all
sting out of the pursuit for the rest of the day. Whenever,
therefore, troops are hard pressed, the best solution of
the difficulty will generally be some form of counter-
stroke, for success may always be expected to bring
relief; a decided check early in the day will almost
infallibly secure an easy retirement.

    * " Field Service Regulations," Part I., section 73 (2).

2. "Ravines should be avoided unless their exact course is known, and the heights on either side are held;"* and, again, "No defile through which the troops will have to pass in retiring, and no commanding point from which an enemy could harass the retirement, should be left unguarded."†

Both the maxims quoted above deal with the passage of defiles, and give warning of the danger of crowding which is inevitable at such places. The retirement from Saran Sar (November 9), the annihilation of the piquet of Kapurthala Infantry (November 6), and the withdrawal from Shin Kamar (January 29, 1898) are instances of the severe loss which may be sustained if high ground commanding a defile is not held.

3. "In advancing up-hill the force should be slow, so as not to distress the men,"‡ to enable—

(*a*) The men to keep together;
(*b*) The troops to be ready for action on reaching the top, where they may have to meet a counter-attack;
(*c*) Supports and reserves to close up;
(*d*) Flanking movements to develop.

4. "All movements should be as rapid as possible."§

The point of this maxim lies in the difference between rapidity and hurry, for a hurried retirement before an enterprising enemy like the Pathans will often be far from rapid. To avoid the encouragement which anything approaching a hurried retirement gives the enemy, as well as to avoid the loss of *moral* which the same is apt to cause among one's own troops, withdrawals should be conducted with the utmost deliberation. At the outset the frontier tribesmen may always be trusted to treat the regular soldier of a civilized army with respect, but his respect is founded only on a belief on the latter's prowess, and he knows no intermediate stage between respect and contempt.

The ultimate success of all the rear-guard actions of 1897 is largely due to the observance of this principle: the British loss on some occasions was considerable, but the troops were never out of hand, and the Afridis always paid dearly for any excessive daring.

---

* "Field Service Regulations," Part I., section 142 (3).
† *Ibid.*, section 146 (5).
‡ *Ibid.*, section 142 (3).   § *Ibid.*, section 142 (4).

The boldness displayed by the Pathans in pursuit
may, however, be turned to account in the employment
of ruses. If the enemy can be induced to mistake a
rapid retirement for disorderly flight, he will in all
probability follow up with recklessness, proportionate to
the panic which he imagines he sees before him, and, if
arrangements have been made beforehand with hidden
supporting troops, the result may be a rude and unexpected check to the hostile daring. This, it will be
remembered, constituted the Gurkha ruse of November 11,
during the second retirement from Saran Sar, which
was also employed with success two days later by the
Dorsets.

The foregoing remarks apply to the withdrawal of a
rear-guard as a whole; the case of fractions of it is
different. The last troops covering a withdrawal such
as piquets should retire at the fastest pace possible,
either for their own safety, if the enemy is following up
with resolution, or to get a good start before the enemy
discovers that they have retired at all. It does not
follow in the least that because a small fraction of the
force may have to retire quickly, or even precipitately,
the general retirement is not marked with the most
perfect deliberation. As has been pointed out already,
moral considerations alone are the *raison d'être* of
deliberate retreat ; neither side would expect the withdrawal of the last detachments of the retiring force to be
anything but as rapid as circumstances would allow ;
therefore, since it is only the expected that happens,
there is no surprise, and consequently neither loss of
moral on the one side, nor corresponding gain on the
other.

5. " The rear-guard commander is responsible for relieving the outposts, and also for withdrawing all flanking
parties by whomsoever posted."*

The necessity for having something definitely laid down
as to whose duty it is to see that all outlying detachments
are called in is exemplified by the disaster to the Kapurthala piquet on November 6, and by the critical situation
of Captain Ryder's company of the 35th Sikhs on September 16, during the first day's operations in the
Mamund Valley. To insure the withdrawal of flanking
parties and outposts at the right time, the commanders
of these parties should be acquainted with the situation
as well as the intentions of the officer commanding the

* " Field Service Regulations," Part I., section 146 (1).

force, and means of communication should be as good as circumstances will permit. In a mountainous country the use of mounted orderlies is, of course, out of the question, and even men on foot will only move slowly. Hilly country is often favourable to visual signalling, but it must be remembered that a rear-guard is frequently split up into small detachments, all of whom cannot be supplied with signallers and signalling apparatus ; moreover, mist or darkness may constitute another disturbing element. In any case the support to a group of piquets should be able to insure that one is not overlooked ; or, if there is no support, a sentry posted on the line of march below his piquet should be sufficient to secure the same object. When instructions are being sent to the commander of an outlying detachment, an ample margin should be allowed for the time required for the message to reach him.

6. "All retirements must be conducted by bodies of troops in succession. The rearmost troops must retire through the successive supporting lines, the latter covering the withdrawal and holding on to their position until their own retirement can be similarly covered by other troops in position in rear ;" * and, again, " The principle of always having bodies of men in rear or on the flanks covering by their fire the advance or retirement of the troops nearest the enemy is especially important in hill fighting."†

The principle of covering fire holds good in any class of military operation, whether offensive or defensive ; but in a rear-guard action against an active and well-armed adversary it is absolutely essential that the enemy should be kept off by the fire of troops in rear, while the last detachments withdraw, particularly if the latter are encumbered by wounded. Men must avoid crowding in such a way as to present a favourable target to the hostile marksmen. It should be remembered that whenever a man is killed, or wounded so severely that he is unable to walk, at least four others are out of action for the time being. Duli bearers are not remarkable for their bravery, and are seldom available when wanted most, so fighting troops have to take their place. In any case a little group is formed at once which presents an irresistible target to the tribesmen.

7. "It is of the first importance that the main body

* " Field Service Regulations," Part I., section 146 (2).
† *Ibid.*, section 142 (2).

should keep touch with and regulate its pace by the rear-guard."*

This was one of the great lessons of the numerous rear-guard actions of 1897. It is the exact reverse of the practice of civilized warfare, but then civilized warfare is conducted on civilized methods. In this class of campaign wounded men are not the same encumbrance as against a savage enemy who gives no quarter and knows not the Hague Convention, for, if absolutely necessary, they may be left on the ground—often to their advantage in the case of some wounds—with the certainty that nothing worse will befall them than being made prisoners of war. In savage warfare rear-guards are frequently so hardly pressed that they require every available man to use his rifle or to help with the wounded, and may need reinforcement at any moment. It is not too much to say that the timely arrival of the 36th Sikhs during the first retirement from Saran Sar, and again during General Kempster's withdrawal from the Waran Valley, in all probability averted a serious disaster.

8. "If the rear-guard commander considers it impossible to reach camp before nightfall, it will generally be advisable for him to halt and bivouac for the night in the most favourable position for defence, informing the commander of the force of his action. The rear-guard should halt in time to make the necessary dispositions for defence before dark."†

By night civilized troops lose many of those advantages wherein their strength against irregular foes lies by day. For the former, discipline, combination, and superior armament constitute the secret of success; but, when daylight fails, the two last at any rate are often completely neutralized. Moreover, superior knowledge of the ground is an asset of greatly enhanced value by night. Fortunately, night attacks on a large scale by irregular warriors are very much the exception, although the history of Indian frontier wars shows that attacks on piquets and desultory firing into camp are very favourite enterprises for small parties. Nevertheless, when uncivilized enemies, elated by real or imaginary triumphs won during the day, find regular troops unconcentrated after dark and impeded by the ground and wounded men, they have everything in their favour: a decisive victory is within their grasp, and they are swift to seize the opportunity. The mishaps to

---

* "Field Service Regulations," Part I., section 146 (3).
† *Ibid.*, section 146 (4).

the parties of Northamptons and Dorsets in the first retirement from Saran Sar, and the withdrawal from the Aka Khel valley, are melancholy examples of the fate of isolated detachments caught in the open after dark. When, in the presence of the enemy, it is impossible for a rear-guard to reach camp before darkness sets in, the fact will almost always be apparent long before daylight fails, so the troops should be concentrated in the best possible position in good time. If a distinct success can be achieved at this juncture, either by ejecting the enemy from a group of buildings, or other coign of vantage which he may have occupied, as was done by Colonel Haughton on November 16, and Captain Uniacke on December 11, or by the decisive repulse of an attack such as that by General Westmacott on December 13, the troops will take up their defensive position on good terms with themselves. The enemy, on the other hand, will see that the rear-guard, though hard pressed, is by no means disheartened, and the result will probably be a comparatively quiet night, as was the case in each of the three instances quoted. During the Tirah Expedition circumstances compelled rear-guards to spend the night in the open again and again; other examples will come to mind from a short mental survey of the campaign, but the three occasions mentioned above are the most familiar, and furnish the best lessons.

In illustration of the consequences of not occupying and clearing a defensive position of the enemy before dark, the critical situation of a portion of the 2nd Brigade of the Malakand Field Force on the evening of September 16 may be recalled to mind with advantage here. It will be remembered that on this occasion the British troops and the enemy occupied opposite ends of a village, that firing took place at only 20 yards' range, and several casualties occurred both among the men and gun-mules before the force was relieved by the timely arrival of four companies under Major Worledge.

Two other principles which are worthy of note may be added :

9. Retirements should be begun in good time.

After the first reconnaissance of Saran Sar the retirement did not begin till 2 p.m. At that time of year less than four hours of daylight remained, and five and a half hours were eventually taken. To avoid the danger of conducting a withdrawal in the dark, time must either be given for the troops to reach camp before daylight fails,

or the latter must be prepared to entrench and pass the
night in the open. The time taken to conduct a retirement varies directly with the difficulty of the ground and
courage of the enemy, and inversely with the loss that
can be inflicted on him. From examination of the time
taken over various retirements it may be deduced that, if
fighting of any severity takes place, it is not safe to
reckon on a speed of even one mile per hour.*

10. When a withdrawal is about to take place the fact
should be concealed from the enemy.

Both negative and positive instances are afforded by
this campaign. On the occasion of the first retirement
from Saran Sar it is related that the enemy were made
aware of what was about to take place by seeing the
movement to the rear of covering troops; the former then
crept up under cover of the woods, and lay in wait for the
last company of the Northamptons, with the results
already described. When General Westmacott began
his withdrawal from Dwatoi to Bagh on November 24,
however, the baggage was loaded up under cover of
darkness, and the whole force had gone some distance
before the Afridis had any idea of what was happening.

This principle of surprise can be carried out in a
variety of ways. In addition to beginning the movement
by night, a successful attack immediately followed by
retreat will often deceive the enemy completely.† The
marvellous system of intelligence, which all uncivilized
tribes seem to possess, may be turned to account by
spreading false reports ; even if no false report is spread,
a change of date will often find the enemy unprepared,
as the Afridis were when Sir William Lockhart began
his withdrawal from Tirah a day earlier than had been
originally intended ; and ruses may be most effectively
employed especially by small parties.

Such, then, are the principles governing the withdrawal

* Example.	Date.	Distance (Miles).	Approximate Time (Hours).
First retirement from Saran Sar	November 9	4	5½
Second retirement from Saran Sar	November 11	4	4½
Retirement from Waran Valley...	November 16	5	9
Retirement from Dwatoi	November 24	7	12
Retirement down Bara Valley ...	December 11	7	7
Retirement down Bara Valley ...	December 13	6	9

† This is advocated by Colonel Callwell in " Small Wars," p. 328.

of troops in the presence of an active enemy in country such as that to be found on the North-West Frontier of India. They are merely amplifications of the two main points to be observed in the action of a rear-guard in any class of warfare : (1) "To show as strong a front as possible to the enemy ;" (2) "to make sure of good lines of retreat."* All are illustrated by actual events in a comparatively recent campaign which are the foundation of the instructions formulated by the official text-books of the day. For a full discussion of these principles the reader is recommended to refer to Colonel Callwell's "Small Wars" Chapter xix. The word "rule" has been avoided purposely throughout the foregoing examination of rear-guard tactics, for, though rules are not laws, it has been thought better to employ terms of still more elastic significance such as "principles" and "instructions." There will then be no suggestion that the conclusions to which history points are laws to be followed blindly on every occasion, but merely warnings of what may happen if they are disregarded without good reason. It has been said that there is no such thing as a normal procedure in battle, but a knowledge of general principles is essential for the adoption of the correct course of action in a particular case.

The principles governing rear-guard actions are of universal application, whether the retiring troops are a whole brigade or merely piquets withdrawing from neighbouring hilltops, so it is just as necessary for the most junior officers, and even the non-commissioned officers, to be thoroughly acquainted with them as the senior officer holding an important command. Indeed, it is not too much to say that no officer or non-commissioned officer should be entrusted with the lives of his fellow-men who has not made all possible insurance for the future by adequate study in the past. Neglect of some principle on the part of a small detachment, when it should clearly have been observed, may easily compromise the whole force in any class of warfare; but when fighting against a savage enemy who gives no quarter, the penalty to the detachment itself for neglect is almost invariably such as will serve as a warning for the future only to others.

There is one great difficulty, however, about the practice of rear-guard actions in peace, which, though common to all other forms of training, is particularly

---

* "Field Service Regulations," Part I., section 72 (3).

pronounced in this class of operation, and that is the absence of moral influences. It has been pointed out already how moral considerations lie at the root of the necessity for the avoidance of any appearance of undue haste in the retirement of a rear-guard as a whole, more especially when dealing with uncivilized foes. Now, moral influences, except fatigue, are the very things that it is impossible to introduce into peace manœuvres. With a trifling transposition of Mr. Jorrocks' definition of hunting, peace manœuvres may be defined as the image of war without the danger, and only five and twenty per cent. of the gilt. It is impossible to reproduce in peace the depression of the troops after a reverse, the corresponding exultation of the enemy, the embarrassment caused by wounded men, the *pht!* of the small-bore bullet, the sight of a comrade's fall, the uncertainty of food and rest, and that magnetic personal influence which brings out the best qualities in men at a critical time. There are many men, officers as well as rank and file, who appear listless and even lethargic at ordinary times, but are totally different individuals when the din of battle is in their ears. British soldiers are phlegmatic by nature, probably to their advantage on the battlefield, but this *trait* is a handicap to their training in peace ; on the other hand, the more imaginative Indian soldier sometimes infuses a semblance of realism into his warlike education which reflects more credit on his zeal than his discrimination. Moral influences, however, such as have just been mentioned, which are so conspicuous a feature of rear-guard fighting, cannot be represented even by the strongest imagination ; but, since it is certain that the soldier's instinct in war will be to act as he has been accustomed in peace, it must follow that the best way to neutralize the disturbing moral factor in time of stress is to make what can be taught in peace so much a second nature that men will do the right thing involuntarily when, maybe, they have to act on their own initiative.

After rear-guard actions the next most noticeable feature of the Tirah Campaign is the growth of the practice known as "sniping." Sniping is a method of warfare adopted by individuals against a mass ; it is a direct outcome of the introduction of the long-range rifle to the frontier hills. Men are snipers when they fire out of hours, as it were, when no regular fight is in progress to make their efforts legitimate. Sniping may be either by day or by night, but, of course, the risk to the sniper is much smaller by night, for which reason the hours of darkness are much more popular with this class of individual than those of day. The target presented by some portion of a camp is a large one ; shots fired in the dark must necessarily be fired more or less at random, but much can be done by day to reduce the element of chance so as to insure that the line of fire passes through some part of the camp where the effect of a lucky bullet, from the sniper's point of view, will be most telling. Mention has been made already of how it was noticed that sniping was unusual during the night following arrival at a new camp, but that during subsequent nights on the same ground firing was the rule rather than the exception, so much so in fact that it seems almost superfluous to chronicle that sniping took place. The inference, of course, is that the enemy marked down by day the position of the headquarters of the larger units, of officers' messes, of piquets and other important points, and turned their knowledge to account by night.

It is largely from the experiences of 1897 that the principles of the present day have been evolved regarding protection at rest in Indian frontier warfare. These are :

1. To establish an outer line of "strong, self-contained piquets, placed so as to deny to the enemy all ground from which he could fire into camp." *

2. To have "a defensive perimeter, which must be clearly defined round the whole encampment."

3. To allow no movement outside the perimeter after dark, except for some special purpose, such as the laying of an ambuscade for snipers.

The Pathan has a strong dislike to having an enemy above him, so, by holding the commanding points in the vicinity of a camp, he is not only prevented from using them as positions for his sharpshooters, but the best posts of observation — the necessary preliminary to accurate sniping—are denied to him. The strength of the piquets detailed to hold these points may be anything from about twenty upwards, and the instructions laid down for their guidance may be summed up thus :

1. Against a well-armed enemy they must be thrown out sufficiently far from camp to prevent hostile marksmen establishing themselves within 2,000 yards.

2. If attacked, they must hold their own without retiring on camp or expecting reinforcements.

* " Field Service Regulations," Part I., section 147.

3. Their position must be prepared for an all-round defence, and be protected against fire from the camp.

4. Their position should be known to all units in camp and to each other, and they should be in signalling communication.

This system of protection proved most successful in 1897, for, though the piquets were often fiercely attacked, no single instance occurred of one being overwhelmed. A defensive perimeter clearly defined by an obstacle or entrenchments is necessary to check a charge of swordsmen, to prescribe beyond possibility of mistake the limits outside which no movements must take place after dark, and to facilitate the allotment of the troops for the defence and their immediate effective action.

When operating against an uncivilized enemy by night, regular troops are generally at so great a disadvantage in the matter of mobility, and knowledge of the ground, that it has to be laid down as a general rule that "after dark none should on any pretext go outside the perimeter, unless specially ordered to do so, in which case the sentries should be previously warned."* The latter precaution is, of course, to prevent the sentries firing on their own side by mistake. The case of ambuscades, however, has already been mentioned as an exception to the general rule. In 1897 the Gurkha scouts, men selected for their physique, activity, and marksmanship, did much to damp the ardour of the nocturnal sniper by several successful ambuscades and stalks. The Gurkhas, being hillmen and hunters by nature, were certainly not inferior to the Pathans at the latter's own game ; but courage, activity, and huntsman's craft are not exclusive perquisites of the Gurkha. Natural ability, of course, counts for much, but practice and perseverance are good substitutes ; and among the rank and file of any regiment, European or Indian, there are always men of the necessary aptitude in sufficient number to form a small patrol which could be trusted, after some practice, to go out and do good work at night, even among the frontier hills, without furnishing material for a regrettable incident. Many men of the army in India are fond of shooting as a sport ; many indulge their taste, and become skilled shikaris. It would seem, then, that there is a very valuable resource lying latent in the army, which at present is developed only to a limited extent. A mono-

* "Field Service Regulations," section 147 (4).

poly is bad for any trade. When men once get an idea into their head that they cannot do a thing, it is often very difficult to persuade them even to try; but, when they are persuaded, it is astonishing how often hidden talent comes to light, which surprises none so much as the possessors themselves. The only occasion on which British troops went out after dark during the Tirah Campaign was after General Kempster's rear-guard action of December 11, when a company of the King's Own Scottish Borderers went up the Bara Valley to see what had happened. Unfortunately for the cause of history, no enemy were met, but this party succeeded in collecting a large number of followers and transport animals, and the record of the battalion throughout the campaign certainly conveys the impression that, if opposition had been encountered, the men would have acquitted themselves with the most perfect credit.

The exploits of the Gurkha scouts in Tirah served to raise the question as to whether it would not be advisable to revive the old light companies of Peninsular days. The services of these are well known, but the formations of to-day are very different even from the line formations of Wellington. The company commanders who fought at Salamanca had no difficulty in controlling their men in action, but the accurate firearm of the present day, whose effective range extends to 1,400 yards, has produced a totally different set of conditions. The necessity for greater extension, the use of all available cover, and the supersession of volley by independent firing, have all combined to make the control of his men by a company commander more difficult, when once the former are committed to action. The result is decentralization of command, and a demand for greater individual intelligence.

Now, the light companies of Wellington's armies were composed of picked men, and, if re-introduced, they would have to consist of picked men to-day. The effect on the rest of the battalion could hardly fail to be unfortunate, for at least a dozen of the most efficient and most intelligent men would have to be taken from each of seven companies and replaced by those rejected from the favoured eighth. Owing to the lowering rather than the raising of the standard of individual intelligence in seven-eighths of the battalion, the necessity for further centralization of command, and not the reverse, would immediately follow. For modern war, an army composed of divisions, brigades, battalions, and companies of a uniform, though not brilliant, degree of efficiency is a fighting machine of far greater value than one which has a few *corps d'élite* and a large number of what may be described as "others."

One more point deserves mention before leaving the question of sniping, and that is that no attempt should be made to reply to the fire from camp. Even if his fire is ineffective, the midnight prowler derives great satisfaction from the fact that it apparently causes so much annoyance as to compel reply. All noise at night is to be deprecated, and there is very little chance of a lucky bullet removing the cause of the disturbance ; the best weapon against nocturnal marauders is the bayonet or its equivalent.

Night attacks on a small scale on the British camp were common, but the history of all these supports the statement that as long as vigilance is maintained, the men are well in hand, and proper arrangements have been made, disciplined troops have nothing to fear from the attacks of uncivilized enemies, even if the latter are considerably superior in numbers. In "Field Service Regulations," Part I., section 147, attention is drawn to the necessity for allotting alarm posts to non-combatants, provision of flanking fire, obstacles, a general reserve, and means of illuminating the foreground, but there are one or two other points which might be mentioned.

In the allotment of troops to the defensive perimeter the flanks of adjacent units should not meet at the corners of a camp ; units posted near a corner must hold both arms of the angle. The reason for this is obvious: corners are vulnerable points, as it is harder to develop the same intensity of fire as along the faces. The tendency of troops in action, especially when their strength is reduced by casualties, is to close towards the centre of their unit ; consequently, if men of different units meet at the corners, there will always be a tendency for a gap to occur at the corner.

Machine guns may sometimes be placed at the corners with advantage, but it must not be overlooked that machine guns are apt to jamb at critical times, so there must be men available to fill the gap without delay if this misfortune occurs.

Guns can defend their front, but the ordinary interval of 20 yards by day is too great for safety at night, if the guns are not quick firers. Ten yards is the maximum safe interval if the field of fire is at all restricted.

Precautions against the outbreak of fire in camp must not be overlooked, and internal communications should be unimpeded.

In 1896 there were some parts of the Indian borderland to the north-west that had never been visited by Europeans, but the campaigns of the following year afforded opportunities for filling in all the irritating blanks in the frontier maps which Sir Thomas Holdich and his intrepid band of surveyors were prompt to seize. In the " Indian Borderland " Sir T. H. Holdich says:

" It is a curious fact that far beyond the rugged line of those frontier mountains, in the deep recesses of which dwelt those tribes that loved to call themselves 'independent,' we were, in the year 1896, better acquainted with geographical details than we were as regarded our own immediate border. Most of Afghanistan we knew by then, all of Baluchistan, and much of Persia; but the comparatively narrow width of border hills which we could scrutinize with our telescopes from the windows of Peshawar houses and the stations of the Derajat was but a sketchy outline in our maps, an outline derived from such information as a few daring native explorers might bring, or from what we ourselves could gather when surveying on either side of it."*

The secret of the success of disciplined armies against superior numbers lies in effective combination, if armament and *moral* of both are about equal, but strategical combinations depend largely for success on accurate calculations of time and space. Without good maps reliable estimates of these important factors are well-nigh impossible; the result is either delay in the progress of the main plan of campaign while reconnaissance supplies the deficiency, or the risk has to be taken of committing troops to a definite line of action with insufficient data.

The pages of history are full of warnings of the danger attending military operations in an unknown country. In 1847 the United States troops would have paid a heavy price for their passage of the broken ground south of Mexico City if General Santa Anna's army had been better armed and better officered. The failure of the Dutch in 1873 to realize that they had reached Kota Raja, the capital of Achin, when the place was at their mercy, necessitated another attack the following year. The French difficulties in Madagascar, the disaster to the

* "The Indian Borderland," p. 351.

Italians in Abyssinia, and the British reverses at Stormberg and on the Tugela in 1899, are chiefly attributable to inadequate topographical information. The first march of the Mohmand Field Force from Shabkadr to Gandab furnishes yet another illustration of a potential disaster. Instead of an easy road along which camels could march without difficulty, the troops found "nothing but a stairway of boulders up which the transport had literally to be hauled."* And instead of the twelve mile march which was expected, twenty miles of waterless mountain-track lay between one night's camping-ground and the next. Whatever the reason may have been, there was, fortunately, no opposition; but one prefers not to think what the possible consequences would have been if a determined attack had been made in any strength on the attenuated British column as it toiled up the Karapa Pass.

The question of choice of objective has not been dealt with before in the preceding pages, but as that is a matter for high authority only, it can be referred to very briefly here. In civilized warfare the destruction of the enemy's field army is always the first objective, but, in savage warfare, there is as often as not no organized field army to destroy; the enemy's forces usually consist of gatherings of armed inhabitants, often without any recognized leader, and ignorant of all discipline. No single individual, nor yet any one section of the hostile population, has the power to sue for peace on behalf of the whole, consequently each tribe or clan has to be reduced to submission in turn.

To compel the surrender of guerillas, such as the frontier tribes of India, by the usual process of breaking down the means of defence would entail operations so prolonged and costly as to be out of all proportion to the interests at stake. Other means, therefore, must be found to achieve the same result, such as the destruction of villages and personal property, which has always been the only effective way of dealing with the elusive tribesmen beyond the North-West Frontier of India. At the same time this is only the last resource when other means fail, and even then must be resorted to with caution, or exasperation rather than submission may be the result.

Throughout the Tirah Campaign the protection of the baggage was a constant source of anxiety, in spite of

* "The Indian Frontier War" p. 26.

the fact that the class of transport generally showed a great improvement on that which had been got together hurriedly for past expeditions. The unsatisfactory nature of transport (both the animals and their drivers) collected at short notice and great expense is now, of course, fully recognized ; but notwithstanding improved transport, the amount of personal baggage that can be allowed on active service has decreased in even greater ratio.* "Rapidity of movement has always been an attribute of success." The 25 pounds of baggage, the maximum allowance of the rank and file of the Army in India on active service, seems very little ; but if only an extra 5 pounds were allowed, this would mean an addition of 100 pack mules or 40 camels to the transport of an infantry brigade,† to say nothing of drivers or the food required for the additional men and animals. But another point must not be overlooked when dealing with the question of impedimenta in the field. Sir Ian Hamilton says, " The finest transport in the world will not compensate for want of carrying power on the part of the men."‡ The meaning is obvious : occasions sometimes arise when men do not see their regimental transport for days together ; they themselves must therefore be prepared to carry whatever else the climate or military requirements may render necessary. In the review of the Chitral Campaign some remarks have been offered on this subject which is undoubtedly one for the consideration of the junior as well as the senior ranks of commissioned officers.

In the history of Indian frontier warfare an inferior class of transport animal has often been the cause of delay or even mishap, but his driver has also been frequently to blame. The enforcement of march discipline among non-combatants is one of the most difficult tasks which fall to the lot of transport officers and their assistants. During the last stages of the march down the Bara Valley the state of demoralization of the followers due to the attacks of the enemy and the weather was such that nothing short of direct supervision of each individual would have prevented the disorder which ensued. It was a case of every man for himself, and if the mules of which he had charge stayed with him, so much the better ; where the valley

---

* "Modern Strategy," p. 144 (Colonel James).
† Taking the strength of a battalion at 800.
‡ "A Staff Officer's Scrap-Book," vol. i., p. 54.

widened out those behind tried to press forward by
increasing the front, and many animals got bogged
in swampy rice-fields ; when the valley contracted again
to a narrow defile, the whole mass converged on one
single channel, and was packed tighter and tighter every
moment by the pressure of those behind. In each case
the delay caused had to be reckoned in hours, and the
penalty in the lives of men composing the hard-pressed
rear-guard.

Two more points deserve notice :

In broken mountainous country a moving flank-guard
is usually unable to keep pace with, and at the same time
be a proper protection to, the main body. The normal
method of crowning the heights along a line of advance
through this class of country is for the force to move off
with a strong advanced guard, which detaches men as
it goes along to occupy all commanding points. These
detachments remain stationary till the rear-guard comes
up, when they themselves fall back and act as a reinforcement to it. Reference to the account of General
Westmacott's reconnaissance to Dwatoi and General
Kempster's rear-guard action of December 11 will show
how rapidly whole battalions are swallowed up when
flanking parties have to be detached to hold some
commanding point, or dislodge a small hostile party
which is harassing the progress of the column. In
order to give the piquets time to gain the heights along
the line of march, the advanced troops may have to start
some hours before the main body. For instance, on the
occasion of the reconnaissance to Dwatoi General Westmacott's leading troops started some three hours before
the rest of his force.

The danger of division of force without facilities for
mutual support is a feature of any class of campaign, but
is particularly great in savage warfare. Weak, isolated
detachments have been again and again the victims of an
enterprising enemy, and a mishap or even delay to one
such detachment may easily compromise the success
of the whole plan of action. The first expedition into
the Chamkanni Valley was quite abortive, because one of
the two detachments into which the force was divided
was so delayed by the enemy and the difficulties of
the road that, when it was extricated at last, the day was
so far advanced that the object of the expedition had
to be abandoned, and a harassing rear-guard action
fought instead before camp was reached.

CHAPTER XXI

THE MAHSUD BLOCKADE, 1900-1902

(*Map III.*)

AFTER the restoration of peace in 1898 the Mahsud Waziris were the only tribe who disturbed the tranquillity of the North-West Frontier of India during a period of ten years. The marauding proclivities of the Mahsuds have already been noticed in previous chapters— in fact, the members of this tribe appear to be a people who court publicity, for they have never permitted themselves to sink into unconsidered obscurity since they first came in contact with the British Government. Between 1898 and 1900 Mahsud raids rendered life and property in the Tochi and Gomal Valleys so insecure, and the perpetrators of these outrages established such a terrorism over not only the inhabitants of British villages, but many of the native officials as well, that retaliatory measures became absolutely necessary. The following extracts from a report by the Assistant Commissioner of the North-West Frontier Province,* dated February 1, 1902, give a good idea of the attitude of the Mahsuds during 1899-1900:

"It would, of course, be an exaggeration to say that the Mahsuds ever attempted directly to intimidate British officers; they were far too clever for this. But they actually did intimidate superior native officials. Bhanju Lal, Tahsildar, told me that on one occasion during the hearing of a case in his court a Mahsud deputation had commenced with petitions, and proceeded to direct threats regarding his decision of the case. Karimdad . . . who was deputed to superintend the demolition of a tower illegally erected by Futteh Khan . . . went long afterwards in fear of Futteh Khan's

* Mr. P. Pipon.

revenge. A notorious raider . . . was got in, and Deputy-Inspector Thana Ram let him go rather than remand him to custody.

*   *   *   *   *

" Practically no cases under the Arms Act were ever sent up from the Gomal Thana. Notwithstanding this, I believe armed Mahsuds were everywhere. I was confirmed in this view by an incident in November, 1899, when I happened to be riding to Murtaza at a time when tongas do not ordinarily pass. I met a Mahsud carrying a gun down the highroad in broad daylight. He was arrested, proved to be a well-known badmash, and was sentenced to nine months' imprisonment. I do not believe for a moment that had the police in any way attempted to enforce the Act against Mahsuds such an occurrence would be possible. Indeed, before the beginning of 1899, the Arms Act seems not to have been enforced at all against Mahsuds.

*   *   *   *   *

" The Border Military Police were useless from fear. During these two years, so far as I know, not one Mahsud was ever killed or even wounded by the Border Military Police. . . . It was well known that no Border Military Police sepoy would ever shoot a Mahsud. He would fire, but be careful to miss.

" It was a generally recognized fact that the Mahsuds had become more and more dangerous of late years. I have had many conversations with our own maliks on the subject, and they attributed the fact to their receiving large allowances with which to buy rifles, to the disarmament of British subjects, to the invariable consideration shown to Mahsuds of all classes in British territory, and to the Mahsud colony. The last-named scheme gave every Mahsud badmash an explanation for his presence, afforded a perfect rendezvous for raiding gangs, and a handy repository for arms and stolen property. . . . It was as a Gundaspur Khan dryly described it, 'a school of badmashi opened by Government for the instruction of our young men.'

*   *   *   *   *

" Two cases were brought before me in which the Hindu shopkeepers had rushed off to the police, but on being confronted with the Mahsud prisoner in court refused to open their mouths against them, evidently in abject fear.

*   *   *   *   *

" When I first came to Tank even the chaprasis used to announce that a Mahsud was waiting, in a manner which showed that all other work, however important, was to be thrown to the winds. When I refused to let Mahsuds interrupt the court on all occasions, they complained on the subject to the Political Officer."

In view of the state of affairs disclosed by the foregoing extracts, it is not surprising that outrages of all kinds were of frequent occurrence. It must be admitted, however, that in most of the cases in which troops or police were concerned, and the Mahsuds scored a distinct success, this result was due to want of vigilance, or the neglect of some ordinary precaution. On the night of January 9 and 10, 1900, a band of Mahsuds entered the Zam police post, the door of which was open, killed six men, and carried off seven firearms. On August 27, 1901, a tonga carrying four passengers, travelling after sunset contrary to orders, was ambuscaded near Murtaza, and one man was wounded.

Again, on June 18, 1901, a party of Mahsuds sent a man forward to reconnoitre the police post at Baran. The man entered the fort on the pretext of asking for a drink of water, satisfied himself as to the laxity of discipline, and returned to his companions. When the raiders advanced against the post an hour later, shortly before noon, the sentry was absent from his post, and with regard to the remainder of the garrison it is said that " it consisted of twenty-two men and a dafadar, of whom eleven were absent either on duty, without leave, or in gaol, leaving eleven men and the dafadar in the post. The whole of these men appear to have displayed the most contemptible negligence and cowardice, and their statements as to what occurred are so tinctured with puerile exaggeration and desire to save themselves as to be practically worthless. . . . Finding the wicket gate open, the raiders rushed in and surprised the entire guard— asleep or engaged in music. These men allowed themselves to be overpowered, without a shot being fired or even a loud cry being raised. The raiders then took from the dafadar his keys, and proceeded to collect the garrison. During the confusion the dafadar managed to slip out of the gate and get away. Had he gone straight to the nearest village much might have been done, but he seems to have gone mad with fear, and probably hid himself in a ravine till the gang were well away. The rest of the garrison were collected by the raiders, and driven into a room in the post the door of which was padlocked."* Fifteen firearms, seven bayonets, and 548 rounds of ammunition were carried off by the Mahsuds.

Yet another instance occurred near Murtaza on November 3, 1901, when the escort to a survey party neglected to take proper military precautions on its return march, was ambushed in a ravine at short range, and half their number were killed.

In November, 1900, the unpaid fines due from the Mahsuds on account of various raids amounted to nearly 2 lakhs of rupees.† There seemed to be no prospect of settlement, and the general situation had become so intolerable that the tribesmen were informed that Rs. 50,000 must be paid by the end of the month, or a blockade of their country would be begun. No satisfactory reply being received, the Mahsuds were therefore cut off from intercourse with the outside world with effect from December 1, 1900, by means of a chain of police posts, supported by movable columns of regular troops. During the next six months part of the fine imposed was paid, but, as fresh outrages were committed entailing further claims for compensation, it was recognized that the effect of the passive blockade would have to be intensified by more active measures. Accordingly mobile columns were organized at Datta Khel, Jandola, Sarwakai, and Wana to carry the war into the enemy's country by means of rapidly executed counter-raids. These operations were conducted under the direction of Major-General C. C. Egerton, C.B., who had the troops named below at his disposal.

1st Punjab Cavalry.	3rd Sikhs.
5th Punjab Cavalry.	17th Bengal Infantry.
Gujrat Mountain Battery	23rd Pioneers.
(27th Mountain Battery).	27th Punjab Infantry.
1st Punjab Infantry.	28th Punjab Infantry.
2nd Punjab Infantry.	29th Punjab Infantry.
32nd Pioneers.	23rd Bombay Infantry (123rd
35th Sikhs.	Outram's Rifles).
38th Dogras.	24th Bombay Infantry (124th
45th Sikhs.	Baluchistan Infantry).
9th Bombay Infantry (109th	North Waziristan Militia.
Infantry).	South Waziristan Militia.

* Report by the Deputy-Commissioner of Bannu, dated August 2, 1901.
† Rs. 200,000 = £13,333.

There were four series of raids at intervals of about a fortnight, beginning on November 23, 1901, during which many villages were destroyed, nearly 400 Mahsuds were killed or wounded, others captured, and a large number of cattle driven off; the British casualties amounted to 146. Some sharp fighting occurred now and then, but the troops were well handled, and the result of these operations was that within forty-five days the Mahsuds had made their submission, and the blockade was raised on March 10, 1902.

Before the end of 1902 an expedition had to be undertaken against the Kabul Khel Waziris under Major-General C. C. Egerton, C.B. The troops operated in four columns, formed from the troops named below, and after taking some 300 prisoners, destroying hostile villages and fortifications, and capturing over 5,000 head of cattle, returned to Bannu in eight days, having met with but little opposition.

1st Punjab Cavalry.	5th Punjab Infantry.
3rd Punjab Cavalry.	22nd Punjab Infantry.
5th Punjab Cavalry.	1st Sikh Infantry.
Kohat Mountain Battery.	3rd Sikh Infantry.
Derajat Mountain Battery.	4th Sikh Infantry.
Gujrat Mountain Battery.	Kurram Militia.
2nd Punjab Infantry.	North Waziristan Militia.
4th Punjab Infantry.	

Since 1902 Mahsud raids have not ceased; from time to time the news of some such escapade reaches the newspapers of India and the mother country, and serves to remind their readers that the military history of Waziristan is not closed yet, but may require an addition at no very distant date. The story of the Mahsud blockade is interesting from a political rather than a military point of view. It furnishes striking evidence of the truth of the assertion that war is after all the surest instrument of diplomacy. Six weeks of active operations procured the submission of the refractory tribe after twelve months of passive blockade had failed to produce any important result, in spite of the strategical facilities afforded to the Indian Government by the occupation of the Tochi and Gomal Valleys. The question of cost and the well-known difficulty of obtaining decisive results among the rugged mountain fastnesses of Mahsud territory appear to have been the chief objections to active military operations in the first instance, but neither of these was justified by events.   Not only had a large force to be employed eventually, but the enemy's territory was successfully penetrated from several directions, and considerable loss inflicted on the fighting strength of the tribe.

Military operations which are not recognized officially as part of a regular campaign are always unsatisfactory to the troops engaged. The risks and hardships incidental to an expedition, a blockade, or a mission on the Indian frontier, are practically identical, but not so the compensations.   In the case of the Mahsud blockade the size of the force employed, the hard marching, the sharp fighting on some occasions, and the important results achieved in a short time, undoubtedly entitle the record of the services rendered by the troops to a place among those of the recognized frontier campaigns.

CHAPTER XXII

1908

THE ZAKHA KHEL EXPEDITION. *(Map II.)*

AFTER the stirring events of 1897-98 ten years elapsed
before military operations against the tribes living north
of Kohat again became necessary, although occasions
were not lacking when there seemed to be some danger
of the door of the temple of Janus being thrown open and
the god of peace permitted to escape. The British policy
enunciated in 1898 of refusing further political responsibility in the tribal hinterland was steadily maintained in
spite of a definite request for annexation on the part of a
section of the Orakzai tribe in 1904.

During the ten years which followed the conclusion of
the Tirah Campaign, the Zakha Khel remained the persistent enemies of tranquillity and progress. Numerous
raids in British territory were proved to have had their
origin in the Bazar Valley, and in March, 1907, the state
of affairs in the district adjoining the Khaibar Pass
became so unsatisfactory, that, if British prestige was
to be maintained, it was clear to the Government of India
that something more than remonstrance or even stoppage
of allowances was necessary to deal with a clan which
was rapidly becoming a menace to the peace of the whole
frontier.

It will be remembered that the Zakha Khel are the
most important section of the powerful Afridi tribe, and
that their territory adjoins the Khaibar Pass on the south
side; but the Bazar Valley, where their most important
villages are situated, lies off the main channels of communication between India and Central Asia. A description of the Bazar Valley has already been given in the
account of the expedition of 1897. Further, it will be
recalled how during the Tirah Campaign the Zakha Khel
maintained an attitude of uncompromising hostility
throughout, and were responsible mainly both for the

attacks on the Khaibar posts at the beginning of the outbreak, and for the severe fighting which took place in the Bara Valley during the withdrawal of the 2nd Division from Tirah. Prior to the expedition which is about to be described their territory had been invaded three times by British armies : in 1878 and 1879 by General Maude, in consequence of their attacks on British convoys passing through the Khaibar Pass to or from the troops in Afghanistan, and in 1897 by General Sir William Lockhart at the end of the Tirah Campaign.

In 1908 the Zakha Khel were well armed with rifles, mostly Martinis, with the use of which they were well acquainted, and once more they justified their reputation as adepts in the class of warfare which is their speciality. In April, 1907, it was thought that the question of the despatch of a punitive expedition against the Zakha Khel might be postponed till the autumn. The autumn came, and the raids were renewed with such daring that even Peshawar city itself became the scene of wholesale robbery under arms. A military expedition was then sanctioned at the beginning of February, 1908, "limited strictly to punishment of Zakha Khel, and not occupation or annexation of tribal territory." * The mobilization of two brigades from the 1st (Peshawar) Division with divisional troops and the necessary departmental services was ordered; the concentration at Peshawar was smoothly and expeditiously carried out, and on February 13, within twenty-four hours of the order to move, the advanced troops were not only in occupation of Jamrud, eleven miles from Peshawar, but detachments had been pushed up the Khaibar Pass to occupy all strategical points as far as Landi Kotal. In the meantime it had been ascertained that the remainder of the Afridi tribe were not in sympathy with the Zakha Khel, so that it seemed unlikely that complications due to the intervention of other clans would arise.

Major-General Sir James Willcocks, the General Officer Commanding the 1st (Peshawar) Division in peace, took command of his troops in war, and the Staff was as far as possible the same as before mobilization, so that for the first time a British force took the field in a frontier campaign under the commanders and Staff who had been responsible for its training in peace. The composition of the Zakha Khel Field Force was as shown in Table XXVI.

* Telegram from Secretary of State to the Viceroy.

TABLE XXVI

ZAKHA KHEL FIELD FORCE, 1908

Major-General Sir James Willcocks, K.C.M.G., C.B., D.S.O.

First Brigade.	Second Brigade.	Third Brigade (Reserve).	Divisional Troops.
Brigadier-General C. A. Anderson.	*Major-General A. A. Barrett.*	*Major-General Watkis.*	37th Lancers, 2 Squadrons.
1st Battalion Royal Warwickshire Regiment.	1st Battalion Seaforth Highlanders.	1st Battalion Royal Munster Fusiliers.	No. 3 Mountain Battery Royal Garrison Artillery.
53rd Sikhs.	28th Punjabis.	55th Coke's Rifles.	22nd (Derajat) Mountain Battery, 4 guns.
59th Scinde Rifles.	45th Sikhs.	1st Battalion 6th Gurkhas.	Nos. 6 and 9 Companies Sappers and Miners.
2nd Battalion 5th Gurkhas.	54th Sikhs.	23rd (Peshawar) Mountain Battery.	23rd Sikh Pioneers.
			25th Punjabis.

The main body left Peshawar on February 13, and halted for the night west of Jamrud. On the next day Sir James Willcocks entered the Khaibar Pass and concentrated near Ali Masjid. The tribesmen were reported to be preparing for resistance near Alachi and Chora, but the rapidity of the British advance had taken them so completely by surprise that all the principal entrances to the Bazar Valley were occupied before the Zakha Khel could combine for concerted action. The tribesmen were completely deceived also as to the intended line of advance by a demonstration on the 14th carried out by two battalions, which were sent out to repair the road along the Alachi-Karamna route. This led the Zakha Khel to think that the Alachi road would be taken, and that the British force would wait near Ali Masjid until the work had been carried out ; the tribesmen therefore made no haste to assemble their forces, though their piquets remained in observation near Karamna. Sir James Willcocks, however, instead of halting near Ali Masjid, marched his two brigades early on February 15 to Chora. The 1st Brigade stopped at Chora for the night, but the 2nd Brigade, pushing on without their baggage, reached Walai the same afternoon, the rearguard arriving in camp at 7 p.m. The distance covered was about sixteen miles, a fine performance on bad hill-tracks which was only possible for troops unaccompanied by baggage. The effect was to upset the enemy's calculations completely; the tribesmen fired some long-range shots at the flanking parties, and the Mountain Battery attached to the 2nd Brigade fired a few rounds, but otherwise no opposition was encountered.

On February 15 another column consisting of Gurkhas and Khaibar Rifles left Landi Kotal for the Bazar Valley over the pass of the same name, under Lieutenant-Colonel Roos Keppel. This move was also a surprise to the Zakha Khel, for, though they had originally expected some such movement, and had established piquets on the Bazar Pass, the ostentatious return of the transport, which had taken supplies and ammunition to Landi Kotal, led them to believe that no such advance was intended from this direction ; their piquets, therefore, had been withdrawn.

Comparing the route taken by Sir James Willcocks with that followed by the commanders of former expeditions to the Bazar Valley, it will be remembered that in 1879 the Jamrud Column marched by way of Chora, and the Ali Masjid Column through Karamna, and that in 1897 General Gaselee's Brigade took the road through Chora while General Hart advanced by way of Alachi and Karamna. It will also be remembered that the Chora route was found to be much easier than that by Karamna, and that General Hart was so delayed in his advance by the difficulties of the road that Sir William Lockhart was able to advance into the heart of the Bazar Valley with General Gaselee's Brigade and carry out the work of destruction before General Hart's men were able to arrive on the scene.

On February 16 the 53rd Sikhs and Derajat Mountain Battery joined the 2nd Brigade at Walai, taking with them the whole of General Barrett's baggage, and on the same day Lieutenant-Colonel Roos Keppel's column from Landi Kotal marched into Walai, having passed the previous night at China. After leaving troops to guard the line of communication the remainder of General Anderson's Brigade joined the rest of the force on the 17th.

From Walai part of the force was sent out daily to destroy the important village of China and to disperse bodies of the enemy who appeared in the neighbourhood. Small skirmishes occurred, more especially when the retirement to camp began, but the British troops showed that they had learnt the art of hill warfare so well since 1897, and the tribesmen were so roughly handled on the few occasions when they ventured to come to comparatively close quarters, that they soon realized the futility of further resistance. During the Zakha Khel Expedition the enemy had to face for the first time the fire of breech-loading guns using smokeless powder. The 10-pounder breech-loading gun, the new weapon of mountain batteries, was seen on active service for the first time, and its increased range, added to greater rapidity and accuracy of fire, gained for it the general approval of the British force and the unqualified respect of the enemy.

On February 21 a combined attack of the two brigades was made on Halwai, the 1st Brigade from the north, and the 2nd Brigade from the east. The village was occupied and destroyed without difficulty, but the enemy pressed the retirement with considerable determination, though without success. Sniping was often indulged in at night, but men and animals were well under cover, and very little damage was done.

On February 27 the Zakha Khel tendered their sub-

mission, being urged thereto by the representatives of
the remaining Afridi clans, as well as the obvious
futility of resistance, and on March 1 the whole British
force returned to Jamrud. No fighting took place during
the withdrawal from the Bazar Valley, but the return
march was rendered an unpleasant experience by heavy
rain. Within three weeks the Zakha Khel Expedition of
1908 was carried through and passed into history; the
principal villages of the Bazar Valley had been destroyed,
and the actual physical loss inflicted was unusually
severe. Sir James Willcocks in his despatch states:
"The enemy's losses as far as can be ascertained at
present have been at least seventy killed, and the wounded
may reasonably be put at a much higher figure."

The success of the expedition, apart from the personal
skill of Sir James Willcocks and those under him, is
attributed to—

1. The rapidity with which both preparations and
execution of the plan of campaign were carried through.

2. Improvement in musketry.

3. Increased skill on the part of the infantry in the
methods of hill warfare.

4. Rapidity in improvising cover and obstacles.

5. Efficiency of the transport.

Sir James Willcocks says also that "the good conduct
of the Khaibar Rifles, many of whom were actually
serving against their own kith and kin, is a remarkable
testimony to their efficiency and loyalty. Not a rifle
was lost by the corps, nor was there a single desertion."
The British casualties during the expedition were one
British officer killed, four wounded; two non-commissioned officers and men killed, thirty-three wounded. The
health of the troops was good throughout. The cost of
the expedition was estimated at £57,000.

THE MOHMAND EXPEDITION. *(Map I.)*

The echoes of war had scarcely died away in the hills
bordering the Bazar Valley when disquieting reports
reached Peshawar from the north. The official information published on April 21 ran: "During the past
few weeks there have been considerable signs of unrest
in the Mohmand country, north-west of Peshawar. It
appears that during the recent Zakha Khel Expedition
mullahs were inciting the tribesmen in the Mohmand
country to combine with the Zakha Khel against the

Government. Their efforts were so far successful that they actually raised a small lashkar, which arrived on the scene of operations too late, owing to the rapidity with which the operations were brought to a conclusion. Not unnaturally, the tribesmen, once excited, were disinclined to return quietly to their homes. The immediate outcome was a series of raids committed along the Mohmand-Peshawar border towards the end of March. . . . In consequence of these raids the military detachments at Abazai and Shabkadr were strengthened at the request of the civil authorities, and a military garrison was placed in Matta Mughal Khel, so as to set free the Border Military Police for patrolling duties."

Late on the night April 19/20 news was received that the Mohmands were preparing to attack the border posts, that shots had been exchanged already, and that casualties to British troops had occurred at Matta. Strong reinforcements of all arms were sent out to Shabkadr early on the morning of April 20, accompanied by Sir James Willcocks, and troops were brought into Peshawar from Nowshera to replace those that were now watching the Mohmand border. It was estimated that the gathering of tribesmen mustered some 10,000 men, but that this number was being increased rapidly by reinforcements from all directions, including Afghan territory. Some anxiety was felt as to the attitude of the Zakha Khel, but throughout the Mohmand Campaign the whole Afridi tribe abode loyally by their engagements, and turned a deaf ear to all the efforts of their neighbours to the north to involve them in a new conflict.

Between April 20 and 23 further long-range shooting was indulged in by the enemy, but by day all attempts to approach to undue proximity were frustrated by the fire of the 18th and 80th Batteries, Royal Field Artillery,* in whose hands the 18-pounder quickfiring gun saw active service for the first time. At night the enemy made several attacks on the British posts, but were invariably repulsed without difficulty; as usual, sniping was the rule rather than the exception.

That the Mohmands should have broken out into open hostilities at this time of the year, when their crops were still unharvested, was a matter for considerable surprise. The loss of their crops is a serious matter for frontier tribesmen, and it was thought that their readiness to

---

* Four guns only of the 80th Battery Royal Field Artillery.

risk them pointed to the existence of powerful influences in the background. The mullahs were known to be on the warpath once more, and it seemed as if another tidal wave of fierce fanaticism was gathering among the Mohmand hills. The conduct of the Amir's frontier officials further tended to aggravate the situation. Large bodies of well-armed Afghans passed through Dakka to join the Mohmands, apparently without let or hindrance, thus giving considerable material, as well as moral support, to our enemies.

On the night April 22/23 an incident occurred at Matta which showed that the reputation of cavalrymen among the tribesmen had lost nothing by the lapse of time. The correspondent of the *Pioneer* says that during the usual sniping at the piquets on the night in question "some of the cavalry horses in Matta camp took fright and stampeded. In their fright they rushed into the barbed wire entanglements with which the camp is surrounded, and ten of them were killed; others were so badly injured that they had to be shot. The men who were amusing themselves by sniping into the camp evidently thought that the cavalry were making for them, and apparently decamped hastily, as the sniping instantly ceased."* In all probability there were many among those gathered together who had been eye-witnesses of the charge of the 11th Bengal Lancers in 1897, and perhaps some who had been ridden over by the 7th Hussars in 1864. Both exploits took place in the immediate neighbourhood; even darkness might be no protection in such an ill-omened place.

The line Michni-Abazai was still further reinforced by artillery and infantry on April 23, in consequence of the formidable force in which the enemy were seen to be, and the mobilization was ordered of two complete brigades, with divisional troops and a reserve brigade at Peshawar. The Khaibar and Malakand Movable Columns were also to be completed to full strength, so as to be ready for eventualities. The composition of the Mohmand Field Force will be found in Table XXVII.

During the night April 23/24 the tribesmen made a determined attack on the British posts at Matta and Garhi Sadar, but the garrison (part of General Anderson's brigade) was so well entrenched, and the barbed wire entanglements proved such efficient obstacles, that there was never any danger of the defence

* *Pioneer*, April 25, 1908.

TABLE XXVII

MOHMAND FIELD FORCE, 1908

MAJOR-GENERAL SIR JAMES WILLCOCKS, K.C.M.G., C.B., D.S.O.

FIRST BRIGADE.*	SECOND BRIGADE.*	THIRD BRIGADE.*	DIVISIONAL TROOPS.
Brigadier-General C. A. Anderson.	*Major-General A. A. Barrett.*	*Brigadier-General J. Ramsay.*	21st Cavalry.
1st Battalion Northumberland Fusiliers (replaced by 22nd Punjabis).	1st Battalion Seaforth Highlanders.	1st Battalion Royal Munster Fusiliers (replaced by 1st Battalion West Yorkshire Regiment).	No. 8 Mountain Battery Royal Garrison Artillery.
53rd Sikhs.	28th Punjabis.	21st Punjabis.†	23rd (Peshawar) Mountain Battery.
57th Wilde's Rifles.	55th Coke's Rifles.	22nd Punjabis (replaced by 19th Punjabis).	28th Mountain Battery.
59th Scinde Rifles.	Guides Infantry† (replaced by 54th Sikhs).	40th Pathans.	Nos. 1 and 6 Companies Sappers and Miners.
			34th Sikh Pioneers.
			One Native Field Hospital.

* To each Brigade were attached—Two Sections of a British Field Hospital ; a Native Field Hospital (two extra Sections to 3rd Brigade) ; a Brigade Supply Column.

† The Guides Infantry were employed on the line of communication, together with the 21st Punjabis.

being penetrated. For about half an hour the firing was incessant, but, thanks to the good cover under which the troops were, very little damage was done. After their repulse the tribesmen took up a position north-west of Matta, where they threw up sangars. At 6.30 a.m. on the 24th Sir James Willcocks ordered an attack on the enemy, which resulted in their complete discomfiture and general retirement towards the hills. Our casualties amounted to 62, while those of the enemy were estimated at 500.

Nothing further of note occurred during the next six days, but all reports that came to hand agreed that the Mohmands had received a very severe lesson, and that their losses had not been exaggerated. News, however, was received to the effect that large bodies of men were assembling on the Afghan border, nominally forbidden to proceed, but practically not restrained in any way. These were reported on May 1 to be moving on Landi Kotal, which was garrisoned by 600 men of the Khaibar Rifles, under Lieutenant-Colonel Roos Keppel. Consequently the 3rd Brigade in reserve at Peshawar was moved at once up to Landi Kotal, together with the 80th Battery Royal Field Artillery and a detachment of the 18th Lancers, and the 2nd Brigade (General Barrett) was brought into Peshawar from its posts on the Mohmand border, and transferred thence to Ali Masjid.   These   movements   were   no   sooner ordered than the enemy appeared in force before Landi Kotal, and made a series of determined attacks on the defences of this end of the Khaibar Pass on the night May 1/2, and the two following days. The Khaibar Rifles, however, stood firm, and on the arrival of Sir James Willcocks and the 3rd Brigade an attack was made on May 4 on the Afghans— for so they must be called—which had the effect of driving them back across the border, with the loss of about sixty men, at the small cost of one officer and two men wounded. Sir James Willcocks moved out from Landi Kotal in two columns, one on each side of the Khaibar gorge. So resolute was the advance, and so effective the covering fire of the guns, in spite of bad weather, that there was no check till the Afghan frontier was reached, when, for political reasons, the advance was continued no farther, and the return to Landi Kotal began. The enemy followed up the retirement of the left column with considerable determination, but the rear-guard, consisting of the Munster Fusiliers and the 40th Pathans, supported by the mountain guns, did their work well, and kept the most venturesome of the tribesmen at a respectful distance. During the day an interesting example of the effect of a bullet on modern small-arm ammunition occurred—"the pouch of a man in the Munster Fusiliers being struck, with the result that all five cartridges in a clip inside exploded. Though the man's coat was penetrated by the bullet, he himself was unhurt." *

The possibility of complications infinitely more serious than any which the Mohmands could cause was at this time very real; practically all officers of the Northern Army on leave in India were recalled, and all preparations were made for concentrating a large force at short notice on the North-West Frontier. Fortunately, however, the Afghan contingents were so disheartened by their repulses at Matta and Landi Kotal that all danger of serious trouble soon passed away. Nevertheless, it is only too probable that matters would have been very different if anything in the shape of a reverse had occurred to the British forces, either on the Mohmand border or at Landi Kotal. If the defence had been less impenetrable in the one case, or the reinforcement of the Khaibar garrisons been less prompt in the other, it is not improbable that the subjects of the Amir would have committed themselves so deeply as to leave the Government of India no alternative but to demand and, if necessary, exact by force of arms sufficient reparation to restore its prestige in the eyes of its impressionable neighbours.

The successful defence of one of the small Khaibar blockhouses by a handful of the Khaibar Rifles during the crisis on May 2 and 3 deserves mention. The blockhouse in question was at Michni Kandao, and was garrisoned by fifty men under a Subadar.† "The enemy, some 4,000 strong, invested the blockhouse for about seventeen hours, and actually planted one scaling-ladder on to the wall of the blockhouse. The Subadar and his men, however, drove off the attackers, and now have the scaling-ladder in their possession as a trophy of war, of which they are naturally very proud." ‡

The fort at Landi Kotal, and the blockhouses in the neighbourhood, were rebuilt after the suppression of the

* *Pioneer*, May 8, 1908.   † Subadar Torkhan.
‡ *Pioneer*, May 6, 1908.

rising in 1897-98, during which, it will be remembered, they were destroyed by the Afridis. Masonry and steel, the materials used in the construction, combined with facilities for the storage of ample supplies of food and water, render these important posts practically impregnable to an enemy not provided with artillery.

On May 5 and 6 the aspect of affairs was so satisfactory as to justify the withdrawal of the 2nd and 3rd Brigades from the Khaibar Pass. Accordingly, the 3rd Brigade began its return march to Peshawar early on the morning of the 7th, preceded by the 2nd Brigade from Ali Masjid. Unfortunately, the withdrawal was not unattended with loss. In an attempt, in spite of approaching darkness, to recover seven camels which had been carried off from Ali Masjid by a party of raiders, an officer * was wounded in the chest, and died before reaching camp.

No military operations took place on the 8th, and it was reported that the Afghans who had crossed the border were returning to their homes; also that all was quiet among the tribes inhabiting the region north of Mohmand territory. On the whole the troops were fairly fortunate in the matter of weather. For the time of year the heat was not oppressive; it was hot in the daytime, it is true, but all through the nights were cool, and as long as it is cool at night, heat by day is of comparatively little consequence. Unfortunately, cholera broke out early in May, but, though several cases occurred, it never assumed a virulent form and was speedily stamped out. Other parts of the frontier having been secured and satisfactory guarantees for the future received from the Amir, preparations were pushed forward for the necessary punitive expedition against the Mohmands, who still persisted in maintaining an uncompromising demeanour.

The Mohmands, it will be remembered, inhabit a barren and waterless district north-west of Peshawar of about the same size as the counties of Middlesex and Surrey combined, and bordering the main highway into Afghanistan through the Khaibar Pass. They may be divided roughly into two sections—an agricultural and comparatively peaceful portion inhabiting the villages near Peshawar along the banks of the Kabul River, and the fanatical and bloodthirsty clans who inhabit the barren and hilly country farther to the north-west.

* Major Coape Smith.

The roads through Mohmand territory are extremely bad; the road constructed by General Elles during the 1897 Campaign was found to have been allowed to fall into complete disrepair. For water the inhabitants are dependent partly on springs whose supply is uncertain, but mainly on tanks constructed for the storage of rainwater. In spite of the natural disadvantages of the country, villages—each with their arrangements for defence—are far from being few or far between, and, like many other barren-looking regions in the world, wherever irrigation is possible, the soil gives evidence of remarkable fertility.

The presence of cholera among the troops necessitated certain changes in the composition of the Field Force which will be found shown in Table XXVII. On May 10 representatives of the southern sections of the Mohmand tribe put in an appearance at Shabkadr, but were told that they were not sufficiently representative of the tribe to render political negotiations possible on behalf of the whole. They were assured, however, that their pacific intentions would receive due acknowledgment by the issue of orders forbidding the destruction of their villages and crops, provided that they did nothing to hinder the advance of the troops.

Profiting by the experiences of General Elles' division in 1897, Sir James Willcocks made no attempt to cross the arduous Karapa Pass on the first day of the advance. Marching independently, with the 1st Brigade leading, the head of the column reached Dand, the site of a ruined village, where there were some trees and good water, on May 13. The next day General Anderson crossed the Karapa Pass and camped at Ghalanai, but a lightly equipped advanced guard consisting of two squadrons, four guns, one section of sappers and miners, and two battalions, pushed on to Nahaki in the hope of surprising some of the Mohmands before they could escape to the hills. Both brigades concentrated at Nahaki, a village some 600 feet below the pass of the same name, on May 16, when the 1st Brigade pushed on over the pass to Dawazagai.

Few signs of the enemy were seen, and it was found that the houses passed by the wayside had been dismantled, and all property removed. Great difficulties were experienced on account of the execrable nature of the road, and the Sappers and Pioneers had a busy time making it passable for transport without undue difficulty.

The road constructed during the last Mohmand Campaign had not been kept up, and in many places had disappeared entirely.

From Dawazagai and Nahaki detachments were sent out in various directions to destroy the hostile villages and collect any supplies that might be found.   Practically no opposition was ever encountered during the advance, but, when the withdrawal to camp began, the tribesmen usually pursued their favourite tactics of harassing the retirement.   The troops, however, were well handled, and no mishap occurred.

On the night May 16/17 the piquets of the 1st Brigade were attacked in a most determined manner during a heavy thunderstorm.   One of the piquets belonging to the 22nd Punjabis was so hard pressed that reinforcements had to be sent to it between 10 and 11 p.m. Further reinforcements arrived about 1 a.m., but the tribesmen were not driven off finally till an hour later, when they withdrew, leaving many of their men dead on the hills round the Punjabi piquets.   The British loss amounted to nine killed and twenty-four wounded.   No further fighting occurred on the 18th, but the work of destruction went on.   Already signs were not wanting that some of the clans, particularly those near the border, had received punishment enough and were ready to tender their submission ; moreover, all danger of external complications seemed to have passed away.

On May 18 General Barrett continued the advance into Mohmand territory, moving up the Bohai Dag, a fertile valley inhabited by the Khawazais and one of the principal centres of hostility.   General Barrett was engaged with the enemy all day, during which thirty-three casualties occurred; but the hills round camp were cleared with great gallantry before leaving by the 28th Punjabis and 55th Rifles.   Two villages and several towers were destroyed, but, during one of these operations, twelve ghazis made a sudden charge, and succeeded in killing three and wounding two of the working party before they themselves received the bayonet thrust which was expected to throw open the gates of paradise. In the meantime General Anderson took charge of the camp at Nahaki and turned his attention to the Safis, who appeared to have been chiefly responsible for the night attack on his camp at Dawazagai.   Another attack on the 1st Brigade was repulsed on the night May 19/20.

On May 20 General Anderson moved out in a

northerly direction, the 2nd Brigade returning to Nahaki the same day, and taking over the duty of guarding the camp. At the village of Umra Killi the 1st Brigade again had some sharp fighting with a large body of Dawazais, Utman Khel, and Safis, who were found holding a strong position on some hills, with a deep nala in front. The 57th Rifles on the right, and the 53rd Sikhs on the left, with No. 8 Mountain Battery in the centre, dislodged the enemy from their position; but, as soon as the troops gave up the pursuit and returned to the village, the tribesmen, now reinforced, also turned and attacked the British position. The enemy were severely handled, and lost over 200 killed, but fought with great determination, their swordsmen charging frequently, and at times getting to within 100 yards of our troops. Further attacks were made during the night, but these lacked resolution, and were repulsed without difficulty.

Continuing his advance, Sir James Willcocks, who accompanied the 1st Brigade, received deputations from the Mitai Khel and Safis on May 21. The former tendered their submission at once, but the latter prevaricated to such an extent that they had to be dismissed from the British camp. The 1st Brigade therefore advanced against their position at Lakarai the next day, and the attack was about to be commenced when the white flag went up, and resistance was at an end.

The Utman Khel were the next to receive attention. On May 23 a force of about 2,000 tribesmen were found holding a fortified position on the right bank of the Ambahar River. The 57th Rifles turned their left flank, while the remainder of the Brigade, supported by the 21st Cavalry and 8th Mountain Battery, advanced directly towards the river. The enemy were soon in full flight, pursued by the cavalry, who succeeded in closing in on the rear of the fugitives, and accounting for twenty in the open.

After his defeat of the Utman Khel on the banks of the Ambahar River, Sir James Willcocks marched in a southerly direction into the country of the Pandialis, a clan who inhabit the country between Nahaki and the Swat River. There the 1st Brigade was given a two days' rest before returning to India, which was a welcome change from the hard marching and severe fighting of the past fortnight. After many days of muddy water from village tanks, the clear, refreshing water of the Ambahar gave joy unutterable to man and beast. The men had

had a hard time since they left Shabkadr. The heat by day had been intense during the last few days, and the sniping by night persistent. This scarcity of water, and above all, dust, had added considerably to the difficulties to be surmounted.

Those whose experience of dust does not go farther than an occasional storm on a metalled road, or that caused by a passing motor-car, can have no conception of what the dust caused by a long column of men and animals on a dry, unmetalled track is like. When there is no cross-wind, it may be so thick that a man is quite invisible a couple of yards ahead. The ordinary traveller, who is inconvenienced by dust, may turn his back till it has blown by or increase his distance from the cause of the annoyance; but for troops in the presence of a watchful enemy, ready to take advantage of the least confusion or over-extension, this is impossible. They must keep closed up; comfort is a secondary consideration. In open country there may be some escape by moving off the road, but in a mountainous district where the track is only a few feet wide there is none. It is often little better in camp. The ground may have to be defended, therefore its area must be strictly limited, and every time a string of animals goes to water some quarter of the camp is sure to be made fully aware of the fact. None of the difficulties mentioned, however, made any difference to the success of the campaign. The tribesmen received several rude shocks, and the memory of the Mohmand Expedition of 1908 will remain fresh for many years. Almost the whole country was overrun by the force under Sir James Willcocks, and it was demonstrated to the tribe in the most practical manner possible that any part of their territory is within reach of British arms at any season of the year.

By May 28 only one section—the Baizais—still remained unrepentant. The Baizais are the most westerly of the Mohmand clans, and live on both sides of the Afghan border, consequently their geographical position is their safeguard to a large extent. For political reasons it was obviously impossible to carry punitive measures beyond the Durand line, and so reduce them to the same degree of submission as their more easterly neighbours, but they were not allowed to go unpunished. On May 28 Sir James Willcocks, rejoining General Barrett at Nahaki, moved out against the Baizais with the 2nd Brigade, reinforced by the 34th Pioneers and Guides

Plate VI

REPRESENTATIVES OF THE INDIAN ARMY

To face p. 346

Infantry, and destroyed their villages and towers as far as the border. Some opposition was encountered, but none of a serious nature, the British casualties numbering only sixteen in all. The 2nd Brigade then began its march back to British territory.

In a very short time all the fines imposed were paid, or hostages for their payment given. The Field Force took back with it to Peshawar Rs. 10,000,* which had been collected from the tribesmen, the readiness with which the money was handed in indicating that our late enemies were not so poverty-stricken as was generally supposed. The destruction of villages and crops may seem at first sight a barbarous method of carrying on war, but it is generally the only way of meting out punishment for raids in British territory committed by our predatory and elusive neighbours on the North-West Frontier of India. They have no trade to dislocate, no stocks and shares to depress, and the Hague Convention is to them not even a name. War with uncivilized enemies must be waged with the methods they understand. The Zulu, the Turcoman, the Arab, the American Indian, recognize and respect superior military power, and invariably accept the consequences of defeat with good grace. They admit the justice of retribution, but entirely misinterpret its non-exaction. To them vengeance is the prerogative of might, forbearance the corollary of weakness.

Though the Mohmands again showed that they could be brave enough, yet their discretion stood equally high. On the occasions when they stood to fight during the operations just narrated, they were heavily punished; but the fruits of victory can only be reaped by pursuit, and effective pursuit is just what is so difficult in these mountain fastnesses. The tribesmen move with astonishing rapidity; ground suitable for the movements of cavalry is the exception, and infantry moving with the cohesion necessary even in pursuit are easily outdistanced. Foes such as the Mohmands are not bound to any line of communication; each is his own supply column. They disperse in all directions after defeat, and the bloodthirsty swordsman of to-day may be the peaceful and, if necessary, humble husbandman of to-morrow. Submission by day will not necessarily prevent him sniping by night.

On May 31 the whole of Sir James Willcocks' force was back in British territory, and received by telegram

* £666.

the approbation of their Excellencies the Viceroy and Commander-in-Chief. The Mohmand Expedition of 1908 was thus brought to a close. Twenty days sufficed since the invasion of their country began to reduce this important tribe to submission, and it is to be hoped that closer mutual relations in the future will convert them into staunch allies who will take service under the British flag with the same freedom and happy results which now characterize their powerful kinsmen, the Afridis.

The cost of the Mohmand Expedition was estimated at Rs. 150,000,* and the casualties, including deaths from disease, were:—British troops, 52 deaths and 42 wounded; Native troops, 45 deaths and 176 wounded. It is believed that the tribesmen lost at least 400 killed and a large number wounded.

* £10,000.

CHAPTER XXIII

1908 : REVIEW

ATTENTION has already been drawn to the striking fact
that every Indian frontier campaign has some special
feature which stands out conspicuously from all others.
The truth of the statement is again exemplified by the
study of the operations of 1908, in which rapidity of
action was a most striking characteristic. Rapidity of
action is a very general term, and may include rapidity
in many different ways ; it is intended to do so.
Absence of hesitation and swiftness of execution are
noticeable during the operations under review from
beginning to end. The mobilization and concentration
of the troops was smoothly and expeditiously carried
out, testifying to the care with which preparation for war
had been made in peace ; the advance into the enemy's
country was unexpectedly swift; there was no pause
before the troops got to work; neither in attack nor in
retirement was there ever the smallest doubt as to the
issue, and when the work of the expedition was done, the
brigades withdrew as quickly as they had come.

Some of the marches accomplished by the men commanded by Sir James Willcocks must undoubtedly be
inscribed on the pages of history devoted to the record
of the more memorable of such achievements. There
are no less than three performances of more than
ordinary merit in a total period of six weeks. When
General Barrett marched his brigade from near Ali
Masjid to Walai on February 15 the distance covered
was sixteen miles ; the same officer two and a half
months later transferred his battalions from their
posts along the Mohmand border to Ali Masjid (thirty-
eight miles) in twenty-four hours ; and on May 14
General Anderson led the advanced troops of the
Mohmand Field Force over the arduous Karapa Pass
from Dand to Nahaki, covering eighteen miles before

4 p.m. When it is remembered that these marches, at any rate the first and third, were carried out, not on a broad, smooth road, but a narrow mountain-track strewn with boulders, that in each case the force was, for mountain warfare in a small war, one of considerable size,* and that in each case the men arrived in a compact body, ready for immediate action, the merit of the achievements enumerated will be apparent. It may be said that long distances had been covered often enough before in Indian frontier warfare, and the march of the division under General Elles in 1897 over the very same ground as that traversed by General Anderson may be quoted in support of the statement. General Elles' march was certainly, if anything, longer, but how many of his troops reached the camp at Gandab the same day? The bulk of the division was strung out along the road leading over the Karapa Pass, and if the Mohmands had made a determined attack, the position of the whole force would have been, at least, most critical. On the day after Sir James Willcocks' leading troops reached Walai and Nahaki during the Zakha Khel and Mohmand Expeditions respectively, they were out destroying villages and searching for supplies. Whenever the enemy were found in position, whether it was at Halwai, Umra Killi, or the Ambahar River, they were attacked without delay; they were given no time to gather an increase of either *moral* or numbers. Neither in any of the retirements, nor in any of the various night attacks, did the tribesmen ever succeed in surprising the British defence.

Decisive results can only be obtained by getting to close quarters with the enemy, but the longer the range of the hostile firearms the greater does the difficulty of attaining this object become. The distance at which battle is joined increases in every succeeding campaign; consequently, if disciplined troops are to close to decisive ranges with their elusive foe, and *a fortiori* bring the bayonet into play before the enemy can make good his escape, the men must be able to move with the utmost rapidity. It is more than probable that a stiff climb will be inevitable, a fact which emphasizes the necessity for practising men frequently in peace in traversing broken ground at a rapid pace under service conditions. At the same time the difference between rapidity and hurry must not be overlooked. No advantage will be gained by getting troops to a certain point in an abnormally

* A brigade.

short time if they are not in a position to profit by their exertions. No one can do two things at once, and it is useless to expect good work from a man whose first care is the recovery of his wind.

The foregoing remarks deal with tactical mobility; but, however mobile troops may be on the field of battle, their activity will be of little avail if the force as a whole is unable to move with rapidity in the theatre of war. The enemy will be able in this case to get ample warning of any intended movement, and to concentrate his resources at the decisive point. In the case of the Zakha Khel Expedition half the work of the division was accomplished before the main body left Jamrud. In twenty-four hours advanced troops, pushed rapidly up the Khaibar Pass, had secured the issues from the Bazar Valley, and were engaged in mystifying the enemy as to the real line of advance. In both expeditions of 1908 a British force was established in the heart of the enemy's country long before the dilatory Eastern mind had evolved the necessary course of action. An initial success was scored, the influence of which was felt far beyond the immediate theatre of operations.

Physical fitness on the part of the fighting troops, however, is not the only requisite for securing strategical mobility. Its absence will render abortive all efforts towards rapidity of movement in the theatre of war, but its presence alone will never insure a great result. Other coefficients have to be considered in determining the rate in miles per hour at which a force can move as a whole. The quality of the work of the Staff, and the efficiency of the transport are matters quite as important as the weather and condition of the road; but these are points which it is not proposed to discuss here. The climate of India and neighbouring countries at different seasons is practically constant from year to year, the terrain is now well known, so these are matters which need cause no great uncertainty. The practice of the Staff and the organization of transport for war are points that can receive attention in peace; their discussion is beyond the scope of this work, but the physical fitness, both of themselves and their men, is a matter which is the direct concern of junior regimental officers.

After examples of rapid movement, the next most striking feature of the expedition of 1908 is the number of night operations undertaken by the tribesmen. All their great efforts—the attacks on Matta, Landi Kotal, and on General Anderson's piquets at Dawazagai—were made at night. They made, it is true, a determined attack on the 1st Brigade at Umra Killi on May 20, but that is the only instance of serious fighting by day ; neither near Landi Kotal on May 4 nor at the Ambahar River did the tribesmen really mean business. Night attacks were, of course, common enough in former campaigns, but there seems to have been a much more definite object in view than usual in the attacks on Matta and Landi Kotal, and they were made in considerable force ; the penetration of the British line of defence and the moral effect of the capture of the Khaibar post would have been productive of important results. The question may well be asked : Is this a sign of the times ? Have the lessons of Manchuria reached the tribes of the Indian frontier? Has the Pathan realized that what the magazine rifle has made impracticable by day may be possible by night ? History asserts that uncivilized warriors are usually averse from night operations. If, therefore, modern science has compelled a conservative people to move with the times and adapt their tactics to the firearms of the day, the year 1908 will indeed mark the advent of a new era in Indian frontier warfare.

Even if events in 1908 showed that the armament and tactics of the frontier tribes (to say nothing of their strategy) had improved during the ten years of peace which followed the great rising of 1897, reassuring proof was also given that the power of disciplined troops in defence is as great as ever. The attacks on Matta and Landi Kotal show again that as long as discipline and *moral* are maintained, well-posted troops have nothing to fear from the attack of a considerably superior force of irregular warriors. During both expeditions our men showed that they had learnt the use of cover both natural and artificial; practice in peace in the art of throwing up hasty defences quickly enabled the troops to take full advantage of their superior discipline and equipment.

From an artillery point of view the Zakha Khel and Mohmand Expeditions just narrated presented some features of exceptional interest. Two new natures of gun, forming the chief weapons of the British mobile artillery, underwent the test of war for the first time. The work of the 18-pounder quick-firing (representing also the 13-pounder) and the 10-pounder mountain gun, both recently issued, was watched with great interest, not only by artillery officers, but by the Army in general. The increased range and power of both guns were matters of common knowledge before operations began, and the effect of these improvements was soon apparent.

The moral effect of artillery on undisciplined armies has always been considerable, even if the physical results attained by their fire have been only moderate; but in 1908 the increased efficiency of the new weapons, particularly the 18-pounder, was quite unmistakable, and the tribesmen proved that the familiar Napoleonic ratio of moral to physical effect still held true. In fact, if Napoleon had carried out his famous project of following in the footsteps of Alexander, Nadir Shah, and other invaders of India, and joined battle with the imaginative hosts of Asia, he would probably have fixed the preponderance of moral over physical influences even higher than as three is to one.

But improved weapons are not always an advantage to regular troops—in fact they may be the reverse. One of the greatest difficulties experienced by the commander of a civilized army operating against guerillas lies in the reluctance of the enemy to commit themselves to decisive combat. Some of the most memorable victories of disciplined troops in small wars have been won by avoiding a premature display of strength, and by inspiring a spurious confidence which leads the enemy on to his destruction. The retirement of the mounted infantry before the Zulus at Kambula, and the feigned retreat of the 5th Punjab Cavalry before the Mahsuds near Tank in 1860, are good examples of what is meant. If guns are not very judiciously handled, they are apt to defeat their own object by frightening the enemy, so that he dissolves in flight before material loss can be inflicted on him. Guns are auxiliaries to the other arms; they can never gain decisive victories by themselves, but only prepare the way for the rifle and *arme blanche*. It has been said that "Napoleon won Friedland and saved Wagram by the fire of his artillery"; * but, whatever the French artillery may have done on these and other occasions, they could never have been on the field at all without the presence of other arms. In campaigns against an enemy unprovided with guns, who seldom stands to fight a pitched battle, it is an undeniable truth that guns may save loss to their own side either in attack or retirement, but, at the same time, they often prevent the decisive action of the

* " Modern Strategy," p. 168 (James).

other arms simply because the latter have not got time to get to close quarters before the shells of the batteries in rear, or the fear of them, have driven the enemy from the field.

The efficiency of the new artillery weapons, no less than the flat trajectory rifle, may have had a good deal to do with the preference displayed by the tribesmen in 1908 for operations by night. At any rate, the effect of shell-fire by day was most noticeable. During the operations in the Bazar Valley, and near Landi Kotal on May 4, the guns made the work of the infantry quite easy, and an occasional round of shrapnel from the field-guns on the Michni-Abazai line was sufficient to insure immunity from attack by day.

The infantry received the close support of the artillery throughout—in fact in one attack on a hostile position in the Bazar Valley the ground was such that the guns were able to continue firing till the assaulting infantry were within 60 feet of the crest.*

Many advocates of the system of providing batteries with the means of finding their own escorts will be found among artillery officers, but this would necessitate an increase of *personnel* and therefore of expense, which is the great obstacle to many improvements. A compromise has been made by the issue of a better class of small arm to artillery units, and increased attention to its use; but in action, as matters stand now, the energies of every individual in a battery are so absorbed in his own normal duties that no instance prior to 1908 comes to mind in which a battery commander has been able to detach a portion of his men to a threatened point to take up the duties of an escort. The more critical the situation of the guns, the greater, of course, is the need for an auxiliary arm; but, at the same time, the supply of ammunition, and the replacement of casualties call for such increased exertions that the difficulty of finding men for other duties, without impairing the efficiency of a battery, will always be very great. Nevertheless, an instance occurred during the Zakha Khel Expedition in which this combination of the two different kinds of armament of a battery was used with effect. The number of men detached was small, as only a single section was concerned, but it was sufficient for the purpose, and the incident is interesting from its excep-

* "Notes on the Bazar Valley Expedition," by Brevet-Major C. de Sausmarez, D.S.O., R.A. (*Royal Artillery Journal*, vol. xxxv., p. 282).

tional character.   Major de Sausmarez, who commanded the Derajat Mountain Battery, says :

"On February 18 the 2nd Brigade went out to destroy China Village two and a half miles west of Walai.   Two guns of the Derajat Battery on a hill to the north-west of camp helped to cover the retirement.   The enemy pressed home their counter-attack (if one may use the expression in a non-technical sense) and the section was fired on before withdrawal.   As there was no escort or other troops near except a piquet of the 25th Gurkha Rifles within a few yards of the guns' right flank, a Lance Naik and five gunners had been sent on to a ridge about 200 to 300 yards to the guns' right front, and they, with carbine fire, prevented the enemy from creeping up close."*

The last frontier war on the Indian frontier has now been recorded.   The Muse of History has wearied for the time being of Pathans and rugged mountain scenery. Clio has turned her face to the civilized West, but she is fickle in her favours, and ere long will turn to the East again.   In the foregoing chapters practically all the data are to be found from which the principles of hill fighting are deduced.   These principles are tabulated in the section of Field Service Regulations (Operations) devoted to mountain warfare, but are necessarily much compressed therein.   An attempt, however feeble, has been made to find illustrations for them, and impress the moral which adorns the tale.   It only remains, therefore, to summarize in compact form the lessons that should be learnt for use in the present, and to undertake the hazardous task of endeavouring to forecast any modifications that are likely to become necessary in the future.

* "Notes on the Bazar Valley Expedition," by Brevet-Major C. de Sausmarez, D.S.O., R.A. (*Royal Artillery Journal*, vol. xxxv., p. 283).

CHAPTER XXIV

PRECEPTS AND EXAMPLES FOR MOUNTAIN WARFARE

Precepts.	Reference to "Field Service Regulations," Part I., 1909.	Warnings of what may happen if insufficient importance is attached to such precept.	Examples of successful practice of precept.
(1) The constant maintenance of communication between the various parts of an army is of urgent importance.	Section 8 (1)	(1) November 6, 1897, Tirah: Mishap to detachment of Kapurthala Infantry.	(a) 1888, Black Mountain Expedition: Good signalling arrangements throughout.
(2) Piquets should always be in sight of the supports, or of the main column. When this is impossible, sentries should be posted to keep connection.	Section 144 (2)	(2) September 16, 1897, Malakand Field Force: Isolation of a company during first invasion of Mamund Valley.	
(3) It is of the first importance that the main body should keep touch with, and regulate its pace by, the rear-guard.	Section 146 (3)	(3) December 21, 1852, Waziris: Mishap to party of the 4th Punjab Infantry. (4) November 6, 1863, Ambela: Mishap to escort to working party.	
(4) A force can only be regarded as secure, when protection is provided in every direction from which attack is possible.	Section 64 (1)	(1) November 3, 1894: Attack on British camp at Wana. (2) April 23, 1860, Mahsud Expedition: Attack on British camp at Palosin.	

(5) Timely information regarding the enemy's dispositions, and the topographical features of the theatre of operations, is an essential factor of success in war.	Section 90 (1)	(1) October 20, 1863: Difficulty in the Ambela Pass. (2) March 8, 1895, Chitral: Mishap at the Koragh Defile. (3) 1897, Mohmand Expedition: Inaccurate information regarding the road to Gandab.	(a) April 13, 1895, Chitral: Careful reconnaissance of Nisa Gol led to discovery of way across ravine. (b) October 29, 1897: Attack on Sampagha Pass. (c) December, 1891, Hunza and Nagar: Reconnaissances before Maiun and Thol.
(6) Time spent in reconnaissance is seldom wasted.	Section 93 (1)	(4) October 18, 1897, Tirah: Delay to turning movement, owing to bad ground at first attack on Dargai.	
(7) Decisive success in battle can be gained only by a vigorous offensive.	Section 99 (1)	(1) 1863, Ambela Campaign: Fights for Crag Piquet; no decisive success till advance began.	(a) January 7, 1898: Attack on the Tanga Pass. (b) July, 1897: British counter-attacks during defence of Malakand. (c) Sorties at Reshun, Mastuj, Chitral, and Gulistan.
(8) The guiding principle in all delaying action must be that when an enemy has liberty to manoeuvre, the passive occupation of a position, however strong, can rarely be justified, and always involves the risk of crushing defeat.	Section 114	(2) March 8, 1895, Chitral: By prompt attack, the party stopped at Koragh Defile might have escaped with less loss than eventually occurred. (3) September 12, 1897, Saragarhi: A death-trap.	
(9) In uncivilized countries success is to be achieved by discipline and vigour rather than by force of numbers.	Section 141 (5)	In the Hunza-Nagar Campaign, though it is a brilliant example of the success of a small force, difficulty was found in supplying even that number during the long check at Nilt, and Spedding's Pathans had to be sent down from the front.	(a) 1891, Hunza-Nagar Campaign. (b) March 13, 1860: Successful cavalry affair at Tank. (c) October 29, 1888: Visit of flying column to Thakot during Black Mountain Expedition. (d) December 2, 1897: Success of Gurkhas against Chamkannis.

Precepts.	Reference to "Field Service Regulations," Part I, 1909.	Warnings of what may happen if insufficient importance is attached to such precept.	Examples of successful practice of precept.
(10) The principle of always having bodies of men in rear or on the flanks, covering by their fire the advance or retirement of the troops nearest the enemy, is especially important in hill fighting.	Section 142 (2)	(1) November 9, 1897, first reconnaissance of Saran Sar: Loss sustained by Northamptons. (2) January 29, 1898, Shin Kamar.	(a) December 20, 1891, Hunza and Nagar: Attack on Maiun-Thol position. (b) November 11, 1897, Tirah: Second reconnaissance of Saran Sar. (c) November 22-24, 1897, Tirah: Reconnaissance to Dwatoi. (d) January 7, 1898, Buner: Attack on Tanga Pass.
(11) As a general rule, salients should be used for advances and retirements rather than re-entrants.	Section 142 (3)	(1) August 27, 1897, Ublan Pass: Loss during retirement caused by enemy's marksmen on inaccessible heights.	
(12) Ravines should be avoided unless their exact course is known, and the heights on either side are held.	Section 142 (3)	(2) November 6, 1897: Mishap to Kapurthala Infantry caught in a ravine.	
(13) In all movements involving subsequent retirements, such as reconnaissances, foraging, etc., no defile through which the troops will have to pass in returning, and no commanding point from which an enemy could harass the retirement, should be left unguarded.	Section 146 (5)	(3) November 9, 1897, first retirement from Saran Sar: Loss sustained in the nala. (4) January 29, 1898, retirement from Shin Kamar.	

(14) In advancing uphill, the pace should be slow so as not to distress the men.	Section 142 (3)		
(15) Preparations to meet a counter-attack should always be made when the summit is approached.	Section 142 (3)	(1) May 4, 1860, Mahsuds: Attack on the Barari Pass. (2) March 11, 1868, Ublan Pass: Repulse of the 3rd Punjab Infantry. (3) October 26, 1863, Ambela: Attack on enemy on Guru Mountain carried too far.	
(16) If the rear-guard commander considers it impossible to reach camp before night-fall, it will generally be advisable for him to halt and bivouac for the night in the most favourable position for defence, informing the commander of the force of his action. The rear-guard should halt in time to make the necessary dispositions for defence before dark.	Section 146 (4)	(1) September 16, 1897, Mamund Valley: Rear-guard of 2nd Brigade Malakand Field Force benighted at Bilot. (2) October 31, 1897: Loss to baggage crossing Ashanga Pass.	(a) November 16, 1897, Tirah: Withdrawal from Waran Valley. (b) November 27-28, Tirah: General Gaselee's expedition against the Chamkannis; march to Esor. (c) December 11 and 13, Tirah: Withdrawal down Bara Valley.
(17) If for any special reason a piquet is left out at night, it should be made safe from fire from the camp and also from surprise. In no case should it fall back on camp during an attack.	Section 154 (4)	(1) November 13, 1863, Ambela: Retreat of men from Crag Piquet, causing confusion in camp. (2) November 3, 1894, Wana,	(a) May 16/17, 1908, Mohmand Expedition: Defence of piquets at Dawazagai. (b) October to December, 1897, Tirah.

CHAPTER XXV

IN FUTURO

It may seem that to indulge in speculation as to the future is to enter upon ground which none but those who know not their peril can tread without misgiving. But, just as no commander in the field can win great results without accepting risks often of the gravest description, so, it is argued, the author of a volume of this description could never hope to fulfil his purpose if he allowed himself to be so deterred by the pitfalls before him as to decline the risks, and be satisfied with only the partial attainment of his end. There is one comforting encouragement open to the commander who aspires to wander from the beaten track which leads to respectable mediocrity, and to seek the tortuous paths by which the flanks of Fame may be turned, and that is that the greater the difficulties, the greater the gratification attendant on success, and the greater the readiness of the impartial critic to condone a failure, provided the reasoning which prompted the plan, as well as the method of execution employed, was reasonably sound. It is submitted that some measure of the same encouragement is permissible to him who would probe the mysteries of the future.

The object of history is not merely to place on record the deeds of this or that individual, or the process which marked the rise or fall of this, or that, nation. It is true that a narrative of this kind may be fascinating and engrossing enough, but there is an utilitarian value as well. It is well known that the methods of the Muse of History are not remarkable for their originality; they have been employed again and again at varying intervals since the manufacture of history began, and they will appear again and again in the future. The only difference is the manner in which they are disguised; the penetration of the disguise is the difficulty. What, then, can be done to facilitate this metaphorical lifting of the veil? The proper study of warfare is war. Clearly a knowledge of the disguises in which the problems of the past have been presented must be of immense value to him who would solve with success the problems of the future. History presents the list of these disguises, and he who knows the list thoroughly has secured for himself a great advantage over a rival who has neglected to forearm himself thus while he had the opportunity.

The relation between cause and effect varies only in degree, consequently it is not unreasonable to suppose that the effect of some future cause may be deduced, without arriving at altogether fanciful results, from an examination of the effect of a similar cause disclosed in the pages of history. In the records of the past, therefore, an augury for the future is to be found, which is the surest clue obtainable to the truth.

There are some who take the view that it is sufficient to deal with problems as they come, that the present furnishes quite enough to engross the attention without the assistance of the future. This may be a sound enough view to take of the ordinary trivial round of the daily life of an individual, but is it sound when applied to a nation? The outbreak of war is an event which can seldom be long predicted. But if the opponents are equally matched in number, *moral*, and the capabilities of their commanders, and there is no intervention by other parties, it is perfectly certain that victory will be to the nation which has prepared itself for the struggle the better in time of peace. In other words, that nation will emerge triumphant which has looked ahead, which has studied the lessons of the past the better, and has applied them to the problems of the future with the greater care and intelligence.

The day is not in sight yet when the nations of the world are to lay down their arms, and regard them merely as interesting relics of an unregenerate age. The force of sentimental considerations is admitted to the full, but the claims of national vigour and probity, of individual courage and unselfishness, are also deserving of attention. It has been said that peace is the dream of the wise, war the history of man. War is a purge which invariably promotes a purer and healthier action of the character of a nation. Much has been said of the horrors of war and the blessings of peace; but is there no compensation on the one hand, or drawback on the other? It is at least possible that the two expressions are merely catch phrases, formulæ so familiar that they are chanted without question as to their origin or universal application. Sir Ian Hamilton says with regard to what is called the military spirit that "it is heroism, self-sacrifice, and chivalry which redeem war and build up national character."* He also quotes in the same connection the forcible words of Ruskin on this subject:

"All the pure and noble arts of peace are founded on war; no great art ever rose on earth but among a nation of soldiers. There is no great art possible to a nation but that which is based on battle. . . . When I tell you that war is the foundation of all the arts, I mean also that it is the foundation of all the high virtues and faculties of men. It is very strange to me to discover this, and very dreadful; but I saw it to be quite an undeniable fact. The common notion that peace and the virtues of civil life flourished together I found to be wholly untenable. Peace and the vices of civil life only flourish together. We talk of peace and learning, of peace and plenty, and of peace and civilization; but I found that these were not the words which the Muse of History coupled together; that on her lips the words were peace and sensuality, peace and selfishness, peace and death. I found, in brief, that all great nations learned their truth of word and strength of thought in war; that they were nourished in war and wasted in peace; taught by war and deceived by peace; trained by war and betrayed by peace—in a word, that they were born in war and expired in peace."

War is essentially a study involving anticipation of the future; provision must be made, therefore, for the effect of the progress of education, science, and civilization, or unpreparedness will be the result. Difficulties are overcome most easily by precautions taken in advance, rather than by measures hastily adopted when trouble arises. "Surprise is the greatest of all foes"; every effort should be made, therefore, to reduce to a minimum the chance of surprise by a problem which has not already received adequate consideration.

It may be objected, however, that the preparation of a

* "A Staff Officer's Scrap-Book," vol. i., p. 168.

nation for war is the duty of statesmen and military officers of senior rank, rather than the care of those junior officers for whom, as has been explained, this work has been mainly undertaken. This is, of course, perfectly true as regards national policy and the general training and equipment of the army, but the junior officer is the agent who is entrusted with the task of giving effect to the wishes of those in superior authority. If the Army is to be up-to-date in every respect, in other words, if it is to be really ready for war, the instructors of the rank and file must be themselves thoroughly abreast, or even a little ahead, of the times. To fulfil their duty in this respect it is not sufficient for officers to drift with the tide of general progress, and appreciate new developments only when their freshness has begun to wear off. With the help of the literature to be found in all libraries, in the club, and in the mess, supplemented by personal experience and the teaching of the lecture-room, it is possible to be thoroughly up-to-date, to appreciate the direction in which progress of all kinds is being made, and to extract therefrom much interesting food for reflection. The speculations which result may turn out to be wide of the mark, or they may be justified by events to an extent which gives their author a pleasant, if surprising, sense of his own shrewdness. In the former case no harm is done, and in the latter no small encouragement is given to renewed explorations of the unknown regions of the future by the light of knowledge of the past.

When considering the effects of the progress of education, of science, or of civilization, on warfare of the future, three questions, which lead up to one another, must be asked. They are:

1. What are the new conditions which may have to be faced?

2. How can science help us to deal with them?

3. To what points must special attention be devoted in peace?

These three questions will have to be dealt with from two aspects—the aspect of strategy and the aspect of tactics. To appreciate the distinction between the two points of view, the difference between strategy and tactics must be clearly understood. Unfortunately, there is no classical definition, either of the one or the other, as there is of a geometrical figure; but the definitions given by some of the standard writers on the art of war will make their meaning clear, if not already perfectly familiar.*

The practice of tactics marks the climax of a preparatory phase, which is the province of strategy. Now, the manner in which the practice of any art is carried out, or the method of execution of any allotted task, depends entirely on the facilities and implements available. The tools, in fact, govern the method. On the other hand, a preparatory phase is, as the term implies, essentially a period during which all contingencies are foreseen, and all possible preparations made, with a view to rendering the manipulation of the instruments at hand both effective and expeditious. It matters little what the peculiar use of these instruments may be, but here we are concerned only with one particular set—the instruments of war. If, then, arguing from the general to the particular case, it is conceded that the manner in which war is waged depends on the weapons in use and the facilities offered by science, it must also be admitted that any marked change in the two agents named will produce a corresponding effect on the methods of war of the time. That is to say, progress in science and change in tactics go hand in hand.

But what of the period of preparation—the province of strategy ? Are the conditions here as unstable as those under review in the case of tactics ? Such words as preparation, foresight, and calculation, suggest at once predominating influences of a totally different character ; there is something very human about the note they strike, and further investigation strengthens the impression until it becomes a conviction. What are "the operations which lead up to battle"? The most prominent of these are the choice of objective, the selection of the theatre of war, the distribution of the troops within that area, and their maintenance in the field. These in their turn are governed respectively by the character of the prospective enemy, the relative size and efficiency of the naval and military forces of both sides, the nature of the country, political considera-

---

* *Strategy*.—" The theatre of war is the province of strategy " (Hamley).
" Strategy is the theory of the use of combats for the object of the war " (Clausewitz)
" Operations which lead up to battle, and those which follow battle " (Henderson).
Tactics.—" The field of battle is the province of tactics " (Hamley).
" Tactics is the theory of the use of military forces in combat " (Clausewitz).
" Those stratagems, manœuvres, and devices by which victories are won (grand tactics), and the formation and disposition of the three arms for attack and defence (minor tactics) " (Henderson).

tions, and the protection of the chain of supply. The progress of science or civilization can affect but little questions of this kind ; the logic, or, if it is preferred, the strategy, of Alexander, Hannibal, and Cæsar, is the same as that of Marlborough, Napoleon, and Von Moltke. In fact, it would appear that there is a tenth Muse on Olympus, whose existence has been overlooked. It may be that she has been overlooked because her favours are rarely bestowed, and often at wide intervals; but, nevertheless, it is undeniable that all the great conquerors of the world have been inspired with the same divine afflatus.

If, then, the art of strategy has remained unaffected since the days of chariots, arrows, and armour by such fundamental innovations as the introduction of firearms, or the various uses to which steam and electric power have been applied, it is not too much to infer that developments of science not more remarkable, such as aerial navigation or noiseless guns, will leave equally little impression.

Improvement in the various means of communication employed in war, and the introduction of long-range weapons have respectively facilitated and extended the scope of strategical operations, without affecting the character of such operations, or the reasons for which they are undertaken. In short, every invention or discovery of an important scientific nature marks the regeneration of an old, and not the evolution of a new species. The conclusions which have been drawn may now be summed up to the effect that the saying *autres temps, autres mœurs* is very true in the case of tactics, but is practically inapplicable to the case of strategy. The effect of these conclusions on the questions arising out of new military conditions then follows that, strategically speaking, little remains to be said, but that the tactical aspect requires careful treatment.

In the case of wars with the tribesmen on the northwest frontier of India there are two main directions in which a change of conditions may be expected—

1. Improvement in the armament of the enemy.
2. Increase of their knowledge of war.

It has been remarked already how improvement in the armament of the tribesmen first became noticeable in the Hunza-Nagar Expedition of 1891-92, and has been steady and continuous ever since. The Kanjutis, it will be remembered, were found to be in possession of all kinds of firearms of European manufacture ; during the defence and relief of Chitral in 1895 the followers of

Umra Khan were as well armed as the troops at the disposal of the Political Agent and Colonel Kelly, and even the greater part of Sir Robert Low's army; two years later in Tirah a further advance was marked by the appearance of the "·303" rifle in place of the "·450" Martini. It is true that small-bore rifles had not reached the tribesmen in any great number in 1897, but still they were available in sufficient quantity to have a marked effect on the campaign by the great encouragement they gave to the activities of the midnight sniper. Eleven years later the Bazar Valley and the Mohmand Expeditions proved that the "·303" rifle was in still more general possession by the inhabitants of the frontier hills.

After 1908 the traffic in arms across the north-western border of India grew to such an extent as to render systematic measures on a considerable scale necessary to cope with this serious menace to the peace of the British Empire in India. The difficulties of the situation, however, were aggravated considerably by the sensitiveness of the Amir of Afghanistan to anything in the shape of interference in the internal affairs of his kingdom. The line of communication was therefore for political reasons as unassailable as the front; the rear alone was open to attack, thanks to the command of the sea.

The process known as gun-running is, as far as it affects India, briefly this. The arms are shipped from Europe—largely from Antwerp—to Muscat, the capital of the independent State of Oman, which flanks the entrance to the Persian Gulf on the western side. Thence they are conveyed by native vessels across the Gulf of Oman to the Persian coast, and handed over to the Afghan caravans, which convey them to their ultimate market. The connivance of the local chiefs, of course, has to be purchased in order to secure both their goodwill and the use of their forts as storehouses pending the arrival of a caravan. The caravans are strongly escorted, so opposition on the part of the weak-kneed Persian authorities is unlikely. The amount of "palm oil" necessary to insure the smooth working of a trade of this kind must be enormous, but it says much for the profits to be derived when the heavy working expenses are apparently no deterrent. Although British influence predominates at Muscat, the State of Oman is, as has been stated already, independent; consequently the sphere of British activity for the prevention of gun-running lies in the Gulf of Oman, which covers an area in round numbers of 30,000 square miles.* The difficulty of patrolling an area of this extent with the limited means available is, of course, immense, without taking into consideration the enervating nature of the climate ; but much has been done to give a decided check to the very undesirable traffic which has lately assumed such formidable proportions. In spite of ruses of all kinds important captures have been made at sea, and a striking force carried on board ship has landed on both shores of the Gulf on some occasions and made successful raids on the forts of chiefs discovered to be giving assistance to the caravans. These raids have done much to make the local chiefs pause to reflect whether they are on the right side after all when they open their doors to their truculent-looking visitors from the north, and many of them are already, as the phrase is, coming in.

Improvement in the armament of the frontier tribes, however, is only to be expected as time goes on ; civilization, which is only, after all, a comparative term, cannot stand still for long even among the most inaccessible mountain fastnesses. Arms will reach the Pathans from somewhere or other in spite of all precautions that can be taken. A few rifles—but very few nowadays—may be stolen from the Government of India ; some may be got from the arsenal at Kabul, but the majority must be imported, and, as long as the returns are adequate, there will always be traders willing to supply the market. Since, then, it is useless to expect to put a stop to the supply of arms entirely, it is better to accept the evil as inevitable, and consider how it can best be neutralized, or, at least, mitigated

But there is another cause which may have some effect on the military equipment of the frontier tribesmen, and that is the great improvement which has taken place in their financial position by admission to practically unrestricted trade with British India. Thanks principally to the extension of irrigation in the Punjab and North-West Frontier Province (to say nothing of parts of India farther afield) the wealth of the population has risen enormously, their spending power has increased, the influence of which must be felt by their neighbours on the north-west, and so a modern rifle has ceased to be the rich man's luxury it once was.

Having admitted that improved firearms are inevitable,

* Or approximately the size of the English Channel.

the disagreeable fact cannot be ignored ; their effect on the mountain warfare of the future must therefore be seriously considered.   The chief obstacle to decisive action encountered by regular troops in this class of campaign is the difficulty of closing with their elusive opponents, consequently any cause which tends to increase the distance at which battle is joined must aggravate that difficulty.   Deployment means some loss of control with its attendant risks, and must be accompanied by some sacrifice of mobility ; turning movements with a wide radius may give rise to delay from unexpected natural obstacles, miscalculations of time and space, and even defeat in detail ; and the difficulties of reconnaissance and protection, both on the march and at rest, are greatly increased.

It might appear from the foregoing remarks that the fact had been overlooked that improvement in armament does not take place on one side of the Indian border only, but, since it is generally acknowledged that accurate firearms, which can be loaded quickly and range to long distances, favour the defence much more than the attack, and since attack and not defence is the guiding principle of the operations of regular troops against ill-organized enemies, it follows that the advantages conferred by the use of modern weapons are almost entirely on the side of the frontier tribesmen.

But is there nothing to be said on the other side ?   It has been said that life is full of compensations.   Now, war is an incident in life, and the weapons which have to be encountered are incidents in war, consequently it may be argued that there are compensations as well as difficulties attached to the methods required for dealing with those weapons.   In the case of the weapons of civilization in the hands of Pathans the compensations are that arms of this kind have a tendency to make those who use them more dependent on the arts of civilization. The strength of irregular foes lies not so much in their military prowess as in their freedom from the cares which clog the movements of a disciplined army.   They have no line of communication to protect, no convoys to escort through difficult country with a minimum escort, and no second line transport, consequently they are mobile to a degree which always proves an embarrassment to regular troops ; but directly provision has to be made for such matters as the replenishment of ammunition, their degree of mobility immediately begins to approximate to that of their civilized antagonists, and then the advantage is all on the side of the latter.

The other condition which has to be faced besides improvement in armament is increased knowledge of war. This may be due to natural causes, such as the progress of civilization; but, at any rate among the Afridis, it may also be due to military training in the ranks of the Indian Army. Some remarks have already been offered on this subject when dealing with the Tirah Campaign of 1897, and it was pointed out then that the adoption of tactics suitable for a disciplined army would be a source of weakness rather than strength to the elusive mountaineers of the border hills. Their strength lies in their guerilla characteristics, in the difficulty of compelling them to fight a decisive action, and in their faculty for baffling pursuit by rapid dispersion. Directly they become committed to the defence of a position, or involved in a systematic retirement, regular troops are on familiar ground. The presence of a definite objective immediately gives scope for the exercise of the advantages conferred by superior armament, organization and *moral*.

The possibility that the Pathans might eventually reach the same standard of tactical skill and moral qualities as that to be found in the Army in India would be only worth consideration if it were possible for progress of all kinds to mark time in India for about one hundred years. As this contingency can be dismissed at once as ridiculous, the conclusion remains that the only hope the frontier tribesmen can have of resisting the advance of our columns with success lies in the practice of those guerilla tactics, of which they are already past masters.

But increased knowledge of war, or, to use a still more general term, improvement in education, may remove some of the most conspicuous weaknesses to which all savage races are heirs, and so add materially to their military prowess without any fundamental change of a positive kind. Want of cohesion and sensitiveness to moral influences have always been strongly marked *traits* in the character of uncivilized warriors; but, in a country where a man's nearest relatives are often his bitterest enemies, and insane religious fervour is accounted a profession of faith, it is not surprising to find that the two *traits* mentioned are particularly characteristic of the people. If the Waziris could make common cause with the Afridis, or the hereditary ravagers of the Swat Valley be capable of contemplating with greater equanimity the presence of cavalry in their neighbourhood, or the smiles of Fortune cease to be absolutely indispensable for sustained effort from the Hunza River to the Zhob, Indian frontier warfare would be a much more serious and costly affair than it is even at present.

As usual, however, there is the possibility of a result of quite another character. A higher standard of education among the inhabitants of the border hills may have the effect of making them recognize the advantages of friendly intercourse with India, the disastrous effect on themselves of a stoppage of trade, the resources of the British Empire, and the futility of kicking against the pricks. But fundamental changes are not made in a day ; it is idle to expect an unscrupulous people, whose pastimes are bloodshed and rapine, to become peaceful and law-abiding members of society in a single generation. Nevertheless, the change is going on. Service in the Indian Army, increased wealth with a disinclination to forfeit it, and diminished influence of the priests, are all powerful agents which are at work. Those who have known the Pathans best agree that they are not without good qualities ; it is impossible not to sympathize with their love of independence, and respect them in spite of all their graceless ways.

To sum up the foregoing conclusions, it would appear that the following are the new conditions which will in all probability have to be faced sooner or later in Indian frontier warfare :

1. Improved weapons in the enemy's hands, entailing—

    (*a*) Early deployment ;
    (*b*) Wide turning movements ;
    (*c*) Increased difficulty of reconnaissance and protection ; and generally
    (*d*) Rareness of decisive actions.

2. Spread of education, supplying the remedy for—

    (*e*) Want of cohesion ;
    (*f*) Fanaticism ;
    (*g*) Extreme sensitiveness to moral influences.

Allusion has been made to the countervailing effect of increased dependence on the products of civilization, and possible unwillingness to fly to arms at the slightest provocation. These factors may influence the situation, or they may not; at any rate, it is better to be on the safe side and place no reliance on them whatever, so that any surprise which may result will be of a pleasant and not a disappointing description.

It is now necessary to pass on to the second question, and inquire in what way science may be expected to assist the British columns who may be called upon in the future to penetrate the tangled mass of hills and valleys which constitute "the Indian borderland" on the north-western side.

Superiority of equipment always goes far to insure success in any class of warfare, and, in the case of campaigns against irregular enemies, can be made the undisputed prerogative of civilized troops. What, then, does science offer to restore the superiority which the general possession of modern rifles by the frontier tribes-men threatens to destroy? At the present time the choice is both generous and varied. Wireless telegraphy may almost be called an old friend; we have already an acquaintance with air vessels, and the mono-rail; noise-less guns are not unknown by name; and the telephone —quite an old friend—is making vigorous efforts to rid itself of the bonds which limit its activity, and announce its freedom to the world by adopting the prefix of wireless to its name.

It has been shown already how these inventions can have but little influence on the strategy of the future. Improved means of reconnaissance and communication merely facilitate strategical movements without affecting the necessity for them or altering their general character, but directly the province of tactics is entered the case is very different. Wireless telegraphy and, when it comes, the wireless telephone seem to be the keys to success of those extended operations which modern long-range weapons impose. The power to carry out combined movements on a wide front is an advantage which is denied to ill-organized armies. The successful employ-ment of operations on exterior lines is the aim of every attacking commander who looks for decisive results. The point has been brought out already, but there is no harm in emphasizing it, that both the strategy and tactics of regular troops against an uncivilized enemy should be offensive, and the use of exterior lines is the deadliest weapon of offence. Anything that can be done, there-fore, to facilitate the use of this weapon is worth a trial.

The decisive success of concerted movements of any

kind depends on the efficiency of the means of communication between the different columns. The subject of the foregoing sentence has been qualified advisedly, for it is not to be supposed that success is impossible in spite of unforeseen contingencies, or some miscalculation of time or space. Sir Robert Low's attack on the Malakand position in 1895 was entirely successful, although it had to be launched before the turning movement had developed; and the Dargai Heights were carried by General Westmacott on October 18, 1897 without the direct assistance of General Kempster's brigade operating on the enemy's flank. But, although victory may be won, it is improbable that it will be decisive, or that the fruits of victory will be reaped.

Improved means of communication will therefore be particularly welcome to the side whose normal *rôle* is the offensive, and in this direction the wireless telegraph and telephone offer important compensation for long-range weapons in the hands of the defence. Orderlies may lose their way, or become casualties; mist may render visual signalling impossible; a wire may be cut at a critical time; but the wireless electric apparatus mentioned rises superior to such disabilities. It is admitted that at present wireless installations are impracticable for general use on account of the amount of transport required, but in all probability science will find a remedy for that, and when this consummation is reached the difficulties that beset the commander of a line of outposts, a convoy, a rear-guard, or a turning movement will lose many of their terrors. Even now the wireless telegraph is available for the co-ordination of important strategical movements. It is easy to imagine the assistance which it would have given to General Maude during the concentric advance on the Bazar Valley in 1879, or again in the same part to Sir William Lockhart in 1897, when no news could be obtained of General Hart's Brigade. If Sir Robert Low could have shot a message over the Lowarai Pass into Colonel Kelly's camp or the fort at Chitral, and received an answer in return, his chief anxieties would have faded away.

From the point of view of defence wireless installations only appear to be of conspicuous value strategically. Tactically speaking, the small number of troops ever engaged in this class of operation on the Indian frontier, and the comparatively restricted area involved render the use of what may be called a long-range weapon unnecessary. Strategically, however, the case is different. It is only necessary to call to mind such positions as that of Sir Neville Chamberlain at the Ambela Pass in 1863, when he was compelled to remain on the strategical defensive for eight weeks pending the arrival of reinforcements, or that of the garrisons of Malakand and Chakdara in 1897, to realize the advantage of uninterrupted communication with the base of operations.

As regards air vessels, these would seem to have a great future in store in Indian frontier warfare as well as elsewhere. As soon as they are sufficiently reliable in their action for use in savage warfare, and some of the transport difficulties can be overcome, or the radius of action of these machines increased, several important uses to which they might be put suggest themselves at once. For reconnaissance or police work air vessels would be invaluable, or indeed for any purpose requiring the employment of a small self-contained detachment—such as a counter-raid—or for action from a central station secured within the enemy's country. For purposes such as these the number of men necessary would not need to be large, nor would the latter require arms more powerful than the rifle. The rapidity with which large tracts of otherwise most difficult country could be covered is of course obvious.

For the attack of inaccessible or otherwise formidable positions air vessels would be most powerful auxiliaries. With assistance of this kind there would have been no seventeen days' check before the Maiun-Thol position on the road to Hunza and Nagar in 1891, nor would the second capture of Dargai in 1897 have cost the 2nd Division 200 casualties. An air vessel used for transferring a few marksmen to a point whence they could bring an enfilade or reverse fire to bear on such a position might soon render the latter untenable. In the case of the former instance there is some justification for the retort that, if an air vessel had caused the immediate evacuation of the Maiun - Thol position, the tribesmen would have escaped the loss suffered when the successful attack was delivered. On the other hand, it will be remembered that, as things were, the strategical situation of the British force, cut off from all hope of reinforcements or additional supplies from India, was becoming somewhat grave, and would have been extremely serious if the Kanjutis, or any of their neighbours, had made the most of the opportunity. At the second storming of Dargai the actual loss inflicted on the enemy could not have been great, so there would have been no loss of decisive effect even if an air vessel had rendered an infantry assault unnecessary.

When considering, however, the effect of any of the aids to victory offered by science, the fact must be borne in mind that uncivilized races, or, for that matter, civilized nations as well, will not be reduced to permanent subjection without the infliction of actual loss of their fighting strength. In campaigns, therefore, where the destruction of the enemy's field army is rendered extremely difficult by reason of their cautious and elusive methods, it is highly desirable to avoid any premature display of strength. Decisive results can never be obtained unless the opposing tribesmen can be induced to hold their ground while the plan for their discomfiture can be put into execution. It may be necessary sometimes to sacrifice decisive effect for rapidity of movement, as in the case of operations for the relief of a besieged garrison, and then any device which may cause the early evacuation of a hostile position is worth adoption. Even if the tactical situation will often render the use of air vessels undesirable in Indian frontier warfare, there is no reason why they should not be in readiness for use if required. Their great mobility would enable them to remain in some position of safety well in rear of the scene of operations till called up by wireless telegraphy or other means. Enough has been said to indicate the great possibilities for effective action; the number of air vessels employed in a North-West Frontier campaign need never be large. Two or three * would be quite sufficient for the purposes suggested, and even if their manufacture should reach such a pitch of perfection that invasions of tribal territory can be carried out entirely by their means, their great mobility, to say nothing of their moral effect, would render a large force of men unnecessary. For transport purposes flying machines hold out no hope of relief from the difficulties inseparable from even the most efficient service for a very long time to come. It would be rash, and probably erroneous, to say that such relief will never come, but, at present, the lifting power of air vessels is so small that they could never deal in a practical manner with the enormous

---

* There should be more than one if any are used at all, so that relief may be sent on an emergency.

quantity of stores and baggage that has to accompany even a small force of lightly equipped troops.

The negotiation of the lofty passes of the Himalayas will no doubt present no difficulty ere long to the future aviators of the Army in India, but, unless their vessels can cross passes in safety under their own motive power, the difficulty of transport on land will be so formidable as to forbid the use of flying machines on a line of operations crossed by passes of any considerable height.*

It stands to reason, of course, that before air vessels can be definitely adopted for military purposes they must be fairly reliable in their action, they must be protected from rifle fire, and they must be capable of starting and landing without the necessity for specially prepared stations. The crew should be capable of independent action for at least twenty-four hours, and, when this is possible, be provided with wireless electric apparatus for communication with the base or the remainder of the force. It goes without saying that the lot of a crew isolated through one cause or another in the midst of an enemy who gives no quarter is most unenviable; but if communication is possible, other machines are available to render prompt assistance, and the mishap does not take place in an utterly indefensible position, the situation need not be irretrievable. There is a platitude which says that war cannot be made safe, and flying machines can never be expected to give rise to an exception. After all, the risk involved is probably a great deal less than that incurred by the crew of a submarine, and there is no suggestion that any difficulty will be found in manning this class of marine vessel in time of war.

During the foregoing discussion on the possible uses of air vessels for military purposes no reference has been made to the relative advantages and disadvantages of the two main classes into which these machines are divided. The matter has been treated entirely from a general point of view, but it may be well to summarize briefly the principal characteristics of each type before passing on to another subject.

The two main classes are, of course:

1. Machines lighter than air, or dirigible balloons, dependent for lifting power on gas.

---

* A height of 9,714 feet above the horizontal plane has been reached by an aeroplane (1910).

2. Machines heavier than air, or aeroplanes, dependent or all power on their mechanism.

For military purposes the former possess four great advantages over the latter, for they are able to—

    (*a*) Rise vertically;
    (*b*) Alter their altitude quickly and easily;
    (*c*) Afford better facilities for observation;
    (*d*) Make marksmanship easier.

Aeroplanes, on the other hand, have the advantage over machines lighter than air in the matter of—

    (i.) Being less vulnerable;
    (ii.) Cost;
    (iii.) Rapidity of construction;
    (iv.) Storage.

Owing to the much smaller mark it presents an aeroplane may easily escape detection, or injury, when a dirigible balloon would not, for at a height of 5,000 feet the former is only a speck in the sky. Cost and rapidity of construction are of course greatly in favour of aeroplanes, and the immense improvements which have taken place in their construction from every point of view, within a short time, may be due to these advantages, since so many more people are financially in a position to carry out experiments than in the case of the much more costly lighter than air machines. The matter of storage speaks for itself. As regards carrying capacity and ascensive power the advantage lies at present with dirigible balloons, but such extraordinary improvements have been made by aeroplanes in these respects in a very short time that it is not unlikely that both classes of vessel will be on terms of equality before very long.

The case of noiseless firearms now comes up for examination, and here again science has come forward to supply, or rather anticipate, the demand, and presented the silencer to the world. The type of silencer which has already given good results with small arms consists of a metal cylinder divided into compartments by partitions of varying shape, which have the effect of liberating the powder gases from the barrel so gradually that no noise results. It is screwed on to the muzzle, is 5½ inches long, and weighs 10 ounces. It has been found that the muzzle-velocity of a bullet is unaltered when fired from a long rifle with silencer attached, but is slightly increased when a short rifle, or carbine, is used ; also that the advantage of increased fire-control due to the absence of noise is discounted by the following draw-backs :

1. The alteration of the centre of gravity of the piece is tiring to the firer.
2. Increased heating of the barrel tending to make the air round it quiver, and so interfere with the firer's aim.
3. Increased weight.
4. The silencer blocks the line of sight at long ranges.
5. Silencer and bayonet cannot be used together.
6. The silencer must be carefully screwed on, or the bullet will foul the partitions inside.

For artillery purposes the length of the silencer would be a great impediment to movement across broken ground, and if it had to be detached in anticipation of such move-ment the delay caused might be a serious matter.

Means will be found no doubt of remedying, or at least mitigating, these disadvantages, so the important question becomes whether they are good in principle or not. Here we are confronted with a difficulty arising out of the difference between the principles governing attack and defence. Now, concealment is one of the chief weapons of the defence, but in attack it is practically impossible, particularly at decisive ranges, consequently it may be assumed that the silencer will strengthen the defence rather than the attack. Whether an ambuscade laid by unseen foes using noiseless rifles would be more demoralizing than one attended by a sudden outburst of noise is open to question.

In the particular case of North-West Frontier wars the normal *rôle* of British troops is offence, and there is one important matter in which we, as the normal assail-ants, would run the risk of being distinct losers by the use of the silencer, and that is in *moral*. Even disciplined troops are intensely human. Sir Edward Hamley says : "Any study of war which fails to take the human factor into account can only result in false conceptions."* In attack the *moral* which discipline and cohesion confer is required to carry men across a bullet-swept zone in face of an unseen foe, and the knowledge that his comrades are at hand is an aid of unquestionable value to both cohesion and discipline. Noise-producing firearms afford

* "The Operations of War," p. 6.

a ready means of supplying this helpful information, and the moral effect of gun-fire is well known. Weapons of war may change with the flight of ages, but human nature does not, so its weaknesses cannot be disregarded.

The timely arrival of a single battery will sometimes contribute more to the success of an infantry attack than a whole brigade of the same arm ; it is the moral effect of the sound of the discharges of artillery, quite as much as the magnetic attraction which guns always seem to have for hostile bullets to the relief of the infantry, that puts vigour and cohesion into the assault. The sensation is well described in the words of Rudyard Kipling :

> " Ubique means that warnin' grunt the perished linesman knows
> When o'er his strung and sufferin' front the shrapnel sprays 'is foes ;
> An' as their firin' dies away the husky whisper runs
> From lips that 'aven't drunk all day, 'The guns ! thank Gawd, the guns !' "

It may be inferred, therefore, that, when the objections which now limit the use of the silencer have been overcome, this contrivance will rank as one more of those inventions which make war more difficult without increasing the destructive power of the weapon to which it is applied, and its use is to be expected with small arms rather than pieces of a heavier nature.

One other invention of the present age remains to be discussed, and that is the mono-rail. The following is an extract from a report on the capabilities of Mr. Louis Brennan's mono-rail system which were demonstrated in the grounds of the Brennan Torpedo Factory, Gillingham, Kent, on February 25, 1910 :

" The car which has been constructed in the form of a military vehicle has a length of 43 feet, and a width of 10 feet, and a height of 13 feet. It weighs 22 tons unloaded, and is designed for a load of from 10 to 15 tons. . . . The demonstration was carried out on a circular track one-eighth of a mile in circumference and a straight course of a quarter of a mile. . . . The sharpest curves in the line are of 35 feet radius. . . . Petrol engines have been used on the present car, but steam or electricity may be used for the purpose of propulsion. . . . In a trial which took place a few days ago 100 soldiers were carried on the platform of the car. . . . Yesterday 50 visitors were accommodated on the platform during each test journey. The car, which attained a maximum speed exceeding twenty miles per hour, ran with great steadiness throughout, and satisfactorily passed the sharp curves on which the line is laid."*

There would seem to be great possibilities for the mono-rail in war which have hitherto not received the attention they deserve. No doubt progress in this direction is being closely watched by the high military authorities, but very little has appeared on the subject in the military journals of the day. The invention is certainly in its infancy, but, even so, anything which may help to solve the great problem of transport in war is of deep interest to all officers, and an occasional article in the *Times* or other newspaper, like the one from which quotation has been made, may catch the eye of only a small percentage, whereas the majority of officers make a point of studying at least one or two of the various service magazines.

Whenever the nature of the country would render its use possible there seems to be no reason to suppose that a mono-rail could not be laid with very little trouble or worked without difficulty, and, if these objects were accomplished, it would prove a valuable substitute for a regular railway; its carrying capacity would not be so great, of course, as that of the latter, but it would in all probability prove sufficient for the needs of comparatively small forces such as those which take part in frontier expeditions. At any rate it would cause an immense saving of animal transport. The negotiation of the curves and gradients of even the best hill roads is where failure may be expected; but we are told that the large car used at Gillingham, during the demonstration described, travelled successfully on the arc of a circle of 35 feet radius, and the steepness of the slope which can be ascended depends on the power of the engines installed. The loss of carrying capacity caused by making the car smaller would be amply repaid by the resulting gain of tractability; in fact a width of 10 feet would be impossible on an Indian hill road apart from any considerations due to curves. The stability of the Brennan mono-rail when going round a corner is secured by mechanism which causes the car to lean over in the required direction. Very sharp curves would no doubt be extremely uncomfortable, if not impracticable, for passengers; but, since the mono-rail would be used chiefly for transport purposes, this drawback is of little real significance.

* *Times*, February 26, 1910.

We now come to the third great question: To what points must special attention be devoted in peace? It has been shown that the surest way of bringing the Pathan tribes to reason is the same now as it always has been, namely, by the infliction of loss in battle, that the great tactical object is still to close with the enemy as soon as possible, but that this end has a tendency to become more and more difficult of attainment. The solution of the problem is therefore to be found in—

1. Mobility;
2. Good marksmanship.

These two qualities are complementary to each other; the one is of no avail without the other, for what is the use of swiftly moving troops if they can hit nothing; or again, of what benefit are the most infallible marksmen if they only arrive in time to see the enemy disappearing in the distance?

Some remarks have already been offered on the subject of mobility, in the course of which it was pointed out that collective as well as individual mobility is absolutely necessary. The rate of progress of a force as a whole depends on the efficiency of its transport and accurate information as to the route to be passed over, both of which can be secured to a large extent in peace; but the junior regimental officer is not concerned with these precautions. Individual mobility—tactical rather than strategical—is what it is his business to insure. Now that every tribesman is able to take the field with a modern rifle and a plentiful supply of ammunition, deployment has to be made earlier, turning movements have become more extended, and the zone in which all movements must be made at the highest possible speed is very much wider. All these new conditions demand increased mobility, that is to say, greater physical activity and powers of endurance which must be cultivated in peace. There is at least no reason to think that there is any falling off in the marching power or offensive spirit of our infantry, but both are very sensitive to neglect, and it is the duty of junior officers to protect them from that most harmful of all dangers. In an age when there is a tendency to make what is carried on the person as little as possible, it should not be overlooked that occasions may arise when men have to be absolutely independent of their second line transport, so they should be given practice in peace in the art of folding, securing, and carrying things like great-coats and blankets, which is not so simple as it may seem. Sir Ian Hamilton says : " The finest transport in the world will not compensate for want of carrying power on the part of the men."*

Even the simplest things require practice, so to adopt the line that it will be all right on the night seems to mean leaving yet one more thing to chance, and the uncertainties of war are quite numerous enough without adding to their number unnecessarily. In war the loss of marching power, and therefore of efficiency, due to inexperience as to how to adjust a load which has to be carried, and to want of development of the muscles used, may easily prejudice the success of the operations, so it hardly seems worth while, to say the least of it, to risk much at a critical time for a little personal discomfort when one day is much the same as another.

To insure strategical and tactical mobility, therefore, there are wanted on the part of those in high authority :

1. Good preparations in peace to insure—

    (a) Rapid mobilization and concentration ;
    (b) A knowledge of the topography of all possible theatres of war and the characteristics of the inhabitants ;
    (c) An efficient transport service ;

and on the part of the regimental officers and men—

2. Endurance.
3. Ability to move for short distances at a fast pace.
4. Weight-carrying power.

The necessity for good marksmanship needs no comment, except that in Indian frontier warfare, where opportunities are few and hard to get, its importance is all the greater.

Much has been made of the dangers, the hardships, and the lack of decisive results which are the features of Indian frontier campaigns ; but there is one comforting reflection to throw into the other side of the scale, and that is, " so long as our troops are in strength and tolerably commanded we have no cause for apprehension. They [the Pathans] have numbers and physical strength, but they are poor, they are under no control, have no

* "A Staff Officer's Scrap-Book," vol. i., p. 54.

cannon, are badly armed, without commissariat, and usually (until united against infidels) every man's hand is against his neighbour, so they are powerless except to sweep over the country like a whirlwind." *

We have seen that there has been some modification of the characteristics of the tribesmen since Sir Neville Chamberlain wrote the foregoing lines, but in substance they are as true to-day as in the days when the names of the Crag Piquet, Kam Dakka, Chitral, and Gulistan were first recorded in the temple of Fame. It will be noticed that, in order to avoid disaster, Sir Neville Chamberlain lays down only two postulates—the troops must be in strength at what is for the time being the decisive point, and they must be tolerably commanded. Now, strength may lie in number, *moral*, equipment, position, or in any combination of these, and its presence or the reverse may be accidental, for it is impossible to be equally strong at all points, but there is no element of chance about the second condition. The troops need only be tolerably commanded; that is not much to ask of any officer or non-commissioned officer who may be entrusted with the honour of his country, and the lives of his fellow-men. The future is foreshadowed by the past; the details may be blurred, but the shape is sufficient to give a clue, and history is the glass which makes the outline distinct. Moreover, the patent protecting the glass has run out long ago; no fancy price need restrict its use, which may be had for the asking. What defence, therefore, is open to him who fails because he has not taken the trouble to ask?

But the responsibility for national honour and safety does not rest with statesmen and soldiers alone. Success in war is not to be expected by a people whose martial instincts have become atrophied through neglect; the virtues and failings of soldiers are not theirs alone, but those of the nation they represent. Sir Edward Hamley says: " No great deeds have ever been performed by an army in which the qualities of courage and steadfast endurance were wanting. No commander has ever risen to fame who has not displayed great energy, perseverance, and resolution. No nation has ever become great without fostering such qualities in its sons, nor has any remained great which ceased to foster them."† However efficient

* Extract from a letter by Sir Neville Chamberlain to his mother (" Life of Sir N. B. Chamberlain," by G. W. Forrest, p. 302).
† " The Operations of War," p. 7.

the Army in India may be, "the key of India is in London,"*
and its guardians are not only the men but the women of
the British race. As long as the latter can command the
love, the confidence, and the respect of their sons
during their youth, these will grow to be sturdy and
high-minded defenders of the Empire which is their
heritage.

* Said by Lord Beaconsfield in the House of Lords (1881) on the subject
of British policy in Afghanistan. The complete quotation is: "The key of
India is not at Kandahar; the key of India is in London."

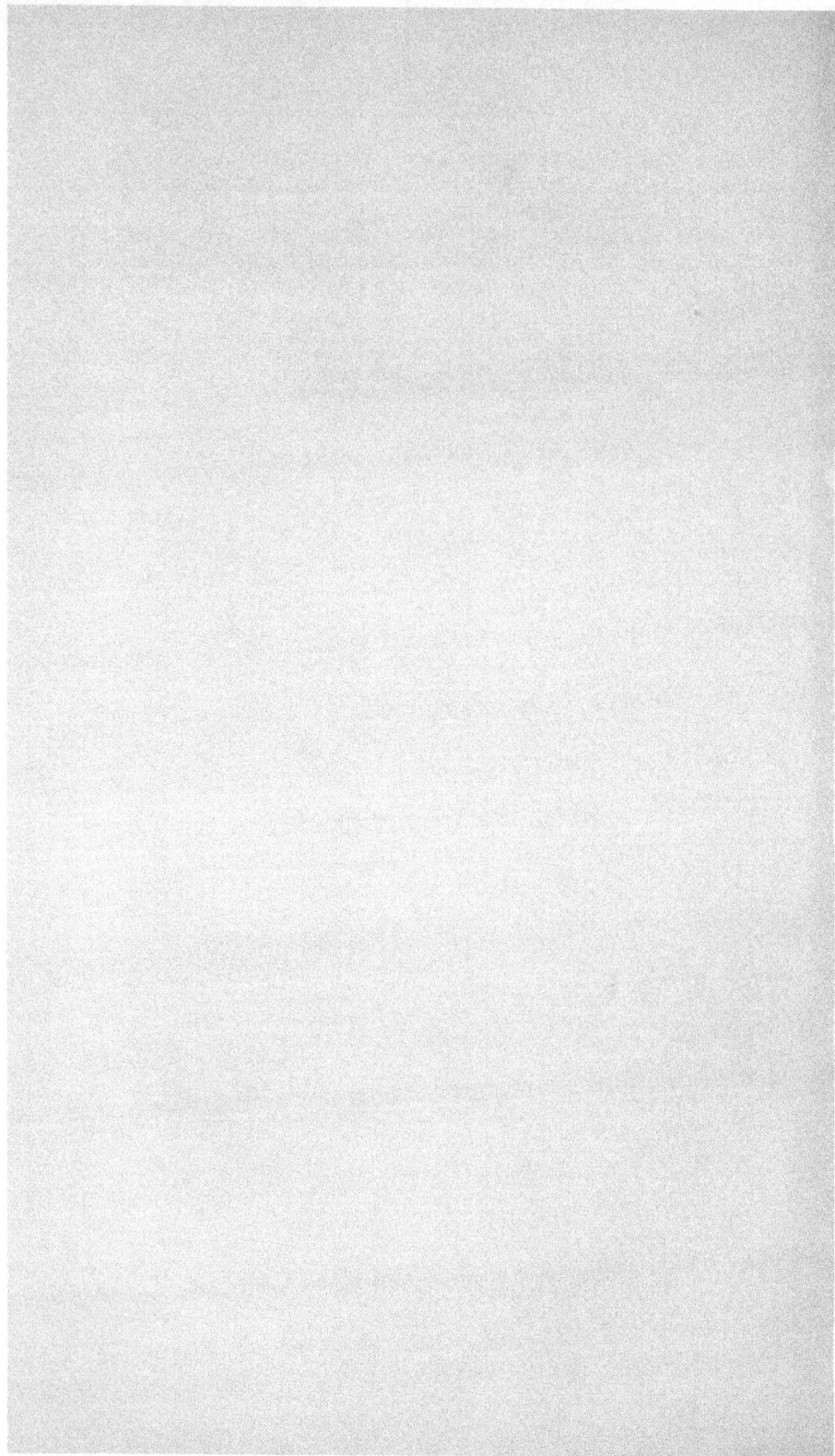

APPENDICES

APPENDIX A

EXTRACTS FROM ORDERS ISSUED TO THE FIELD FORCES UNDER HIS COMMAND BY BRIGADIER-GENERAL SIR N. B. CHAMBERLAIN, K.C.B.

ARTILLERY.

EVERY shot and shell is to be re-gauged before being taken on service.

CAMP AND BAGGAGE.

A doolie and a pair of kajawahs are to accompany the rear-guard

A guard is to be told off to prevent baggage crowding upon the road leading out of camp before the troops march.

The doolies, dandies, and bhistis of corps and detachments are to follow in rear of their own corps.

Soldiers and camp-followers are to be warned not to injure trees.

No soldier or camp-follower is on any account to go beyond the piquets.

No person in camp is to stir, or the least noise to be made, until the first bugle has sounded.

No baggage or followers of any kind are to move until the advance has sounded.

No dogs are to be allowed, as they disturb the camp at night.

Grass cutters are never to go beyond the cavalry piquets.

Commanding officers are always to take measures to prevent any injury to houses, fields, or other property, and are responsible for the cultivation in the immediate vicinity of their camps.

Camp colour men are to march in rear of the advanced guard.

When camps are pitched on ground subject to irrigation, care is to be taken that the dams are well secured.

Great care is to be taken that the water near camps is not polluted, and animals are to be watered down-stream.

No firing is to be allowed in camp or its vicinity without permission, or any unnecessary noise permitted.

Camp-followers and baggage are always to keep to the high-road, and not to take short cuts through fields.

No soldier or camp-follower is to enter a village on the line of march, or after reaching camp, without permission.

The desecration of shrines or burial-grounds is strictly prohibited.

All supplies are to be paid for on the spot; and plundering, however trifling, will be severely punished.

Every soldier or camp-follower having occasion to go beyond the piquets is to carry his arms; but none are to be permitted to roam about the country. When going to cut wood, they are to keep close to the piquets.

No person is to be allowed to go beyond the line of camp sentries after dark.

The greatest sanitary precautions in regard to the cleanliness of camps and their vicinity are enjoined.

The people of the country are not to be permitted to enter the camp armed.

No women or children or superfluous followers are to be allowed to accompany the troops. Shelter is to be provided for all followers.

ORDERLIES, GUARDS, AND PIQUETS.

The employment by officers of guards or orderlies with their baggage, whereby the services of a large number of soldiers are misapplied and lost, is strictly prohibited. The protection of the baggage is otherwise provided for, and officers are to leave their baggage to the care of their servants.

The infantry camp guards and sentries are to stand fast until all the baggage has left the ground, when they are to form up by regiments and follow the column in succession at intervals of a quarter of an hour under the orders of the officer in command of the rear-guard.

While the troops are employed on field service, four sentries are to be allowed to each post instead of three.

Cavalry piquets are to be withdrawn at dusk.

The outlying piquets are to stand fast until the whole of the baggage has moved off, when they are to be called in, and marched into camp under the orders of the officer commanding the rear-guard.

During rainy weather every sentry is to be posted under shelter as far as may be possible, for it is of the utmost importance to preserve the men in health; and standing in the rain for two hours, and then having to lie down in wet clothes, must be injurious.

The men are also to be instructed always to sling or secure their arms when exposed to the rain, and not to carry them at the shoulder or support. This order applies to sentries as well as others.

Tents are to be provided for guards and piquets.

The officer in command of the advanced guard is always to

report overnight that he has made himself acquainted with the road leading out of camp.

INFANTRY.

The ammunition of regiments of infantry is to be completed to 200 rounds per man.

Such corps and detachments as are not provided with sickles for cutting green crops are to provide themselves with some. Every corps and detachment are also to have one or more adzes for the purpose of making new or repointing old tent-pegs.

The men are to be allowed to wear what shoes they like, and are to be allowed to carry their native swords, but are not to take pistols with them on piquet.

Every man is to be provided with a haversack and canteen.

SICK AND HOSPITAL.

All sick and weakly men are to be left in cantonments.

All soldiers or camp-followers who fall sick, or are unable to travel previous to the force marching, are to be sent to the depôt hospital.

Arrangements are to be made regimentally for the provision and carriage of hospital stores, medicines, doolies, etc.

Medical officers are to see that the doolie-bearers are well provided with shoes.

CAMELS.

The officer in command of the grazing guard is to see that sufficient space is allowed for the camels to graze, and that they are not brought back before sunset. Unless the animals are properly fed, they cannot carry their loads. Camels are to be sent out of camp by sunrise to graze.

HORSES.

Strong head and heel ropes are to be provided, as well as hobbles for vicious horses, for hobbling them at night.

The artillery and cavalry horses are to be well found in horse-shoes.

ELEPHANTS.

The elephants are to be all females, selected with regard to their docility and thorough soundness. They are to be equipped for the conveyance of a field battery, and are to be provided with leathern pads for kneeling on, shields or aprons for their foreheads, and an ample supply of chains. In selecting them the feet are to be carefully examined.

SUPPLIES.

Every regiment and battery is to arrange to have carriage for four days' supplies for all men and camp-followers, as well as for that amount of grain for the transport animals.

BUGLE-SOUNDING.

No regiment or detachment is to sound any bugle between the first bugle and the assembly. Corps and batteries are to learn to have their horses saddled and harnessed and put to by verbal order, as a multiplicity of bugle-calls causes confusion.

The assembly and advance are to be repeated by every corps and detachment. In like manner the advance and halt are to be repeated by all on the line of march.

The assembly is to be sounded one hour after the first bugle, when corps are to take up their places according to their order of march, ready to move off on the advance being sounded from the head of the column by order of the commander of the force.

APPENDIX B

WAR SERVICES OF BRITISH AND INDIAN REGI-MENTS ON THE NORTH-WEST FRONTIER OF INDIA

I

REGIMENTS, ETC., WHICH HAVE NO MODERN REPRE-SENTATIVE THAT CAN BE TRACED

CAVALRY.

Designation.	War Services.	Subsequent History.
10th Light Cavalry ...	Mohmands, 1854	—
13th Irregular Cavalry	Baizais, 1849	Mutinied Benares, June 4, 1857
15th Irregular Cavalry	Kohat Pass Afridis, 1850 ; Mohmands, 1851-52 ; Ranizais, 1852	Disbanded, 1861
16th Irregular Cavalry	Black Mountain, 1852	Disbanded, 1882
16th Bengal Cavalry	Black Mountain, 1868	—
Peshawar Light Horse	Hindustani Fanatics, 1858	Composed of detach-ments from 1st Bat-talion Inniskilling Fusiliers, 2nd Bat-talion East Surrey Regiment, 1st Bat-talion Irish Fusiliers, mounted on horses taken from the dis-banded 5th Bengal Light Cavalry; strength, 90
4th Punjab Cavalry ...	Orakzais, 1855; Miran-zai, 1855-56; Mah-suds, 1881	—

ARTILLERY.

Designation.	War Services.	Subsequent History.
No. 1 Punjab Light Field Battery	Miranzai, 1855 - 56; Bozdars, 1857; Waziris, 1859; Bizotis, 1868-69	—
I — C Royal Horse Artillery	Jowakis, 1878; Mohmands, 1880	Broken up, 1882
Mountain Train Battery	Black Mountain, 1852	—

INFANTRY.

3rd Native Infantry...	Black Mountain, 1852	Disbanded, 1861
20th Native Infantry	Jowakis, 1853	Mutinied Meerut, May 10, 1857
23rd Native Infantry	Kohat Pass Afridis, 1850	Mutinied Mhow, July 1, 1857
28th Native Infantry	Ranizais, 1852	Mutinied Shahjahanpur, May 31, 1857
29th Native Infantry	Ranizais, 1852	Mutinied Moradabad, June 3, 1857
71st Native Infantry	Mohmands, 1851-52	Mutinied Lucknow, May 30, 1857
3rd Punjab Infantry...	Sheranis, 1853; Orakzais, 1855; Miranzai, 1855-56; Waziris, 1859; Mahsuds, 1860; Ambela, 1863; Bizotis, 1868; Mahsuds, 1881	—
12th Punjab Infantry	Hindustani Fanatics, 1858	—
14th Punjab Infantry	Mahsuds, 1860	—

II
REGIMENTS NOW SERVING

BRITISH CAVALRY.

Present Designation.	War Services.
4th Dragoon Guards	Punjab Frontier (Khaibar), 1897
6th Dragoon Guards	Mohmands, 1880
7th Hussars	Mohmands, 1864

ARTILLERY.

Present Designation.	War Services.
F Battery R.H.A.	Ranizais, 1852
K „ „	Punjab Frontier (Khaibar), 1897
O „ „	Zakha Khel, 1878-79
S „ „	Mohmands, 1864 ; Black Mountain, 1868
T „ „	Black Mountain, 1852
3rd Battery R.F.A.	Punjab Frontier (Kurram), 1897
9th „ „	Punjab Frontier (Miranzai), 1897
10th „ „	Malakand, 1897 ; Buner, 1897-98
15th „ „	Chitral, 1895
18th „ „	Mohmands, 1908
35th „ „	Hindustani Fanatics, 1857-58 ; Ambela, 1863
52nd „ „	Baizais, 1849 ; Kohat Pass Afridis, 1850
56th „ „	Mohmands, 1851-52
57th „ „	Punjab Frontier (Khaibar), 1897
59th „ , ...	Black Mountain, 1868
80th „ „	Mohmands, 1908
No. 1 Mountain Battery, R.G.A.	Mohmands, 1851 ; Jowakis, 1877-78 ; Black Mountain, 1888, 1891; Malakand, 1897 ; Tirah, 1897
No. 2 „ „ „	Jowakis, 1878
No. 3 „ „ „	Miranzai, 1891 ; Chitral, 1895 ; Mohmands, 1897; Punjab Frontier (Khaibar), 1897 ; Zakha Khel, 1908
No. 4 „ „ „	Black Mountain, 1868
No. 6 „ „ „	Ranizais, 1852 ; Black Mountain, 1888
No. 7 „ „ „	Zhob, 1890; Malakand, 1897 ; Buner, 1897-98
No. 8 „ „ „	Chitral, 1895 ; Tirah, 1897 ; Mohmands, 1908
No. 9 „ „ „	Black Mountain, 1891 ; Tirah, 1897
53rd Company R.G.A.	Jowakis, 1878
62nd „ „	Mohmands, 1854
65th „ „	Zakha Khel, 1878-79 ; Mohmands, 1880 ; Marris, 1880
92nd „ „	Zaimukhts, 1879 ; Waziris, 1880 ; Mahsuds, 1881
21st Kohat Mountain Battery...	Sheranis, 1853 ; Bozdars, 1857 ; Waziris, 1859 ; Mahsuds, 1860 ; Bizotis, 1868-69 ; Zaimukhts, 1879 ; Mahsuds, 1881, 1894, 1902
22nd Derajat „ „ ...	Orakzais, 1855 ; Miranzai, 1855-56 ; Bozdars, 1857 ; Mahsuds, 1860 ; Ambela, 1863 ; Tochi, 1872 ; Mahsuds, 1881 ; Black Mountain, 1888, 1891 ; Miranzai, 1891 ; Chitral, 1895 ; Punjab Frontier (Miranzai), 1897 ; Tirah, 1897 ; Mahsuds, 1902 ; Zakha Khel, 1908

ARTILLERY—*continued.*

Present Designation.	War Services.
23rd Peshawar Mountain Battery	Jowakis, 1853 ; Orakzais, 1855 ; Miranzai, 1855 - 56 ; Hindustani Fanatics, 1857-58 ; Waziris, 1859 ; Mahsuds, 1860 ; Ambela, 1863 ; Black Mountain, 1868 ; Mahsuds, 1881 ; Miranzai, 1891 ; Mahsuds, 1894 ; Tochi, 1897 ; Mohmands, 1908
24th Hazara ,, ,, ...	Hindustani Fanatics, 1858 ; Waziris, 1859 ; Mahsuds, 1860 ; Ambela, 1863 ; Black Mountain, 1868 ; Jowakis, 1878 ; Mahsuds, 1881 ; Sheranis, 1883 ; Black Mountain, 1888 ; Miranzai, 1891 ; Hunza and Nagar, 1891
25th Mountain Battery	Mohmands, 1897 ; Tirah, 1897
26th ,, ,, ...	Tochi, 1897
27th ,, ,, ...	Zhob, 1890 ; Mahsuds, 1901-02
28th ,, ,, ...	Malakand, 1897 ; Buner, 1897-98 ; Mohmands, 1908

INDIAN CAVALRY.

1st Lancers	Zaimukhts, 1879
2nd Lancers	Mohmands, 1851-52 ; Ranizais, 1852 ; Mohmands, 1864
3rd Skinner's Horse	Punjab Frontier, 1897
5th Cavalry	Mohmands, 1851-52 ; Jowakis, 1853 ; Hindustani Fanatics, 1858
6th Cavalry	Mohmands, 1864; Punjab Frontier (Kurram), 1897
8th Cavalry	Hindustani Fanatics, 1858
9th Hodson's Horse	Black Mountain, 1868 ; Punjab Frontier (Khaibar), 1897
10th Lancers	Kam Dakka, 1879 ; Malakand, 1897 ; Buner, 1897-98
11th Lancers	Ambela, 1863 ; Zakha Khel, 1878-79 ; Black Mountain, 1891 ; Chitral, 1895 ; Malakand, 1897
13th Lancers	Zakha Khel, 1878-79 ; Zaimukhts, 1879 ; Mohmands, 1897
15th Lancers	Mahsuds, 1860 ; Black Mountain, 1888
17th Cavalry	Mohmands, 1880

INDIAN CAVALRY—*continued*.

Present Designation.	War Services.
18th Lancers	Zaimukhts, 1879; Waziris, 1880; Mahsuds, 1881; Zhob, 1890; Punjab Frontier (Miranzai), 1897; Tirah, 1897
19th Lancers	Miranzai, 1891; Mohmands, 1908
21st Cavalry (Frontier Force) ...	Kohat Pass Afridis, 1850; Miranzai, 1855-56; Tochi, 1872; Mahsuds, 1881; Sheranis, 1883; Zhob, 1890; Mahsuds, 1894; Tochi, 1897; Mahsuds, 1901-02; Mohmands, 1908
22nd Cavalry (Frontier Force) ...	Waziris, 1852; Bozdars, 1857; Hindustani Fanatics, 1857; Tochi, 1872; Jowakis, 1877-78
23rd Cavalry (Frontier Force) ...	Bozdars, 1857; Mahsuds, 1860; Bizotis, 1868-69; Marris, 1880; Zhob, 1890; Mahsuds, 1894; Punjab Frontier (Miranzai), 1897; Mahsuds, 1902
25th Cavalry (Frontier Force) ...	Sheranis, 1853; Miranzai, 1891; Mahsuds, 1901-02
37th Lancers	Zakha Khel, 1908
38th Central India Horse ...	Punjab Frontier (Kurram), 1897
39th Central India Horse ...	Punjab Frontier (Kurram), 1897

BRITISH INFANTRY.

Royal West Surrey Regiment (1st Battalion)	Malakand, 1897; Tirah, 1897
East Kent Regiment (1st Battalion)	Chitral, 1895; Malakand, 1897; Buner, 1897-98
Northumberland Fusiliers (1st Battalion)	Zakha Khel, 1878-79; Mohmands, 1880; Black Mountain, 1888
Royal Warwickshire Regiment (1st Battalion)	Black Mountain, 1868; Zakha Khel, 1908
Royal Fusiliers	Ambela, 1863
Liverpool Regiment (2nd Battalion)	Zaimukhts, 1879
Norfolk Regiment	Jowakis, 1878
Devonshire Regiment (2nd Battalion)	Tirah, 1897
Suffolk Regiment (1st Battalion)	Black Mountain, 1888
Somersetshire Light Infantry (1st Battalion)	Mohmands, 1897
West Yorkshire Regiment (1st Battalion)	Mohmands, 1908

BRITISH INFANTRY—continued.

Present Designation.	War Services.
Bedfordshire Regiment (1st Battalion)	Chitral, 1895
Leicestershire Regiment (1st Battalion)	Zakha Khel, 1878-79
Royal Irish Regiment (2nd Battalion)	Black Mountain, 1888 ; Punjab Frontier (Miranzai), 1897
Yorkshire Regiment (1st Battalion)	Black Mountain, 1868
Yorkshire Regiment (2nd Battalion)	Tirah, 1897
Royal Scots Fusiliers (2nd Battalion)	Punjab Frontier (Miranzai), 1897 ; Tirah, 1897
Cheshire Regiment	Jowakis, 1853 ; Mohmands, 1854
Royal Welsh Fusiliers (1st Battalion)	Black Mountain, 1891
King's Own Scottish Borderers (1st Battalion)	Zakha Khel, 1878-79 ; Mohmands, 1880
King's Own Scottish Borderers (2nd Battalion)	Chitral, 1895 ; Tirah, 1897
Royal Inniskilling Fusiliers (1st Battalion)	Hindustani Fanatics, 1857
Royal Inniskilling Fusiliers (2nd Battalion)	Punjab Frontier (Khaibar), 1897
Gloucestershire Regiment (2nd Battalion)	Baizais, 1849 ; Kohat Pass Afridis, 1850 ; Mohmands, 1851-52
East Surrey Regiment (2nd Battalion)	Hindustani Fanatics, 1857
Duke of Cornwall's Light Infantry (1st Battalion)	Ranizais, 1852
Border Regiment (2nd Battalion)	Mahsuds, 1894
Royal Sussex Regiment (2nd Battalion)	Black Mountain, 1888
South Staffordshire Regiment (1st Battalion)	Black Mountain, 1868
Dorsetshire Regiment (1st Battalion)	Tirah, 1897
Oxfordshire Light Infantry (2nd Battalion)	Mohmands, 1897 ; Punjab Frontier (Khaibar), 1897
Derbyshire Regiment (2nd Battalion)	Tirah, 1897
Loyal North Lancashire Regiment (2nd Battalion)	Hindustani Fanatics, 1858
Northamptonshire Regiment (1st Battalion)	Tirah, 1897
Royal West Kent Regiment (1st Battalion)	Malakand, 1897 ; Buner, 1897-98
King's Own Yorkshire Light Infantry (1st Battalion)	Jowakis, 1878 ; Zakha Khel, 1878-79
King's Own Yorkshire Light Infantry (2nd Battalion)	Zhob, 1890 ; Punjab Frontier (Khaibar), 1897

BRITISH INFANTRY—*continued.*

Present Designation.	War Services.
King's Shropshire Light Infantry (1st Battalion)	Mohmands, 1851-52
King's Shropshire Light Infantry (2nd Battalion)	Zaimukhts, 1879 ; Waziris, 1880
King's Royal Rifle Corps (1st Battalion)	Black Mountain, 1891 ; Miranzai, 1891 ; Chitral, 1895
King's Royal Rifle Corps (2nd Battalion)	Marris, 1880
King's Royal Rifle Corps (Battalion unknown)	Baizais, 1849 ; Kohat Pass Afridis, 1850
North Staffordshire Regiment (2nd Battalion)	Kohat Pass Afridis, 1850 ; Mohmands, 1851 - 52 ; Hindustani Fanatics, 1858
Highland Light Infantry (1st Battalion)	Ambela, 1863
Highland Light Infantry (2nd Battalion)	Malakand, 1897 ; Buner, 1897-98
Seaforth Highlanders (1st Battalion)	Zakha Khel, 1908 ; Mohmands, 1908
Seaforth Highlanders (2nd Battalion)	Black Mountain, 1891 ; Chitral, 1895
Gordon Highlanders (1st Battalion)	Chitral, 1895 ; Tirah, 1897
Royal Irish Fusiliers (1st Battalion)	Hindustani Fanatics, 1857
Argyll and Sutherland Highlanders (2nd Battalion)	Ambela, 1863 ; Tochi, 1897
Royal Munster Fusiliers (1st Battalion)	Ambela, 1863 ; Mohmands, 1908
Rifle Brigade (3rd Battalion) ...	Mohmands, 1864 ; Tochi, 1897
Rifle Brigade (4th Battalion) ...	Jowakis, 1878 ; Zakha Khel, 1878-79 ; Mahsuds, 1881

SAPPERS AND MINERS.

1st Sappers and Miners ...	Mohmands, 1851-52; Ranizais, 1852; Black Mountain, 1852; Mohmands, 1854; Mahsuds, 1860; Black Mountain, 1868 ; Zakha Khel, 1878-79 ; Zaimukhts, 1879; Mahsuds, 1881 ; Black Mountain, 1888, 1891 ; Miranzai, 1891; Hunza and Nagar, 1891 ; Mahsuds, 1894; Chitral, 1895 ; Tochi, 1897 ; Malakand, 1897 ; Buner, 1897-98 ; Punjab Frontier, 1897 ; Zakha Khel, 1908 ; Mohmands, 1908

Sappers and Miners—*continued.*

Present Designation.	War Services.
2nd Sappers and Miners ...	Zakha Khel, 1878-79; Mohmands, 1880; Malakand, 1897; Buner, 1897-98; Tirah, 1897; Zakha Khel, 1908
3rd Sappers and Miners ...	Baizais, 1849; Jowakis, 1853; Zhob, 1890; Mahsuds, 1894; Malakand, 1897; Tirah, 1897
Not ascertained	Miranzai, 1855; Bozdars, 1857; Hindustani Fanatics, 1858; Waziris, 1859; Ambela, 1863; Jowakis, 1878

The Guides.

Queen's Own Corps of Guides: Lumsden's (Cavalry and Infantry)	Mohmands, 1851-52; Ranizais, 1852; Black Mountain, 1852; Jowakis, 1853; Hindustani Fanatics, 1858; Waziris, 1859; Mahsuds, 1860: Ambela, 1863; Black Mountain, 1868; Jowakis, 1877-78; Zakha Khel, 1878-79; Black Mountain, 1891; Chitral, 1895; Malakand, 1897; Buner, 1897-98; Mohmands, 1908

Indian Infantry.

1st Brahmans	Hindustani Fanatics, 1857-58
2nd Rajput Light Infantry ...	Kohat Pass Afridis, 1850
6th Jat Light Infantry	Zakha Khel, 1878-79; Tochi, 1897
8th Rajputs	Mohmands, 1880
11th Rajputs	Black Mountain, 1891
12th Pioneers	Black Mountain, 1852; Hindustani Fanatics, 1858; Punjab Frontier (Kurram), 1897
13th Rajputs	Zaimukhts, 1879
14th Sikhs	Ambela, 1863; Jowakis, 1878; Mahsuds, 1881; Black Mountain, 1888; Mahsuds, 1894; Chitral, 1895; Tochi, 1897
15th Sikhs	Miranzai, 1891; Chitral, 1895; Punjab Frontier (Miranzai), 1897; Tirah, 1897
16th Rajputs	Buner, 1897-98

INDIAN INFANTRY—*continued.*

Present Designation.	War Services.
17th Infantry	Mahsuds, 1901-02
19th Punjabis	Black Mountain, 1891; Miranzai, 1891
20th Punjabis	Hindustani Fanatics, 1858; Ambela, 1863; Black Mountain, 1868; Jowakis, 1878; Zaimukhts, 1879; Waziris, 1880; Mahsuds, 1881; Hunza and Nagar, 1891; Mahsuds, 1894; Mohmands, 1897; Buner, 1897-98
21st Punjabis	Mohmands, 1854; Hindustani Fanatics, 1858; Mahsuds, 1881; Malakand, 1897; Buner, 1897-98; Mohmands, 1908
22nd Punjabis	Jowakis, 1878; Mohmands, 1897; Punjab Frontier, 1897; Mahsud-Waziris, 1902; Mohmands, 1908
23rd Sikh Pioneers	Ambela, 1863; Miranzai, 1891; Mahsuds, 1901-02; Zakha Khel, 1908
24th Punjabis	Hindustani Fanatics, 1857; Black Mountain, 1868; Zakha Khel, 1878-79; Black Mountain, 1888; Malakand, 1897
25th Punjabis	Chitral, 1895; Tochi, 1897; Zakha Khel, 1908
26th Punjabis	Hindustani Fanatics, 1858
27th Punjabis	Jowakis, 1878; Zakha Khel, 1878-79; Black Mountain, 1891; Miranzai, 1891; Mahsuds, 1901-02
28th Punjabis	Black Mountain, 1891; Mahsud-Waziris, 1901-02; Zakha Khel, 1908; Mohmands, 1908
29th Punjabis	Zaimukhts, 1879; Black Mountain, 1888; Miranzai, 1891; Mahsuds, 1901-02
30th Punjabis	Mohmands, 1880; Mahsuds, 1881; Tirah, 1897
31st Punjabis	Black Mountain, 1868; Mohmands, 1880; Malakand, 1897; Buner, 1897-98
32nd Sikh Pioneers	Waziris, 1859; Mahsuds, 1860; Ambela, 1863; Mahsuds, 1881; Black Mountain, 1891; Chitral, 1895; Mahsud-Waziris, 1901-02
33rd Punjabis	Mahsuds, 1894; Tochi, 1897
34th Sikh Pioneers	Black Mountain, 1888; Punjab Frontier (Khaibar), 1897; Mohmands, 1908

INDIAN INFANTRY—*continued*.

Present Designation.	War Services.
35th Sikhs	Malakand, 1897 ; Mahsud-Waziris, 1901-02
36th Sikhs	Samana, 1897 ; Tirah, 1897
37th Dogras	Black Mountain, 1891; Chitral, 1895; Mohmands, 1897
38th Dogras	Mahsuds, 1894 ; Malakand, 1897 ; Mahsud-Waziris, 1901-02
39th Garhwal Rifles	Malakand, 1897 ; Punjab Frontier, 1897
40th Pathans	Black Mountain, 1888 ; Mohmands, 1908
44th Merwara Infantry	Zakha Khel, 1878-79 ; Kam Dakka, 1879
45th Sikhs	Zakha Khel, 1878-79; Black Mountain, 1888 ; Malakand, 1897 ; Punjab Frontier (Khaibar), 1897 ; Mahsud-Waziris, 1901-02 ; Zakha Khel, 1908
51st Sikhs (Frontier Force) ...	Black Mountain, 1852 ; Mohmands, 1854; Bozdars, 1857 ; Tochi, 1872 ; Jowakis, 1877-78; Mahsuds, 1881 ; Sheranis, 1883 ; Zhob, 1890 ; Mahsuds, 1894 ; Tochi, 1897 ; Mahsud-Waziris, 1902
52nd Sikhs (Frontier Force) ...	Hindustani Fanatics, 1858 ; Marris, 1880 ; Black Mountain, 1888 ; Zhob, 1890
53rd Sikhs (Frontier Force) ...	Bozdars, 1857 ; Ambela, 1863; Black Mountain, 1868; Jowakis, 1877-78; Marris, 1880 ; Black Mountain, 1888 ; Miranzai, 1891 ; Mahsuds, 1894 ; Tirah, 1897 ; Mahsud-Waziris, 1901-02 ; Zakha Khel, 1908; Mohmands, 1908
54th Sikhs (Frontier Force) ...	Waziris, 1859; Mahsuds, 1860; Mohmands, 1864; Tochi, 1872; Jowakis, 1877; Mahsuds, 1881; Black Mountain, 1891 ; Chitral, 1895; Mahsud-Waziris, 1901-02 ; Zakha Khel, 1908; Mohmands, 1908
55th Coke's Rifles (Frontier Force)	Kohat Pass Afridis, 1850 ; Ranizais, 1852 ; Waziris, 1852 ; Sheranis, 1853 ; Orakzais, 1855 ; Miranzai, 1855-56 ; Bozdars, 1857 ; Waziris, 1859; Mahsuds, 1860 ; Ambela, 1863; Bizotis, 1868-69; Tochi, 1872; Mahsuds, 1881 ; Miranzai, 1891 ; Tochi, 1897 ; Mahsud - Waziris, 1901-02 ; Mohmands, 1908

INDIAN INFANTRY—*continued.*

Present Designation.	War Services.
56th Punjabi Rifles (Frontier Force)	Waziris, 1852; Orakzais, 1855; Miranzai, 1855-56; Bozdars, 1857; Mahsuds, 1860; Black Mountain, 1868; Mahsuds, 1881; Zhob, 1890; Miranzai, 1891; Mahsuds, 1894; Punjab Frontier (Miranzai), 1897; Tirah, 1897; Mahsud - Waziris, 1901-02
57th Wilde's Rifles (Frontier Force)	Waziris, 1852; Bozdars, 1857; Waziris, 1859; Mahsuds, 1860; Bizotis, 1868-69; Jowakis, 1878; Zaimukhts, 1879; Mahsuds, 1881; Sheranis, 1883; Black Mountain, 1888; Miranzai, 1891; Mahsud-Waziris, 1901-02; Mohmands, 1908
58th Vaughan's Rifles (Frontier Force)	Miranzai, 1855 - 56; Hindustani Fanatics, 1857; Ambela, 1863; Jowakis, 1878; Mahsuds, 1881; Sheranis, 1883; Miranzai, 1891; Punjab Frontier (Miranzai), 1897; Mahsud-Waziris, 1901-02
59th Scinde Rifles (Frontier Force)	Miranzai, 1855 - 56; Hindustani Fanatics, 1857-58; Waziris, 1859; Mahsuds, 1860; Ambela, 1863; Bizotis, 1868-69; Jowakis, 1877-78; Mahsuds, 1881; Miranzai, 1891; Mahsuds, 1894; Zakha Khel, 1908; Mohmands, 1908
61st Pioneers	Mohmands, 1880
64th Pioneers	Mohmands, 1880
81st Pioneers	Tirah, 1897
103rd Mahratta Light Infantry	Baizais, 1849; Buner, 1897-98
109th Infantry	Mahsud-Waziris, 1901-02
123rd Outram's Rifles	Mahsud-Waziris, 1901-02
124th Baluchistan Infantry ...	Mahsud-Waziris, 1901-02
128th Pioneers	Mohmands, 1897; Tirah, 1897
129th Baluchis	Zhob, 1890
130th Baluchis	Zhob, 1890
1st Gurkhas (1st Battalion) ...	Mohmands, 1851-52; Ranizais, 1852; Jowakis, 1853; Miranzai, 1855-56; Black Mountain, 1868; Mahsuds, 1894
1st Gurkhas (2nd Battalion) ...	Mohmands, 1897; Tirah, 1897
2nd Gurkhas (1st Battalion) ...	Mohmands, 1864; Black Mountain, 1868; Zakha Khel, 1878-79; Tirah, 1897
2nd Gurkhas (2nd Battalion) ...	Punjab Frontier, 1897
3rd Gurkhas (1st Battalion) ...	Tirah, 1897

INDIAN INFANTRY—*continued.*

Present Designation.	War Services.
4th Gurkhas (1st Battalion) ...	Ambela, 1863 ; Black Mountain, 1868; Zakha Khel, 1878-79; Marris, 1880 ; Mahsuds, 1894
4th Gurkhas (2nd Battalion) ...	Chitral, 1895 ; Tirah, 1897
5th Gurkhas (1st Battalion) ...	Mahsuds, 1860 ; Ambela, 1863 ; Black Mountain, 1868 ; Jowakis, 1878 ; Marris, 1880; Black Mountain, 1888, 1891 ; Hunza and Nagar, 1891 ; Miranzai, 1891 ; Mahsuds, 1894 ; Punjab Frontier (Kurram), 1897
5th Gurkhas (2nd Battalion) ...	Zakha Khel, 1908
9th Gurkhas (1st Battalion) ...	Mohmands, 1897 ; Punjab Frontier (Khaibar), 1897

APPENDIX C

RULERS IN INDIA

Viceroys and Governors-General.	Year.	Commanders-in-Chief.
—	1767	Brigadier-General Carnac
—	1767	Colonel R. Smith
—	1769	Brigadier-General Sir Robert Baker
—	1772	Colonel Charles Chapman
Right Hon. Warren Hastings	1774	Lieutenant-General John Clavering
—	1777	Brigadier-General Giles Stibbert
—	1779	Lieutenant-General Sir Eyre Coote
—	1783	Brigadier-General Giles Stibbert
Sir John Macpherson, Bart.	1785	Lieutenant - General Sir Robert Sloper
General Earl Cornwallis, K.G.	1786	General Earl Cornwallis, K.G.
Sir John Shore, Bart. ...	1793	Major-General Sir Robert Abercromby
—	1793	Major-General Sir Charles Morgan (temporary)
—	1796	Colonel Sir Alexander Mackenzie (temporary)
Lieutenant - General Sir Alured Clarke, K.C.B. Earl of Mornington, P.C.	1798	{ Lieutenant - General Sir Alured Clarke, K.C.B.
—	1800	Major-General Sir James Craig (provincial command)
—	1801	Lieutenant-General Gerard (Lord Lake)
General Marquis Cornwallis, K.G. (second time)	1805	General Marquis Cornwallis, K.G. (second time)
Sir George Barlow, Bart., K.C.B.	1805	Major - General W. Dowdeswell (provincial command)
Earl of Minto	1807	Major-General Sir Ewen Baillie (provincial command)
—	1807	Lieutenant - General Sir George Hewitt
—	1810	Major-General W. St. Leger (temporary)
—	1812	Lieutenant - General Sir George Nugent

Viceroys and Governors-General.	Year.	Commanders-in-Chief.
General the Earl of Moira, P.C.	1813	General the Earl of Moira, P.C.
Mr. John Adam ... Earl of Amherst, P.C.	1823	General Sir Edward Paget, G.C.B.
—	1825	General Viscount Combermere, G.C.B., G.C.H.
Mr. Butterworth Bayley General Lord William Cavendish Bentinck, G.C.B., G.C.H., P.C.	1828	—
—	1830	General Earl of Dalhousie, G.C.B.
—	1832	General Sir Edward Barnes, G.C.B.
—	1834	General Lord William Cavendish Bentinck, G.C.B., G.C.H., P.C.
Sir Charles Metcalfe, Bart., G.C.B.	1835	General Sir Henry Fane, G.C.B.
Earl of Auckland, G.C.B., P.C.	1836	—
—	1839	General Sir Jasper Nicholls, K.C.B.
Earl of Ellenborough ...	1842	—
—	1843	General Lord Hugh Gough, G.C.B.
Mr. William Wilberforce Bird Right Hon. Sir Henry Hardinge, G.C.B.	1844	—
Earl of Dalhousie, P.C. ...	1848	—
—	1849	General Sir Charles Napier, G.C.B.
—	1850	General Sir William Gomm
Viscount Canning, P.C. ...	1856	General Sir George Anson
—	1857	General Sir Colin Campbell (Lord Clyde), G.C.B.
Earl Canning, G.C.B., G.M.S.I.	1858	—
—	1860	General Sir Hugh Rose, G.C.B.
Earl of Elgin and Kincardine, K.T., G.C.B., G.M.S.I.	1862	—
Major-General Hon. Sir Robert Napier Colonel Sir William Denison, K.C.B.	1863	—
Right Hon. Sir John Lawrence, Bart., G.C.B., G.M.S.I.	1864	—
—	1865	Lieutenant-General Sir W. R. Mansfield
Earl of Mayo, K.P., G.M.S.I.	1869	—
—	1870	General Robert Cornelius Lord Napier (Baron Napier of Magdala), G.C.B., G.C.S.I.

Viceroys and Governors-General.	Year.	Commanders-in-Chief.
Hon. Sir John Strachey, K.C.S.I. Lord Napier of Merchistoun, K.T. Lord Northbrook, P.C., G.M.S.I.	1872	—
Lord Lytton, G.C.B., G.M.S.I., G.M.I.E.	1876	General Sir Frederic Haines, K.C.B.
Marquis of Ripon, P.C., K.G., G.M.S.I., G.M.I.E.	1880	—
—	1881	General Sir Donald Stewart, G.C.B., C.I.E.
Earl of Dufferin, K.P., G.C.B., G.C.M.G., G.M.S.I., G.M.I.E.	1884	—
—	1885	General Lord Roberts of Kandahar, V.C., G.C.B., C.I.E.
Marquis of Lansdowne, K.G., G.C.M.G., G.M.S.I., G.M.I.E.	1888	—
—	1893	General Sir George White, V.C., K.C.B., G.C.I.E.
Marquis of Elgin and Kincardine, K.G., P.C., LL.D., G.M.S.I., G.M.I.E.	1894	—
—	1898	General Sir William Lockhart, G.C.B., K.C.S.I.
Right Hon. George Nathaniel Baron Curzon of Kedleston, G.M.S.I., G.M.I.E.	1900	General Sir Arthur Power Palmer, K.C.B.
—	1902	General Right Hon. Horatio Herbert Viscount Kitchener of Khartoum, G.C.B., O.M., G.C.S.I., G.C.M.G., G.C.I.E.
Right Hon. Arthur Oliver Villiers Baron Ampthill, G.C.I.E. Right Hon. George Nathaniel Baron Curzon of Kedleston, G.M.S.I., G.M.I.E.	1904	—
Right Hon. Gilbert John Elliot Murray Kynynmond, Earl of Minto, P.C., G.C.M.G., G.M.S.I., G.M.I.E.	1905	—
—	1909	General Sir O'Moore Creagh, V.C., G.C.B.
Right Hon. Charles Baron Hardinge of Penshurst, P.C., G.C.B., G.M.S.I., G.M.I.E., G.C.M.G., G.C.V.O., I.S.O.	1910	—

APPENDIX D

CHRONOLOGICAL TABLE OF NORTH-WEST FRONTIER CAMPAIGNS

1849	...	Baizais
1850	...	Kohat Pass Afridis
1851	...	Mohmands
1852	...	Ranizais
1852	...	Utman Khel
1852	...	Waziris
1852	...	Black Mountain Tribes
1853	...	Hindustani Fanatics
1853	...	Shiranis
1853	...	Kohat Pass Afridis
1854	...	Mohmands
1854	...	Afridis
1855	...	Orakzais
1855	...	Miranzai
1856	...	Kurram
1857	...	Bozdars
1857	...	Hindustani Fanatics
1859	...	Waziris
1860	...	Mahsuds
1863	...	Ambela
1863	...	Mohmands
1868	...	Black Mountain Tribes
1868	...	Bizotis
1872	...	Tochi
1877	...	Jowakis
1878	...	Utman Khel

1878	...	Zakha Khel
1878	...	Mohmands
1878	...	Zaimukhts
1879	...	Zakha Khel
1880	...	Marris
1881	...	Mahsuds
1883	...	Shiranis (Takht-i-Suliman)
1888	...	Black Mountain Tribes
1890	...	Zhob Valley
1891	...	Black Mountain Tribes
1891	...	Miranzai
1891	...	Hunza and Nagar
1894	...	Mahsuds
1895	...	Chitral
1897	...	Tochi
1897	...	Malakand
1897	...	Mohmands
1897	...	Orakzais (Miranzai and Kurram)
1897	...	Afridis (Khaibar and Tirah)
1900	...	Mahsuds
1908	...	Zakha Khel
1908	...	Mohmands

INDEX

BILLING AND SONS, LTD., PRINTERS, GUILDFORD.

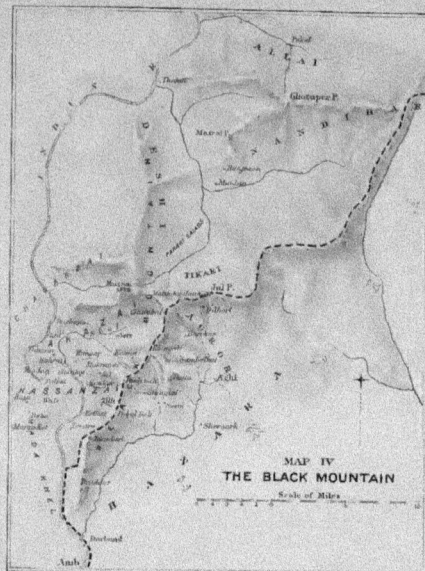

MAP IV
THE BLACK MOUNTAIN

Scale of Miles

Lightning Source UK Ltd.
Milton Keynes UK
UKHW011423170123
415497UK00004B/156

9 789353 299866